DIPLOMATS AND DREAMERS

The Stancioff Family in Bulgarian History

Mari A. Firkatian

University Press of America,® Inc.
Lanham · Boulder · New York · Toronto · Plymouth, UK

Copyright © 2008 by
University Press of America,® Inc.
4501 Forbes Boulevard
Suite 200
Lanham, Maryland 20706
UPA Acquisitions Department (301) 459-3366

Estover Road
Plymouth PL6 7PY
United Kingdom

Library of Congress Control Number: 2008924049
ISBN-13: 978-0-7618-4069-5 (paperback : alk. paper)
ISBN-10: 0-7618-4069-9 (paperback : alk. paper)

⊖™ The paper used in this publication meets the minimum
requirements of American National Standard for Information
Sciences—Permanence of Paper for Printed Library Materials,
ANSI Z39.48—1984

For Anahid and Maral, my family.

Contents

Part II A Second Generation of Diplomats

Preface

This book is a chronicle of a family of diplomats who experienced the world in transition. Subjects of capricious fate they forged a destiny as a family that overcame some of the most cataclysmic events of the twentieth century. *Diplomats and Dreamers* is a family biography that begins with the careers of the parents in 1887 and ends with the death of Nadejda Stancioff, their eldest child, in 1957.

The context of the historical developments in an uncertain period of European history highlights their lives. This accomplished family is noteworthy for an unflagging ability to survive and persist with success and grace.

Members of the *haute bourgeoisie*, the Stancioff family parents issued from elite families—a Bulgarian wealthy merchant family and French nobility. Their professional participation in diplomacy and their personal and professional involvement in Bulgarian court life added to their cachet as cosmopolitans at ease in any social and international setting. They upheld the political system monarchy necessitated; a conservative world view that supports the crown, the church, and the class system as the three pillars of public life.

Furthermore, this book addresses issues of gender by using the careers of the Stancioff women as exemplars of how a woman could develop her life in an atmosphere of strict gender divisions of labor—in elite society. The Stancioff women's way of fitting into the mainstream of elite society is yet another model of a new generation of women who came into sharper focus after the turn of the last century women who stepped beyond the narrow expectations of what their gender could achieve.

The fact that Nadejda became a relatively high-ranking member of the Bulgarian diplomatic corps in the 1910s and 1920s, following her father's example, is a testament to her intelligence and talent. Ultimately, she was named first secretary to the Bulgarian legation in Washington, D.C. Her achievements were impressive: author of dozens of scholarly articles in at least two languages; author of scores of newspaper articles; presenter and producer of countless radio broadcasts, some in two languages, for the British Broadcasting company and the National Radio London; officer of various charitable organizations such as the Scottish Red Cross and the National Council of Women of Sterling; friend and playmate of Bulgarian royalty.

Her rise offers a glimpse into the opportunities available to women of unusual talent and drive. In fact, her life offers a great many perspectives on European society: female diplomat, English Lady, and Bulgarian patriot. She had a talent for shaping her persona and an ability to assume the role of propertied lady who is expert in foreign affairs while she also was capable of doing the mundane chores of preserving fruits for winter. She associated with the ruling classes, published on foreign affairs, traveled the world, championed the Red Cross, was a wartime nurse, produced for the BBC, tirelessly supported the war effort when she converted her Scottish estate into a hospital during World War II and all the while continued to document her life.

Based on unexplored, unpublished primary materials, my translations from chiefly Bulgarian, French, and Russian texts, this book, enriches both women's history and European history. I have tried to let the documents speak for themselves. Where possible and valuable, I have quoted from journals, memoirs, letters, published articles, and transcripts of oral communications with members of the family.

Not only did the Stancioffs experience a great deal but also they documented their observations. With a keen sense of history, they preserved important documents. Mostly through the prism of Nadejda Stancioff Muir's (1894-1957) journals and letters as well as her family's correspondence to each other, I have compiled a family biography. No other member of the family kept journals as regularly or as methodically as Nadejda and no other member's surviving correspondence is as voluminous as hers. She kept a journal from 1906-1957. What's more, she maintained an epistolary conversation with her family.

The problems associated with working with primarily a private archive, ego documents in particular, are clear to me. There is, nonetheless, value in these private musings among the members of one family and their correspondence with others of their acquaintance. The family memoirs, journals, letters serve to illustrate the world through the Stancioffs' social, family-specific lens, and bring the reader closer to an appreciation of a specific world view. Contextualizing their perceptions by using western and east European historians I have created this historical reflection.

The Stancioffs represent the observers from the Bulgarian perspective who through their unique blend of cultures, could see from both an eastern and a western lens. They served kings and princes of Bulgaria and an Agrarian Party prime minister. There exists dialectic between their personal experiences and their public lives.

Opinions in Nadejda's journal entries were those shared by all the members of her family. She expected her journals to be available to her family as a kind of chronicle, a clan record of their collective family history. These chronicles cannot avoid being revealing. By their very fundamental nature, the methodical recording of the mundane and the extraordinary, they reveal the principles and morals this woman and her family found natural. (*Nota Bene*, Feodora Stancioff, who came into possession of her sister Nadejda's archive, did exercise censorship on some documents.)

This book presents a view from the perspective of a small power looking at worldwide transformations. *Diplomats and Dreamers* is not prepared to tackle the complex nature of diplomacy in the era, but to examine the lives, reactions, and traditions that make this family history a paradigm of a transitional type of family created from the fading of the romantic era and the birth of the twentieth century.

This family biography or history is also a prototype for everyday life of the elite classes. Using the framework of their daily occupations, I have revealed the quotidian context of a family life that was a reflection of thousands of others who sought to maintain certain standards of life customary for their class. The Stancioff family history illustrates how families coped with the impact of wars, social unrest, and attendant economic hardships. Their lives illuminate the social history of the later 19th century through the middle of the 20th century.

The Stancioffs originated from a country considered the "Other" by western Europeans. The positioning of Bulgarians as orientals placed even an elite family in the situation of having continually to prove their membership in the upper classes among the diplomatic and social elites of Europe. Yet, they managed to self-identify simultaneously with the Orient and with the heights of western elite cultural circles.

Bulgaria has the distinction of being a Balkan state of slight repute in the western consciousness because of its proximity to the eastern parts of a (western) Eurocentric world. Viewed through the historical telescope that puts exaggerated distance between the eastern and western parts of the European continent, the stigma of being a southeast European territory and part of the Balkan Peninsula has been virtually impossible to lift. This text provides some insights into how perceptive and at other times, how equally blind contemporary observers of Bulgarian domestic and foreign policies could be. Had contemporary observers, the political leadership of powerful states, paid closer attention to evolving developments, instead of focusing on their dated perceptions of the oriental part of Europe, the historical outcomes of Bulgarian and Balkan destinies could have changed dramatically.

The era illuminated here, late nineteenth century through World War II, brought about dramatic changes on the political map of the world. Those changes were driven by the fruits of modernity, the Industrial Revolution, leaps in scientific innovation, the emancipation of women, the transformation of social hierarchies into less rigid forms, and several revolutions in the arts.

Historically the period is rich and complex and by its nature attractive for contemporary readers, because it most clearly defines the world we live in today. The legacies are evident in every aspect of our modern, culturally western lives: the roles of men and women, the place of family in society, the expectations of populations of their governments, the birth, and development of mass consumer culture, the spread of cosmopolitan trends in all aspects of human experience. This rich period laid down the blue print for human development and interactions of our era. Our future is largely rooted in this past.

This book is intended primarily for a general audience however, specialists too may find it useful. I envisioned a history class which approached the period from the micro perspective by reading a family history. Such a course would then aim to broaden the scope of the material to encompass the larger questions of history: diplomacy, class, economics, gender, geography, leadership, monarchy, and politics.

Mari A. Firkatian;
West Hartford, Connecticut;
October, 2007

Acknowledgements

This work began, in my imagination, at the American University in Bulgaria, where I first met members of the Stancioff family in 1995. A few years later, Johnny Stancioff, who was collecting the family documents that would eventually become the Stancioff family private archives, generously allowed me access. In the summer of 1998 I first visited his home in Scotland where the heart of the document collection was housed.

With my initial examination of the documents, which would become the Private Archives of the Stancioff Family (PASF), I experienced something another researcher described as "archive faintness." The materials were not only voluminous but also not organized. In a small room in Scotland, I encountered steamer trunks full of letters carefully folded and returned to their original envelopes, packets of pressed flowers, sweet smelling sachets, childhood memorabilia in the form of clipped bits of hair and ribbons, boxed medals and trophies, post cards tied in stacks of dozens of exemplars, bound inventories of household contents for multiple residences as well as household account books, all packed together.

Thus, my first years with the documents were spent organizing and cataloging the collection. Further complicating my task was that years ago the archive had been divided among family members. As I worked, over several years, the documents were slowly being gathered into one central repository. The restitution of formerly confiscated properties in Bulgaria permitted the Stancioffs to reclaim the family homes on the Black Sea in Varna. The former residences *Les Trois Sources* and *Villa Marion* provided an apt resting place for the Stancioff family archive. Documents penned at these residences were returned to their place of origin.

Based on unpublished and unused family documents, using both western and East European historians' work, this book is a historical reflection of a family's history and the national history of Bulgaria.

For reading the first few and very rough chapters I thank Barbara Greif Wolfe. I am grateful to Robert Berry for his thorough reading of the book and his many helpful suggestions and support through the writing process. I am especially indebted to Krassimira Daskalova for her critical and objective comments and bibliographic help. Johnny Stancioff's editorial comments were extremely helpful, especially in filling in gaps about family members.

A short-term travel grant from the International Research and Exchanges Board which facilitated initial research in Bulgarian archives was one of my first sources of support for this project. A Visiting Faculty Fellowship from Yale University gave me access to their wonderful library. Later, a Greenberg Junior Faculty Grant from the University of Hartford helped to fund some research expenses, a Vincent Coffin Grant also helped with a course release so that I could continue with my research. Hillyer College, at the University of Hartford, generously funded several research trips to Bulgaria over the years. I thank each funding institution for their support.

I thank my Dean, David Goldenberg, for being willing to share my vision of the ultimate creation and his support for the project. I am grateful to my department chairs who have also been patient and supportive over the years when research and teaching had to coexist in harmony.

The book has been made possible with the help and work of many historians who wrote so much of the material which I came to depend upon, librarians, archivists, colleagues all of whom helped to make the book possible; to them I am grateful. For any errors of omission or commission, I am solely responsible.

I thank my friends for their kind support during the years' long process. I cannot thank my family enough, Anahid, my mother, and Maral, my daughter, for their patience and support during years of travel and time I spent away in order to finish this book. They suffered the depravations and frustrations most and I cannot express the full measure of my gratitude to them who know me best.

Alex K. Kyrou created a fine map for my book and I thank him. I wish to thank Johnny and Alexandra Stancioff, Dimitri and Charlotte Stancioff for their hospitality. I am deeply grateful to them all for opening their hearts and homes to me and offering their support for the project. Finally, I gratefully acknowledge the Stancioff family's permission which provided me exclusive and unrestricted access to their documents.

Part I:
A Bulgarian Diplomat and a French Courtier

1
Mass Culture and Politics

"We fear for [Papa] ... Bulgaria is a bit agitated."
Nadejda Stancioff, journal entry[1]

June ushered in a balmy summer, and London was in bloom with a luxuriant display of color. The public gardens and parks exhibited their verdant finery, as did the fashionable women of the city. London society enjoyed spending its leisure time in public spaces. Moreover, it was the Saturday of what should have been an ordinary weekend.

In 1923, Nadejda Stancioff, at twenty-nine, had an astonishing amount of first-hand diplomatic experience, if one takes into account her gender and the era. On that day, she had completed her domestic chores, done some shopping for small necessities, and had already taken a walk in the park, when she heard the terrible news. It was not the news that she had been anticipating.

She was waiting for her superiors in the Bulgarian ministry of foreign affairs to send instructions on her next assignment. Her father, Dimitri, was Bulgarian minister plenipotentiary to the Court of St. James. She was already designated the next first secretary for Bulgaria in Washington, D.C. She waited, anticipating the finalization of her date of departure and additional details of the appointment.

Long after the official announcement of her posting to Washington in 1921, she had managed to keep herself assigned in Europe. She participated in the final economic and territorial conferences of the post-war era so that she could stay close to her family for as long as possible. Her next professional move, as the first Bulgarian woman appointed to a position of significance in that country's diplomatic service, would be in the United States of America. She had been dreading as well as anticipating the moment of her departure.

When she was only twenty-seven, Aleksandûr Stamboliiski, Bulgaria's prime minister, had specifically earmarked her for this post, not only because of her talents as a diplomat but also because of her gender. She and Stamboliiski both understood the power of the appointment. A small Balkan agrarian state took the forefront in promoting gender equality by appointing a female to a diplomatic post and making the decision to send her to the emerging power across the Atlantic.

Stamboliiski liked playing the iconoclast, acting in ways both his patrician and plebian servitors would find incomprehensible. Nadejda was perfect for the post, and he had worked with her closely over enough contentious and critical issues to believe that Bulgaria could trust her implicitly. He had personally nominated her, and she was appropriately flattered.

The Military Coup of 1923

The news she received that June day in London came via a terse telephone call. Stamboliiski was dead and his government destroyed. On June 9, 1923, his government was overthrown in a military coup; Stamboliiski was hunted down in his native village of Slavovitsa and savagely killed. His brutal political assassination would change the future of Bulgaria as well as the professional and personal life of Nadejda Stancioff forever.

Over the next days and weeks, Nadejda and her family were barraged with inquiries from the press about the coup d'état. The family received letters of personal condolence as well as official communications on the coup and its results. Those who were close to Nadejda understood well how deeply she was affected by the murder of her superior, who had, over their four years of collaboration, grown close to her and her family. The Stancioffs had played the role of Pygmalion with Stamboliiski. They focused their effort on his rough, peasant-like manners and gruff ways and attempted to instill some refinement and a sense of cosmopolitanism in the man who had achieved his position abruptly after the ignominious end of King Ferdinand's reign. The King abdicated his throne in disgrace when Bulgaria was defeated in 1918.

The prime minister's death and the expulsion of his supporters from government was a defining moment in the history of Bulgaria and in the fate of a dynasty of diplomats—the Stancioffs. Soon, after they understood the impact of the coup, the Stancioffs, father and daughter, were out of the diplomatic service and on to another chapter in their lives. The new powers in office encouraged them to leave, and they both chose to exit the service.

Nadejda Stancioff's letters to her family reveal some of her emotional turmoil. She exposed nothing to the British press, who deluged the legation with calls, nor did she reveal her sadness to her friends and admirers. She was distressed and apprehensive about her own future. As a twenty-nine-year-old spinster, she would have had few prospects in marriage and fewer still in employment. Her life experiences, as well as her professional résumé precluded her taking on any kind of lower-echelon work. She was not suitable material for shop employment or secretarial work. Furthermore, a woman of her social position would not have willingly sought out work outside the home except for a few specific types of acceptable employment such as governess, nurse, or teacher.

Diplomacy was a perfect venue for her talents and experiences; however, a diplomatic career was now denied her. She could have reverted to the genteel but poorly remunerated role of lady-in-waiting. However, both her younger sister, Feodora, and her mother, Anna, were frequently called to service, and one more Stancioff woman would have simply diluted the family's pool of opportunity.

A World in Transition

Most of the European world which had shaped the Stancioffs and which they, in turn, would attempt to change had undergone incredible transformations during period following the Napoleonic Wars and culminating with the peace settlements ending the First World War. (Historians refer to the period as the long nineteenth century, 1815-1923.) It was a period of significant change in society, and the transformations occurred in every area of life—economic, political, scientific, social, and artistic. It was a time of exuberance, frivolity, and gaiety in Europe when the upper middle class and the aristocracy could almost converge because money had begun to replace rank in social life. Those whose fortunes permitted an elite lifestyle, managed to buy themselves the accoutrements of wealth and position.

The rituals of daily life revolved around obligations and duties in the form of regimented calling hours, dinner parties, theater outings—all of which lasted late into the night—and attendance at the horse races and the other social events of the season. In addition, etiquette required "card-leaving," following a rigid protocol of leaving a calling card could, in some instances, fulfill visiting obligations.[2] As members of the elites were harnessed into a system of set forms of social interactions, this practice helped to maintain their class bonds.

The elites of society spent large portions of their day changing clothes and fine-tuning their appearance. It was extremely important to have the right tailors. Women and men had extravagant costumes for each type of mandated activity: promenades, horseback rides, soirées, bridge parties, and dinner parties, clothes to receive guests in, and clothing for taking walks in the park. A gentleman could not be seen without his walking stick or hat. The list of must-haves and must-dos was exhausting.

It was also an era of the great fashion houses, such as, Whits, Worths, and others, that custom-designed elaborate clothing for Europeans of breeding. Rue de la Paix was an address pronounced with reverence on the lips of well-heeled elites the world over. The era also witnessed the rise of large department stores like Printemps and Selfridges. These stores began to supplant the expensive and exclusive offerings of couture houses with more ready-to-wear merchandise at prices accessible to the *haute bourgeoisie* (A class distinction that denotes a group above the ordinary middle class and just below those of pure aristocratic extraction.).

Remarkable achievements in mechanical inventions and the sciences were the hallmarks of the age. In Europe, the automobile was in its barest infancy at the beginning of the twentieth century; a driver of an automobile had special status, and certainly, the owner of an automobile was an exceedingly wealthy individual. Rail lines shrank distances on continents, and telegraphs and telephones were soon to become commonplace. Perceived as an age of progress in which no feats were impossible, western civilization greeted the beginning of the century with enormous optimism. Opening a vista onto a boundless new horizon, the twentieth century promised modernity, life in a new age.

Rank and Privilege Rule

Although most people earned their living by their labor in the fields and increasingly, in factories at industrial jobs, society continued to focus on strict hierarchies. Rank and privilege were indicators of superiority or inferiority based on the nineteenth century's notions of quality in breeding. The fact that one had to work rather than simply come into one's wealth was one indicator of inferiority that had persisted since the emergence of medieval Europe with its emphasis on rank distinctions.

Although the Industrial Revolution permitted a completely new class to emerge, the bourgeoisie or middle class, their acquired wealth was still not quite *comme-il-faut* (not quite acceptable). In order to become and remain a member of the aristocratic elite, one had to have inherited wealth. As the noble, aristocratic elites struggled to find a way to accommodate the *nouveau*, untitled, *riche*, change swirled around the group.

High culture reflected the changes. The transformations were new and exciting; it was a heady time to be an artist. On May 18, 1909, the Ballets Russes, under the direction of Serge Diaghilev, put on their premier show in Paris with Russia's top soloists: Anna Pavlovna, Tamara Karsavina, and Vatslav Nijinsky. It was a remarkable time to witness the collaborations of some of the most spectacular artistic talent of the age. Rimsky-Korsakov, Stravinsky, Debussy, Ravel, and Mussorgsky composed for a ballet company that would set the gold standard for the dancing world. The bold and innovative use of peasant themes, combined with classical ballet virtuosity, made the Ballets Russes the focal point of an artistic renaissance in Europe.

Art and artists were sovereign; they could rule hearts and minds. Aristocrats, however, felt separate and above the masses; the domains of honor and privilege were theirs. Thus in March 1914, the assassination of the editor of the French newspaper, *Le Figaro,* by the wife of the French minister of finance, Mme. Caillaux, was the biggest society scandal in West Europe before the cataclysmic events in Sarajevo that led to the First World War.

Mme. Caillaux had shot the editor in his own office to avenge her husband against a defamation campaign by the newspaper. The shooting was a matter of honor that both horrified and appeased social expectations. Acquitted in the end,

Mme. Caillaux' case illustrates the tolerance of the Belle Époque society for this kind of expression in defense of honor.

During this period, honor continued to be appeased by fighting a duel, a rare but still legitimate form of reproach and vindication. Europeans did not feel particularly alarmed over the political situation in Central Europe, specifically, the tension between Austria and Russia. Yet the old quarrels between those two powers would lead to a war that would devastate the continent.

The Great Powers

Europe, as well as most of the world, was governed by the whims and plots of five Great Powers by 1900. These powers were the five states that had come to dominate not only European politics but, through their colonial interests, to rule the world. Chief among the colonial powers was Great Britain. Germany and France vied with each other in an attempt to close the gap in territorial acquisitions between themselves and England. Austria-Hungary, or the Habsburg Monarchy, was an empire whose complex domestic situation did not permit foreign adventure, but it too engaged in expansionist schemes. The Russian Empire was the largest in territory of the five and had the least developed domestic state of affairs.

As the most powerful and dominant states in the world, these five powers permitted themselves the arrogant luxury of dictating the fate of millions. However, they also had little regard for the consequences when they sought to win minor skirmishes on the battlefield of honor. Increasingly, the Great Powers behaved as individuals rather than responsible states and leaders of their subjects. They behaved as aristocrats who, ever watchful of slights to their honor, issued a challenge. Their governance was still, especially in the Russian and the Habsburg realms, in the hands of an autocratic monarch or a small powerful clique. Therefore, their governance style reflected more the personal ambitions of the players involved rather than a well thought-out master plan.

As a system of checks and balances, the Great Power system prevailed in a world that was still largely colonial and subservient to the whims of the states. However, bad leadership, noble arrogance, and favoritism created, in virtually every state, cadres of powerful individuals whose personal abilities did not coincide with their ambitions. The political tensions that roiled Europe from the 1890s to the Great War and beyond can be attributed, directly and indirectly, to Great Power courts and (mis)governments. The modern state of Bulgaria was conceived in this turbulent era, through the machinations of the Great Powers; and the course of Bulgaria's development occurred largely a result of the country's neglect or mismanagement by those powers.

Small States, Little Powers

For any minor state to survive in this environment, it was natural for a single Great Power patron to take on that country's "direction." Each lesser power had a Great Power patron, not by choice on the part of the lesser state, but by necessity. Protector status endowed the power to intervene, legally, in the domestic affairs of their protégé. The treatment of the Southeast European states was more akin to the treatment of colonial possessions on other continents, like Africa. These satellite relationships permitted the powers to feel comfortable to project their will onto the Balkans because they perceived them as worlds apart from European civilization, the eastern or oriental "other." Survival of the lesser state depended on easy and smooth relations with the appropriate patron. The patron state had the duty to anticipate the well-being of her client and make certain that the lesser state maintained appropriately supine and deferential foreign and domestic policies. Should relations become untenable, then the small state could look forward to trouble abroad and at home.

The Sick Man of Europe

One important and large state captivated Great Power attention—the Ottoman Empire. Once a powerful state, vigorous enough to launch an attack on Vienna in the center of Europe, the Ottoman Empire had become weak to the point of imminent collapse. By the nineteenth century, common diplomatic usage referred to the Ottoman Empire as the Sick Man of Europe. Its fate was a topic of diplomatic debate, as the Great Powers understood that it was not a question of *if* the empire would collapse but rather *when*. To that end, most of their negotiations centered on the principal subject—the distribution of the empire's remaining territories.

The most nagging question was the issue of access to the Straits of the Bosphorous, which linked the otherwise landlocked Black Sea to the Sea of Marmara, the Aegean Sea, and ultimately, the Mediterranean Sea. Control of this land, on either side of the strategically important water channel, was an issue that heightened tensions among the powers.

As there could be no agreement that would suit them all, the tacit decision of the powers was to do nothing and avoid precipitating a conflict. The powers actually propped up the decrepit state so that the decision would not be forced upon them by its premature demise; "premature," in this case was a relative judgment based on their inability to create a viable alternative to a weak state controlling the critical waters.[3] The alternative of one dominant, European power with armies and navies that could threaten her neighbors was not desirable.

The situation was complicated further by the (re)birth of the medieval Balkan states, which Ottoman armies had once conquered. The primary contenders among these relative newcomers for Ottoman territories in the European provinces of the empire were Bulgaria, Greece, Romania, and Serbia. These states planned to reclaim territories that revived historic entities. The difficulty lay in the definition of which historical incarnation was the most authentic, hence, which demand for land was most justifiable.

For that reason, while the Great Powers debated and fought over the future of the quickly disappearing Ottoman state sovereignty over its territories, the

Balkan states sought to do the same among themselves by taking matters either into their own hands or by getting the help of a Great Power patron. For the most part, the Balkan states could do little on their own without the approval of their more powerful protector.

After the Young Turk Revolution of 1908, however, the temptation to grab land from the empire, now in the grips of deep domestic turmoil, was great. Although Great Power counter-pressure was significant, the Balkan states could not miss the opportunity to carry out their plans. From 1908 onward, the race was on among the Balkan states and the Great Powers to secure for themselves as large a piece as possible of the dying Muslim empire. Those struggles produced much bloodshed and unrest, including, in time, two Balkan wars—in 1912 and 1913—and eventually, the Great War in 1914.

The New Bulgaria

Liberated from the Ottoman Empire in 1878, Bulgaria's modern historical development begins much later than that of other European countries. As a vassal but autonomous state, the Bulgarian principality in 1878 bore little resemblance to the territory her nationalists desired.

Bulgaria was reborn in the Peace Treaty of San Stefano at the end of the Russo-Turkish War (1877–1878), and then torn apart, a few months later in 1878 through the Treaty of Berlin. With the indispensable help of Russian armies, the Bulgarians had achieved a modest form of liberty. Then, chiefly due to the insistence of Chancellor Bismarck of the ascendant German state, the new Bulgaria was broken into three parts in the Treaty of Berlin.

One third of the territories came to life as the Principality of Bulgaria. Prince Alexander von Battenberg (r. 1879-1886) became the ruler. The province of Eastern Rumelia, a second third, existed as a semi-autonomous entity. Eastern Rumelia, joined the autonomous Principality of Bulgaria in a revolt in 1885. The revolt also led to the toppling of Bulgaria's first leader, Prince Alexander von Battenberg, and the eventual ascension of Prince Ferdinand (r. 1887-1918) to the same post. The last third had reverted to direct Ottoman rule in 1878. It was that third part, Macedonia that became the center of the most inflammatory issue in modern Balkan history.

Reborn with a substantial territorial deficit to make up, with a largely illiterate agrarian population (though the most literate among the modern Balkan nations), the Bulgarian Principality had little wealth with which to build a modern, industrial state.[4] The late nineteenth-century incarnation of Bulgaria was a weak reflection of past glory. The political parties in the Principality of Bulgaria, liberals and conservatives, vied for political power primarily as a way to attain government sinecures. Their foreign policy positions were secondary to this goal of personal rewards.

The issue that splintered the Bulgarian political climate, however, was what diplomats called the Macedonian Question of the Balkans. Political opponents could undo Bulgaria's political stability, tenuous for decades after its recreation, on the question of the eventual reincorporation of the last third of San Stefano

Bulgaria—Macedonia, a territory as well as an idea, which over the years has caused incalculable suffering, pain, and, thousands of deaths.

The newly independent Balkan states of Bulgaria, Greece, Romania, and Serbia, ravaged the region in their race to claim as much territory as possible from the disintegrating Ottoman Empire. The scramble was real as the Great Powers also sought to divide the larger bits of the Sick Man of Europe, while the Balkan states too fought over the prostrate body.

Bulgaria in 1886 was a troubled Balkan state with no ruler. The country, which had just unified in defiance of the stipulations of the Treaty of Berlin, was politically adrift. It was not recognized by other countries and could have no diplomatic relations with them. Prince Ferdinand would step into a shaky position on a European scale when he accepted his new title. He also would accept the responsibility for the resolution of a dangerous issue when he set out to tackle the realization of that lingering national desideratum—Macedonia.

This territory, contested between Bulgaria, Greece, and Serbia and for the entire span of the twentieth century, has been witness to scenes of tragedy for centuries. The overwhelming majority of Bulgarians, both in the Principality and in the unredeemed territories, was united on that one issue; in the future, the territory had to be incorporated into Bulgaria, and every Bulgarian leader had to address the issue in his policies.

Without Great Power protection, Bulgaria in 1886 could have reverted to direct Ottoman rule. In order to preserve the autonomy that had been so dearly won in the Russo-Turkish War, Bulgaria needed someone at the helm to give the country's political system a focus and relative stability. Prime Minister Stefan Stambolov (1854-1895), and key members of the Narodno Sûbranie, the Bulgarian National Assembly, desperately sought to find a replacement for Prince Alexander. The new prince would have to fulfill two deceptively simple criteria: he would have to be a member of a European royal house and to be willing to steer an anti-Russian foreign policy. Very few members of European royal houses were interested in the delicate position.

Ferdinand Saxe-Coburg-Gotha

After a laborious, exhausting search, the Bulgarians settled on Prince Ferdinand Saxe-Coburg-Gotha, an ambitious descendant of the Bourbon dynasty whose mother, Princess Clementine, was daughter of the last Bourbon French King, Louis-Philippe. It was a choice born out of necessity; Ferdinand and Bulgaria each got what they wanted out of the bargain, but neither was overjoyed about being shackled to the other.

Both the Bulgarian state's and her new ruler's positions were precarious; no European power would recognize the country until Russia had given her consent by being the first to bestow diplomatic recognition. However, Ferdinand's position was untenable to Russian sensibilities; he was unacceptable for three reasons: he was a Catholic, he was half Hungarian, and he was a Coburg. All three circumstances made his candidacy the obverse of what the Russian emperor would have desired in a man who would hold a geopolitically important post in the Balkans as Bulgaria's new prince. Furthermore, Ferdinand was not a Russian choice but one made by the extremely Russophobic prime minister Stambolov.

Much of the difficulty in recognizing a Bulgarian prince lay with the inability or unwillingness of Russian diplomacy, Tsar Alexander III, (r.1881-1894) in particular, to appreciate the Bulgarians' sense of national unity. Russian political sensibilities could not recognize a country that did not slavishly make a bow to Russia's importance and power by maintaining a careful, respectful, and unreasonably low profile. Young upstart states did not have license to behave as they wished until their Great Power patrons acquiesced or in some way approved of their actions.

Therefore, Russia took years to consent to Bulgaria's existence in its newly constituted form. It is telling that the young prince could not leave his newfound country for two whole years after stealing into Bulgaria via a Danube port with his small entourage in 1887. At least one Russian agent based in Bucharest was charged with hatching several assassination plots. Alexander III's vehement dislike of Ferdinand led to renewed attempts to neutralize him over the course of several years and to the tune of hundreds of thousands of francs in payoffs to potential assassins or revolutionaries.[5]

In the interim, Ferdinand, although well aware of the situation before he accepted the position, took the rejection as a personal insult. He proceeded to do everything in his power to make himself comfortable in Bulgaria and to help the country regain some domestic stability and economic well-being, but he was supremely aware of how delicately he would have to tread when the time came for negotiating all-important international recognition.

It appears he never held any regard for what might have been perceived as his natural foreign-policy allegiances. He did not favor France, Germany, or Austria-Hungary (his father was a Hungarian) over Russia or England in his actions; instead, he pursued, as long as it was practicable, a policy of playing one power off another by promising much but giving nothing away to either. To his credit, there was no other viable option for his adoptive people in that diplomatic atmosphere.

Ferdinand of Saxe-Coburg-Gotha lived his entire life with a heightened sense of inferiority, and this sensitivity made him excessively vulnerable to personal affronts, real or imagined. His self-consciousness about his outward appearance made him exceptionally aware of other people's judgments of reactions to him; therefore, he took all negative statements or postures as personal slights. He could not bear to be ridiculed, and this sensitivity made him an impolitic political leader. He was, too easily riled and too difficult to assuage. His character was further complicated by his and his mother's drive to attain the dream of a throne, any throne. Therefore, he tended to be imperious and unnecessarily cruel with his social equals and his subordinates alike, even when they were the very people who could assure his success as a leader.

Europe on the Brink of War

Europe, from the end of the Treaty of Berlin in 1878 through the outbreak of the Great War, had been on the brink of war numerous times. Each new alarm brought the increasingly rigid power camps closer to a military solution to territorial disputes that focused primarily on the Balkans; the resolution of the Eastern Question had become the primary flash point for the major European states.

Squabbles over the fate of territories such as Morocco or Ethiopia or the Liaoning Peninsula in Northeast China brought European states to the brink of open war. Yet the issue that led to the creation of battle plans drawn on the continent of Europe was the disposition of the remaining European territories of the decrepit Ottoman Empire. The Treaty of Berlin can be viewed as the shot of the starter's pistol that began the race of rapacious European states for Ottoman territories. Ferdinand knew his history well and understood that Bulgaria and the Balkans would be at the center of the next continental war.

Bulgaria's Domestic Climate

As an upstart, aspiring kingdom, the Bulgarian court had no legitimacy in the international community, and it had a shaky support base domestically. Retainers and "friends" of the court were well treated and almost cosseted by the royal family in an attempt to build a loyal support base and a comfortable social milieu. Since the international community did not recognize Prince Ferdinand Saxe-Coburg-Gotha as sovereign of Bulgaria until well into the twentieth century, his legitimacy and stature as a monarch were always in question.

Bulgaria was also politically unstable because the process of nation building was in its infancy. As the young state struggled to develop its domestic political culture, it was also building the institution that would give it its international visage, the diplomatic corps. Political parties were enormously polarized in their positions; party affiliation pitted members against one another. At the extreme, this polarization resulted in physical attacks and bloodshed. Disagreements over political positions led to personal attacks in party-sponsored newspapers; these defamation campaigns became the stuff of public discourse.

Bulgaria had lost the stability of a sitting ruler with the kidnapping of Prince Alexander of Battenberg, returning the country to sectarian politics and violence. The situation in Sofia from 1886 until Russia bestowed her official recognition, in 1896, was, at times, dangerously close to political anarchy. The threat of invasion by Turkish forces, which had a legitimate claim to what was, after all, a vassal state, and by Russian forces, who saw in the illegal unification of the two parts of Bulgaria in 1885 a deliberate provocation, were real. Therefore, Bulgarian society was at loggerheads by very passionate affiliations to political parties who were either vehemently Russophile, like the Conservative Party, or Russophobe as in Stambolov's National Liberal Party.

Stambolov's reign as prime minister was dictatorial, and in many respects, his heavy-handed system of governance denied basic civil rights to any who would oppose his rule.[6] However, the necessity for stability and the need to attach Bulgaria to another Great Power patron forced his hand. By presenting the country as well-run and stable, his seven years of rule steadied Bulgaria and put the country on a course of modernization and economic stability.

In Bulgaria, modernization developed haltingly. Part of that culture included the quickening of class differentiation. Increasingly, being modern meant adopting an urban, bourgeois culture and rejecting agrarian, rural ways of life. Liberation from the Ottoman Empire prompted a reexamination of the nation's identity, and those who could, as a mark of national pride, chose to emulate western models of class distinction instead of eastern models.[7] Thus, they based class distinction largely on attempts to be more "civilized," that is, more western, and less "oriental" or Turkish.[8] Introducing western models of class distinction, versus eastern models, constructed a dichotomy of western versus eastern ways. One was modern if one exhibited western modes of behavior and the reverse if one clung to eastern ways. Furthermore, Bulgarians owed most of their attitudes toward the life of the family and the role of women in society, regardless of class differentiation or the west/east divide, to tradition and religious education, a conservative view. However, urbanization, in this sense, was beyond the reach of most Bulgarians; the country remained largely an agrarian state which created a sharp divide between urban western oriented Bulgarians versus the slower to change rural population.

The Bulgarian Orthodox Church

Historically, the Bulgarians are Orthodox Slavs. The Bulgarian Orthodox Church is a national church and defined the nation as much as its ethnicity or imagined geography. Under Ottoman Muslim rule for 500 years, they developed a method of maintaining identity by acquiring a close affinity with their religion. A Bulgarian is a member of the Bulgarian Orthodox Church or vice-versa. By maintaining strong family bonds, which centered on patriarchal power, religion played a leading role in the process of national preservation. So important was religion in the historical development of the Balkan peoples that it was considered a transgression against the nation to convert to any other religion, even to another Christian religion.[9] One's religion was closely associated with one's membership in the society.[10]

National Liberation and Class Distinctions

Class differentiation, up until the Liberation, had both external and internal forms. If Bulgaria had classes, these included two basic social groups. A small group of the wealthy elites included large landowners and businessmen who dominated the society through their hold on the economy; the majority of the population, however, were peasants who worked the land. There existed a growing Bulgarian intelligentsia as well; however their relatively modest numbers and their fragmentation among various foreign schools of thought had a reserved impact on Bulgarian society in the latter part of the nineteenth century.[11]

Liberation meant a blurring of this division, but for the peasant class, the transformation would be extremely slow. The wealthy could attempt to experience the changes made possible through freedom from Ottoman influences. The rejection of all things "oriental" became a way of asserting independence, both politically and culturally. Everything that could be changed in the environment of the household to western styles was made to fit that particular model: clothing, décor, leisure activities, and occupations for both men and women. Education was the most enlightened form of differentiation.[12]

Those families who believed in the importance of emulating the west to a great degree sent their (mostly) sons to the best schools abroad (mostly Russian), even as nearly all of their contemporaries, if they could afford it, sent their sons away to school and kept the daughters at home.[13]

The Bulgarian principality took up the challenge of educating the population. Despite the frequent turnover of ministries, the national educational system managed to produce remarkable results. By the end of the first decade of the twentieth century, Bulgarian children attended four years of primary school, three years of (pre)gymnasium, and five years of gymnasium. Sofia housed the first Bulgarian university by 1888.[14]

While boys became heads of households and breadwinners, the occupational horizons of girls continued to be traditional and conservative. As the Industrial Revolution produced an increased demand for women in the work force, the numbers and types of jobs open to the female population increased. However, as in most industrial societies, the jobs were limited in scope and offered no hope for advancement. It was extremely unusual for women to rise above basic, entry-level types of positions.[15] In fact, the principal role of women remained that of wife and mother. Societies made certain that female citizens fulfilled that role by making most jobs inaccessible to women and by pressuring those who chose to remain single into marriage. Societal opprobrium made it clear that remaining single and, therefore, childless was unacceptable, practically deviant, unnatural, and utterly unpatriotic.[16]

If a woman were fortunate enough to be educated, her education did not necessarily "emancipate" her from traditional roles. There is no evidence to suggest that after the liberation of Bulgaria, a woman's education inspired her to change her world view or aspirations as an individual. Although Bulgarian women had the opportunity to study at Sofia University as early as 1901, as one historian put it: "Women seldom set themselves apart from their families . . . unthinking self-identification and devotion to the family unit to the point of self-abnegation seems to have been the common inner stance."[17] Rather than attempting to change the established system, educated women tended to become a part of it. Professionally and personally, they perceived themselves as members of the nation first.

When women attained "male" jobs, they did not necessarily behave as "women." Women had a better chance of gaining support for change in the status of women through a generalist approach, by manipulating public opinion, rather than directly through their roles as executive officials, diplomats, or politicians.[18] Thus, the presumption of gender-specific roles such as motherhood placed women at once in a position of unique importance while subjecting them to the authority of the state and the whims of the men in their lives.

The Stancioff patriarch, Dimitri, through his service to king and country, stood for the preservation of the established order, and he used the proper execution of his duties to set an apt moral example to his children and society.[19]

From the late nineteenth to the mid-twentieth century, the Stancioffs were in a profession that eased them into the transition of the world. The ritual of practicing diplomacy did not eliminate the possibility of change, but it did slow the process. In the less developed parts of Europe, educated and cultured people, and ideally, people of social status, could aspire to careers in diplomacy; they had little competition from the masses. An education abroad, preferably in a West European institution, guaranteed success in a profession in which fluency in several languages, tact, and delicacy in a myriad of formal occasions, were the *sine qua non* of a successful career.

The Stancioffs: *Haute Bourgeoisie*

The Stancioffs were members of Bulgarian elite society. Dimitri and Anna Stancioff came from very different backgrounds and cultures; together, the unique mixture of their individual heritages gave the family a firm foundation of resilience. Dimitri eventually became minister plenipotentiary (a status similar to ambassador) to several European courts, and Anna was mistress of the robes to Princess Clementine, the mother of Prince Ferdinand. Later, Anna was lady-in-waiting to three princesses.

The Stancioffs had four surviving children, Nadejda (1894-1957), Feodora, (1895-1969), Ivan, (1897-1972), and Hélène (1901-1996); their first-born, Alexander, (1890-1891), died in infancy. A daughter and a son, Nadejda and Ivan, served in the Bulgarian foreign service. Diplomacy and court life were this family's calling.

The matriarch's father was lord chamberlain to the Bulgarian Court; one of Anna's brothers was briefly in the horse guards. The patriarch's brother, Nicolas, was in the Bulgarian diplomatic corps, and Dimitri Stancioff served his entire career in various diplomatic and government capacities culminating with the position of prime minister.

The best class definition of the Stancioffs is *haute bourgeoisie* given the "mixed" nature of their parents' respective backgrounds. Anna was of Savoyard noble lineage and Dimitri was the son of Bulgarian merchant elites. Their family was unique, and Nadejda's journal entries repeatedly note that the Stancioffs found few families in Bulgarian society with whom they could share mutual interests or have views in common. Bulgaria had few families with equally cosmopolitan backgrounds. Furthermore, their milieu is difficult to pinpoint because of the amalgamation of Anna and Dimitri's social and national cultures. Neither fully of the aristocracy nor fully of the middle class, they existed in a middle ground between those groups with the understanding that they could and did exhibit the traits of both groups, as dictated by circumstances.[20]

While the men, Dimitri and Ivan, could fit into the emerging professional cadres, the women, Anna, Nadejda, Feodora, and Hélène, defied their gender roles. Neither fully emancipated nor completely in the arms of the suffrage movement, these women created a unique path for themselves and, as public figures, for other women.

Dimitri Stancioff Family Roots and Branches

Dimitri Stancioff's family lived in Svishtov, Bulgaria, for three generations; having migrated from Berat in Albania. A family of prosperous merchants in the port city of Svishtov, they acquired control of the Danube Navigation Company operations in the town in 1833, and from that point, their material fortunes were assured. The Stancioffs then traveled abroad on business and formed a marriage alliance with the Panitza clan another wealthy family, from Tûrnovo.

Dimitri Stancioff, (1863 – 1940), was the first son in a family of four children. He had two older sisters and a younger brother, Nicolas Stancioff. Sister Elena married Grigori Natchevich, (1853-1901) minister of finance and sister Eudoxia, (1867-1947), married Stefan Teodorov. The Stancioff family was wealthy and privileged but lived life with little or no pretension. Dimitri's parents owned a variety of scattered properties, primary among them were fishing rights on a stretch of the river, and the controlling interest in the Danube Navigation Company. They were extremely religious, and regular church attendance was part of their weekly rituals of work and worship. The Stancioffs, as Bulgarian patriots, supported the notion of gaining independence from the Ottoman Empire; they even hid the famous freedom fighter, Vasil Levski, in their home as well as, Stefan Stambolov, who would marry a Stancioff cousin, Poliksena.

An Austrian governess taught Dimitri and Nicolas in preparation for their studies at the Theresianum Academy in Vienna. Dimitri began his education there at the age of ten and stayed for eight years. In a school established initially by Habsburg Empress Maria-Theresa (r. 1765-1780) for the sons of the nobility, the boy from Bulgaria received a thorough education in more than academic subjects. Dimitri's schoolmates were noblemen and princes; they were not only Austrians but also noblemen from other European states. At the Theresianum Dimitri acquired the bearing and, most importantly, the outlook of the privileged classes, who still controlled the destiny of Europe.

The curriculum was rigorous; among other subjects, Dimitri studied the classics, mathematics, science, history, and Latin, as well as swimming, fencing, and riding. He presented an elegant figure as a boy, with lithe limbs, dark, deep-set eyes, and short brown hair. His visage and bearing projected seriousness and, intelligence. An impassive deep thinker, Dimitri was, by virtue of his education and experiences, a candidate for any professional occupation. He exuded a self-assured presence in photos taken in his early twenties.

Their uncles Panitza were businessmen and bankers in the city; therefore, Dimitri and his brother had relatives in Vienna. At the Panitza home, the boys met some of the better-known personalities in Bulgarian history. The two returned home only for summer vacations, and the contrast between the cosmopolitan Austrian capital and the provincial Ottoman river-port town was striking. How did they reconcile the differences between their birthplace and their educational environment? They both pursued careers in government service. They eschewed business careers, leaving those occupations to others. A career in government was prestigious, relatively well-remunerated, and more secure than other pursuits.

Dimitri Stancioff's tenure at the Theresianum coincided with the liberation of Bulgaria and the accession of her first prince. It is possible that his Austrian schoolmates' adulation of their Habsburg heir apparent, Prince Rudolph, inspired and awakened in him the need to have a like focus. Teachers steeped in imperial traditions schooled him; and he was surrounded by fellow students who lived in an important empire at a time in history when empires, nobility, and social distinctions seemed to be destined to last indefinitely. Thus, it was only natural that a youth from a country seized by nationalist fever to be free of foreign domination would yearn for all those institutions that his fellows took for granted. He too wanted a prince to worship and to whom he could swear allegiance and devotion.

In this atmosphere, he grew to admire and support, unquestioningly, the institution of monarchy and the supreme role of the king in the lives of his subjects. The role of the church as the main support to the monarchy was naturally a part of the structure. Dimitri Stancioff could not have failed to make, and eventually become, a supporter of this paradigm. He became a staunch monarchist in the bosom of the Habsburg Empire.

As a student in Vienna, he also participated in all the beloved pastimes of that youthful group. He and his mates pursued all the activities associated with Vienna of the period. They spent time in favored cafés on the Graben, hailed their much-loved coachman while practicing their Viennese dialects, and frolicked in the Prater during their free hours. As a way of creating their own social milieu, Dimitri and his friends started a foreign students' club called *Les Gamins Internationaux*. After graduation in 1881, Dimitri stayed on in Vienna to study law.

Although the Stancioff brothers were not typical Bulgarians in terms of their education and upbringing, they were typical in terms of their devotion to their parents and their piety. Prayers and the evocation of God for all events peppered their lives, and no major or minor event passed without the invocation and practice of religious ritual. This type of atmosphere also created the kind of filial devotion and eagerness to be of use that is emblematic of the period in general and of Orthodox culture in particular. An example of this type of evocation is in an excerpt from a letter Dimitri wrote home when he passed the first of his law exams:

> With the help of God and thanks to your invaluable support during the last few years, I shall soon sit for my final Law examination. My greatest wish is to please you and to deserve the happiness of serving you and my country even in the most humble capacity. I shall strive for this with all my strength and I kiss my mother's hand and assure you of my respect and devotion.[21]

For their part, Dimitri's parents encouraged their sons in their educational pursuits, even though ultimately that education set the boys apart from other Bulgarians, and even their parents.

Anna de Grenaud and the Cinzanos

A photo of Anna de Grenaud (1861–1955) taken in 1887, shows a diminutive woman in an elegant evening dress with long sleeves. She looks directly at the lens; her eyes are light-colored and piercing. She is bold, unabashed, and clearly calm and poised. Her face has angular features, a slightly prominent chin, a straight mouth with narrow lips pressed together, echoed by straight dark eyebrows hovering taut above her clear eyes. Her hair, pulled back, and into a chignon, with small ringlets draping her temples, softens the angular effect. This was a self-assured, intelligent woman.

Anna was one of six children born to a Savoyard French family. She had two sisters and three brothers. On her mother's side, she was a Cinzano. Her father's title was Alexander Joseph Bonifort Count de Grenaud de St. Christophe and her mother's full name was Gabrielle Della Chiesa Marquise de Cinzano. Her family did not have exceptional means. Their lineage reached back to heraldic medieval Europe, and the parents raised and educated their children to perpetuate an aristocratic heritage; however, by the late nineteenth century, they lived in strained financial circumstances.

Anna was educated at a convent school administered by Catholic nuns. A convent education held girls in a special kind of ignorance; it prepared them to be perfect mates, with refinement and enough general knowledge to maintain salon and dinner-table conversations. The purpose of their education was to create future pillars of society who would acquire a certain polish. A strictly enforced schedule governed the students' lives and imposed an order created by the nuns. The girls would one day learn to transfer that structure to their lives as proper matrons in society.

The convent curriculum included literature, history, arithmetic, religion, sewing, painting, and especially music. Graduates had to have just enough education to make them shine in society but not enough to allow them to pursue inquiry into any field of study with any great profundity.

Another aspect of the convent education was to direct any propensity toward individualism into cooperative undertakings. Conformity of mind and purpose led these girls to the ultimate accomplishment of losing themselves in the rigid structure of patriarchal and, ultimately, church-inspired hierarchies of the world that awaited them outside the convent walls. Their class segregated the girls themselves; structure inside the convent reflected, in simplified form, the structure to come outside its walls.[22]

Thus the trademark of a convent-educated girl was the controlled, flowing handwriting that each student acquired before graduation. Conformity and acceptance of a standardized form of penmanship instead of an individual style steered the girls away from individualism and toward collectivism; later, the focus would be the family group and not individual wants. Anna de Grenaud's penmanship was startling in its consistency, elegance, and graceful lines.

The symbolism and structure of this type of education not only imbued girls with a sense of devotion to the church but also prepared them to manage a household. Modeling the hierarchy and distinction based on status and power outside the convent walls, girls were educated to accept patriarchy.[23] A young girl was prepared to accept her place in the hierarchy in society by accepting her lack of influence over her own world and the influence of God and His established order in the world she would enter at her maturity. Faith in the Creator explained and compartmentalized so much of the incomprehensibility and random aspects of life for the girls.

In this view, monarchy was completely comprehensible as a viable system, and patriarchy was equally natural and desirable. Convent-educated women became the greatest supporters of the church and of monarchy because within those rigid structures, women could understand the cosmos, the relevance of life, and their roles in it. For the most part, the girls left the convents staunch conservatives.

The future Madame Stancioff was one of a diminishing number of monarchists in France; it was natural for her to continue to champion that social hierarchy. She accepted the patriarchal order, as expected; however, she did not pursue the exact course of obedience and servility one might expect.[24] Educated to believe that the two focal points of her life would be her home and the church, Anna had learned how to create order and structure in her life; that order would later prove useful in her domestic as well as professional life.

Courtship and Marriage of Anna and Dimitri

Anna de Grenaud had accompanied Princess Clementine (daughter of Louis-Philippe of France) in 1887 when the Prince Ferdinand's mother first arrived in Bulgaria. It must have been an epic journey since the last leg of the trip had to be finished in horse drawn carriages over rough terrain and wild country from Belgrade to Sofia. There was no rail link between those territories. Anna had taken up the duties as lady-in-waiting to Princess Clementine.

She met her future husband while she served at the Bulgarian court. She was reserved and tactful with strangers. He must have appeared an unexpected candidate in a society very sparsely populated with eligible men. Then a bouquet of Parma violets delivered at the appropriate moment imparted more meaning than impassioned speeches or ardent glances. Anna and Dimitri pledged their troth by spring 1889. She was more than two years older than her fiancée, but what eventually won over the young Frenchwoman was her love for nature and its splendors.

Dimitri wooed her with the natural beauties of his native land, and she was enchanted. This shared love formed the essence of their mutual yearning for splendor, both internal and external. They understood the same language of beauty, which informed their intimacy. Mountain valleys and streams became the alphabet of their joint language and the foundation of their love. Over the years, they managed to convey that love to all their children. The Stancioffs spoke and wrote with the lexicon of natural beauty: a brilliant sunset, a perfect bloom, a perfumed breeze became metaphors and symbols of life and love.

Dimitri and Anna married in a Catholic ceremony in Prince Ferdinand's chapel in Ebenthal, a relatively modest house compared with the Coburgs' other properties. Twenty-five miles from Vienna, the country house, built in the eighteenth century, was a simple, pleasant structure, surrounded by generous expanses of woodland and vineyards. A nature-lover's paradise, it was an idyllic place for the young Stancioffs to form their union as man and wife. Prince Ferdinand and Princess Clementine attended the ceremony.

The newlyweds were both favorites of Prince Ferdinand, whose feelings for them vacillated between love, lust, and disdain. He honored them by offering his ancestral home for their wedding; however, he also tormented and teased them in some insidious ways. For example, he had the habit of pretending to drop papers in Dimitri's presence and then order Dimitri to pick them up. Dimitri's refusal always elicited a rebuke from the initiator of the scene. Prince Ferdinand deliberately sought out ways to humiliate Dimitri because it assuaged his need to assert superiority. He also made it clear that he found Anna attractive and paid court to her and presented her with expensive gifts.

When he heard that the couple was engaged to be married, the prince ordered, from Paris, a special brooch to be made for Anna in celebration of the event: a spray of lilacs, executed with diamonds, wrapped in a black ribbon of enamel to show that he was in mourning. In his standard *modus operandi,* when the prince needed the services of his subordinates, he would woo and court them in extravagant ways; when his baser nature overpowered his more rational instincts, he let loose his repertoire of insults and barbs.

Faith as a Family Bond

After mutual attraction, for Dimitri and Anna religious faith was the other pillar of their bond that supported the relationship. Although Dimitri converted to Catholicism so that they could marry, throughout his life he worshiped in both Catholic and Orthodox churches. The decision to convert set him apart from his peers in Bulgaria and put him and his family on a different course.

Largely due to this blending of cultural traditions, the domestic structure and dynamics of the Stancioff family were unique.[25] For example, under Ottoman rule, the Bulgarians developed a method of maintaining identity by acquiring a close identification with their religion and maintaining strong family bonds, which centered on patriarchal power. Therefore, religion played a pivotal role in the development of the Stancioff family character, although their father was born Bulgarian Orthodox, and their mother was a French Roman Catholic the resulting blend was firmly anchored in the Catholic Church. This became a basis for their distinctiveness as a family.

The social expectation was that a wife, upon marriage, joined her husband's family and its circle of connections. In this, too the Stancioffs were an anomaly. Her husband, instead, clung to her. So closely did Dimitri cling to his wife and new family that his family was aware of his conversion to Catholicism only at his funeral.

Anna and Dimitri's family celebrated all the major holidays in both churches, and since the difference in the calendar allowed for a 12-day interval between holidays, the dual celebrations did not conflict with each other. Although, the children were raised Catholic, they too attended Orthodox services and practiced that faith's rituals of observance. One characteristic of the entire family was their strong faith, especially, their Catholic faith, which truly sustained them in times of crisis.

The family's world view and special cohesiveness emanated from their strong religious beliefs and the pervasiveness of their faith throughout their lives. This aspect of their character, both collectively and as individuals, shaped them, sustained them, and served as the foundation of their strength as a cooperative unit. However, Dimitri was among a small group of believers who chose to marry outside of his church; the decision was a grave one for Dimitri.[26] To their credit, the Stancioff family managed both to maintain their identification with Bulgaria and sustain their fundamentally unrepresentative religious life.

Family Structure

Anna Stancioff, who perceived herself as a Catholic wife and mother, was the core of the family. Her responsibilities as a pious Christian and devoted wife vested her with the moral authority of her stature in society.[27] From her strong devotion to monarchy was born her link to the French bourgeois women who saw republicanism and democratic values as a dangerous product of modern times. In their insistence on clinging to the structures and values of the ancién regime, they saw the salvation of the family.[28] Since a woman's primary role was the preservation of the family, she would have been remiss in her duties if she had espoused the destruction of the established hierarchical order.

Anna internalized the prescriptive literature of her era and became the parent who instilled moral values in her children.[29] Furthermore, a convent education reaffirmed the primacy of God for her. The Catholic Church, revitalized and rejuvenated in nineteenth century France, further constrained individual initiative by channeling the tradition of women's participation into charity work and thus suppressed female enterprise.[30] In Anna's case, however, it is clear, by the deference her spouse and their children exhibited, that she exacted her power from her efforts to be a good mother. There is no overt evidence of opposition to any of her desires. She earned and kept the power a "good mother" garnered by performing her duties well.[31] She taught her children her philosophy of life: work with a passion for what you do without thinking of the compensation or of its potential for success.[32]

The Stancioff's family hierarchy was skewed by the unique nature of Anna and Dimitri's relationship; they had an egalitarian marriage, one in which both parties had equal say. And in time, the parents sought their children's participation in some decisions.[33] There existed a correlation between egalitarianism and the acceptance of women in society as fully rational beings deserving equal status with men.[34] This trend was a herald of modernism.

The husband and wife of this family did not divide their relationship only along traditional patriarchal and matriarchal duties. Dimitri Stancioff was responsible for order in the family and served as a role model for middle class virtues; Anna was mainly busy with the duties of a nurturing mother. However, both were engaged in professional positions, diplomacy, and court service. At home, they overlapped and traded roles on numerous occasions and so did their children, especially Nadejda. Therefore, when Nadejda later found work outside the home, she did not do so as an opportunity to alter her relationship with her family or to put any distance between herself and them but rather the opposite. She used her work as an opportunity to enhance her family's survival, both professionally and financially.[35] The physical distances that separated them shortened the emotional space among them, and Nadejda worked harder than ever for her family's benefit.

Careers for Diplomats and Courtiers

Dimitri Stancioff's career began because of much larger events than his own efforts to find work. The acceptance and eventual accession to the Bulgarian throne of Prince Ferdinand Saxe-Coburg-Gotha created an opportunity for Dimitri. At the age of twenty-four, Dimitri was in the right place at the right time, and he had the requisite accomplishments for the position of private secretary and later head of the new sovereign's political cabinet. The headmaster at the Theresianum asked Dimitri if he could put himself at the disposal of Prince Ferdinand for translations and other types of work necessitating a facility in German and Bulgarian.

Chosen for a position of responsibility and prestige at the very beginning of his young life, Dimitri was fortunate. Thus, he returned to Bulgaria with an employer who became the second foreign prince to rule the country since its liberation from the Ottoman Turks. By 1888, promoted from the prince's private secretary to chamberlain of the court, Dimitri found time to pursue his future wife.

Life in Sofia was an uncommon mixture of French court elegance and peasant chic. Court life was constrained by the economic feebleness of the country and lack of basic infrastructure. However, Anna performed her duties so well that her relationship with Princess Clementine was warm and friendly until the latter's death some thirty years later.

Anna Stancioff was already in the service of the monarchy, so being a diplomat's wife was not a leap away from that life but rather an extension of it. She and Dimitri were able to attach to each other's professional worlds. Dimitri did not dominate or supersede his wife. Rather, the couple created their own unique family circle. Anna's role as lady-in-waiting helped rather than hindered Dimitri's diplomatic career, just as his career continued to make Anna visible to the monarchy. Anna's influence and visibility, and her good relationship with Princess Clementine and Prince Ferdinand had a part to play in Dimitri's professional life. Later, Anna's position in the court made her daughters eligible for the same posts at court; and her daughter, Nadejda, used her mother's influence to segue into a professional career in the diplomatic service of Bulgaria. The Stancioff women were professionals before the notion was widely accepted, albeit in careers that were within the norms of respectability.

The entire families of diplomatic appointees were expected to form a kind of support network of soft but persistent diplomacy of a different sort at their postings throughout the world. [36]

Social calls were extremely important in the process of establishing a network of professional contacts, and in making these calls; women had an impact on the family's professional future. [37] Diplomatic social life absorbed an incredible amount of time and required enormous amounts of endurance; all family members were required to play their part in accomplishing the business of diplomacy including the children. [38]

Anna and her children were all active participants in the life of the diplomatic communities they joined. The Stancioffs' two eldest daughters were their father's informal secretaries, and had their own desk in his study, where they took dictation, translated, or deciphered dispatches from Sofia. They performed this labor throughout their entire lives.

The younger Stancioff children also had their role to play; they had to be exemplary playmates in order to be permitted the privilege of contact with other diplomatic children. Thus, as the playmates of other diplomat's children, and then as bona fide assistants to their father, the children learned the diplomat's *métier* (calling). A diplomat's wife and children, then, would assist him in his professional capacity by furthering his prestige and social contacts and, therefore, supporting the family enterprise. [39] George Buchanan, (1854-1924) the British ambassador to Bulgaria, 1905-1910 and to Russia 1910-1918, and a contemporary of the Stancioffs, attributed his professional success to his wife and daughter's indispensable services. [40]

Domestic Life and Negotiating Space

Due to the unique nature of their family relationships, these six people, the Stancioffs, especially the women, managed to live and work as a highly effective network of enabling partners. [41] Each individual was instrumental in helping to elevate the others in their professional and personal, lives. [42] Their goal was to advance each other's careers and, at the very least, to facilitate beneficial marriage alliances.

In a patriarchal family structure, daughters would have been forced to marry or *not* at the behest of one or both of their parents. This kind of patriarchy was not the *modus operandi* of the Stancioff family.

Throughout their lives, the Stancioffs functioned as both a close-knit family and a professional unit; they were aware that they were different from other families, however. For example, after a visit to an acquaintance during a time of Stancioff family crisis, Nadejda wrote home, saying "...I told myself that for families as united as ours, it is always easy; we are happy together, at the heights and in the depths and God is always there."[43]

Domesticity, as defined by observers of the development of this new form of nuclear, convivial family life in the nineteenth century, was only part of this family's existence.[44] As the pace and nature of work outside the home changed, genteel women and their children were forced, even more, to remain in the confines of the home.[45] Although this isolation fostered closer relations between mothers and their children, it also kept women confined to strictly traditional pursuits and raised the barriers between men and women even higher. The Stancioff home served to advance the progress and practice of diplomacy.[46] Yet a home designated as both a public and private space was in direct opposition to the way in which bourgeois and aristocratic women would have used their homes.[47] The Stancioff family created the kind of domestic space that shut out the outside, solidified their bonds, and helped them to cling very closely to each other. For this family, the home combined the worlds of work and leisure, it was both a private and a public space.

In this milieu, women were in control of the domestic material content and therefore, material culture was extremely important. They controlled and supervised décor, cooking, and cleaning as well as the family's wardrobe. For the Stancioff women, this domain was even more important than for other women of their social group because the home of a diplomat was more than the family's refuge from the outside world. Their home welcomed, by necessity, the outside, workaday world, as well as a procession of social and political dignitaries. Their communication with each other and society used the semiotics of fabrics and flowers as well as a countless other markers of prestige and social station.

If the comparison were made to the lives of the principal royal families with whom they had the most contact and by whose success the Stancioffs marked their own lives, then it is clear that the Stancioffs came out well ahead of that group. They accommodated and adjusted as necessary and ended by surviving extraordinarily well. The Bulgarian, French, Italian, and Russian royal families were all by the end of the Second World War, in disarray, to say the least. Some families, violently eliminated by wars, revolutions, and civil unrest, did not survive.

Anna and Dimitri Stancioff, however, managed to hold on to the last vestiges of aristocratic honor and even the vision of noblesse oblige well into their children's generation. What preserved the family, aside from the vagaries of chance, were their faith, their hope in the future, and their complete, almost perfect devotion to each other.

The Family in Transition

The Stancioff family played a unique transitional role that spanned the gap between the traditional and the modern periods. As historians of the family have noted, the bourgeois groups emerging in the wake of liberal ideologies of the nineteenth century paved the way for the modern family.[48] Families had a public as well as private role to play.[49] The modern state, which encouraged large, stable families as a national duty, expected its (married) citizens to embody national ideals.

The Stancioffs created a life that employed a variety of techniques for survival and success. Their family most resembles the small number of modern bourgeois families who, at the turn of the last century, strove to blur gender roles and responsibilities while keeping patriarchy intact. The Stancioffs both exemplified and animated this new construct through their collaborative style of communication.

As liberalism nudged its way into their world, families chose to bridge the ever-widening gap between traditional roles and the evolving roles of modern women and to keep a leg in each world. Although essentially a Catholic family, for the Stancioff family, the decision to embrace Catholicism and Orthodoxy imbued not only their religious practice but also their family life with a useful flexibility—a quality that also served them well throughout their public lives. Collective freedom was this family's experience.

The Stancioff women were devoted to God and religion. Although change and modernity threatened the link between their reproductive role and the divine, their strict adherence to religious ritual and dogma kept them firmly in the conservative environment of their forbears.[50] Their strict religious observances served not only as a touchstone to their system of life but also reaffirmed their connectedness to the existing religious and societal structures.

Living in a world in transition Europeans in general and Bulgarians in particular entered the twentieth century with raised expectations. The immediate past and the ghosts of national discourses long past propelled Europeans into a new world. At the cusp of change most people still focused on the past to guide them. Living with one leg planted in their familiar surroundings they stepped onto the changing firmament as it was forming about them. For westerners on the continent change did not seem so drastic. Those living in the Balkans experienced change as fundamental and profound. They, the European others, had so many steps to take to simply achieve parity with the sophistication of the West.

Notes

1. Nadejda Stancioff, unpublished journal, 18 September 1911, PASF.

2. Katie Hickman, *Daughters of Britannia the Lives and Times of Diplomatic Wives* (New York: William Morrow, 1999). Leonore Davidoff, *The Best Circles Women and Society in Victorian England* (Totowa, New Jersey: Rowan and Littlefield, 1973). While in Western European society this practice had already become commonplace in Russian society it was, as late as 1914, still considered a shocking breach of convention. There, only visits in person were *de rigeur*, no substitutions permissible.

3. This dilemma is the Eastern Question. A diplomatic and foreign policy conundrum which bedeviled the Great Powers since the first significant defeat of Ottoman forces by a European power in 1774. The powers were stymied by their indecision of apportioning spheres of influence over the Ottoman Empire. The uneasy compromise, to leave the Ottoman Empire erect, became the Eastern Question.

4. Rumen Daskalov, *Bûlgarskoto Obshtestvo 1878-1939*, 2 vols. (Sofia: IK "Gutenberg", 2005).

5. Stephen Constant, *Foxy Ferdinand Tsar of Bulgaria* (London: Sidgwick & Jackson, 1979). See also Doncho Daskalov, *Anarkhizmût V Bûlgaria*. (Sofia: Universitetsko izdatelstvo "Sv. Kliment Okhridski", 1995).

6. His very controversial personality has been the subject of numerous recent studies and he is experiencing a rehabilitation of sorts. His image has been burnished and now he is referenced as the Bismarck of the Balkans. See Andrei Pantev, *Za Stefan Stambolov V Chasa Na Bûlgariia: Statii, Eseta, Ochertsi.* (Sofia: Edem 21, 1995).

7. While the Ottomans ruled Bulgarians, behaving like a westerner, acquiring western dress, or manners, were considered a betrayal of the state, i.e. the Ottoman rulers, and therefore forbidden. Liberation presented an opportunity, to those who could take it up, to emulate westerners. At the end of the 19th Century, in the countries of the Balkans western culture meant for the most part French, English, and German, for a variety of historical reasons.

8. The Orient for Europeans up to and through World War II began in the eastern Mediterranean and continued all the way to Japan. Orient is a term akin to Near East, which has a specific, time sensitive and geographically specific historical significance. The cultural value given the term was backwardness, inscrutability and a lack of civilization – with a hint of the savage. To be accused of Orientalism ascribed all of the aforementioned characteristics to the individual or nation so named. See Daskalov, *Bûlgarskoto Obshtestvo 1878-1939,* Rumen Daskalov, *Mezhdu Iztoka I Zapada : Bûlgarski Kulturni Dilemi,* 1. izd. (Sofia: Lik, 1998).

9. See Sells, Michael. *The Bridge Betrayed: Religion and Genocide in Bosnia.* Berkley: University of California Press, 1996. For the Serbs and Croats this phenomenon is referred to as *Christoslavism* by Michael Sells. A new religious ideology, *Christoslavism,* is the belief that Slavs are Christian by nature and that any conversion from Christianity is a betrayal of the Slavic race. Further to convert from one's national church was also perceived as a form of betrayal.

10. Among Balkan Slavs, each nation had its own national church and members of the nation were almost exclusively members of the national church. To be a member of any other church made one ineligible for full membership in the nation thus being a Catholic Bulgarian was highly suspect not only because of the potential of subversive leadership from Rome but because a true Bulgarian could only be a member of the Bulgarian Orthodox Church.

11. See the following and other historians on the emerging intelligentsia. Daskalov, *Bûlgarskoto Obshtestvo 1878-1939,* Daskalov, *Mezhdu Iztoka I Zapada : Bûlgarski Kulturni Dilemi,* Ivan Elenkov and Rumen Daskalov, *Zashto Sme Takiva : V Tûrsene Na Bûlgarskata Kulturna Identichnost* (Sofiia: Izd-vo Prosveta, 1994).

12. Nikolai Genchev, *Bûlgarska Vûzrozhdenska Inteligentsiia,* (Sofia: Universitetsko izd-vo "Sv. Kliment Okhridski", 1991). While before liberation education served the purpose of defining and maintaining national identity after liberation modernization forced a choice. After liberation there was an option to go beyond simply the preservation of national identity; an opportunity to cultivate a modern, sophisticated, cultured citizen of a new state. Once educated in the western tradition those newly acquired distinguishing characteristics were institutionalized by the wealthy elites in their modes of behavior, the professions they chose, and the company they sought. It was common for these self-made elites to speak a second or even third language and to expand their business contacts abroad and again mainly in a westerly direction. By the last quarter of the 19th century, the Ottomans had ruled Bulgarian territories for 500 years and the yearning for all things western and therefore not associated with things eastern or oriental was a natural

outgrowth of that history. Furthermore, the economic prospects west were more vigorous and embodied potential growth, not an impression when one looked east from the Balkan Peninsula.

13. Engel, Barbara Alpern. *Mothers and Daughters Women of the Intelligentsia in Nineteenth-CenturyRussia*. Cambridge: University of Colorado, 1983, 14. "Until well into the 19th century, only a minority [of girls] could even read and write; fewer still attended school, and those who did were instilled with religious precepts and the necessity of subordinating themselves to husband and family."

14. Charles Jelavich and Barbara Jelavich, *The Establishment of the Balkan National States, 1804-1920, A History of East Central Europe ; V. 8* (Seattle: University of Washington Press, 1977). 196 Professors Jelavich give the date as 1904 it is rather 1888. See too Daskalov, *Bûlgarskoto Obshtestvo 1878-1939*.

15. See *Victorian Women* and other texts on this trend in the 19th century. While women's labors at home were diminished by "income" producing labor, their workloads only increased. For lower middle class and industrial class women this added burden increased the misery of their lives as they tried to fulfill the societaly and church prized roles of mother while they worked outside the home to generate the income necessary for survival.

16. Daskalova, Krassimira "Bulgarian Women in Movements, Laws, Discourses." *Bulgarian Historical Review*. 1-2 1999:193.

17. Ibid.182.

18. Rhodi Jeffereys-Jones, *Changing Differences Women and the Shaping of American Foreign Policy, 1917-1994* (New Brunswick: Rutgers University Press, 1995).

19. Leslie Tuttle, "Celebrating the Pere De Famille: Pronatalism and Fatherhood in Eighteenth-Century France," *Journal of Family History* 29, no. 4 (2004).

20. Edward Shorter, *The Making of the Modern Family* (New York: Basic Books., 1977), Randolph Trumbach, *The Rise of the Egalitarian Family Aristocratic Kinship and Domestic Relations in Eighteenth-Century England* (New York: Academic Press, 1978). I believe the best evidence to the unique nature of this family's make-up and philosophy of family togetherness lies in an examination of the father's last will and testament. If we are to understand how the family functioned and perceived their roles in the family, then we need only to look to the very practical and egalitarian inheritance document. Although the son was left more property than the daughters were, they were all given equal shares in the main family estate and properties. The mother was provided for without leaving her dependent on the children and the children were enjoined to take care of their mother. There was nothing bequeath to anyone outside the nuclear family.

21. Nadejda Muir, *Dimitri Stancioff Patriot and Cosmopolitan* (London: John Murray, 1957). 25.

22. Bonnie Smith, *Ladies of the Leisure Class: The Bourgeoisies of Northern France in the Nineteenth Century* (Princeton: Princeton University Press, 1981).

23. Ibid.

24. Ibid.

25. Pat Jalland, *Women, Marriage and Politics 1860-1914* (Oxford: Clarendon Press, 1986), Karl Kaser, *Mact Und Erbe. Mannerherrschaft, Besitz Und Familier Im Ostlichen Europa (1500-1900), Zur Kunde Osteuropas Ii/30* (Wien: Bohlau Verlag, 2000), Karl Kaser, *Vom Nutzen Der Verwandten: Soziale Nezwerke in Bulgarien (19. Und 20. Jahrhundert)* (Wien: Bohlau Verlag., 2000), David Ransel, ed., *The Family in Imperial Russia. New Lines of Historical Research* (Urbana: University of Illinois Press, 1978), Shorter, *The Making of the Modern Family*, Louise with Joan Scott Tilly, *Women, Work and Family*. (New York: Holt, Rhinehart and Winston, 1978), Trumbach, *The Rise*

of the Egalitarian Family Aristocratic Kinship and Domestic Relations in Eighteenth-Century England.

26. In Southeast Europe religion has played a significant role in the development of national consciousness. In the Balkans, given the historical reality of non-Christian, Muslim domination, one's religion was worn as a protective cloak, a shield against conversion and a convenient way to define oneself when among "others." "Others" was anyone who is not of the same religion, ethnicity, and race.

27. Eileen Janes Yeo, "The Creation of 'Motherhood' and Women's Responses in Britain and France, 1750-1914," *Women's History Review* 8, no. 2 (1999). 206.

28. Smith, *Ladies of the Leisure Class: The Bourgeoisies of Northern France in the Nineteenth Century.*

29. Jennifer J. Popiel, "Making Mothers: The Advice Genre and the Domestic Ideal, 1760-1830," *Journal of Family History* 29, no. 4 (2004).

30. Renat Bridenthal and Claudia Koonz, eds., *Becoming Visible Women in European History* (Boston: Houghton Mifflin Co., 1977).

31. Rachel G. Fuchs, "Introduction to the Forum on the Changing Faces of Parenthood," *Journal of Family History* 29, no. 4 (2004). 228.

32. Anna Stancioff, unpublished letter to Dimitri and Nadejda at Neuilly, 6 October 1919, DSF IV, PASF. "This is how we should live our lives. Not by attaching importance to futile or useless gestures: all that glitters can be a [false lure] fight for life, to do good, and for that contented feeling of knowing that I was true to myself."

33. Jessica Tovrov, "Mother-Child Relations among Russian Nobility," in *The Family in Imperial Russia*, ed. David Ransel (1978).

34. Trumbach, *The Rise of the Egalitarian Family Aristocratic Kinship and Domestic Relations in Eighteenth-Century England.* 228.

35. Barbara Alpern Engel, *Mothers and Daughters Women of the Intelligentsia in Nineteenth-Century Russia.* (Cambridge: University of Colorado, 1983). Engel had different findings on this subject. "The need to look for work...made a girl less subject to the power of her parents and altered her relations with her family."51. In Bulgaria married, divorced and widowed women could vote in 1937. Therefore, women, although permitted to vote, were still recognized by virtue of their connection to the men in their lives; as Krassimira Daskalova noted, the present, past and even the already dead men in their lives.

36. Janet Finch, *Married to the Job: Wives Incorporation in Men's Work* (London: G. Allen & Unwin, 1983). 25-26. In the United States the wives of diplomats were assessed along with their husbands in the latter's efficiency reports to the Foreign Service as late as 1972.

37. Jeanne Petersen, *Family, Love, and Work in the Lives of Victorian Gentlewomen.* (1989).

38. Hickman, *Daughters of Britannia the Lives and Times of Diplomatic Wives.*

39. Davidoff, *The Best Circles Women and Society in Victorian England.* Dimitri Stancioff taught his children to be effective at networking. Years after his daughter Nadejda was old enough to network on her own her father reminded her still to "write [him] a word of greeting...it will please him a great deal and *for you—for us—*it is always good to maintain contacts." He was referring to the primary Turkish negotiator at Lausanne in 1923, Ismet Pasha.

40. George William Buchanan, *My Mission to Russia, and Other Diplomatic Memories.*, 2 vols., vol. 1 (1923). 78. Buchanan acknowledged that he accomplished his official work "in Sofia...with a chancery composed of a single vice-consul, reinforced by the voluntary services of my wife and daughter."

41. Trumbach, *The Rise of the Egalitarian Family Aristocratic Kinship and Domestic Relations in Eighteenth-Century England*. Trumbach has pointed out that domestic ideal favored a very close association of the nuclear family with the key actors including a man's: "father's and mother's family.. and his siblings an siblings-in-law, his closest ties [beyond] this circle were with his paternal uncles."288-289. The Stancioffs modified the model by clinging most closely to each other, husband and wife, next were the close ties to their children. Finally, the next closest ties were with the wife's siblings. Connection with the husband's family was distant. They formed a very loosely defined patriarchal household, which in reality comprised of a domestic ideal, which encompassed the most convenient and beneficial aspects of domesticity and patriarchy. However, this intersection is not as contradictory as it may appear at first glance since Trumbach also asserts that: " domesticity...increased patriarchal control over women and children since men believed they could not love what they did not own."

42. Tovrov, "Mother-Child Relations among Russian Nobility." 16. "It was assumed that individuals in an extended family...would find, in the family unit, the satisfactions and fulfillment lacking in any particular relationship." The Stancioffs came to exemplify this search for 'satisfaction' to a highly developed degree.

43. Nadejda Stancioff, unpublished letter, 10 June 1923, PASF.

44. Shorter, *The Making of the Modern Family*. 227.

45. Judith Newton, "Engendering History for the Middle Class: Sex and Political Economy in the Edinburgh Review," in *Rewriting the Victorians Theory, History, and the Politics of Gender*, ed. Linda M. Shires (London: Routledge, 1992).

46. Smith, *Ladies of the Leisure Class: The Bourgeoisies of Northern France in the Nineteenth Century*. Unlike Smith's examples where "the culture of the home often stood in opposition to the imperative of industrial progress," the Stancioffs' home life differed.

47. Yeo, "The Creation of 'Motherhood' and Women's Responses in Britain and France, 1750-1914."207.

48. Philippe Aries, *L'enfant et la vie familiale sous L'ancien regime* (Paris: Librarie Plon, 1960). See also Leonore Davidoff, *Worlds Between: Historical Perspectives on Gender & Class* (London: Routeledge, 1995), Gracia Gomez Urdanez, "The Bourgeois Family in Nineteenth-Century Spain: Private Lives, Gender Roles, and a New Socioeconomic Model," *Journal of Family History* 30, no. 1 (2005).

49. Fuchs, "Introduction to the Forum on the Changing Faces of Parenthood.", Popiel, "Making Mothers: The Advice Genre and the Domestic Ideal, 1760-1830."

50. Smith, *Ladies of the Leisure Class: The Bourgeoisies of Northern France in the Nineteenth Century*. 95-98.

2
The Young Family

*"From their earliest childhood my children spoke several languages with the
ease of some diplomats and most hall porters!"*
Anna Stancioff, *Recollections of a Bulgarian Diplomatist's Wife*[1]

Sofia, at the turn of the century, was a city with few paved roads; most were
packed dirt that turned to rivers of mud during the rainy season.[2] Initially the
capital of an autonomous principality that was vassal to the Ottoman Empire, it
was never developed or planned as an important center. In 1878, after the war of
liberation, the town was designated as the seat of the reigning prince and nominally an administrative center. It was little more than an Ottoman provincial
town. That nascent bloom did not encourage the creation or construction of a
substantial city. Only with the unification of Eastern Rumelia with the Principality of Bulgaria in 1885, did Sofia receive the impetus to expand.

Sofia the City

Unification made Sofia much more important politically and economically and
attracted the disenfranchised and those who hoped to find suitable employment.
Expansion and growth occurred at such a rapid pace that the government was
caught unprepared and ill equipped to handle the influx of refugees and urban
poor. By 1886, the city planners had doubled the size of the terrain available for
the construction of homes, but the invasion of people did not allow a suitable
interval to help plan and lay out a well-thought-out grid.[3] The unsanctioned
building of homes beyond the zoning boundaries was further spurred by the high
prices of plots available within the city limits. The construction of dwellings
became a matter of competition among the authorities who tried to enforce zon-

ing ordinances and the poor and homeless who sought to create a life for themselves in the emerging capital. Thousands of squatters erected their houses on the fields and farmland on the city's periphery.[4]

By the post World War I period, city sprawl began engulfing surrounding villages.[5] What contemporaries would have recognized as a city center were terrains built up around the palace: the Military Club; the Union Club; Hotel Bulgaria; the Alexander Nevski, Sveta Nedelia, and the Sveta Sofia Cathedrals; the mosque; the synagogue; the post office, and the Central City Baths. The most substantial and imposing structures in Bulgaria's capital city were insurance companies, banks, and brokerage houses. The city erected a university complex and national library, but early in the twentieth century, there was no national theatre or opera buildings and no city parks. These latter structures were *de rigueur* for a proper European society and its cultural season.

This Balkan capital east of Vienna would have been unfamiliar and exotic to anyone from Western Europe. Sofia was just emerging as a modern city when Paris and Vienna were already in cultural decline. In fact, denizens of Bulgarian Danube port cities like Svishtov and Ruse found Sofia backward. One contemporary informant thought the city both ill conceived and poorly organized—a jumble of neighborhoods with no clear city plan or charm.[6]

The primary forms of transport into the 1920s were by horse, donkey, oxcart, or on foot. The population was still largely unsophisticated, much less cosmopolitan and, therefore, would have appeared backward and the city unkempt to anyone who had traveled to western European capital cities. The few wealthy Bulgarian families of Sofia might have had a landau or some simple carriage for transport. No one owned an automobile in the country until Prince Ferdinand imported his. The river that ran through the city was barely contained. Projects that Prince Ferdinand proposed finally banked and bridged the river in several spots with elegant stonework bridges.[7]

Sofia had few amenities and no glittering storefronts; instead, in Ottoman era tradition, merchants relied on private shops located on the ground floor, or even the basement, of their homes. Most of the local population preferred peasant dress, and their clothing colored the city streets with a rainbow of hues. Furthermore, the Sofiotte dialect of Bulgarian could be unintelligible to Bulgarians from different regions, so the language in the streets of Sofia would have been mellifluent. The city had a mixture of inhabitants not only the Bulgarian peasants of the region—the Shopi and the Makedontsi—but also a good mixture of other ethnic groups Armenians, Greeks, Jews, Turks, and a sprinkling of others from neighboring states.

The city's development was uneven at best and woefully backward at worst. With no real fashionable core of residences, it offered instead, sprawl, a mass of neighborhoods, most of them poor, with no real local public amenities for rest and relaxation. In contrast, Prince Ferdinand and his mother were largely responsible for the plan and execution of the city's grand public parks, which resembled some of the same type of great expansive public greens found elsewhere in Europe, with walks, tree-lined lanes, fountains, and cultivated flowerbeds. Ferdinand also built botanical, zoological, and ornithological gardens to house his collecting mania for rare species of flora and fauna. He imported the first elephants into the city and could joke that he liked to keep them because his facial features—small eyes and oversized nose and ears—so resembled the pachyderms.[8]

Bulgaria had no rail link to central and western Europe. What came to be known as the Orient Express, the train and the line that linked Paris to Constantinople, was not completed until 1888. Sofia had just constructed its first train station and Princess Clémentine funded the Bulgarian portion of the line with her personal fortune.[9] The completion of the line allowed for a direct link to all the elegant capitals of Europe and indulged Ferdinand's fascination with rail travel and locomotive engines. With a city populated by peasants from the provinces, the brightly colored clothing and work carts in the streets made Sofia an exotic destination.

In other parts of the country, development was slow. The most advanced cities were Bulgaria's Danubian port cities. River traffic reached into the heart of Europe—Budapest and Vienna—and endowed river-town citizens with a more cosmopolitan perspective, especially those of Lom and Ruse. Proximity to the large Bulgarian émigré communities in Romania further enlivened Bulgarian cultural development on the Danube.

With the exception of the Black Sea, where the seaports of Varna and Burgas were built and linked via rail lines with the rest of the growing commercial transport network in the country, Bulgaria remained largely a land of small landholders, peasant farmers. The completion of major transportation arteries, and the facilitation of both road and rail traffic, helped Sofia to resemble more closely western European cities. Tourists had freer access to the country, and Bulgarians could more easily travel abroad. The broadening transportation network did not assure a concomitant enrichment of the economy. These improvements to the transportation network, however, did lead to a modest increase in economic activity via the new ports.

In 1892, Prince Ferdinand inaugurated the first international trade fair in Plovdiv, transforming the city into a major commercial hub. That same year witnessed the inauguration of the first telephone line in Bulgaria between the capital city and Plovdiv. All of these developments hastened modernization and offered the possibility of parity with the West. The advent of the new prince coincided with the quickening pace of the country's internal development. Bulgaria began the twentieth century with a sizeable agenda in both domestic and foreign development.[10]

Life at Court

Bulgarian court life, in its infancy, offered opportunities for advancement and promotion as well as many occasions to garner influence with the royal family. Compared with other European courts, more significantly, other western European courts, the pomp and circumstances of the Bulgarian court was woefully inadequate.

As a member of Prince Ferdinand's entourage, Dimitri Stancioff accompanied the prince on his inaugural voyage from Vienna to Bulgaria.[11] When Prince Ferdinand arrived in Bulgaria to take over a shaky, uncertain throne, he was twenty-six years old. His self-confident and imperious air impressed those who first encountered him.

At first, Ferdinand employed two French Orleanist noblemen, Comte de Grenaud and Comte de Bourboulon, at his court; the latter was marshal of the court, the former grand chamberlain of the court. These were largely ceremonial duties, which included being constant companions to the prince when he desired. Both men were French noblemen from Savoy whose personal fortunes had seen better days. Later, when he wished to fill more positions, the prince invited other members of the Grenaud family to form his entourage and court. Count Aynard who was the Comte's son and Countess Anna de Grenaud, the Comte's daughter, were part of the expanding de Grenaud presence at the Bulgarian court. Over time, other members of their extended family served Prince Ferdinand. As the longest-serving member of the original entourage, Count de Bourboulon, through his frequent correspondence with his mother, and later with his wife, painted the prince's personality and the nature of court life in Bulgaria from a unique perspective.[12]

To play the role of a sounding board on all types of questions, Prince Ferdinand brought his former tutor, Dr. Fleischmann, to court. Included in this first group of royal appointees were his personal physician and a press attaché. The prince named a Bulgarian Army chief of staff, Colonel Popoff.

At the turn of the twentieth century, diplomats from western Europe bemoaned the lack of restaurants, theatre, and opera—in general, a social scene worthy of a season. They found Sofia a rather drab backwater of a capital, where the inhabitants often remained close to their peasant roots. The combination of foreign cultures, languages, architecture, cuisine, personal habits, attire, and norms of social intercourse set a colorful, if unfamiliar, backdrop to an incomprehensible mélange, that Western sense of the mysterious "East." Before the arrival of Prince Ferdinand, few visitors saw anything resembling the western European norms of court ritual, the trappings of wealth and station that were commonplace in Paris, London, Rome, Vienna, and St. Petersburg. Thus, an appointment to Sofia left most foreign functionaries cold and desperate for reassignment.

According to de Bourboulon's letters, the palace staff was poorly trained and could, at times, be odiferous; also, disputes among the staff members often disrupted the smooth running of the prince's households.[13] Since there were multiple residences, and the prince acquired dozens by the end of his reign, the potential for staffing problems was enormous. All these difficulties complicated the existence of the ruler's foreign-born, mostly French, servitors. In response to discomforts, they, in turns, decried their burdensome duties or satirized both their master and his adoptive country's population. Prince Ferdinand did nothing to ease or facilitate his entourage's labors. He was a procrastinator of the worst sort, and although he recognized the inefficiencies of his court, he did nothing about them. In fact, he joked about himself and his people by referring to himself as King Petaud, a reference to the French proverb in which the king is in charge of beggars, and in his court, all are equals.[14]

The country's new prince was a curious member of aristocratic elites. Born to nobility with an exceptionally brilliant pedigree, his predilection for self-ornamentation, insistence on fine clothing, and embellished surroundings served to emphasize his somewhat effeminate posturing.[15] His social milieu found his manner, his affectations, even his extraordinary gifts as a naturalist, off-putting; they could not understand his passions.

Prince Ferdinand was a serious ornithologist and a dedicated botanist; the scientific community accepted works he wrote as legitimate contributions to these fields. Instead of pursuing the manly art of horseback riding, Ferdinand preferred to take a butterfly net on long walks in the woods. This image made him a puzzle of an aristocrat, a descendant of one of the prominent royal houses of Europe, the Bourbons. As a descendant of the Sun King of France, his behavior was unbecoming. Furthermore, his dalliances with lovers of both genders and his rather comical appearance—his prominent Bourbon nose and small blue eyes—made him the subject of ribald jokes and stinging comments throughout his life. He was sensitive to these slights, both perceived and real, and behaved consistently as though they were a constant subtext to others' perception of him.[16]

Although Prince Ferdinand spent an enormous amount of time, energy, and money on furnishing his palaces and assorted public spaces in the best and most luxurious décor, the sheer diminution of scale and lack of social season aristocratic elites followed elsewhere made the entire effect inadequate. Despite his and his mother's best efforts to create a court of equal stature to the brilliant ones of the West, at least in outward appearance, the persistent impression of foreign observers was that Sofia, so close to Constantinople, the capital of Byzantium, was much more akin to its eastern roots than its western aspirations. Unfortunately, for Ferdinand and his subjects, Byzantium, as a perceived construct, was very much in vogue at the turn of the twentieth century; western Europeans refused to see in Bulgaria anything but a shadow of the former empire's culture. They sought to find that which was exotic, opulent, and oriental in a place in which the elite among the population desperately wanted to be considered on equal terms with the supposedly civilized West.

Ferdinand was known throughout Europe for his taste for all sorts of luxuries as well as for his exceptional vanity. He was also exceedingly fond of jewelry. Reputedly, he had a habit of carrying unset gemstones in his pockets to fondle and admire at his leisure.[17] He kept jewelers busy with commissions to create elaborate items of personal adornment set with precious gems, and he was generous to those who served him well. Inevitably, those who had earned his favor could expect a gift of the utmost fineness and artisanship, often adorned with jewels of highest quality.

What complemented that sense of luxury and high standards in appearance was also a sense of his exalted destiny as a man and, specifically, as a monarch. Attaining the position of prince of Bulgaria was just the beginning of what he imagined for himself and his country; he felt his career would culminate in nothing less than the establishment of a new Byzantium with himself as supreme ruler. He felt entitled to surround himself with exceptional quality in everything if for no other reason than to assure himself and his visitors that he was worthy to be a descendant of his grandfather, Louis Philippe of France, the last, albeit bourgeois, king of France. He was also extremely susceptible to flattery, a characteristic that could not fail to escape notice and to be exploited.[18]

Certainly, he first had to overcome tremendous obstacles to achieve recognition from the Great Powers. While a lesser man might have felt fainthearted at the prospect of his grand plan, Ferdinand's personality combined a rare mixture of pessimism and megalomania. These traits permitted him to plot and scheme to attain his ultimate desires while maintaining an ever-constant refrain of dark views about the future of his dynasty.

Establishing the Coburg Dynasty in Bulgaria

In 1892, the prince and his prime minister, Stefan Stambolov, were often at loggerheads over domestic and foreign policy issues; however, they were of one mind on the question of an heir. Ferdinand had to perpetuate the monarchy by founding a true dynasty with an appropriate wife and especially with a male heir to the throne.

There were few princely families willing to take that risk of earning the displeasure of the Russian emperor. The search for a suitable wife was exhaustive and exhausting, since Ferdinand, despite his enormous wealth and his princely seat, had little to offer a bride and her family except the enmity of Russia. The quest for a consort was successful when the Duke of Bourbon-Parma offered his eldest daughter, Marie-Louise, (1870-1899), on the irrevocable condition that the article in the Bulgarian constitution stipulating that the heir to the throne should be a member of the Orthodox Church be rescinded. Count de Bourboulon negotiated the engagement in 1892.[19] In order to found a dynasty, the Bulgarian prime minister did the unthinkable—politically and, as a member of the Orthodox Church, religiously—he cajoled and threatened members of the National Assembly (Narodno Sûbranie) to agree to the amendment. These actions placed him at risk, both personally and spiritually, but his political will triumphed in the end.

The marriage alliance was a bold step for Prince Ferdinand, and the Narodno Sûbranie bowed to his will to change the Bulgarian constitution for the sake of the alliance. The following summation of the impact of the alliance by the Comte de Bourboulon accurately assesses the audacity of the act:

> This little Cobourg of nothing at all . . . . dares to raise his head to the great and sainted Russia and who, because of personal ambition, risks putting all of Europe to flame . . . and who will ally himself to the oldest, the most noble of royal houses, blessing and making blessed his people with monarchical traditions of real legitimacy! And this royal house consents to give its daughter to this kinglet, this parvenu! . . . this Slav nation, linked for centuries to the Church of the East, a fanatical religion, jealous of its rites, of its form, for the

purity of its ecclesiastical language . . . [over it] will reign a Catholic-Roman dynasty, and truly, it is an amazing thing to try to comprehend.[20]

This marriage would reunite the Bourbon and Orleans dynasties; both partners had royal French blood in their veins. Princess Marie-Louise Bourbon-Parma was exceptionally gifted and intelligent; she spoke five languages, was musically talented, a voracious reader, and witty. She lacked any sense of haughtiness and was a deeply religious and kind person.[21]

A Catholic Marriage

As soon as the announcement of the prince's engagement was made public, the two courtiers most likely to be the new princess' constant companion, de Bourboulon and Anna Stancioff, discussed how they would enhance their future mistress' rather plain, unattractive looks with improvements in wardrobe and hairstyles. The two took up the role of close confidants to their mistress, who reciprocated in a like manner. Marie-Louise appreciated their ministrations. Rather than treating them as servants, she preferred their company to her two Bulgarian ladies-in-waiting.[22] Princess Marie-Louise shared their propensity for sarcasm and mockery for entertainment's sake, and she grew to rely on both de Bourboulon and Anna.

The wedding ceremony in Villa delle Pianore, Parma, included a special blessing from the Pope; the bride was not only a fervent Catholic but also a goddaughter of Pope Pius IX. This bit of spiritual loftiness would return to haunt her husband's future foreign policy. The wedding party was a picture of traditional pomp and elegance with elaborate public and private celebrations in Parma. When the newlyweds arrived in Bulgaria, the celebrations continued.

Dimitri and Anna Stancioff were witnesses at the wedding of Prince Ferdinand with Princess Marie-Louise of Bourbon-Parma. In fact, Anna de Grenaud Stancioff and the Comte de Bourboulon were charged with preparing the honeymoon suite for the new royal couple.[23] The courtiers amused themselves with all sorts of speculations about what would transpire in that room on the first night. The two court servitors were both prone to sarcasm and mockery, so they were a good foil for each other.

Bulgaria's new princess promptly produced an heir nine months after her marriage, and the country was jubilant. The young princess had not only to endure the labor of childbirth but also the indignity of having to suffer the presence of the Prime Minster Stambolov, the minister of justice, and the court chamberlain. At the insistence of the prince, the men witnessed the legitimacy of the heir apparent's lineage, in the time-honored way of being present in the birthing room.[24] The birth of a son meant that the realization of the dream of establishing a dynasty was within reach for the Coburg mother and son.

Princess Marie-Louise's Court

Initially, the Bulgarian royal couple was quite affectionate and grew close. Ferdinand actually reveled in the fact that they shared the trademark Bourbon nose and that their progeny would carry that particular genetic trait on to posterity. He was extremely fortunate to marry into not only a grand, old, royal house but also one, which did not necessarily tie him to an alliance with England, Germany, or Russia. Princess Marie-Louise was not beautiful, however, and her directness in manner would quickly become irksome to her husband. She was also much younger than her spouse, and her tendency to be playful, cheerful, and vivacious irritated his vanity.

Since Ferdinand had an overwhelming need to be the focus of any gathering, his spouse's attractiveness as a companion—even to members of his court—nurtured a jealousy that turned venomous. Ultimately, the marriage was an unhappy one. Ferdinand soon treated his wife with little dignity and as simply his reproductive agent in the dynastic creation game. She responded with public displays of her own venom, making it clear how little they enjoyed physical intimacy, even before members of their entourage.[25]

Anna became *Grande Maîtresse* of Princess Marie-Louise's court, a position that was borne with some resentment in Bulgarian society; the expectation had been that the position would be filled by a Bulgarian lady. However, the royal family was not overly concerned with public opinion when it came to decisions about court life and structure.

Soon the royal family and the Stancioffs had much in common and began to share a life of mutual interests in issues involving family and child rearing. Nadejda Stancioff and Prince Boris were born days apart in the same year, 1894. Apparently, Nadejda was quite a gifted child even as a toddler. She was bright and the kind of child that made adults tremble (given her precocious intelligence).[26] She was "covered in hair" at birth, Prince Boris was handsome, with his blue eyes dotted with black lashes. The princess and her *Grande Maîtresse* were able to commiserate together on the developments of pregnancies, childbirth, and childrearing. The two women ended up having the same number of children, four. Anna had already endured the death of her firstborn son.

The women grew close, and the princess shared all the most intimate details of her married life with her confidante. Although at first, the princess viewed her conjugal life as satisfactory, she found Prince Ferdinand's moral and philosophical positions insupportable.[27] What is more surprising is that the young princess was not intimidated by her husband in the least. The letters and notes, which Princess Marie-Louise and Anna shared, are tender and warm.[28] It was only the premature death of the princess, in 1899, that ended the relationship between the two women.

The Stancioffs had a rocky relationship with the prince. Although happy to have the prestige and security of their positions, the couple was often in a dither about whether to leave the service of a court that caused them such headaches by its chaotic and irregular rhythm, which emanated from the pernicious personality at its center.[29] This quandary was a permanent feature of the Stancioffs' lives as part of the court and diplomatic services. Years of service did not soften the tension; the final rupture did not occur, however, until Ferdinand decided to enter World War I on the side of Imperial Germany.

A New Kind of Family

In contrast to the very authoritarian and patriarchal royal family style of interacting with one another, the Stancioffs followed a different system than the traditional roles of gender-segregated parenting. In fact, the Stancioffs exercised their parental roles and duties in a variety of ways. Ultimately, the differences in parental power and the corresponding relationship with their children were markedly dissimilar from their contemporaries.

The role of fathers as ideal citizens was revived by national states in the twentieth century, and Dimitri Stancioff, a good provider, educator, and moral compass, fit that image.[30] He did not insist on a patrilocal dynamic for his family. The Stancioff father was not always the central character in the family drama, despite the perpetual verbal cosseting he received. Instead, the power relationships remained fluid and reverted from member to member, as the situation dictated. The Stancioffs were malleable enough to readjust the family hierarchy and power structures to suit the needs of the moment with no ill effects on any family member. There were times when Anna and not Dimitri would take the lead in manifesting authority. Later, when the children grew up, Nadejda and Feo stepped in when it would benefit the family interests. The father did not feel the need to assert or reassert his authority, nor did the women, his wife and daughters, rebel against or usurp his proper place at the head of the family enterprise. What the family did manage to achieve was a complex maneuvering of positions, which to the outside observer seemed to perpetuate the *pater familias* image of the father, while the real drama was quite different.

First Diplomatic Post

Dimitri was singled out for his first diplomatic post to Romania because relations between the two countries were so important. In addition, the posting served as his entrée from a regional mission to a Great Power level assignment. It seems provident that Dimitri Stancioff began his diplomatic career after the end of Stambolov's reign in Bulgarian politics. The departure of the powerful political leader from the scene ushered in a new era in Bulgarian domestic and foreign policy, an era that allowed the new prince to put his own stamp on Bulgaria's future. The prince felt free to choose and support "his" ministers and to chart a new course for a country that was so much on the periphery of European diplomacy. Stancioff's diplomatic career began at this point, and his career would reflect the vicissitudes of Bulgaria's history from this point on.

In 1894, the Stancioffs moved to Bucharest, where their second daughter, Feodora, was born in 1895. This training opportunity in Bucharest was a segue from work at court to work abroad and assured Dimitri Prince Ferdinand's consideration by for the future post of future minister of foreign affairs. Court and society life in Bucharest were quite luxurious and met Parisian standards of dress and entertainment.

Anna Stancioff enjoyed herself immensely, but the expenses of maintaining that lifestyle were a strain on the family finances. Stambolov's resignation and the rise of Ferdinand's involvement in Bulgarian political life began a period of unreasonable exuberance and sometimes adventurism on the European continent that was increasingly tense politically.

Stambolov was vehemently against wooing Russian acceptance. The course of this initiative—to simultaneously maintain an amicable relationship with Russia's rivals in Europe while getting Russia to finally acknowledged Bulgaria as a legitimate, legally constituted state—led Prince Ferdinand on a torturous political journey. Increasingly, war and aggression would replace diplomacy and patient negotiations in Europe as a whole. Such actions led, Dimitri Stancioff during the course of his career, to feel ever more frustrated by Bulgaria's foreign policies.

Assassinations and Changes

Stambolov's mission as co-regent after Battenberg's departure, was to steer a steady course for the country while he found a new prince and settled him into the position, all of which he accomplished by 1893. However, his inability to gain international diplomatic recognition for Bulgaria and his intransigence on policy decisions that Ferdinand favored, diminished his usefulness to the prince. Forced from office, he was assassinated on a Sofia street, his hands severed and his body stabbed multiple times in the summer of 1895.

Prince Ferdinand's first political decision after the assassination was to convert his heir apparent to the Orthodox Church in order to initiate a proper rapprochement with Russia. Summoned from Romania and briefed, Dimitri Stancioff then traveled to Rome with the mission to try to persuade the Pope to grant a dispensation based on reasons of state.[31]

The mission was a failure (even after Ferdinand visited the Pope in person to plead his case). Prince Ferdinand had tried to persuade the Pope to consider this improbable concession with a wild suggestion that the decision might gradually convert the schismatic Bulgarians back to the one true faith! Ferdinand then took the unprecedented step of initiating the conversion of his heir to the Orthodox Church on his own.

His wife was predictably devastated, and their relationship as husband and wife deteriorated further. This move essentially forced Ferdinand out of the Catholic Church; the Pope anathematized the prince. because he converted his son to what the Catholic Church considered a heretical sect. Until Boris attained maturity, Prince Ferdinand was denied the sacraments of communion and confession in the Catholic Church. However, a close relationship with Russia was paramount to the development of a strong kingdom, and he was willing to pay the spiritual price.

The timing of the conversion was propitious, since Tsar Nicholas II had newly ascended the throne. None of the stigma attached to old personalities or quarrels lingered, and the process created a clean slate on which to chart successful state relations. The christening in 1896 launched the strengthening of diplomatic ties between the Russian Empire and the Principality of Bulgaria. Once the Russians recognized Bulgaria officially, the remaining of the signatories of the 1878 Treaty of Berlin lined up to do the same.

Concurrently, Dimitri Stancioff's career took an enormous leap in stature; he was the first Bulgarian named diplomatic agent to the court of the tsar. Prince Boris was christened in the Orthodox faith on February 15, 1896, and the Russian emperor acted as his godfather, cementing the warming Bulgaro-Russian relations. When the Stancioffs moved to St. Petersburg in the fall 1896, Dimitri was only 32, and the posting was an enormously prestigious honor, especially as it came at the start on the heels of this new chapter in Russo-Bulgarian relations.

St. Petersburg 1896-1907

The city of St. Petersburg, to the uninitiated, resembles an elaborate stage set floating on canals and riverbanks, illuminated by a northern light that exists, seemingly, solely for this purpose. At the turn of the century, it was still largely Peter the Great's city, untouched by later attempts at modernization. It was a showpiece with a carefully constructed look meant to impress and transport the visitor to a European state of mind. In fact, its purpose was to make its noble Russian residents more European and their estates and clothing and manners more western.

The building of a family residence in Peter's city, according to the specifications of his imported European architects, marked the definitive break from a Russian nobleman's past into his European future. As a showpiece, the city made its mark. No other city could be so alluring, distinctive, and as un-Russian as St. Petersburg. The capital of the Russian Empire had a glitter as unique as its grand palaces and parks. Its society observed all the rituals of European elites, and the social atmosphere was as proper as in Paris. This was the Russia familiar to the diplomatic representatives of foreign states, who had little business outside the city. Apart from taking summer vacations on the Gulf of Finland and possibly visiting Moscow, Kiev, or the Crimea, these foreigners' contact with Russia and Russians was limited to this unique showpiece and its Russian servants.

A post in St. Petersburg was desirable because the society and its season were most brilliant. Professionally, a diplomat posted to this city considered it a special coup and an honor. Russia was one of the Great Powers of Europe, and governments trusted only their gifted diplomats to represent their states to the tsar and emperor of all the Russias.

Russia on the Brink of Modernity

The turn of the century Russia to which the Stancioffs moved, was a country undergoing a slow, deliberate drive to liberalize and modernize. Although the court and its most loyal supporters refused to acknowledge it, the hopelessly backward-looking ways of their governance could not keep the impetus for change at bay. The liberal and populist movements of the 1870s, impelled by the sons and daughters of the nobility and rising gentry, fueled the change. Although not joyously welcomed by the peasantry, these new ideas and initiatives for reform filtered back into all levels of Russian society in louder and more frequent calls for transformation. Therefore, Russian culture, politics, the arts, the economic life, and even aristocratic society faced a restructuring of the traditional order. As artists, writers, and musicians experimented with changing the Russian psychological landscape, their counterparts in the political and social arenas pushed for change as well.

To have lived in Russia—Moscow and St. Petersburg—at that time, one would have experienced two countervailing pressures. One force was the conventional, historically true ship of conservative aristocratic values, which did not welcome change and sailed into the future as keepers of the traditions of these ancestors, sacred and inviolate. These conservatives were the social elites who sought to emulate European culture rather than anything native. The other force was an agitation that roiled below the surface in some segments of polite society and among the rising gentry and working classes. This latter force pressed for change because the old traditional ways of steering the Russian ship of state were moribund and certain to founder the entire culture if the true, Slav, peasant, and Russian nature of the people was not recovered and elevated to its proper place. Among their goals, those who sought change wanted to unearth, preserve, and elevate the unique culture of the Russian peasantry.

While the conservative members of the traditional nobility continued to live their absurdly lavish lifestyles based on the labor of hundreds and sometimes thousands of peasant laborers, their ideological opponents, left leaning groups of many different shapes, were creating and recreating what they perceived as the true Russia. It was a struggle for the definition of what it meant to be Russian, and at its core, was an answer that was still obscure when the trigger of the Sarajevo assassination set the society on its apocalyptic course.

Russians struggled long to come to define themselves as simultaneously unique and a part of European culture, not apart and exotic, but a *sui generis* blend of native and imported characteristics. They were the inheritors of the Mongol traditions and the descendants of Peter the Great's efforts at westernization.[32] When the Great War began, Russia was at the brink of full self-discovery. The catastrophe of the war retarded that process.

The Season

The Russian social season began in fall, October, and pressed on until spring. With balls and banquets on practically every night during that long period, Russian society had a host of merry-making opportunities. Traditionally a time for gaiety at a lively pace, these events also provided an important vehicle for finding and securing marriage alliances. Even those who normally would not have been inclined or predisposed to partake in the fray, rented houses for the season and brought their marriageable-aged daughters to town, escorted them to coming-out balls, and planned on making a marriage pact. The season was a meat market for the elite, and it was the acceptable way to enter polite society up until the revolution in 1917.

St. Petersburg was a rather sophisticated host during the season. As the seat of government, the city remained rather formal and aloof in its entertainments. The elites were truly among select company there. The Moscow season had a homier feel; conventions about dress and social standing were looser, and to the natives, Moscow felt Russian. Nonetheless, both cities witnessed an exuberant frivolity, with champagne flowing at sumptuous suppers, and in balls that lasted until daylight. With breakfast at daybreak, Russians would go home to sleep and rise to lunch at 8 or 9 p.m. Both cities' elite populations became nocturnal and perked up only after 11 p.m.

These social events were the focal point of life for Russian and foreign elites in the big cities. Although attendees were actually in the minority, the armies of staff required were staggering. The staff supplied every imaginable aspect of the manual labor involved in these society entertainments, including servants, cooks, musicians, coachmen, footmen, stable hands, and tailors. Foreigners, even from wealthy countries, were astounded by the number of domestic servants each household employed. Diplomats remained scandalized at the number of Russians they were forced to employ to run their embassies.

The lavish spending on the social season was not an exaggeration of the non-Russian imagination. There were still noblemen who could put on extravagant balls night after successive night and not exhaust their fortunes (although much of the nobility was heavily in debt). Conversely, there were those who spent their fortunes in one season. The servants' gold-thread embroidered livery and the opulence of the musical and other entertainments was a means for famous hosts and hostesses to vie with each other for that elusive title of most opulent. Balls that began near midnight included breakfast at daybreak. Some households covered their windows to mask the arrival of daylight so that their amusements could proceed longer. Although St. Petersburg enacted an ordinance against loud music after 4 a.m., the ordinance was unenforceable, and reveling Russians usually ignored it.

Since entertaining guests was such a large part of their ritual of hospitality, Russians practiced the longstanding custom of opening their doors for lunch and dinner to persons of rank, even without specific invitation. Once a guest had dined at an aristocrat's residence, it would have been the height of boorishness not to return to partake of the host's hospitality. Thus, permanent hangers-on developed strange relationships with hosts whom they did not necessarily know well. For the fabulously wealthy Sheremetevs of St. Petersburg, entertaining fifty guests for lunch every day was a common occurrence.[33]

As an affirmation of their different natures, the two most important cities in Russia observed social rituals in their own unique ways. In St. Petersburg, the elite observed a custom of set times for visits; in Moscow, the elite kept a virtual open house. In addition to these types of constant exchanges of visits, there were the additional opportunities for guests to make appearances, such as the special occasions of birthdays, name days, religious holidays, or when some unusual event created an excuse to socialize.

The Stancioffs' Russia

The Stancioff family remained in Russia for a total of ten years, and they enjoyed their time there enormously. Anna de Grenaud Stancioff fell in love with the mythical Russian soul and was prepared to take up the beauty and the profundity she found. She enjoyed the literature and splendor that are unique to Russia, and she had no trouble adjusting to the move. She did not embrace Russia blindly, however, and she had many negative things to say about the "Russian mentality" and the thoughtless exuberance of the "race."[34] However, she was in love with the romance of the country, the vast spaces, the sleigh rides in winter, the Gulf of Finland in summer, the pageantry, and the solemnity of court events—in sum the glory that was the Russia of history and fairy tales. Moreover, although she understood the vast differences between the lot of the peasantry and the nobility, it was a social order she comprehended and supported.

Conversely, Dimitri saw through the Russian mystique; he perceived the capital as the showpiece for the West and not an indication of the true essence of the Russians. The Russian elites lived as though they were part of the western cultural tradition. He cast a wary eye on the nobility and kept them at a respectful distance, although he and his wife enjoyed the benefit of their hospitality and the welcome they received as the representatives of a small Balkan state at the Great Russian court.

In Russia, the Stancioffs were accepted into polite society because of their status as diplomats and as members of an elite class. They had acquaintances among the other diplomatic families and as well as some Russian families.

Raising a Family in Russia

In St. Petersburg, the family grew to three children with the birth of Ivan in 1897. The growing family eventually found a residence large enough for their needs—and their servants and governesses and pets and horses and the attendant mass of requisite domestic accoutrements. It was an imposing compound, at Mohovaia number 29. The Bulgarian legation in St. Petersburg had wrought iron gates and fence, which encircled a building that evoked the Winter Palace and boasted a forecourt large enough for a formal garden.

Anna and Dimitri's lives revolved around the social scene of the twilight of St. Petersburg high society. In addition to the official ceremonies to which diplomats were invited, the Stancioffs found a warm reception among many of the Russian aristocratic families. The children, especially the eldest two, had fond memories of their time in Russia. The country was mysterious but beautiful.

Early in the family's history the Stancioff children were impressed by their social environment in St. Petersburg, that imperial show-piece. There, the Stancioffs observed the Russian elites wrestle with their sense of "otherness," on a daily basis. Orthodox and of the East Russia was perceived by Europeans as part of the Orient. However, Russian elites had managed to overcome that perception by embracing fully French language and culture. Furthermore, Russia's size, her presumed military superiority and her dominance in the arts assured her aristocrats a place among the highest ranks of European elites.

Russian aristocrats reconciled their dual natures by playing at being peasants, putting on costume balls with oriental themes, building opulent mansions housing proudly displayed trophies of wars against savage orientals, peoples whose territories were now part of the Russian empire and finally, some of these "savage orientals" had been incorporated into the Russian elites, for example the Yusupovs (a Russian noble family of Tatar origins). Yet, Russian aristocrats appeared, on the surface, to exemplify the manners of western cultural elites.

The Stancioff children, especially the eldest, internalized the symbolism of separate selves, for the private and public realms, in the very instructive environment of the Russian imperial capital. They witnessed how the private and public self also reconciled the clash of cultures from East and West.

Among the Stancioffs' social acquaintances in St. Petersburg were some of the wealthiest people in Europe. One of the children even made a list of all the exquisitely beautiful things that impressed her young mind in a Russian playmate's home. Most of all, she recalled the full-size cherry tree in the Russians' greenhouse.[35]

Anna was enthralled with court life and found that she even had a relative among the foreign diplomats: the Italian ambassador, General Count Morra di Lavriano, who was related to her on her mother's side. Thus she felt perfectly at home in these elite social circles, and since French was the language of diplomats and all well-educated people, she was never out of place.

The duties of the Bulgarian representative to the court increased as the relationship between the two countries became more cordial. Russia sponsored more Bulgarian students and cadets in her schools, and the Bulgarian community grew.

Education and Training

The Stancioffs' breeding and education set them apart from other Bulgarians, but those qualities positioned them perfectly in the world of European diplomacy. They moved in circles in which educated women were not a drawback but an asset to their husbands as hostesses with polish.[36] For Anna, raising and educating her children was a key responsibility that she took seriously. She drew inspiration from the Bulgarian royal family governess, Miss Fraser, when developing and carrying out her plans to educate her own children.

Miss Fraser was maid of honor to Princess Marie-Louise and governess to Prince Boris. She embodied the virtues that Anna considered essential in a great governess—devotion and self-sacrifice—although she also instilled the morals and ethics that were essential to a well brought-up child. Academic curriculum was not enough; teaching "based on truth, and moral and physical security" was the key to producing well-rounded pupils according to Anna.[37]

Mrs. Hose was the Stancioff children's governess throughout most of their childhood. Affectionate and devoted, she had Anna Stancioff's complete approval for her methods of educating her two daughters. According to their mother, Nadejda and Feodora were two very different characters, but Mrs. Hose managed them equally well, and the governess was an enriching addition to the household.

The overall supervision of her children's moral and intellectual training was Anna's sole responsibility, but she did take on two governesses to do the job by the time her fourth and last child, Hélène, was born in 1901. The second governess, Miss O'Sullivan, became not only a servitor of the household but a friend.

From this point on, when Nadejda was already six, her attachment to her father was facilitated by his injunction for her to write to him on a *daily* basis when he was called away by work. As a duty and a privileged contact with her Papa, Nadejda began what would become a life-long habit of letter writing. In the future, this habit of prolific letter-writing made her the intermediary for her father and the family when they were apart. This duty also helped to develop Nadejda's natural tendency to worship her father. He became, over the years, the ideal man in her eyes, both as a paternal figure and as a masculine ideal. Handsome, intelligent, charming, talented, and accomplished, he was perfect. Dimitri Stancioff may have perceived his eldest daughter as a son. This special father-daughter bond strengthened the family. Dimitri Stancioff was the only other member of the family whose output in letters and cards exceeded his eldest daughter's. When separated from his family, through this medium, he continued to instill in his children his love of country, their sovereign, and the beauty of nature—Bulgarian nature above all.

The tradition of hiring English governesses was common among the nobility, and the Stancioffs continued in this tradition with these women. Each was hired with a written contract, which specified her duties, her pay, and her benefits, which included a return ticket home contingent on minimum two-year duration of employment. Occasionally the women renegotiated their pay as their workload increased.

Although they were called on to be companions as well as educators to the children, the governess' personalities occasionally clashed as disparities in character led to jealousies, rivalries, and animosity. Eventually, as the children grew, a Miss O'Donnell, a nursery governess, was hired in March 1906, and a Miss Clark was hired as tutor a few months later that same year. For Ivan, the only son, education began with tutors when he was young, then a lycée in Paris, and then education by Assumptionist Fathers when he enrolled in their school in Plovdiv. He became fluent in four languages and learned to play the violin.

In general, families with resources had tutors and governesses educate their daughters, who stayed home. The daughters learned second and third languages and became accomplished in the arts, such as painting and singing or playing an instrument. They wore the latest Paris fashions and held soirées in their homes. At these soirées, both the invitees and hosts entertained each other with their musical and artistic talents. Afternoon teas were a part of this world, as were regular walks, horseback riding, dance lessons, tennis, or other sports. In sum, the world of the elites of Bulgaria, such as the Stancioff family—and for the most part, the rest of the Balkans—emulated western social life as much as possible and rejected the traditional life of peasants.[38]

Winter in Paris 1906

Most probably in response to the series of strikes and disturbances that characterized most of 1905 in Russia, mother and children went to France for part of that year. In Paris, 1906, during the winter season, Anna rented an apartment for herself and the four children. She combined sightseeing with searching out and finding a correspondence school for her daughters. She decided to sign the girls up in the French Lycée de Jeunes Filles, a school organized and supervised by an acquaintance, Mlle. Pouzadoux, who was the superintendent.

The school predetermined the curriculum, and the children would study at home, wherever their father's assignment took them, and send in their exercise books every three months initialed by their governess, who possessed a French diploma. The work would then be reviewed, comments written, and returned to the children. This type of study worked perfectly for the household, since the children augmented their book learning with visits to museums, music lessons, and outings to notable sites; their education would be continuous no matter their location. Each Stancioff child learned to play at least one musical instrument and they often created a family orchestra, with their mother at the piano. Commenting on this system, Anna Stancioff wrote, "I was lucky in securing an excellent Scotch governess [Miss Clark], Diplomée de l'Université de Caen, with complete mastery of both languages." [39]

Anna chose this system of education because she believed that she could avoid several pitfalls at once. She avoided the possible vagaries of changing teachers, the separation and anxiety inherent in sending her children to a boarding school, and the expense associated with that kind of arrangement. In addition, the girls were safe from foreign, undesirable influences by staying at home near their mother.

By 1907, the two governesses who had charge of the family of four children were Miss Clark, the Scotswoman, and Miss O'Donnell. Miss Clark took charge of the education of the three eldest, according to the curriculum of the French lycée; in addition, she taught the children English and music. Miss O'Donnell was in charge of Hélène and her first lessons. In addition, when they spent extended periods in Bulgaria, the children learned their "native" tongue.

The eldest Stancioff child developed many of the qualities, which would make her unique in Russia. Nadejda began keeping a journal in 1906 and kept up that practice until the end of her life; her siblings were not quite as diligent. She recorded the weather as methodically as she recorded the developmental progress of her siblings. She recorded her synopses of family affairs as well as noting international affairs that were subjects of discussion at their dinner table.

As a young child in St. Petersburg, Nadejda took on the role of leader and organizer of her siblings' playtimes. The other children remembered her as the one who loved to tell stories, fairy tales, and organize games to play with them.[40]

Her talent for being a weaver of tales and a conjuror of verbal images would be legendary among family and a few close friends. She made her stories fresh and exciting by incorporating real events and personalities so that her listeners were titillated by that hint of veracity, while they could indulge in explorations of fantastic possibilities limited only by the storyteller's imagination. The family's travel and life experiences enriched Nadejda's stories and gave them substance. She gave free reign to her fantastic musings, especially with her sister Feodora, who was her closest friend. In Russia Nadejda's character defined its place in the family—commanding, binding, and loving.

The Stancioff children visited museums and monuments from an early age. Both older girls accompanied their mother to lectures at the Sorbonne and visited old churches and neighborhoods in Paris, where ancién regime structures still stood. These types of cultural pursuits remained customary throughout the family's lives together. The Stancioffs either lived in or visited the cultural capitals of Europe, where an education beyond the classroom was a standard practice for children of the elite. The bonds between siblings were strengthened by their shared experiences and by their ability to enjoy and be nourished by each other's company.

Diplomacy in the Age of Tsars and Chancellors

Diplomacy dictated all aspects of the family's life; diplomatic protocols dictated everything from the style of literary expression of official correspondence to appropriate attire and dinner seating (according to the importance of one's country in the power pantheon of nations).

One anecdote reported in Dimitri Stancioff's biography, entitled *Dimitri Stancioff Patriot and Cosmopolitan*, illustrates the pettiness and ephemeral nature of this world of power negotiators. The Bulgarian mission to Russia was not an embassy; thus its status, honors, and privileges ranked lower than those afforded to accredited embassies.

On one occasion, the Romanian diplomatic representative in St. Petersburg reminded the Stancioffs that they, in their less-exalted position, were not permitted the privilege of having their coachman wear the Bulgarian tricolor rendered in plumes on his hat! This kind of discourse was part of the diplomat's mission. It had its amusing moments as well as its more somber displays.

The lives of diplomats consisted of a combination of subtle indicators and some overt markers of rank and privilege associated with rank. With a constant barrage of signals in the form of dress, gestures, visiting cards, and similar semiotics diplomats had to negotiate carefully every aspect of their professional image. Protocol was meant to shore up distinctions, cement standing in the community of nations, and assure due respect to the state one represented. One had to follow detailed protocol or risk offending and possibly destabilizing international relations.

Dimitri Stancioff was conscious of this subtext and had occasion to reprimand others when they ignored the rules. When Stancioff later was minister of foreign affairs, a foreign diplomat dared to keep an appointment with him dressed in tennis clothes. Stancioff issued a warning that such casual attire was unwelcome at the ministry of foreign affairs of Bulgaria.[41]

By 1898, relations between the Bulgarian principality and the Russian Empire had warmed to such a degree that the Bulgarian royal couple and the Tsar's godson, Prince Boris, received an invitation to St. Petersburg for a state visit. The Stancioff family played a key role in making all the arrangements for the visit and acting as guides to their sovereigns. While the royal couple stayed in Peterhoff palace, the principal venue during their visit, they reinstated Anna temporarily as an attendant to the Princess Marie-Louise. Prince Boris, at age four, attended some of the ceremonies but generally retreated to the Romanovs' nursery to play with the Princesses Olga and Tatiana.

According to Dimitri Stancioff, even though the tsar and tsarina welcomed the Bulgarian royal family, the grand dukes, the tsar's siblings and their spouses, were not entirely warm and friendly. It was the only time Stancioff saw Prince Ferdinand hesitant: "Generally so sure of himself and inclined to be arrogant rather than gracious, [Prince Ferdinand] appeared more timid at the Russian Court."[42] In a visit in which personal charm and tact were used as powerful tools to garner social acceptability, Princess Marie-Louise was the most successful at the task. According to the Stancioffs' observations, she was charming, particularly in those areas in which wit and engaging conversation won converts. Her natural tendency as a vivacious conversationalist and a lively companion contrasted with her husband's common attitude of reticence with everyone. The visit was a modest success.

Royal Married Life

The royal couple had a tempestuous relationship that strained court life. Ferdinand spent most of his free time either complaining about his health or his wife to his court. Although Princess Marie-Louise's carelessness in conversation at times angered her spouse to the point of open resentment, their relationship had devolved into an ongoing verbal sparring match in which each said and did things for the sole purpose of irritating the other.

Marie-Louise did not survive long enough to develop the role of the compliant and helpful consort she could have become; she died on January 30, 1899, as a result of complications from the birth of her fourth child in five years. She had not rebelled against her conjugal duties as a princess consort but had been quite vocal about all the other burdens she had assumed with her position. In fact, while in the throes of profound spiritual pain at having to submit her eldest to rebaptism, she found enough inner strength to mock her husband before her two trusted servitors, Anna Stancioff and Comte de Bourboulon. She took out a guitar and composed an impromptu verse, to the tune of "Roi Dagobert," in the tradition of French street political pamphleteers:

C'est le Prince Ferdinand   Au Czar Nicolas!
Qui fait r'baptiser son enfant!   Un perjure n'est rien
Il donne le p'tit gars   Quand c'est pour le bien!

- C'est vrai qu'j'avais promis;	To Tsar Nicholas!
- Maintenant j'ai change d'avis![43]	A calumny is nothing
	When it is for a good cause!
[It is Prince Ferdinand	- It is true that I did promise;
Who had his child re-baptized	- But now I have changed my
He gave the little tike	mind!]

The princess' death was a loss most of all for her children, Boris, Eudoxie, Cyril, and Nadejda. Her life had been dedicated to duty, and it had been an onerous assignment becoming the consort of Prince Ferdinand.

The Diplomatic Old Guard and International Crises

In 1899, Dimitri Stancioff represented Bulgaria at the International Peace Conference at The Hague. An inspiration of the Russian emperor, this international affair was a key end-of-century event in terms of pomp and protocol. The same group of diplomats who faced each other over the negotiating table in the major capitals of Europe sat down at The Hague to work out an agreement on what was to be an international court of arbitration to settle disputes before they turned violent. In the words of the Italian representative, Count Nigra, the conference was, "a delightful family party," since most of the delegates had brought their wives and children.[44] In its parties, balls, and excursions to the Dutch countryside, the conference resembled the long list of peace conferences that had preceded it.

The results of the diplomatic efforts at The Hague were insignificant, in the end; peaceful arbitration lacked the necessary might with which to back up any decisions. Prince Ferdinand was astute enough to understand the conference for what it was: an ego-stroking enterprise for the monarchs of Europe, and especially, Tsar Nicholas II of Russia. In a letter to Stancioff, Ferdinand called the gathering a nineteenth century imposition on the twentieth conjured up by an "assembly of rancid diplomatists"[45]

The prince was writing this letter, in April 1899, just months after his wife's death. Incapacitated with gout he was at Rila, the medieval monastery which is nestled in a steep valley surrounded by alpine peaks where the variety of flora and fauna is unmatched elsewhere in the country. It was Bulgaria's most important repository of sacred texts. Once, Ivan Rilski, a hermit, inhabited a cave in the vicinity of the monastery.

It was spring, and the beauty of the mountains was unsurpassed. Prince Ferdinand complained of feeling useless as a leader and as a role model for his sons, who had preferred to leave for Sofia rather than remain in Rila, which they could not appreciate for its natural beauties. He called them "horrid little urchins – especially Boris who only likes Sofia and his Court; he is becoming very disagreeable and full of authority."[46] The prince was feeling rather gloomy. The Stancioffs passed off the prince's mood as characteristic of Ferdinand, who preferred to describe every event in the most dismal terms.

As a reward for all of his hard work in Russia, Dimitri received a promotion to the rank of minister plenipotentiary and envoy extraordinary to the court of St. Petersburg.[47] As a reflection of the strength of Russo-Bulgarian relations, the promotion was a prize.

The next international crises, which Stancioff faced in his career, were the violent Macedonian violent rebellion of 1903 followed by the Russo-Japanese War of 1905. Informed fully on the Macedonian troubles Dimitri traveled back to Bulgaria several times for briefings. On one of his journeys, the entire family returned to Bulgaria with him. It was the children's first visit to Bulgaria and to their grandparents' home in Svishtov. The family arrived during the grape harvest and enjoyed the bounty of the vineyards, which were abundant on the property. Life there was very different from their experiences in St. Petersburg; the city on the Danube had no electricity and no potable water. Water for household use had to be delivered by donkeys that trotted along perilously steep and winding streets to deliver their burdens twice a day.

The Russo-Japanese War (1904–1905), was a complete disaster for the Russians. Militarily, the Russians were thoroughly humiliated; diplomatically, it was a defeat on par with the debacle of the San Stefano agreement reconfigured at Berlin in 1878. Domestically, it led to demands for reform. The Russian monarchy responded with permission for the creation of a Duma, a representative body with rights to discuss although not legislate domestic issues. The revolution of 1905 also led to a steep rise in the proliferation of political parties which vied for popularity among the largely quiescent Russian population. As the Industrial Revolution finally reached a more steady rhythm of development the worker discontent that had led to disturbances in the western parts of Europe in the nineteenth century finally reached Russia. Political dissent and worker unrest rose to a considerable crescendo over the course of the next ten years. Politically motivated assassinations and strikes led to an increase in domestic tensions in Russia.

Family, Friendships, and Fun

Though still assigned to St. Petersburg, the family had spent the end of 1905 and the beginning of the New Year in Paris. The situation in the Russian imperial capital had been unsettling; riots and demonstrations prompted the Stancioffs to take their children to safety. The family returned to St. Petersburg only in the spring, when the situation seemed to have stabilized.

The process of "democratization" in Russia was slow and stumbling; for every step forward, there were several steps backward, and for the next few years, political developments were constantly in flux.

Back in St. Petersburg, the children were introduced to a new governess, a pretty and vivacious Irishwoman called Miss O'Sullivan. The legation also supported the children's paternal Uncle Nic, who served as an attaché, and a maternal Uncle Ernest, who was employed as private secretary to Dimitri. It was hoped that Uncle Ernest would eventually secure a more remunerative position.

For the most part, however, the glittering social life in St. Petersburg never dimmed, and the Stancioffs continued to enjoy balls, soirées, dinner parties, and evenings of music and bridge, along with the rest of the diplomatic community and the Russian aristocracy. In the summers, the family habitually took a picturesque villa on the Gulf of Finland, in Tarhovka. The villa had carved wooden eaves and veranda embellishments typical of the architectural style of Russian dachas.

Quite often, other diplomats were neighbors, and professional acquaintances turned into summer friends. One summer, during the Stancioffs' stay in Tarhovka, their neighbors were the Aerenthals. Count Aerenthal was ambassador of the Habsburg Empire, and later, minister of foreign affairs. Diplomatic families tended to create a subgroup of social equals who allowed their children to socialize and take lessons together from the same teachers. As the families shared in the specific exigencies of a particular post, they sought out others of their sort and established a loose network of like-thinking and like-suffering equals with whom they hoped to socialize safely.

Another of these friendships of convenience is noteworthy because of the professional rivalry that would manifest itself years later between Nadejda Stancioff and Harold Nicolson. The Stancioff children became playmates with the children of the British ambassador Sir Arthur Nicolson, first when he was stationed in Sofia, and later when he took the post over from Sir Charles Hardinge in St. Petersburg in 1906. Invited to join in a dancing class conducted especially for Gwen Nicolson at the British embassy, Gwen's brother, Harold, also entertained the Stancioff sisters. He (who later served with distinction in the British foreign office) gave his sister and her guests' rides on a Persian carpet he dragged along the parquet floors of the embassy.[48]

The Stancioffs became especially close with a branch of the Tolstoy family and visited them at their country estate. The sisters nurtured a close friendship with Sophie Tolstoy, with whom they corresponded for years after they left the country. Her father, Count Nikolai Nikolaevich Tolstoy had been a general in the Russo-Turkish War in 1878 and had become close friends with Dimitri. A distant relation of Leo Tolstoy, the count owned substantial properties in Tombov *gubernia* (province), and the Stancioffs visited the Russian family at their estate at Troubetchino.

Sophie represented, for the Stancioff sisters, the quintessential Russian soul—*dushichka*. Photographs of the girls playing on the estate show them at that tender age when little girls see the world in that wonderfully radiant way that is unique to their tender psyches.[49] Mysteries and fantasies of childhood blend with reality to make everything seem full of wonder and possibility. Their dresses and hair done in great bows and pigtails, along with the dreamlike quality of their expressions, lure their gaze into that wonderland where childhood begins to brush against maturity.

Minister of Foreign Affairs and Prime Minister

In fall 1906, Prince Ferdinand recalled Dimitri Stancioff to name him minister of foreign affairs in Bulgaria. The abrupt shift was a surprise for him and his family. They now had to prepare to leave Russia.

While they made slow preparations for their eventual departure, they had time to celebrate Christmas. The Tolstoy family came for the celebration of the holiday. Sophie and Nadejda presented a balalaika concert and recited poetry. Already exhibiting her lifelong habit of self-abnegation, Nadejda's commentary on the Christmas tree that day, which she had decorated, was that it was a "pretty tree, well decorated but with no artistic sense."[50]

The Christmas season offered an occasion to entertain other mothers and their children. In addition to the Countess Tolstoy and her children, the Stancioffs invited prominent members of the aristocracy in St. Petersburg, the Countess Rugieri and her children, Lady Nicolson and her daughter, and Mme Sveginsov and her daughter. These children's friendships, which were fostered by their parents, initially survived separation, time, and distance. The connections that the offspring of diplomats made as children served as a kind of networking for future relationships, both personal and professional. Therefore, the mothers with an eye to that potential took turns escorting each other's children, along with their own, to cultural events and play dates together.

Farewell to Russia

In 1907, the family was still in St. Petersburg, where the snow and cold did not deter Russian society from their habitual amusements of elaborate balls and parties. Anna and Dimitri had a series of visits of official leave-taking. Dimitri took official leave of the emperor on his own, and Anna went to bid her leave of the Empress Alexandra. Together they went to Gachina to bid adieu to the Dowager Empress Marie Feodorovna, and on another occasion had lunch with Grand Duke Vladimir. No one in the family wanted to leave St. Petersburg.

When they had finally managed to pack their household goods, along with crates of archives, official and personal correspondence, mementos—like signed menus from court banquets, and cotillion ribbons from balls Madame Stancioff had attended—they took home a considerable quantity and diversity of objects. They left with all their material possessions, plus the Scottish governess, Miss Clark (Miss O'Sullivan had married and left their service), the Irish nursery governess, Miss O'Donnell, a Russian chef, a Bulgarian house cleaner, a thoroughbred horse, and two Borzois. The menagerie of animals had to be culled from a total of seven dogs, two cats, and two canaries.

Nadejda wrote at the end of January, "Where will we be at this time next year?"[51] They had spent ten years in Russia, and their departure was painful. The enormous job of packing, crating, and apportioning appropriate hand luggage to everyone in the family and the servants who would accompany them on their journey was Maman's responsibility.

The good-byes at the train station were both personal and professional. This scene at the station was one that would be repeated often in the Stancioffs' careers. The crowds of well-wishers were made up of Russian notables, members of the diplomatic corps, Bulgarian legation workers, family, and friends. The Stancioffs were showered with armfuls of flowers, bonbons, and warm adieux.

Death of Princess Clémentine

The family headed for Vienna. Dimitri Stancioff, still in the capacity of representative of his country, made official visits to Berlin. While conducting formal business with Chancellor Bernhard von Bulow, he also attended a court ball. There the Emperor Franz Joseph spoke with him for twenty minutes, according to Nadejda, and she records that he told her father, "Your Prince is the most intelligent sovereign in Europe. Before him we must simply vanish and he has proven his intelligence when he named you Minister of Foreign Affairs."[52] Her father was enormously flattered and, by extension, so was the entire family.

While in Vienna, the family had one last brief contact with Princess Clémentine. She had been quite ill and was now feeble and close to death, but on the day before she died, she still had the clarity of mind to say to Anna, "I am very glad to have the chance to see you again dear Anna. I hope to see your children next time."[53] Both parents seemed to shine in their respective circles.

Princess Clémentine's funeral arrangements put a further burden of formal duties on the Stancioffs. Official telegrams of condolences arrived in a flood, and wreaths of mourning came. Papa had to respond to the most important ones in his own hand. Maman oversaw the arrangements at the chapel where the body lay in state.

On February 19, the funeral Mass was conducted in the Hofburg Palace, where the mourners in attendance were a veritable who's who of European nobility. In all, the family spent nearly two months in Vienna, and it is a tribute to their parents—and especially their mother's efforts and insistence for a well-structured life for their children—that with the help of their two governesses, the routine of lessons continued regardless of the parents' professional duties.

Nadejda recorded their regimented schedule in her journal.[54] The entry and many subsequent entries kept a consistent and observant eye on her siblings' development while noting changes in academic performance, physical features, and the children's' unique characters. Nadejda, for example, noted that when her sister Chou was six years old she was "a bit headstrong and a tattletale" while her brother Ivan at eleven was "at times a crybaby."[55] In Vienna the children were escorted to important historical sites; they visited the Capucin Crypt in Vienna, the Habsburg ancestral tomb. They expressed their special feeling for Napoleon and his legacy by placing a bouquet of violets at the tomb of his son, the Duke of Reichstadt.

Settling in Sofia

When they reached Bulgaria, the Stancioffs settled in the capital city. Power outages and water shortages were still common in Sofia. Being close to the prince, and performing their duties at court, were the family's primary occupations.

Akin to foreign diplomats, the Stancioffs, especially Anna, had a hard time adjusting to life in Sofia, which they found lacking in much that was stimulating in the more cultivated capitals of Europe. That is why it was characteristic for Nadejda to assess her mother's state of mind in the following way: "Maman is doing very well, she is very happy but I believe that the intellectual and spiritual life of Sofia is a bit limited for the superior faculties of my dear Maman."[56]

Once they decorated their home to their liking and arranged it with all of their fine imported furnishings, the Stancioffs could entertain others with similar experiences, mostly members of the diplomatic community.

Internally the state was undergoing a period of turmoil. Strikes paralyzed the country, and political parties vied for power, so the domestic environment was unsettled. In fact, soon after his return to Sofia, Dimitri was unlucky enough to witness the assassination of the newly elected Prime Minister Petkov, leader of the Stambolov party. The unfortunate man was shot and died in Stancioff's arms.[57] The recent violence in neighboring Macedonian territories led to anti-government demonstration, repressions, and counter demonstrations in Bulgaria. The violence in Bulgaria was extremely bloody in 1906-1907 as political assassinations punctuated civil discourse.[58]

In Sofia, Dimitri's position as minister of foreign affairs, and briefly prime minister, due to the assassination of Petkov, required frequent entertaining of his colleagues, the other Bulgarian ministers. The rare exceptions were guests like journalist James Bourchier, (1850-1920) whose famously pro-Bulgarian stance earned him a venerated place in Bulgarians' hearts. The Stancioffs associated with him regularly since he lived in Sofia for over twenty years, 1892-1915.

The Stancioffs befriended not only diplomats like the Buchanans who were the English Ambassadors to Bulgaria, Bulgarian court functionaries like the Bourboulons but also scholars like the renowned Byzantinist Steven Runciman. They also were close with some religious figures and with some exceptional Bulgarians. Occasionally a well-traveled, well-educated aristocrat would pass through the Balkans and would receive invitations from Sofia society.

The Stancioff home quickly became the rendezvous point for various foreign and domestic dignitaries, and the children, especially the eldest two, had occasion to observe and become acquainted with the families of the representatives of foreign states in Sofia and to befriend their children. The Buchanans, the Thurns, and the Czernins, the Austrian representatives, were frequent visitors. The mothers and their children shared leisure-time activities. Their children took dancing lessons together and invited each other to teas and to play games like croquet and hide-and-seek. The parents also organized costume balls, suitable for children, for the purpose of preparing the children for entry into the adult world once they achieved maturity. At these parties, the young society children could practice the dance steps they had studied in their classes in a simulated authentic dance. In this way, the small diplomatic community and the nascent Bulgarian society could expand their meager guest lists. The Stancioffs' pattern of diplomatic family life was very similar to that of diplomats around the world.[59]

These diplomatic family communities were a consequence of the oftentimes forced isolation of a group of foreigners who had more in common with each other than with the native culture. As diplomats, they understood the traditions dictating their behaviors, and they could communicate in the language of mores and manners they shared.

French was not the only language of diplomatic intercourse; diplomats also shared another common language—one of manners—which was a kind of refuge amidst a strange, puzzling environment of a foreign state.[60] In each other, they sometimes found suitable and comprehensible companions, and sometimes friends, who remained connected beyond the period of their postings. For example, Meriel Buchanan, (1886-1959), the daughter of the British ambassador, became a welcome companion and lifelong friend of the Stancioff sisters. Nadejda and she corresponded for years, even when the Buchanans were posted to St. Petersburg, Rome, and later on, when the family settled in England. Meriel described Nadejda as a school girl with long, bronze colored braids, with a vivid imagination, a thirst for knowledge, and a keen memory.[61] Feo recorded that Nadejda was, at the age of 14, an avid botanist and hiker, who bounded up mountain paths with ease.

Nadejda, noting her first impressions of her friend Meriel, said, "I find her very fresh, simple, and pretty, and Meriel is as pretty as a cherub of Murillo.[62] The Thurns and Czernins had younger children who played with Ivan and Chouchou (Hélène). For the children of diplomats, choosing and maintaining a friendship with others whose parents were in the same field posed a challenge. The children were first put together by their parents and then drawn to each other when they found their favorites. Nadejda writes:

> Our children friends in Sofia or rather our acquaintances are Hélène Tontcheff, Nadia Markoff, the Tantioloffs, Olga Batorsky, the Petroff-Tchomakoffs, the Thurns. We see them at dance lessons, at drawing lessons and at little parties that we give each other. I do not have a special friend my favorite acquaintance is Olga, nice young girl of 17-18. I will never forget my dear Sophie Tolstoy whom no one can replace.[63]

The Creation of Sanctuary and Feelings of Patriotism

While in Bulgaria, the Stancioff parents made the decision to buy and build on a property that would become a permanent home for the family. They found a shorefront parcel of land on the Black Sea between Varna and Euxinograd and within two years built the family home. This home would become the focus of their energies and a family refuge. Even when they were far away, they would grow to love the home so much that they would use words of longing and melancholy to describe their feelings for the property. It became an oasis of respite from their constant travels.

During these busy months in Bulgaria, the children developed their unique sense of patriotism for a land they hardly knew. Spending months—seasons—in their nominally native land led to a deepening of appreciation for its wonders and beauties. Their father was the one most responsible for nurturing that deep sense of national loyalty, about which Nadejda writes in the following passage:

> We will enjoy a bit longer of this charming fatherland. As it is quite sweet! We have but to look at Vitosha, the dear mountain top! My country! And the good air pure, pure with an ideal climate! What a fatherland, truly.[64]

Perhaps as a thank-you, or possibly because of genuine feeling, Prince Ferdinand invited the couple, along with their two eldest daughters, to spend Holy Week with him and his two eldest children, the Princes Boris and Cyril, at the family residence in Plovdiv. Ferdinand apparently doted on them the Stancioff children and was solicitous enough for the gesture to seem extraordinarily kind and thoughtful. Nadejda writes:

> We were perfectly installed, living with His Royal Highness, and having our meals with him. He himself was charming to us always looking for ways to please us, chatting amiably with us, and paying attention to Feo and me with a perfect grace. What intelligence and what goodness does his brain hold? What soft solicitude for the needs of others! Thrilled to be in his dear Plovdiv, he was constantly in a delicious humor and we savored it.[65]

One of the highlights of this trip in 1908 was riding in Ferdinand's "fast" motorcars, which were still a rarity in Europe. Relations between the families continued to be warm and were certainly closer than those between most court functionaries and their sovereign. The children would have happy memories from their time spent together during these and other holidays and special occasions.

The prince entertained the Stancioffs at his residences, sometimes the entire family, sometimes one or both of the parents; and the Stancioffs reciprocated with dinners at their home in Sofia. The relationship was more than a formal exchange of obligatory visits; it was a special friendship.

Nevertheless, the children had some startling memories of Prince Ferdinand. They were extremely conscious of his acerbic, biting sarcasm, and knew well that their own lives with their parents were in sharp contrast to the lives of the royal children. The Stancioff children did not envy the royals their station because Prince Ferdinand made his children's lives miserable with cruelty and verbal abuse of all sorts. As their only surviving parent, Ferdinand had undue control, which was unrelieved by a parent with a softer touch, over their psyches.[66]

On another occasion, late in 1915, Ivan was witness to the sovereign's dismissive and degrading handling of his sons. While dining with the boys, Ivan once heard the monarch refer to both his sons as dwarfs, in contrast to Ivan, who was tall for his age. When Ferdinand quizzed Ivan on some of his book knowledge, the prince turned to his sons and said, "See, you have no education."[67] He then turned toward Ivan and told him to tell his father to "keep quiet – Bulgaria is going to win the war."[68] The prince was undiplomatic and hard with family members and guests alike.

Royal Celebrations

The year 1907 was also the year of the twentieth anniversary of Prince Ferdinand's accession to the Bulgarian throne. He had accomplished a great deal in his time as prince of Bulgaria, given the dismal beginnings of his reign, and he seemed to be gaining in popularity. He had managed to keep his throne and his head.

The plans for rapprochement with Russia had played out as he had intended, and Bulgaria was beginning to turn a corner domestically. The next steps would include moving forward with more ambitious foreign policy goals. Prince Ferdinand dreamt of a regal throne, but to accomplish that goal he had first to rid himself of his country's vassal-like status in relation to the Ottoman Empire. An opportunity presented itself in due course.

In September 1907, a Russian delegation headed by Grand Duke Vladimir Alexandrovich, Tsar Nicholas II's uncle, and Grand Duchess Marie Pavlovna, his wife, arrived to witness the unveiling of the statue Tsar Liberator dedicated to Alexander II. This event was a high-water mark in Russian-Bulgarian relations. The equestrian statue located in a prominent place in Sofia served to remind Russians, especially Tsar Alexander's son, the grand duke, that Bulgarians were cognizant of their debt and wanted closer relations with their liberators.

The mood was jubilant, and Prince Ferdinand made certain the pageantry surrounding the Russian visit was memorable. He also used the occasion to fashion closer ties with Russia by deliberately asking the grand duke, and especially the grand duchess, for help in finding a suitable spouse.[69] Ferdinand hoped to make clear his intention to be guided by the Russian royal family and, ostensibly, linked to them in some manner. This relatively minor concession on his part would reap big returns in terms of a strengthening Russo-Bulgarian ties. By asking a member of the Russian imperial family to help with his choice, he effectively bound his distant cousin, Nicholas II, closer to him.

Ferdinand's hopes were more than realized when his request was quickly fulfilled. By January 1908, negotiations for an engagement were underway for the hand of Princess Eleanore von Reuss-Köstritz, (1860-1917) a relative and a friend of Grand Duchess Marie Pavlovna. The couple married in a matter of months later that year.

A Second Royal Marriage

Although not a beauty, Ferdinand's second wife came from a lineage with a commendable standing. She was a woman who had dedicated her life to charitable endeavors, and the prospect of being a consort who would have many opportunities for charitable work in a poor country appealed to her. Her focus was hospital work, and she already had first-hand experience when she had been in charge of an ambulance train sent out to Manchuria to attend to the wounded during the Russo-Japanese War. She spoke Russian.

Those who knew Prince Ferdinand and his country prepared her for her duties as consort; they warned her about the erratic moods, biting wit, sarcasm, and sometimes wanton cruelty of her future husband. She also knew that her role would include becoming surrogate mother to his four children, aged eight to fourteen. Although a rather daunting prospect, this was a marriage of convenience and obligation but one she was groomed to accept. Those born to duty and accountability, such as the members of European royalty who took their obligations seriously, did not rebel against their responsibilities. Nevertheless, the marriage was a challenge for the princess.

Work and Leisure

At the beginning of 1908, Dimitri Stancioff was still minister of foreign affairs, and the family lived in Sofia. Eventually, he received the very prestigious simultaneous appointments of minister plenipotentiary to Paris and London.

During his appointment, Dimitri Stancioff spent a considerable amount of time with his sovereign, both in Sofia and in the royal residence in Vrana, a few miles on the outskirts of Sofia. His duties took him away from his family for days at a time when he also accompanied his prince on leisure trips. Both husband and wife were in close contact with Prince Ferdinand during the extended period of time when they lived in Sofia. They either singly or as a pair dined with him and spent their leisure time with him.

In March, the Stancioffs traveled to Germany to witness the prince's marriage to Princess Eleanore. The Stancioff children stayed behind in the care of family, their governess, and friends. Later that year, while the children remained in Sofia with their dour governess, Miss Clark, the parents traveled to Paris to begin the process of finding a suitable residence, which would become the Bulgarian legation in Paris and their new home. The children maintained a careful schedule of mandated school work and play hours. Their utilitarian style of home schooling kept to a predetermined plan, and the governess did her job well. The children's free time and bedtime schedule were tiered according to age.[70]

There is no doubt that the life of a diplomatic family required a great deal of self-discipline, a chore which fell to the mother, whose realms shifted between the domestic and the public. She had to keep her family on track with the mundane tasks of daily life while she also kept up with the deluge of social engagements and hostess obligations that were part of her existence. The wives and daughters of diplomats understood well their delicate role in the entire game in which influence was sometimes dependent on the tact of the women in the family as they made their way through social events. The Stancioffs were supremely conscious of this fact, and Anna instructed her children well.

When their parents were in Paris, the royal family drew the Stancioff children into their family circle. Princess Eleanore invited the children to play time with her stepchildren. Only two weeks after her arrival in Sofia, Princess Eleanore set about creating a homey and welcoming environment for her new charges. She invited the Stancioff children and their governess to the palace for an Easter celebration and egg hunt. Other invitations followed. The Stancioff children felt elect and enjoyed basking in the glow of royal attention. Nadejda writes, "We play games, hide and seek, chase we return late, dirty, tired, enchanted.[71]

The forced playgroup, which began as a way to amuse and keep all the children occupied, eventually developed genuine bonds among the children. Nadejda writes, "The Princesses have the goodness to invite us to a concert violinist Florizel, the Princes are there too, duty before everything!"[72] In later years, the eight children would increasingly enjoy each other's company and begin to create opportunities to spend more time with each other. They found things in common and could relate to each other's experiences; the Stancioff children could relate to them perhaps better than most other Bulgarians.

This relationship among the children began in earnest with the inclusion of Princess Eleanore into the royal family. She amply fulfilled her duty as a good hostess and family member as she developed and maintained the social contacts with which family life prospered. The Bulgarian royal family, such as it was in 1908, cobbled together by need and necessity and a sense of duty as well as destiny, blossomed under Princess Eleanore's supervision. Her need to do good both in her charity work and at home for her new family showed tangible results. She deliberately fostered a strong relationship with the Stancioff family, both children and parents, as evidenced by the flurry of visits she initiated. The following entries in Nadejda's diaries attest to the princess' efforts:

> May 17—While [we are] at lunch the Princess arrives to pay us a little visit. She is so gracious, so amiable. We love her respectfully. Our parents arrive in London.
> May 21—The Princess comes with a automobile to take Ivan to Vrana. He returns enchanted loaded with asparagus that he cut himself.[73]

Once, when Anna was seriously ill with a recurring case of bronchitis, Princess Eleanore paid frequent visits, or when she thought the children might enjoy a particularly special fruit or vegetable, she sent those items to their house.

In August, Prince Ferdinand permitted the Stancioffs to spend their vacation at the Euxinograd residence while the family's villa was under construction. In this way, the Stancioff children got their first taste of a summer vacation on the shores of the Black Sea—the thrill of exploring the large gardens and the cliffs—while their mother could supervise the work on their property, approximately 5 kilometers south of the palace. Commenting on the experience, Nade-jda wrote:

> We are delighted, enchanted, overcome with emotion. This park, this sea, these plants . . . the scent that talks to us of the good generous prince who permits us to come here. We scream with delight at the miracle, - beautiful, grandiose, delicate. The monastery is a gem, our rooms that sheltered princes! We look at everything; we take walks, mute with admiration. This cliff, this view, the sea, the sea above all. We are in delirium![74]

Construction of *Les Trois Sources* or *Tri Kladenitsi*

The situation was ideal for the children. Since their Papa was away seeing to his duties, Maman took care of the construction details and the inevitable headaches associated with the construction project on their property. Their architect, Stav-roff, worked closely with the Stancioffs to achieve the residence Anna and Dimitri had dreamed for themselves. However, as it seems with all construction projects, misunderstanding, delays, and overspending led to friction between owners and architect. Nadejda articulated the family's frustrations in her journal. "Arrival of Stavroff the Liar! New contract, business affairs, reproaches, rules, corrections, and the house is still abandoned, without workers! They say they will begin work on Monday."[75]

Despite some misunderstandings about the timing and quality of the work, the project was eventually finished to the Stancioffs' satisfaction. They built a two-story villa on a sloping bluff by the sea on which they cultivated a vineyard, fruit trees, a vegetable garden, and most importantly, a large garden with flowers, a fountain, walks with trellis works, and eventually a pergola garden. The property, christened *Villa Les Trois Sources* (Villa of the Three Springs) by their mother because of its abundant fresh-water springs, turned into an elegant house with balconies on both floors, a large hall on the first floor, and bedrooms upstairs. The house was whitewashed and tiled with the distinctive coral-colored clay roof tiles of Bulgaria.

Later they created a cozy lunch spot with a table and benches under a large pear tree, duplicating the outdoor dining space the family had in Svishtov. The Stancioffs also built two seaside cabins—large enough to cook in—where the children could amuse themselves, play house, and host their playmates.

The family now had a home; they were located in close proximity to Euxi-nograd, the royal seat by the Black Sea. They could sustain their special relationship with the royal family by maintaining their vacation residence only a few kilometers from the palace north of Varna.

The prince's children made a habit of visiting the Stancioff children virtually at will, like any good neighbors, whenever they were in residence. As they matured and could manage their own transportation, the princely children visited over land, by sea, on horseback, and on motorcycle from the Euxinograd palace to the Stancioffs' estate.

A Turbulent Year

When Dimitri Stancioff returned to his family in Euxinograd on September 4, 1908, after a four-month absence from Bulgaria, his arrival set off a delirium of celebrations and excitations for the children. They wanted to show off everything they had learned and explored in their new paradise. They were thrilled to reveal their favorite fishing and swimming spots, the places where they found baby turtles, and their favorite fruit and nut trees. But his stay, and their joy, was brief. He rushed off after only three days to Sofia, where, according to Nadejda's diary entry, he had politics to discuss. She writes, "He will visit his mother, the diplomats, and the ministers . . . to get busy with politics! He comes with a mission from Carlsbad while he was with Izvolsky."[76]

While he had been away, Dimitri had had an extremely important meeting with Count Izvolsky (1856-1919), Russia's foreign minister. On August 29, Dimitri left Paris for his meeting with the Count in Carlsbad.[77] Izvolsky advised the Bulgarians to take care and not fall into "Austria's trap." He urged Dimitri to advise his sovereign of the danger of declaring independence when Austria announced her annexation of Bosnia-Hercegovina. Izvolsky argued that Bulgaria instead should immediately protest this action before the Great Powers and demand recognition of its independence. In other words, Izvolsky advised against unilateral action for the Bulgarians. Izvolsky stated that Russia would immediately convene a group of sympathetic Great Powers who would aid the Bulgarian cause. However, he underscored that it was important to be sure that the Austrians would be culpable for altering the Treaty of Berlin.

The international climate was tense; no one power wished to appear to cede control over the disputed territories of Europe. If Austria was the sole responsible party, then the rest of the powers would find fault with the Austrians and reward Bulgarian patience. However, if Bulgarians, according to Izvolsky, "opened the door" for the Austrians, then there could be no guarantees of independence.[78] These talks, and the events that would evolve after Dimitri's return to Bulgaria, eventually would lead to Bulgaria's unilateral declaration of independence that fall which isolated Bulgaria once more.

Events in the spring of 1908 prepared the way for the fall salvo. Two processes proceeded simultaneously: one was a cause for incredible political confusion in the Ottoman Empire; the other was a cause for great celebration in Bulgaria—the declaration of Bulgarian independence. These enormously significant events shook the diplomatic world that year. It was a volatile period for Europeans. This large shift in the tectonic plates of power relations in Europe could have disrupted the established order to the point of open hostilities. Dimitri Stancioff's posting to Paris was a critical appointment made during an increasingly tense time in European power relationships.

The Treaty of Berlin is Being Torn Up

According to the Treaty of Berlin, Bulgaria was still a dependency of the Ottoman Empire and had to pay off an indemnity—to her former sovereign—for its autonomous status. The opportunity to achieve independence came in 1908 by way of propitious circumstances outside of Bulgarian control. In a climate of increasingly shaky international relations, Bulgaria found her chance during the Young Turk revolt, which began in the summer. In July of that year a group of young Turks seized control of the Ottoman state and in a series of deft maneuvers pushed the sultan to the periphery of power. They declared their intentions to modernize the state. Their revolt permitted a rearrangement of the geopolitical situation on the Balkans.

Prince Ferdinand used the disruption of the Ottoman state by the Young Turk revolt against their sultan to declare Bulgarian independence. When the Austrians affirmed the annexation of Bosnia-Hercegovina on October 6, the Bulgarians had already gathered their government in Tûrnovo, and with their sovereign, announced their independence from Ottoman suzerainty on October 5.

By international law, Bulgaria found herself in an awkward position, vis-à-vis the rest of the European states, by breaking the Treaty of Berlin and taking independence as a self-propelled initiative. Bulgaria was once again an isolated, rebuffed state. The international community reviled the act and isolated the country by limiting diplomatic links.

Meriel Buchanan, daughter of the British minister to Sofia, Sir George, wrote a passionate letter of support to her Bulgarian friend in Paris. The English girl wrote, "who could sit and speak about the weather when there are such frightfully exciting things going on? ...I said [at a formal dinner in Sofia] that the English government all deserved to be hung...if my own country [has done] something wrong and stupid I should certainly say so."[79] She was grateful to Nadejda for promising to treasure their friendship despite British foreign office's attitude toward Bulgaria. She also bemoaned the fact that as a female and the daughter of a diplomat there was little more that she could do to show her support for Bulgarians.

In Russia, Tsar Nicholas II was furious on two counts. Nadejda writes, "The Treaty of Berlin is being torn up . . . [Great] Powers without power!!!"[80] First, the Austrians outwitted his foreign minister, Count Izvolsky, and annexed Bosnia-Hercegovina without the Russians being able to execute a countervailing measure to benefit themselves. This annexation caused Russia enormous humiliation. Second, Bulgaria, the country that Russia had liberated and whose fate was dependent on Russian good will, unilaterally declared its maturity as a state despite Izvolsky's advice to the contrary! Bulgaria's act was an unforgivable insult to the power and pride of place Russia occupied among the European Great Powers. Although it was the Austrians who had been primarily culpable for Russia's diplomatic drubbing it was the Bulgarians who bore the brunt of Russia's ire.

It took the death of Grand Duke Vladimir Alexandrovich and his official funeral in February 1909 to smooth out the state of affairs between Bulgaria and Russia. Ferdinand successfully managed the situation so that Tsar Nicholas II had to acknowledge him as a king rather than a prince. By April 1909 the rest of the Great Powers had recognized Bulgaria as well, a masterful effort by "King" Ferdinand.

As the Bulgarian minister plenipotentiary to Paris and his family received congratulations on their country attaining "maturity" of a sort, the outlook for Asia Minor's future was cloudy and violent. Sultan Abdul Hamid was deposed in 1908 and he was eventually sent into exile by the Young Turks. The Young Turk Revolution began as a political coup d'état and ended with the massacre of thousands of Armenians in the country's interior. Nadejda comments, "What a shameful conduct for a people in the twentieth century, who pretend to be European even!"[81] Reports on the events there were first received with incredulity in Paris. The news of Turks massacring Christians, including Protestant pastors and especially Armenians, led Nadejda to make a sarcastic statement about Great Power politics: "England can be proud of supporting such a sweet country,"[82] she noted. This statement is a reflection of the ideological camp in which her family's allegiance lay, and since England had been reticent to recognize Bulgaria, the derisive comment was a strike at her power politics.

International calamities aside, Bulgarians were, it seemed, on the verge of gaining a perfect state of happiness. Bulgaria would soon become a kingdom, by the end of 1909 there would be a sense that the country was welcomed into the ranks of European states. Legitimation came at a price yet Bulgarians were optimistic about the future.

Notes

1. Anna Stancioff and Nadejda Muir, *Recollections of a Bulgarian Diplomatist's Wife* (London: Hutchinson, 1931).
2. Konstantin Jiricek and Stoian Argirov, *Bûlgarski Dnevnik, 30 Oktomvri 1879-26 Oktomvri 1884 G* (Plovdiv, Sofia:, Knigoizd. Kh. G. Danov, 1930).
3. Georgi Georgiev, *Sofia I Sofiantsi 1878-1944* (Sofia: Nauka i Izkustvo, 1983). 8.
4. Ibid.15.
5. Ibid.18.
6. Petæur Neæikov, *Zavchera I Vchera : Skitsi Ot Minaloto*, 2. izd. ed. (Sofia: Izdvo na BZNS, 1981). See Daskalov, *Bûlgarskoto Obshtestvo 1878-1939*.
7. Ibid.
8. Ibid.
9. Constant, *Foxy Ferdinand Tsar of Bulgaria*. 106.
10. Daskalov, *Bûlgarskoto Obshtestvo 1878-1939*.
11. Muir, *Dimitri Stancioff Patriot and Cosmopolitan*.
12. Comte de Bourboulon, PASF, *Ephémérides De Bulgarie*, 1-554, 1-71.
13. Ibid.
14. Ibid.

15. Constant, *Foxy Ferdinand Tsar of Bulgaria.*

16. Bourboulon, *Ephémérides De Bulgarie,* Constant, *Foxy Ferdinand Tsar of Bulgaria.*

17. Bourboulon, *Ephémérides De Bulgarie.*

18. Buchanan, *My Mission to Russia, and Other Diplomatic Memories.* 67. "We paid each other compliments and exchanged pretty speeches, for with a character such as his one could, as Lord Beaconsfield put it, and lay flattery on with a trowel."

19. Bourboulon, *Ephémérides De Bulgarie.*

20. Ibid.

21. Ibid. Anna Stancioff confirms this characterization.

22. Ibid.

23. Ibid.

24. Ibid.

25. Ibid.

26. Ibid.

27. Ibid.

28. Anna de Grenaud Stancioff (AGS) file, unpublished letters, PASF.

29. Both Stancioff correspondence and Bourboulon's observations attest to the constant strain of serving Prince Ferdinand.

30. Kristen Stromberg Childers, "Paternity and the Politics of Citizenship in Interwar France," *Journal of Family History* 26, no. 1 (2001).

31. Muir, *Dimitri Stancioff Patriot and Cosmopolitan.*

32. See the following article for an example of one Russian family that worked to combine their disparate heritages into one. Konstantin Bolenko, ""Ruskii Vel'mozha, Evropeiiskii Grand Seigneur I Tatarskii Kniaz'" N.B. Iusupov: K Voprosu O Samoorientalizatsii Rossiiskovo Dvorianstva V Poslednei Treti Xviii-Pervoi Treti Xix Vv.," *Ab Imperio* 3 (2006).

33. Orlando Figes, *Natasha's Dance a Cultural History of Russia* (New York: Holt and Company, 2002).

34. Anna Stancioff, *Recollections of a Diplomatist's Wife.*

35. Feodora Stancioff, Nadejda Memories of Love, 140.

36. Alpern Engel, *Mothers and Daughters Women of the Intelligentsia in Nineteenth-Century Russia,* Muir, *Dimitri Stancioff Patriot and Cosmopolitan.* 16.

37. Stancioff, *Recollections of a Diplomatist's Wife.*

38. Krassimira Daskalova, "Women, Nationalism and Nation-State in Bulgaria (1800-1940s)," in *Gender Relations in South Eastern Europe: Historical Perspectives on Womanhood and Manhood in Nineteenth and Twentieth Century,* ed. M. Jovanovic and S. Naumovic (Belgrade-Graz: 2002), Tuttle, "Celebrating the Père De Famille: Pronatalism and Fatherhood in Eighteenth-Century France."

39. Stancioff, *Recollections of a Diplomatist's Wife.*

40. Stancioff, Nadejda Memories of Love, 3.

41. Muir, *Dimitri Stancioff Patriot and Cosmopolitan.*, 110.

42. Ibid.

43. Bourboulon, *Ephémérides De Bulgarie,* Translation is my own.

44. Muir, *Dimitri Stancioff Patriot and Cosmopolitan.*

45. Dimitri Stancioff, unpublished letter, DS II, 1908-1915, PASF.

46. Dimitri Stancioff, unpublished letter, DS I, 1896, PASF.

47. A position similar to ambassador.

48. Stancioff and Muir, *Recollections of a Bulgarian Diplomatist's Wife.*

49. Family photo albums in possession of Dimitri Stancioff in Camden, ME.

50. Nadejda Stancioff, unpublished journal, 7 January 1908, PASF.

51. Nadejda Stancioff, 1907, PASF.

52. Muir, *Dimitri Stancioff Patriot and Cosmopolitan.*

53. Stancioff and Muir, *Recollections of a Bulgarian Diplomatist's Wife.*

54. Nadejda Stancioff, unpublished journal, 7 January 1908, PASF. "Our regular routine in Vienna. Breakfast at 9, lessons at 10-12. Lunch at 1 walk at 2, 3:30 lessons. At 6 change for dinner, at 7 dinner, at 9 bedtime, a rather full day."

55. Nadejda Stancioff, unpublished journal, 20 February 1908, PASF.

56. Nadejda Stancioff, unpublished journal, 28 May 1907, PASF.

57. Muir, *Dimitri Stancioff Patriot and Cosmopolitan,* Ivan D. Stancioff, *Diplomat and Gardener Memoirs* (Sofia: Petrikov, 1998).

58. The Stancioffs were worried for their Papa since the assassination foisted two additional positions on him. He was temporarily minister of public works and president of the council of ministers. The family prayed that their patriarch would survive the additional burdens of office literally and figuratively. "May God have pity on us." Nadejda wrote on hearing of his decision to accept the additional responsibilities. Nadejda Stancioff, unpublished journal, 12 January 1907, PASF.

59. The following are just a few exemplars of the enormous literature, both primary experiences and comparative works that describe diplomatic life. Fru Lillie Moulton Hegermann-Lindencrone, *The Sunny Side of Diplomatic Life, 1875-1912* (New York and London,: Harper & brothers, 1914), Hickman, *Daughters of Britannia the Lives and Times of Diplomatic Wives,* Katherine L. Hughes, *The Accidental Diplomat Dilemmas of the Trailing Spouse.* (Putnam Valley, New York: Aletheia Publications, 1999), Mary Jane McCaffree and Pauline B. Innis, *Protocol : The Complete Handbook of Diplomatic, Official, and Social Usage*, Rev. ed. (Washington, D.C.: Devon Pub. Co., 1985), Harold George Nicolson, *Portrait of a Diplomatist* (New York: Harcourt, 1939), Harold George Nicolson and Nigel Nicolson, *Harold Nicolson Diaries and Letters 1907-1964* (London: Weidenfeld & Nicolson, 2004), I. Ilchev, *Misiia Na Balkanite,* 1. izd. ed. (Sofia: Univ. izd-vo "Kliment Okhridski", 1987), Anna Viroubova, *Memories of the Russian Court* (New York: The Macmillan Company, 1923).

60. Literature on the social rituals of diplomats is abundant. The work of the German sociologist Norbert Elias is now recognized as a path-breaking study of how the "civilizing process" evolved from post-medieval Christian norms to accepted court etiquette and modern notions of modes of socially acceptable behavior. Norbert Elias, *The Civilizing Process*, 1st American ed. (New York: Urizen Books, 1978).

61. Stancioff, Nadejda Memories of Love, 23.

62. Nadejda Stancioff, unpublished journal, 6 March 1907 and 8 May 1908, PASF.

63. Nadejda Stancioff, unpublished journal, 27 February 1908, PASF.

64. Nadejda Stancioff, unpublished journal, March 1908 recapitulation, PASF.

65. Nadejda Stancioff, unpublished journal, April 1908, PASF.

66. Stancioff, *Diplomat and Gardener Memoirs,* p. 17, and see de Bourboulon.

67. Ibid. 25.

68. Ibid.

69. Constant, *Foxy Ferdinand Tsar of Bulgaria.*, 210.

70. Nadejda Stancioff, unpublished journal, 23 March 1907, PASF. "Our schedule here: Feo and I rise at 7, Ivan at 7.3, Chou at 8 breakfast at 8:30 lessons 9-12, lunch at 1, 2:30 walk. 3:30-lessons-6, 10 min for tea at 4:30, 6 toilette and sewing, 7:30 dinner. Chou bed 8, Ivan 8:15, we 9:15."

71. Nadejda Stancioff, unpublished journal, 9 May 1908, PASF.

72. Ibid. 29 April 1908.

73. Nadejda Stancioff, unpublished journal, 17 and 21 May 1908.

74. Nadejda Stancioff, 18 August 1908, PASF.

75. Ibid. 16 September 1908.

76. Ibid. 7 September 1908.

77. After making an ordinary entry on 29 August 1908, about her father's where-abouts, Nadejda writes "Ooora! Ooora!" Did she know the subject of her father's meeting with Izvolsky? The two men had been discussing the potential for changing the Treaty of Berlin to both Bulgaria's and Russia's advantage. Izvolsky advised Stancioff to make certain that when the diplomatic upset came, fault for the disruption in European relations be laid squarely at Austria's door. He also made clear that Russian interests coincided primarily with Romania's and Bulgaria's. That Bulgaria could eventually expect to have a port on the Aegean Sea and that the difficulty for Russian foreign policy was not to gain free access to the Straits but to impede access to other [great] powers. When the diplomatic crisis arrived in September Izvolsky was not so very much upset as frustrated. He complained to Stancioff, "why did you not listen to us?" He wanted assurances that Austria and Bulgaria were not in league with each other. Once the Russian diplomatic embarrassment of the Russo-Japanese war loss was repaired he had assured Stancioff the Bulgarians could depend on Russia to help them fix the Macedonian question. See also Dimitri Stancioff's reports and official correspondence regarding his conversations with Izvolsky in BIA F13 ae 37.

78. Ibid., BIA, F13 ae 37, 33-79.

79. Meriel Buchanan, unpublished letter, November 1908, Nada VIII, PASF.

80. Nadejda Stancioff, unpublished journal, 10 October 1908, PASF.

81. Nadejda Stancioff, unpublished journal, 2 May 1909, PASF.

82. Nadejda Stancioff, unpublished journal, 17 April 1909, PASF.

3
Growing Up

"At Paris, one is dazed, worn out, one sees and hears too much of too many different things."
Nadejda Stancioff, unpublished journal[1]

The Stancioffs' reward for faithful loyalty and diligence was the prestigious posting of Dimitri as Bulgarian minister to Paris in March 1908. Prince Ferdinand knew how much it would mean to Madame Stancioff to return to her native land. This post was an inspiration. Although demoted from the higher-ranked minister of foreign affairs position, Dimitri Stancioff, in fact, had done very well for himself. On this occasion M. Paleologue, his friend, said "You certainly have fallen without hurting yourself."[2]

The Stancioffs spent seven idyllic years in Paris. They were together in the most cultured capital of the world, the matriarch's native land, at a time when the world seemed to be renewing itself. It was the Belle Époque, an era that witnessed an explosion of high culture and a mushrooming of mechanical inventions in the name of progress.

Paris 1908-1915

The family established the Bulgarian legation at 38 Avenue Kleber. For their home, Anna chose an eighteenth-century building, which had period paneling, a forecourt with stables, a vaulted porch, and a grand winding staircase. A French decorator helped beautify the reception rooms, which were in the style of Louis XVI.[3] Freshly cut flowers—a marker of elegance, wealth, and elite status— adorned the public rooms.

In Paris, the family kept a sizeable staff at the residence to assist them with all of their official duties and with the upkeep of a large and complex household. They kept horses, dogs, and birds. The legation's domestic staff had to prepare for visiting-day rituals as well as for large and elaborate gatherings for the diplomatic community.[4]

Each member of the family had a bedroom; the staff shared accommodations at the top floor of the building, and the governess had her own bedroom. The children's lessons, the shopping and chores, the parties—hosting and attending—all were a constant demand on both family members and staff. Wardrobes were a time-consuming affair. Keeping everyone properly attired for every occasion and seeing to the many needs of the entire household was a full-time occupation for the mistress of the household as well as her domestic staff. Her daughters learned at her side.

The Stancioffs moved their family to Paris on October 1, and a few days later Nadejda could write, "Ooora! Bulgaria has declared her independence, da zhivee [long live] Bulgaria."[5] It was an auspicious beginning for the legation of the newly independent Bulgarian Kingdom.

In their home, the two most important rooms were Dimitri Stancioff's study and the salon, which was used for entertaining visitors. Nadejda, who helped with the unpacking and arrangement of all their furniture and home décor, designated the study as the room where she could, in essence, feel her father's presence and where she felt closest to him. The study contained a large, glass-topped desk, with framed photographs along the edge, two vases for flowers, four or more calendars, an icon in a corner, and a second desk for his two eldest daughters. They were old enough for their father to employ them as his private secretaries. This was serious employment, and the amount of work they accomplished for him grew in quantity and importance as they grew older.

It took the family until mid-December to feel completely installed in their new residence and ready to receive guests other than their family and a few friends. The end of the installation also signaled the beginning of a more regulated life for the children. Nadejda wrote, "Regular life begins today, goodbye disorder, goodbye happiness! At least happiness of the oriental sort!"[6]

They now returned to their regular lessons and a more regimented social life, Ivan at the lycée, the girls at Mlle. Pouzadoux, and Chouchou with her governess Miss O'Donnell. By January 4, the children's vacation from lessons was over, and they returned to their routines of attending classes, keeping up with homework, and chores. Meanwhile, their parents returned to the cycle of entertaining friends and diplomatic contacts: the relentless round of visits, soirées, teas, and matinees. Dimitri and Anna could entertain properly since they also had finished hiring their full complement of eight domestic servants.

Nadejda sometimes had the freedom, at the age of fifteen, to venture out alone to her singing and drawing lessons. The family maids accompanied the girls on walks, and the sisters chaperoned each other when they went to school. At this point, their private college was select enough to offer lectures by professors from the Sorbonne. 1908 Nadejda recorded her thoughts in her new journal,

"Where will we be next year? In 1907, we were in Sofia, in 1906 at Petersburg, in 1905 in Paris! Where will we be in the year to come?"[7]

Parisian Distractions

In 1909 two of Anna's brothers were in Paris simultaneously, Comtes Aynard and Robert. The latter had just returned with his wife and child from his business post in Indochina and was searching for a new position. His moods of despondency and lethargy as a result of being out of work must have irritated his sister and brother-in-law since Nadejda records that although his moodiness was understandable, he had to learn to control himself and evince some energy, to "have a personal sense of will, to never count on others and make one's way by one's own power. Maman and Papa have all these qualities."[8] Uncle Aynard was unmarried, but he too was looking for a suitable position, one befitting his station and talents. His moods seemed to be mercurial as well, but the Stancioff children thought of him as a fun adult, more amusing than his older brother. Therefore, Nadejda characterized him as "very gay and always makes me think of the Duke de Montmorency, the one who Richelieu had decapitated."[9]

In January of that year, the Bulgarian colony in Paris put on a matinee performance of Bulgarian songs, dances, and poetry. The Stancioff children all participated, and the group prepared for the show by holding their practices primarily in the legation on Avenue Kleber. The goal of the performance was to make Bulgaria better acquainted to the Parisians; it was a positive propaganda campaign. The task was vast. Bulgaria and her people were perceived as exotic as any colonial population. Ivan had a shocking encounter with French ignorance and exoticism of his country on his first day at lycée, when one of his classmates disingenuously asked if he was "the new Negro?"[10] Meanwhile, the Russian state began the process of officially recognizing Bulgaria's independence and legitimating the country's existence before the diplomatic community. As the rest of the Great Powers would follow suit, it was an ebullient epoch for Bulgarian citizens both at home and abroad.

In 1909, at the age of 63, Sarah Bernhardt still acted in Paris, and the two eldest Stancioff children were thrilled to see her performance in *L'aiglon (The Eaglet)*, written by Edmond Rostand. Nadejda comments, "We quiver with anticipation . . . what joy, what delirium!"[11] The play's subject was Napoleon's unfortunate son, the prince of Rome, a subject that captured the children's imaginations to such a degree that after seeing the play, the girls organized a reenactment of their own at home. Feo, who had a gift for mimicking people, took the role of Sarah Bernhardt, emulating the same weary, sad timbre of the legendary actress' voice.

As a family of monarchists, the Stancioffs were great admirers of Napoleon Bonaparte. Over the years, they made pilgrimages to sites touched by Napoleon's presence and collected representations of his image. Eventually, Nadejda had letterhead created with her monogram, "N," surrounded by a laurel wreath, similar to Napoleon's own monogram. Anna Stancioff marked and noted the ninety-fourth anniversary of his passing on St. Helena in Nadejda's journal.

Anna and Dimitri also continued their children's unofficial education through excursions to historically significant locales, combining the pleasure of family togetherness with instruction in history, art, and their favorite leisure-time activity, the admiration of all things verdant and flowering in nature. In mid-April, they took a typical excursion to Fontainebleau, a royal residence of the Bourbon dynasty. They spread their picnic on the grass in the estate's woods, toured the interiors, and discussed the events and people that shaped French history.

Social Obligations in the City of Lights

The children and parents were fully aware of the toll the hectic pace of life in Paris exacted on all of them. Nadejda notes one afternoon's activities:

> We go to the dentist with Maman and then she has three teas! Life is very ani-mated in Paris. Papa and Maman go out constantly, without stopping, the after-noons and the evenings. Teas especially are in fashion.
> Plunged into the turbulence of this city [which is] never at peace, at Paris one is dazed, worn out one sees and hears too much of too many different things, all the waves of existence collide here and one great ocean, which is constantly in motion whose noise muffles, deadens one's aspirations. Life is truly intense here; is it good too?[12]

The daily rhythm of family life required that each family member perform duties, both pleasant and otherwise. No matter how young or irresponsible the children were in other ways, each of them was on their best behavior at all times, before guests, Parisian society, and their domestic help. As Bulgaria's diplomatic representatives, the entire family worked in harmony to project a sophisticated, urbane image. They were under scrutiny as actors in the most watched social scene in Europe.

Anna and Dimitri were compelled to attend requisite numbers of socially acceptable modes of ritual bonding. These demands on their time were part of the diplomat's duties and bound his family as firmly as they bound him to do right and, therefore, to adhere to high professional standards.

The Stancioffs were intimately linked to the right circles; they performed all the social maneuvers required of a diplomatic family. In so doing, they garnered acceptability not only for their family but also for their homeland in the eyes of the French and other diplomatic representatives. Nadejda comments:

> Papa goes to see Pichon. He is admired a great deal for his many talents and his fine perspicacity as a diplomat, his noble manners of a Marquis in the court of Louis XIV and his elegant turn of phrase, his fine Slav ideas and his originality, [he is considered] interesting, in all Parisian society.[13]

By the standards of their day, the Stancioffs considered all their accomplish-ments as a collective feat. They were an outstanding family in Bulgarian society and the diplomatic milieu according to their own estimation and their peers. The fact that their father looked noble, had an aristocratic profile and—when dressed in his most ceremonial uniform, covered in a constellation of decorations—could fit into any formal social occasion, was a source of great pride. Appearances were a factor in the constant effort to gain acceptance and keep it. One's potential for professional success was linked to one's ability to appear to belong to the group.

The Stancioffs were not singular in their insistence on the importance of a noble or aristocratic bearing as a means of achieving success in their work. Countless diplomatic memoirs attest to the fact that carrying oneself as regally as possible and appearing to be of the superior strain of the human species in looks and bearing were paramount. Being small, dark, misshapen, or maladroit gave enough license to society wags to take up even the smallest professional infraction and ascribe it to the unfortunate transgressor, and, by extension, to his embassy. In their world, diplomats watched for any symbol—the faintest semiotic indicator—of what really lay beneath the clothes, the facial expressions, and the manners. Just as the languages of European diplomats gave way to French, the diplomats' public image evolved from centuries of court rituals into a social standard that became an accepted part of diplomatic discourse.

Domestic Rearrangements

In 1909, the family let go of their English governess. Miss Clark had been with them for three years, long enough for the children to be attached to and fond of her. They enjoyed her company and she enjoyed them. She taught them to make English toffee; she took them on outings to parks, chateaux, and teas at popular spots in Paris. However, there must have been something disagreeable about her. In her journal, Nadejda noted the decision for Miss Clark's departure: "Miss Clark will leave us soon; she is good but her character is insupportable and makes her not likeable. It is a lesson for us, so that we may correct ourselves while we are young."[14] When she left the Stancioffs, Miss Clark headed to a new position in the former Congress Kingdom of Poland.

Nadejda claimed not to like change, but she had to experience quite a bit of change in a brief period of time. Coincidentally, when Miss Clark left, Nadejda's formal schooling also ended when she graduated from eighth grade. This was the end of what Nadejda called her regular studies—the end of dictations, copying by rote, reading narrations aloud, and other boring and annoying exercises. From this point on, her studies would consist of select history and literature lectures, some language lessons, as well as piano instruction.

Summer in Varna – the Orient East

In August, the Stancioffs left for their summer holiday in Varna. Nadejda wrote, "Au revoir beautiful Paris! West and civilization! On the way to the dear, uncultivated, disordered, and sympathetic Orient-East!"[15] The family was about to enjoy their first extended stay in their new villa by the Black Sea. In France, they had taken the time to order and purchase various supplies for their house. Nadejda writes, "We think a lot about the dear little house in Varna, we order papers [wallpaper], furniture, the bath fixtures, etc."[16] The estate was ideally located four kilometers north of Varna and about five kilometers south from the royal palace at Euxinograd. Sheltered from the dust and traffic noise, the house, which was built in the middle of a bluff planted with vineyards, had a commanding view of the surrounding area, especially the sea.

To descend to the sea, the Stancioffs had a long staircase built from the top of their cliff to the shore, where they also constructed a wooden pier from which they could jump into the water. The main house had enough space to include private rooms upstairs for everyone as well as the occasional guest, a small study, a bathroom, and a washroom. There were balconies from all the bedrooms. The north side of the house looked out toward the vineyards and the distant hills. The south side had an uninterrupted view of the sea. Downstairs, the villa had an immense hall, or salon, with a large fireplace; a dining room, also with a fireplace; and a vestibule with parquet floors.

During their first full-length summer holiday, the family became better acquainted with their environs by taking daylong excursions to notable sites such as the petrified forest at Diklitatch, the spring at Devna, the monastery of Aladja, and the river Kamtchia. They visited the archaeological museum in Varna and learned first about the artifacts excavated in the region from Professor Skorpil, who was supervising the excavations, and then visited the Pliska ruins for a private tour of the remains of the first medieval Bulgarian capital.

The Palace Beckons

On September 30, 1909 the queen invited the children to the palace to commemorate Princess Nadejda's name day. Each princess presided over her own table with the children of Varna's society as her guests. After their tea, the children played games and amused themselves with a lottery in which they won prizes. Invitations to the palace for the Stancioffs or for their children gradually increased with time. However, the newly wed royal couple was still negotiating their communication style, and at least on one occasion, crossed signals. The king invited the Stancioffs for dinner—after the Stancioffs and the royal family had attended mass at the palace chapel—without informing his queen; so she improvised meal plans at the last minute. She had the table reset and the menu stretched to meet the demands of the increased number of guests.[17]

The king also honored the Stancioff family by coming more than once to *Villa les Trois Sources*. On his first visit there, he inspected the residence from top to bottom and voiced his approval. It was high praise for the Stancioffs, since King Ferdinand had a reputation for being finicky about everything that concerned the comforts of life. He had exacting tastes in décor and personal adornment, and his approval meant a great deal; the family felt validated.

In 1910, on the first page of her new journal, Nadejda wrote:

Papa is at this moment Minister Plenipotentiary and Envoy Extraordinary of King Ferdinand I, to Paris. Maman is very well, as well as we children; I am 15 ½ and I have finished my conventional studies; I keep busy with Chouchou's work and I take a few courses. Feo is in 7th grade (out of eight total) she has begun to study violoncello, Ivan is at Lycée Janson in 5th grade; he will end his studies after the 1st at the age of 12. Chou is in 2nd out of 8 grades at Mlle Pouzadoux's institution . . . . She is 8 and ½.[18]

The chronicle of their contented family life, fulfilling for everyone concerned, continued. Nadejda was at a point of transition. She was no longer a child; she was a young woman who was preparing to enter society.

As her journal entries show, she and the family discussed local and domestic politics, Parisian municipal (mis)government, as well as foreign affairs:

The political year begins calmly. France is always inclined a bit toward decadence; there are public crimes which are left unpunished; the administration of Paris especially, leaves a lot to be desired; the people have become common, because they have been too long masters.[19]

As the Stancioff family collectively assumed responsibility for all their accomplishments as well as disasters, they regarded 1910 as a very good year. King Ferdinand's official visit to France would be one of those moments when the entire family worked hard and basked in the glow of a successful occasion.

To Be a Stancioff

As a member of the Stancioff family, one had to be adaptable and equally at ease in a salon of social elites as in a backyard stirring marmalade concocted from the fruits of the orchard. This practicality and adaptability was a reflection of solid family training. Anna and Dimitri's training, to work hard and especially to work for the collective benefit were instilled into the children. In the family, the virtues of a good life and the principles of goodness mingled.

A Stancioff was required to have a proper education, be well traveled, and keep current with international events; a Stancioff, woman or man, was also required to be in tune with the growing and harvesting cycles of fruits, nuts, and flowers. The women primarily organized, delegated, and, in time, worked on domestic projects. However, the very fact that they were able to switch easily from one world to another is another remarkable aspect of this family's resilience and work ethic. They knew how to hire, organize, and manage domestic help, but in times of unusual need or crisis, they could also make do without. The blending of diplomatic airs with the country pursuits of gardening, fruit picking, and preserving—as depicted in Nadejda's journals—appear seamless and virtually effortless.

The Victorian era reexamined and revised the model of the "good life." Being a well-educated country gentleman was a laudable goal. Being able to tend one's garden, as did all the Stancioffs, as well as tend to one's investments and business prospects were part of being a well-rounded person and a model citi-

zen. Therefore, it is no surprise that the Stancioffs managed a house full of domestic servants and governesses. While the children were at home, Anna and
Dimitri traveled the continent and kept at least two residences simultaneously. In
time, they kept three homes: one on the Black Sea, one in the capital associated
with Dimitri's latest diplomatic appointment, and a house in Sofia on Oborishte
Street.

In Paris, the staff at Avenue Kleber was cosmopolitan. The cook was Bulgarian, perhaps by necessity, since the family was responsible for official celebrations: he would serve them for several years. The family also employed a
valet for Papa; Maman had a chambermaid and *femme de confiance*. The family
also employed a French family, the Delbars; the husband was *maître d'hôtel*,
and the wife was a chambermaid. In addition, there was a young valet from
Grenoble.

The ménage worked well together, and the family was pleased with their
staff' services. Servants were a constant in the Stancioffs' lives; often they too
were a cosmopolitan group. As part of engaging his children in the running of
the household, Papa entrusted them to make decisions regarding the staffing of
their households and asked for their input. While away on business Dimitri
wrote to Anna. "The children should verbalize their impressions; they are good
judges for domestic help."[20] This luxury was a *sine qua non* of existence, and
although their lives, professional and private, necessitated the extra help of do-
mestics, the family as a whole did not shrink from work of any sort. Their lives
were replete with chronicles of manual labor, the kind of drudge work associated with domestic order and cleanliness.

In 1910, Nadejda wrote an entry about riding a bicycle. Her way of negotiating around convention to do what she wanted to do, ride a bicycle, is telling.
According to conservative convention, it was a shocking sight to see a woman
riding on a bicycle; such an act was not tolerated in polite society. Nadejda
complained that her billowing skirts were a nuisance, or a danger to her, but the
alternative, bloomers, were unacceptable to society and therefore banned for
girls from "good" families.

Although riding a bicycle was quickly becoming a way for women to show
their emancipation from social conventions in some societies, it was not done in
France. To willfully experience the independence of that kind of freedom of
movement meant that the woman in question was of loose morals. Nadejda nevertheless wanted to experience the sensation, so she compromised. First, she
walked the bike with her chaperones while in the city limits and began riding her
bike once on trails in the woods. Her chaperones were both her brother and their
servants. Naturally, the men could ride from the onset of the excursion. Nadejda
writes:

> We go out with Nemeth and Jeanne [both were servants]. Nemeth and Ivan are
> on bikes, I have mine and I walk with it until the woods. Then, goodbye to
> convention! I jump on the bike and take a long excursion with Ivan. We go to
> Lonchamp, Bagatelle, Neuilly, and find the walkers at Ave Henri Martin. Re-
> turn on foot.[21]

Once the group returned to city streets, Nadejda jumped back into the role of a demure, proper young lady.

Change and Progress as Undesirables

The family had a sense of the absurd well mixed with their conservative, religious foundation. They enjoyed dressing up to amuse each other, for example. The following entries from Nadejda's journal, just days apart in 1910, are typical of the kind of religious training and family spirit that pervaded their home:

> I dress Oriental style after dinner for fun.

> I hope we will profit from this retreat; we are on earth only to prepare ourselves to go to the sky, and nevertheless we rarely think about this aspect of life the weakness of men (and of women) is truly very great.

> I go out with Maman; we visit the cemetery of Passy and tarry among the tombs . . . We too will lie in the earth one day, under the slabs; I would love to die at sea and be thrown in the waves with the sharks.[22]

Nadejda's imagination was active even in those somber moments. When she was just sixteen, she wrote "Live the past always, the future and "progress" do not interest me."[23] These are not the words or the tone of a dreamy, romantic teenager; they are the thoughts of a mature, one could say even cynical, observer of her milieu and world.

In support of empire, change was the enemy, and change is what the Stancioffs opposed in their personal and professional lives. As a motto, the belief that change is by definition damaging, set the tone for a generation of old-world devotees. Those adversely affected by change would, of course, oppose it; some opposed change simply because it was unsettling and, therefore, undesirable. Observing conventional mores was not limited to class or gender but was a manifestation of the prevailing human desire to maintain the status quo because no matter how uncomfortable, the alternative, the unknown, was anathema.

Duties

The death of Edward VII, (r.1901-1910), in early May offered an opportunity for the Stancioffs to reassess their worldviews. They continued to support empire, monarchy, nobility, and rank. Nadejda commented for all of them when she wrote on May 7: "His death is huge loss not only for England but also for . . . all the other states; he was an excellent politician since he worked for peace and justice."[24] The world remained frozen in the last embrace of great empire traditions when the knowledgeable few governed the hapless millions. Nadejda and her family resisted change as much as possible for as long as possible.

Dimitri Stancioff organized King Ferdinand's first state visit to France in June 1910 as he had his visit to St. Petersburg in 1898. These visits were important as a means of cementing good relations between the two states. The event was doubly important for the Bulgarian sovereign because Bulgaria was still considered an upstart state, especially since Ferdinand took the step of crowning himself king without European-wide approval. Each nuanced bow and curtsy, each perfectly organized banquet and reception was part of a larger plan to have Bulgaria and her king accepted by the rest of Europe's royalty. Thus, a successful state visit would reflect well on its organizers, the Stancioffs.

The preparations began weeks in advance and required revision up to the last moment. The revisions were complex enough to require that Dimitri meet with his sovereign in person. Thus, Dimitri left for Bulgaria early in June to work on those details. While he would be completely responsible for the duration of the visit to Paris, his wife would take on the added responsibilities of *Grande Maîtresse de la Cour*. In addition to her usual duties, Anna would escort and see to the needs of her queen. Furthermore, Anna took on the role of her absent husband in all manner of arrangements while he was out of the country and with the king.

In addition to her continued attendance at society balls and soirées, Anna pressed on with arrangements for the Bulgarian royal visit. For example, on the sixteenth of June, she attended a ball that included a sit-down supper given by the wife of the Russian military attaché, Mme. Nostitz, although Anna was busy with her extraordinary duties as the Bulgarian representative's wife. The preparations that led up to the visit actually put the entire family under a strain. Nadejda comments:

> Maman is overwhelmed with duties/chores; she must oversee protocol from the directions Papa sent her via ciphered telegrams; she must see to the decorators, think about our official dinner menu and the reception, which will follow! Today we arranged the freshly cleaned rugs and drapes in Papa's study.[25]

Dimitri kept in constant touch with his wife via a flurry of telegrams; each volley redirected the family's efforts in the rush to do a flawless job. Thus, on the seventeenth, Anna received gardeners and decorators, and she hastened to address the newest directives in her husband's telegrams; in the evening she made time to go to a concert to hear Enrico Caruso.

When Dimitri returned on the eighteenth of June, he began to work on all the details that were his purview, especially on questions of protocol with the French. A soirée for the Bulgarian royal family, including dinner on the twenty-seventh, had to be organized. The family all worked on writing the invitations. As the day of the royal couple's arrival drew near, the pace of work intensified. Nadejda's description is thorough:

> The day approaches . . . Papa works from morning until night so that all will go smoothly, so that the King is satisfied. He is constantly at the Protocol office . . . I go out with Mama to a stylist and to a tailor who are making preparations for the Queen's visit . . . evening in the family circle when all the members become scribes.[26]

Until the very end, there were, of course, problems with tradesmen, gardeners, rug merchants, and the attendant fracas associated with so complex an undertaking. The Stancioffs planned to make the Avenue Kleber residence into as close to a royal-worthy reception space as possible. While Papa was virtually attached to the telephone continuing to arrange protocol, Maman wrangled with tradesmen and their minions. On the evening of the twenty-second, when Dimitri left to meet with his sovereigns at a point outside Paris, mother and children, exhausted by their ordeal, finally paused. Nadejda notes:

> Arranging the rooms, Mama is tired; one night of rest will revive her for our reception . . . our courtyard will be transformed into a salon with a rug, flowers, chandeliers . . . in the exterior courtyard there will be a large tent for a cloak room. We children look drawn. Yes, but mostly enchanted.[27]

The French press wrote complimentary articles on the Bulgarian royal visit; the big circulation newspapers such as *Le Temps*, *Le Siècle*, and *Le Figaro* all welcomed the Bulgarian king and queen. On the first day of their official visit, June 23, the city was decorated and at 1 p.m., traffic was stopped on Avenue du Bois, on the Place de l'Etoile, and on Les Champs Elysées. The sovereigns arrived at the train station accompanied by Dimitri Stancioff and their suite. At the station, M. Fallières, president of the Republic, French ministers, and notables, received the king and queen.

Anna presented her queen with a spray of flowers. The entire company formed a cortege and proceeded to the Palais d'Orsay for an official visit with M. Fallières. Next, the king received the diplomatic corps, while the queen spent time with Anna and her ladies-in-waiting, who had accompanied her from Bulgaria.

That evening the royal couple was feted at a gala dinner at the Elysée Palace. The king and queen were housed at the ministry of foreign affairs; their apartments were deliberately decorated with furniture and ornaments from Fontainebleau used by King Ferdinand's illustrious ancestors, Louis XIV and Louis XV. The bedroom furnishings belonged to Ferdinand's grandfather, Louis Philippe. Ferdinand was overcome with emotion. Possibly at that moment, he felt that he had truly come home to full recognition—equal status with other European monarchs and, perhaps, finally received all the adulation and dignity he and his bloodline deserved.

Protocol and Leisure Pursuits

The visit was full of protocol-mandated meetings as well as more practical concerns. There was a reception for the Bulgarian colony of Paris at the Quai d'Orsay, as well as a dinner and reception at the foreign ministry hosted by M. and Mme. Pichon.

On the next day, June 25th, King Ferdinand paid a visit to the military establishment at Chalons while his queen visited the museums of Paris, the Louvre, Invalides, and others with her *Grande Maîtresse de la Cour* and her Bulgarian and French entourages. Later, the ladies stopped at hospitals. The king surveyed troops, reviewed maneuvers, and firing exercises, and observed aviation displays. Nadejda observed, "The King is interested in everything."[28]

On the twenty-sixth, a Sunday, the sovereigns went to mass at Notre Dame Cathedral. Then, the king and his uncle, the Duke de Chartres, hosted a lunch at the Bulgarian legation. Nadejda's responsibilities included last touches to the flower arrangements and table settings.

After lunch, the entourage left for the Grand Prix. The horse race had been the buzz of Paris for weeks, and the anticipation brought out the entire city to watch the competition. The winner, Muage, was owned by Mme. Cheremetieff. A Russian won the race! Ferdinand was superstitious enough to see this as a propitious omen. That evening, an intimate dinner was held at the Elysée with a mere score of invitees including Dimitri and Anna. Then an evening at the opera followed. Nadejda comments:

> A beautiful royal defile in the grand staircase . . . the hall full of roses and green garlands; the royal loge is superb; then the performance, one act of Damnation of Faust, one act of Samson and Delilah. We children were thrilled to attend this soirée.[29]

On the twenty-seventh, the day for which the entire residence had been transformed, the Stancioffs hosted their reception. First, they held a small family celebration in honor of Feo's fifteenth birthday. The formal dinner and later, the evening reception at the Bulgarian legation included a host of important dignitaries, both diplomatic and aristocratic, in 1910 Paris. Among them were President and Mme. Fallières, M. Paleologue, the Ministers Briand, Pichon, Mouchanoff, Paprikoff, M. and Mme. Dubost, and General Fitcheff. The gala evening included an orchestra and a buffet supper along with formal introductions of the Parisian elites to the visiting sovereigns and the French president. Their majesties appeared satisfied with the event.

On the day after, the sovereigns formally rewarded their servitors, Dimitri and Anna, with tokens of their appreciation. Anna received a diamond brooch from the queen and cuff buttons with pearls from the king. Dimitri received a silver cigarette case from the queen. On July 2, the king decorated Dimitri with the most prestigious honor of the Kingdom of Bulgaria, the St. Aleksandûr cross, which was encrusted with diamonds.

A host of appointments and duties continued to fill the Stancioffs' days. The king lunched with the Stancioffs; it was a last-minute arrangement that gave the visit a homier feel, with the children at the table and with a menu that was simple and not elegant or fashionable. The king dispensed expensive gifts to the Stancioff children as well. Chouchou and Nadejda received bejeweled *coqs* (bantam roosters, the symbol of France) in the French and Bulgarian colors. The king bestowed upon Ivan and Feo watches on gold chains, then remained to work in their father's study and later dined with the family. Nadejda was content that he declared their simple family repast satisfactory; she had some say in the preparations. He left late that evening. Meanwhile, their mother accompanied the queen to *Salome,* sung by the vibrant Mary Garden.

The children continued to be yoked into work on the sixth, when they helped their father sort and complete his paperwork. On this visit, the royal family also required assistance in procuring exotic birds and plants for their menagerie and gardens in Bulgaria. The new acquisitions were housed temporarily with the Stancioffs until it was time for the royal family to leave. Finally, on the eighth, the sovereigns left for Brussels on an unofficial trip.

Later that month Nadejda recorded a candid assessment of her father during this visit. "Papa is agitated and tired these days but one can tell that this is his life; he is in his element, that he loves all this."[30] The family was relieved and proud that in the end, the visit was a resounding success.

Although they made plans to leave Paris at last, the *monde* (Parisian society) had already left for their summer retreats; King Ferdinand and his sons came back to Paris for an unofficial visit incognito, necessitating an even longer stay for the Stancioffs. Nadejda assessed her royal playmates and described Prince Boris as very thin. The prince seemed a bit awkward, although he had beautiful eyes and the promise of growing into a handsome man. Prince Cyril she described as a pretty boy with a fine little head and beautiful blue eyes with a nice little mouth, and a svelte, well-proportioned body. Although they had not accompanied the king on his official visit to Paris, the royal brothers now joined in a round of theatre, museum, and visits to parks with the Stancioffs in assistance.

In addition, while the family began to prepare for their summer trip to Varna, the work of the diplomat continued. According to an entry Feo made on the twenty-eighth of July,

> Papa works constantly with two secretaries to distribute the remaining decorations to regulate the mountains of paperwork . . . The salon is already atrocious with the rugs rolled up, the books in piles etc.[31]

The confusion of packing was augmented by the presence of packing crates that were the king's purchases and acquisitions while on his visit to Paris. The clutter and disorder disrupted the Stancioffs' lives for several days. On the thirtieth, their father, drained by his duties, made the decision when to depart. The date was contingent on his finishing his work, and the royal visit had put off their departure for over two weeks. They took three domestic servants with them, and the husband and wife team remained to take care of the residence in Paris.

Longing to Get Away

The family yearned for their vacation time in their villa. *Les Trois Sources* represented a refuge of their own making; the house was designed and decorated with the gardens planned and tended by them with help from their domestic workers. The property held a special place in their hearts, and summer was the time when they could shed their diplomatic countenance and relax, let down their virtual hair, and be at ease in their own place. Since it was built far from the city of Varna, the property had no access to electrical services until 1927, the atmosphere was decidedly rustic.

When they were finally prepared, the mountain of parcels and crates added up to twenty large pieces of baggage that they would expedite to the luggage car, as well as twelve smaller pieces, which they would carry as hand luggage. They traveled in sleeping cars and traversed an 1870 battlefield (a poetic scene, Nadejda noted) while the train passed Strasbourg, Stuttgart, and Ulm. On this summer trip, they took along their French cousin Lele who stayed with them the entire summer.

In Munich the natives were, according to Nadejda, heavy, sleepy, and beery. The Stancioffs appreciated the fine museums where they admired Van Dyck, Rembrandt, Durer, Lippi, Del Sarto, and Murillo. In Vienna, their uncle Panitza and cousin Stati met them; the latter gave them a ride in one of his late-model cars. The boat crew of the Danube Navigation Company knew their father because of his family's longstanding interests in the business and treated the Stancioff passengers exceptionally well. According to Ivan, the family had free passage on the steamship line from Linz to Ruse at least until 1912.[32] Nadejda wrote with a proprietary air when more passengers were taken on later in the trip:

> We travel all the night in a clean boat unfortunately it fills up with all sorts of crowds of people from the country, more or less clean, smelling of the Orient. . . . we chat with the Banat women, of different nationalities, speaking Serb, Hungarian, and German. They are pious, naive, and nice.[33]

Finally, in the early morning of August 8 they arrived at their villa. The weather was beautiful. They rushed to visit their favorite places and take that long anticipated first swim in the Black Sea. For Nadejda, Bulgaria had a specific smell—a mixture of sea, flowers, peppers, and dust. She inhaled the air with gusto and began to anticipate a long, luxurious vacation.

The next morning, when they had their first breakfast on the veranda with a view of the sparkling sea, she could not help but begin to project her unique feel for the place. Their bread was soft, malleable, and languorous like the Orient and emitted whiffs of a harem! In addition, they cut it with a "good sturdy knife of Samokov [their cook was from Samokov]!" The metro, the Bois the Boulogne, and the opera seemed very distant and alien in contrast to their special refuge. Their joy was boundless. "We are thrilled to be in our dear villa Tri Kladenitsi [the Bulgarian translation of *Les Trois Sources*]. We eat our vegetables and drink our own wine and since we are Bulgarians these two things make us crazy with joy."[34] The Stancioffs reveled in the Oriental ambiance, warm, care-free, relishing the fruits of their labors.

Palace Calls

In addition, almost immediately, in what would become routine over the course of this and countless future stays, an invitation arrived from the palace. Invitations from the royal family—either individually or collectively—streamed into the villa: outings, lunches, teas, and other amusements. On this particular occasion, the queen invited the Stancioffs on a boat excursion. One day later, on the thirteenth, the Stancioffs invited the queen to tea. The family also began work immediately on a major remodeling project—the wallpapering of several rooms by two Austrian workers, who papered the hall in red and installed a fresco. Designed by Anna, it was a Bulgarian motif with two large birds bracing the Stancioff cipher in Cyrillic letters. The study would be green, with the same fresco, and the dining room yellow, again with the family crest done in fresco.

The focal point of the hall was a wood engraving of the Madara horseman. Hung over the large fireplace, the replica was the work of the young artist Schivaroff. (The original, which has inspired imitations, is a dramatic bas relief carving into a high stone face near Varna, possibly an eighth-century creation, intriguing because of its size and its mysterious provenance.) In this manner, the villa, inside and out, was a family creation that reflected the Stancioffs' spirit as lovers of the splendors of nature and as worshipers of the historic, national aspects of their homeland.

Wedding Anniversary Traditions

On the seventeenth of August, the Stancioff children celebrated their parents' twenty-first wedding anniversary with their usual festive and gay uproar. With the wallpapering finished, and the grand piano—purchased in France—installed along with the stone gargoyles and other bits of decorative details and furniture, Anna collected over the course of the family's travels; the villa took on a more polished air. It became a testament to her abilities to decorate and orchestrate an elegant, sophisticated style, and the entire family was quite proud of the work. Their photo albums contain several pages of photographs of the hall; the photos were devoted only to the interior space as the focal point. The family's domestic space was valued as a masterpiece of decorating acumen and as the inanimate symbol of the family's unique essence.

In September, the royal couple hosted the Duke and Duchess of Orleans at their Euxinograd residence. The Count de Grammont, Count de Pimodan, Baron de Fonscolombe, and Mlle. de Villeneuve accompanied them. Maman was called to duty and spent her days in attendance to the queen. Apparently, Anna was extremely pleased with her duties, especially since the duchess addressed her by her Christian name. The duke dispensed traditional gifts to valued servitors and presented Maman with his monogram on a brooch.

The Stancioffs continued the work of diplomats, meanwhile, inviting the consuls of France, Russia, and England for tea. Nadejda assessed them, observing that "the first is common, the second a dreamer and soft and the third honest and heavy; the first wife is vulgar, the second thin and silent, the third is pretty but she knows too much."[35] She took the measure of the diplomats' wives, which was a customary measure of the diplomats' intelligence.

On the very next day, Nadejda and Feo were granted permission to meet the French royal couple. Enthralled by the prospect, they trembled with anticipation. Nadejda observed that the duke was, "big, blond, handsome, elegant, thin, svelte, smart, with eyes that scrutinized, mouth ready to laugh, a voice low and a speech that delivered in rapid fire!"[36] They judged him handsome, and when he bowed to kiss their hands, they were transported to another world. Nadejda referred to herself and her sister as "little savage Bulgarians" who were apparently ennobled by the duke's simple gesture of polite greeting. Feo and Nadejda found the Duke d'Orleans more compelling than Victor Napoleon, and Nadejda confessed they were developing a predilection for the house d'Orleans.

Nurturing Patriotism

The Stancioffs filled their summer days with excursions to various sites in the area, either with their guests, their Baba Frossa (paternal grandmother), Uncle Nicolas (paternal), and cousin Lele (maternal), or with friends from Varna. The Monastery of Aladja, the Madara horseman, the ruins of a French fort from the Crimean War, the Gypsy, Greek, and the Turkish quarters of nearby settlements were all destinations. The family generally traveled in carriages or wagons pulled by horses and their newly acquired donkey.

Relaxation was the order of those days, with picnics in scenic spots and general gaiety. At one point, Nadejda came down with a fever after visiting a Gypsy encampment and blamed the gypsies for her illness. However, she also appreciated the vibrancy and diversity that the gypsies represented:

> Although you were quite colorful in front of your low carriages seated or lying in the dust before the large red fires, at twilight. It is a dirty race, unpleasant, contemptible, vile, but I prefer them to the Finns. Oh, Orient! With your blue sky and your hot colors, you embellish everything; you endow charms and beauty to the most humble swineherd in your lands! Yes! When we spy one at night, wandering the mountain with his troupe playing his flute with a melancholy air, with a distant look in his dark, languid eyes, yes, we look at him with pleasure and think about him for a long time after! Long live the Orient![37]

The family spent the rest of their time on household chores and keeping up with the harvest of ripening fruits and vegetables, since they did a fair amount of preserving of their produce. While Baba was their guest that particular summer, she and Nadejda did most of the preserving, jarring of compote, marmalade, comfitures, *tourshia* (pickled vegetables), tomato puree, and other items. It was anathema to "buy" fruit for preserves according to Baba, who was used to growing everything on her own land. Nadejda and Baba even picked and dried peppers to take with them as provisions for their kitchen in Paris. Baba Frossa represented the mixed Balkan background of the family, since she still read her Bible in Greek and used the Greek alphabet to write letters in Bulgarian.[38] This kind of cosmopolitanism was inherent for the Stancioffs, who were comfortable in a variety of languages and cultures.

Children as Children

In October, all four of the royal children were in Euxinograd, and the eight companions spent hours amusing themselves together. Generally, the royal children had lessons or some other kind of training during early parts of the day, and then they were free to play. On the Stancioff's property, they had the run of the grounds, and they spent a lot of time in the two diminutive cabins built close to the sea. The playhouses where they could cook and serve themselves concoctions of their own creation offered refuge from the adult world and a sense of independence. They made up lemonade and brewed coffee, toasted bread, roasted potatoes, chestnuts, and created more complex dishes. The princelings enjoyed the singular experience of cooking for themselves. They played games in the cabins near the sea or tennis on the courts on the north side of the house. They sometimes harnessed the horses to the carriage or mounted the donkey for fun.

When the Stancioff children were invited to the palace, they had an opportunity to go on motorboat rides, perhaps go fishing out on the water, or, as it happened in 1910, they listened to a phonograph for the first time and danced a quadrille to the music. Quite often, the group organized themselves in *tableaux vivants*. They dressed in various caricatures of types of people and created images of some significant moment or event. These themes were drawn from current or past events or just literary imagery. This amusement occupied them for hours.

Anna Stancioff in effect also "played" with her contemporary in the royal household, the queen. The queen either invited her to the palace or on occasion invited herself to *Les Trois Sources* for tea. When the queen entertained guests, she asked Anna to the palace as her companion. The women spent time together socializing and discussing political current events. Typically, these arrangements could include the entire households of both families as on October 31 when the queen arrived on foot, the princes via boat, and the princesses in a cart pulled by donkeys, and the queen's American guests, Mrs. and Miss Bagg, via chauffeured car. The mixed company shared high tea then broke up into age-appropriate groups for more amusements after they had toured the property with the American guests.

It was fully part of their summer leave to spend entire days with the royal family. Nadejda's journal records the following day, on November 2, 1910:

> We go to Mass at the palace at 10 the King has invited us all to lunch. Meanwhile we take a walk with the Princes and Princesses along the shore; we see the King on the shore with Papa and Weich who takes two photos of everyone. Lunch at the palace excellent; Monsignor Baumbach is part of the company. After the Queen calls Maman, the King takes a walk with Papa and we remain with the Princes and Princesses; we take an excursion via boat, chat, and fish a large catch. Then tea at the palace . . . The King and Papa therefore talked quite a few hours together; Papa is very content. As for Lele, he is under the spell of it all, of our entire royal family. In addition, we Stancioffs feel full, complete with devotion and affection, and cognizant of them [the royal family].[39]

By mid October, it was time for the grape harvest; the Stancioffs hired peasants from the village of Kisteritch to help. The harvest was another opportunity for the family to spend time doing what they enjoyed and to appreciate the refuge their estate represented from the stifling and rigid world of diplomatic protocol. After they had vacationed for two months, they headed to Paris on November 6; the journey took them back to work, urban living, and cooler, less pleasant weather.

In Germany, they woke to much colder weather and Nadejda made a commented on the scenery, "Hilly sad country! Villages very clean; they remind one of children's toys with their houses thatched, symmetric streets, and their little square gardens. They exude order, methodical."[40]

Upon arriving in the first French train station, the scene was quite repugnant; the train station was ugly, dirty, and unkempt; the station workers rude, vulgar, and common. Nadejda opined, "We recognize the headless body, which is this country."[41] The entire legation greeted the Stancioffs at the train station, and at the family's home, all was in order and the animals were well.

Back to Work in Paris

On the next day, the children recommenced their formal studies; vacation was over. Chouchou rejoined her classmates, Ivan was reinstalled at the lycée, Nadejda would take some courses in history, and Feo returned to studies with Mlle. Pouzadox. The Stancioff women also immediately took up the running of errands from buying corsets to exercise books for school lessons. Nadejda was especially pleased to go out with her mother. Their time together, shopping, and criss-crossing Paris was fun. They began with a visit to a milliner, then shopping in the large department stores Printemps, Galleries LaFayette, Potin, and finally an antiquarian shop. Anna must have been enjoying herself immensely, since her daughter noted that the shopping was extra fun because the city appeared lively and gay. Nadejda notes that Maman herself "chats in such a bright and intelligent way!"[42]

The pace of city life changed their habits: no more leisurely walks by the beach or lengthy excursions in the country. Dinners at home for guests and relatives, lessons, office work, predetermined the rigid tempo that became the routine as they resumed visits, soirées, balls, theater, and opera performances.

As Nadejda approached her seventeenth birthday, her uncle Aynard asked her if she looked forward to coming out. She had a little over two years before the event. She answered in the negative, since she found Parisian society "hardly interesting." She also felt that London would be no better; instead she would have preferred Constantinople or Petersburg because they exemplified "the true orient or the true north. I detest the lukewarm; long live the extremes in morals and physical environment."[43]

Parisian Pursuits

In Paris, the family lived the "normal life" of diplomats and their families. Bridge was a fashionable pastime. The duties and obligations of diplomats weighed on Nadejda, and she felt that their life in Paris, although the family was doing a service to their country, was not ideal. Nadejda was at the age when she still felt emotions strongly and longed for Russia, which she perceived as real and authentic as opposed to "false" Paris. She wrote on January 11, 1911:

> I have a desire to live in dear and sympathetic Russia, the country of grand ideas where one thinks still a bit of love, of beauty. In Paris, people do not have a soul, they live for nothing, but society, their existence is completely superficial. There are exceptions, it is true, but they are rare. In this city called Paris love is nothing, one marries for money, marriages in which there is not one day of true happiness. Little of beauty, nothing but the artificial, which is abhorrent [to me].[44]

Meriel Buchanan's father was reassigned to St. Petersburg, and Nadejda was excited for her. Meriel, Nadejda's friend, saw none of the charms in the northern capital but only its remote, cold location. Conversely, Nadejda longed for Russia.

The Stancioffs opened their homes to private and official celebrations, and Nadejda recorded these events with avid interest. She was diligent in reporting about the parties, dresses, manners, menus, and amusements. She also inevitably ended her entries with an assessment of how successful the event was, such in the following notation:

> Vive la Bulgarie et les Bulgares! Morning of preparations—we pick up the rugs, the floors are waxed and shine like mirrors, the books, papers neat . . . At 10:30 the party begins. Officers, students, dames, young girls all Bulgarians and all Bulgarian: soul, body, appearance. . . . in all almost 100 people. The Salons are full. General gaiety. We chat, we play national music, and then the hour arrives, champagne and conversations. Noise and gaiety, supper . . . excellent, appreciated. Midnight! Long Live 1911! Music, dances, horo, walses, Russian dances. Joy, exuberance, at 3:30 we part.[45]

On the day after her seventeenth birthday, Nadejda went out for a walk with her Maman alone. She was very close to her mother, and she reveled in that intimacy of love, but she and her mother also shared ideas, goals, and perspectives. Nadejda never seemed, in her entire life, to have wanted to break away from that bond. In addition, as a teenager she never appeared to exhibit rebelliousness against either of her parents. Instead, when her parents did not permit her to visit her cousin, Vera Stambolouff, in London for the Easter holidays, a much-anticipated journey on her own, she agreed that it was perhaps too soon for her to have undertaken such an adventure far from her paternal home. She muses about her time alone with her mother:

> This evening I go out once again with Maman alone. A delicious walk in the
> Avenue du Bois, dark and deserted; I adore this, this hour, this calm and most
> of all my dear Maman. We talk together; our ideas coincide marvelously this
> eve. Ah, I feel sorry for those who don't have "Maman."[46]

When Nadejda could not realize her fantasies about visiting her cousin, she
dressed up for amusement. "January 22 . . . after dinner. I dress myself up as a
man with Papa's clothes; a droll affect."[47] In the heart of the fashion world, the
Stancioffs had the opportunity to observe the introduction of what Nadejda
called "skirt pants." The women of the family found the article of clothing "un-
gracious, horrid, abnormal, and despised by good society."[48] They labeled the
style depraved and a fashion that robbed a woman of her grace and charm.
Dressing up in men's clothing or any clothing that was not in keeping with socially acceptable norms was solely for family amusements.

Later in her life, Nadejda had difficulty bowing to the prevailing trend in
fashions by, for example, shortening her skirts to a more stylish height. She and
her family were conservative in a variety of ways but especially in their habitual
costumes. Nonetheless, they could enjoy the pleasure of transforming themselves and playing at looking different when they created *tableaux vivants* or
when they chose costumes and poses for their many portraits. Then they could
abandon traditional looks for whatever their imagination inspired. The children
shared that valuable characteristic of all transient families, the ability to amuse
themselves with very little at hand.[49]

Receiving Days and Social Obligations

As part of her duties as a diplomat's wife, as well as a member of the aristocratic
elite, Anna Stancioff observed the practice of keeping receiving days. She received on the second Monday of the month. Those days required extra care with
the hall, fresh flowers, and other embellishments. The reception was from 3:00
to 7:30 p.m., and on those days, it was Nadejda, as eldest daughter, who helped
her pour; she also recorded the list of attendees.[50]

The practice was a continuation of French salon culture which placed
women in the active role of organizers and purveyors of intellectual exchanges
in their homes, as early as the mid-seventeenth century. As the one responsible
for gathering and hosting intellectual and artistic pursuits, such as singing, playing an instrument, and dancing, female hosts not only entertained their guests
but directed the intellectual life of their social equals. The role of the salon hostess was primarily one of supporting artful conversation, of informing and shaping public discourses on topics of mutual interest. For Anna Stancioff, this practice would have been a deeply ingrained practice. She would have held court by
carrying on witty and elegant conversations within a carefully selected circle of
invitees.

Nadejda understood very well that this responsibility was more than the
obligation of a woman of her class. She viewed it as work in which everyone
helped to the best of her ability, and she noted that "Maman talks incessantly,

entertaining, 'working' basically, and we help well and poorly."[51] The guests were, after all, the family members of her father's colleagues and French politicians.

The receiving day ritual reinforced Dimitri's connections with all of these functionaries and helped to smooth relations among diplomatic households so that the work of diplomacy could proceed effortlessly, especially in times of crisis when ordinary niceties were often not observed. These conventional social bonds served a dual purpose. Anna's standing in her social circle was reinforced in an acceptable way; while Dimitri's professional position was strengthened. Furthermore, the bonds among the children of this elite society also strengthened, thereby creating the network of acquaintances that would be their professional and personal mainstays in their respective futures.

Entertaining appropriately and being a proper guest was a large part of the role a diplomatic wife and diplomat's children played throughout their lives. For example, when the Count and Countess Nostitz were beginning his mission as military attaché at the Russian embassy in Paris, the Count was clear about how much of the success of his mission would depend on his wife's talents. "Much of the responsibility will devolve on you as my wife...you can be of utmost help to me. You are adaptable and you are naturally a charming hostess..."[52] The implication here is that a lack of adaptability, charm, and the ability to entertain key guests could be a disaster for the mission. One of his qualifications for the position, other than his long-standing eminence in the imperial Russian horse guards, was his large private fortune. This fortune disposed him to entertain lavishly and to do it on a scale befitting the prestige of the Russian court.

When the Countess Nostitz gave her very first ball in Paris, she invited 500 of the *crème de la crème* of Parisian society. Her guests included the aristocracy and royalty, select members of the French military leadership, and the diplomatic corps. She invited the Stancioffs, and Nadejda had the good fortune to accompany her parents. According to the Countess Nostitz, Dimitri was good looking, distinguished, and willowy; his wife was a pretty blond, and Nadejda was a dreamy-eyed girl.[53] The Stancioffs made a good enough impression to be included in her memoirs, possibly because Dimitri was pro-Russian, and she eventually accepted invitations from them in return. Countess Nostitz, née Madeleine Bouton of Iowa, became one of those rare flowers whom Nadejda kept in her special place of reverence in her imaginary garden because she had all the qualities that Nadejda's imagination sought. One of the leading beauties of her day, the Countess occupied a position of prominence in several societies and had the good fortune to marry well (from a fiscal perspective), not once or twice, but three times.[54]

During the high social season, February through the end of spring, attendance at all the society functions and events was obligatory, and even Nadejda stopped listing them all and simply recorded that her parents attended thousands of teas, games of bridge, dinners, soirées, parties, and conferences. On their afternoons free from other engagements, the women carried cards to the households with whom they mixed, although Nadejda found the custom ridiculous.

On the rigors of the season, Nadejda was less accusatory; however, her parents' routine was monotonous in its predictability. For example, on May 31, 1911, they attended four matinées, had dinner in the city, and attended two soirées. The veritable merry-go-round of social commitments varied little from day to day. With the anticipation of her own entry into society, Nadejda did not relish the prospect of that tiring routine.

Flowers of Her Garden

At seventeen, Nadejda had some unique romantic notions of love and marriage, although she seemed ready to consider appropriate suitors. She seemed also not to be in a hurry to marry and leave her parental home and even found marriage at an early age repugnant. In fact, according to one journal entry in 1911, she considered the prospect rather grim. She opined that

> the marriage ceremony of a young girl resembles that of her death, they are the same white flowers of an insipid perfume, the same disorder in the rooms, the same smile on the lips of those who leave and the same tears in the eyes of those who remain.[55]

This is not the observation of a girl eager to toss her hat into the marriage ring. Instead of indulging in romantic musings about a handsome young man, she created a special place in her heart and mind for her most loved women.

These were women whose beauty, grace, elegance, and poise set them above all others in her estimation. She was especially fond of women who were, in her view, alluring, seductive, and captivating. For these few, she imagined an entire fantasy realm of their dwellings—places where she could join them and enjoy their company when she sought an escape from reality. A small number of them became her idols, and instead of referring to them by name, she named each of them by the flower, which most resembled their unique aspects. These "flowers" were her muses, as she notes:

> My big perfumed garden. . . . The invisible musicians play my favorite tunes all the simple and sad melodies of the Orient. What repose I get from this retreat each night I decorate my room and I hide in my garden. I save for myself the role of vague melancholy slave.[56]

In her imagination, and increasingly, through her contacts with elite women, she shaped her own female persona. As a constant observer and commentator on human nature, she internalized the behaviors and manners of the women she most admired. She saw them in a variety of environments, and that experience gave her opportunities to note and query their nuanced behaviors. She wondered: Were they coquettish? Were they serene? Did they seem sad? Grown weary with the weight of their complex lives? And how did they project that essence of themselves to their public? She, in turn, became a part of that world by creating her own unique projection of female elegance, as the following passages illustrates:

A magnificent soirée at the Prince and Princess Murat in their palace on Rue de Moncdeau. The garden is illuminated and scored with beautiful women. House full of flowers. A dashing ball. I begin to get to know women; we run into each other sometimes two times per day! I love to study the bizarre and the seductive Madame de Rudini, the little Italian, who pleases me![57]

These women had a following. Each of the great beauties of the day had a coterie of admirers; married women had the most admirers, while unmarried girls had fewer, since they had to be circumspect. Married women, on the other hand, could and did have, depending on their allure and unique charms, scores of admirers who vied for their attentions. Admirers simply meant that these women embodied all the socially accepted charms that were essential in a great beauty. For the most part, admirers, male or female, were not lovers. Male admirers had specific ways of displaying their devotion with flowers, gifts, compliments, and often insisting on being present, they could declare their devotion in person. Women, on the other hand, were more subtle and private with their devotion to the great beauties. They admired from afar, praised and compared their favorites with their contemporaries and in general, kept their overt manifestations of admiration to glances at their object of esteem and occasional shy comments in person. Nadejda muses that

My women must sleep in their perfumed niches . . . niches [that are] ensconced in the big southern wall; the women hear the sea without seeing it. They are seated, on thrones behind a veil; Meriel has an azure veil and all white flowers, Nostitz has a red veil, red roses and tiger lilies, Bosdari a purple veil, violets and iris, Anna de Noailles, gold veil, tuberoses ...[58]

A relationship of admiration, even adulation, pervaded these sentiments. These were a natural expression of the kind of platonic love women bestowed on one another.[59]

Women allowed their admiration to blossom into feelings that were warm, passionate, and delicately balanced between veneration and exaltation. This kind of inspired devotion between women, even when it was publicly declared, was a perfect foil for the circumspect and carefully ordered lives they led. It was permissible for women to be carried away with their feelings for the object of their affections, since she was a popular beauty. These emotions served the purpose of embracing the lover and beloved into a wholesome diad. Nadejda writes: "Dear flowers, sweet symbol of purity, of love, of dreams, of folly or languor or passion how I love you! I would love to have the poetic talent to sing about you, to dedicate a long canticle to you, especially to you roses."[60]

As a woman, Nadejda hoped, but did not believe, that she could ever ascend to these women's heights of accomplishment. Instead, she happily admired them from a distance. She remained reserved and shy in her imagined lowly position. Most of these women, not surprisingly, were fair, with smooth alabaster complexions complemented by bright, blue eyes. Their figures were draped in the most fashionable clothes, and their taste in jewelry and perfume and personal adornment she found impeccable. They were also perfect hostesses and enjoyed the heights of social esteem.

These standards were not accidental; Nadejda had one very real, tangible model on which to base her ideal—her Maman. Her mother embodied all the qualities that Nadejda came to prize in her "flowers." Her love affair with exceptional women continued all her life, although, as she matured, her cynicism diminished the numbers of her objects of admiration. While her standards did not diminish her admiration was bestowed on fewer even more elite exemplars of ideal womanhood. As a teenager she chose the kinds of "flowers" among whom she would seek to recluse herself.

> My little room of roses is . . . covered with precious oriental rugs, and it is always full at twilight with flowers and perfumes. And at night when I descend softly, to fall asleep there, and roll myself up in the veils of silk, I live a second existence among the visions of dear beings.[61]

Giving free reign to her youthful imagination, fed by the books she read, the plays, ballets, and operas she attended, Nadejda recreated an imaginative environment accessible only to her. With her own key she could enter the hidden enclave and admire the female beauties ensconced there.

> My moral garden is magnificent at this moment; my female divinities, in their alcoves, behind the gauze of silk breathe in the perfumes, which come from the invisible flowers. The water of my fountains is covered by petals . . . the moonlight gives off blue shadows, the sun throws purple shadows on the alleys . . . I am the only one who possesses the keys of this unique door pierced in the circular wall; [I] water the tuberoses, the lily . . . but it rains quite often in the evenings; a rain that is warm, slow and soft, which I love![62]

Nadejda's romance with all things mysterious is reflected in her love of heroines, real and imagined, who personified her vision of the ideal woman: Salome, Circe, Scheherazade, and Theodora (Byzantine empress). Her favorite literary and real-life heroines were strong women who, by the force of their character, moved men and empires. She, therefore, opined that girls who married young, even for love, were doing something she could not comprehend. The only male hero she admired was her father, with an occasional bow to Napoleon, who was her mother's favorite.

Clearly, Nadejda had a mind of her own. She was not a girl who would be her parents' silent and pliant instrument but rather a thoughtful, active participant in her own future. She fulfilled that promise. In her journal, she articulates her antipathy toward progress, which presaged change in Europe. However, she herself did not remain a member of the cadres of compliant women who, by their willingness to embrace the patriarchal structure, relinquished much of their power. She notes: "I have a horror of being simply a little young girl of . . . the century of progress! Oh, how I despise these modern times and this atrocious progress."[63]

Stancioffs Prefer Conservative Tradition

Despite declaring modernity a horror, Nadejda nonetheless behaved in ways that her female ancestors would have found puzzling. She participated fully in her father's work, fulfilled many of the functions her mother vacated when she was called away, and continued to insist on surrounding herself with intelligent, engaging people. In her life, she modeled a very different archetype of the new woman, whether she was willing to acknowledge herself as such or not. Nadejda was a modern woman who used her intelligence to gain professional status and who sought and reveled in the visibility the diplomatic profession offered. Using the opportunity and training she gained from her experiences as her father's secretary and her mother's primary assistant, she created a path suited to herself. Although her accomplishments could be perceived as groundbreaking, in all endeavors, both public and private, she steered the middle road. She made no completely outrageous forays into professions that were simply unsuitable for a young woman of her station. Moreover, she did not use professional opportunity to unshackle herself from parental control or social convention.

A conservative unbroken chain of tradition did not ease the way for daring change, even on the dance floor, for members of elite society. Naturally, to those people, the tango, which Maman encountered for the first time at an event hosted by Comtesse Nostitz, was "a kind of South American folly," in Nadejda's view.[64] The Argentine dance had become a craze in Paris in summer 1910, and Comtesse Nostitz hosted what she called *leçons de danse* parties in her home.[65] The countess offered the possibly more impressionable younger set of Paris an opportunity to learn the dance from a couple of dance instructors during her afternoon teas in her salon. Among the young and daring, it was an enormously fashionable dance. So along with the one-step and the teddy bear, the tango became wildly popular among those who wished to express their unconventional natures. For the Stancioffs, these dances were not appropriate outward expressions of one's inner nature. Nadejda was content to continue as chronicler of her family's activities and, especially, of the crowd of elites who touched their lives.

When her mother hosted a large tea reception with the accomplished pianist, Sauer, with his performance as its centerpiece, Nadejda recorded the event. She gave details on how they arranged their salon, filling it with irises in purples and mauves as well as lilacs, which filled the room with exquisite perfumes. Sauer's piano was delivered, installed, and tuned by the time the ceremonies began at 4:30. The audience included a host of dukes, duchesses, counts, countesses, princes, princesses, marquis, marquises, and a baron, a sprinkle of ambassadors and their wives, and some military men of rank. Reading the list makes one wonder how all that large elegant company fit in the Stancioff's salon, along with a grand piano and requisite furniture. The evening was another satisfying success for the hostess.[66]

Coronation Fever

The highlight of 1911, for Nadejda, was being given permission to attend the coronation of King George and Queen Mary in London. Her cousin, Vera Stambouloff, invited her for an eight-day visit in June. Nadejda's reaction was predictably effusive. Moreover, she noted that this would be the first time she would sleep somewhere other than her parental home—a grand adventure! This trip gave Nadejda her first experiences in England, and she had a wonderful time. She saw as much as she could of the fashionable neighborhoods, the shops, the museums, and, of course, the two-day long ceremonials of the coronation.

On her first day, she and Vera visited High Street, Knightsbridge, Brompton Road, Regents Street, Oxford Street, and Bond Street. They entered Harrods, Peter Robinson, Selfridge, Fullers, and Barkers. Nadejda found the stores enchanting and quite suitable. She loved London and judged it a noble and dignified city. Decorations for the coronation created a festive backdrop for her visit, and she was impressed.

Of all the museums, she found her visit to the National Portrait Gallery educational; she learned more about English history there.[67] Vera and Nadejda walked around the exteriors of Parliament and Westminster Abbey. On the day of the coronation, the girls rose early—at 5 a.m.—and by 7:30 were installed in the stands. As a member of the diplomatic corps, her father arranged for the girls to have seats in the reviewing stands so that her view was comfortable and close enough to the parade that she could pick out and recognize her father and later, Prince Boris, as they processed into Westminster Cathedral. She admired everything and everyone in the procession. The coaches were impressive; the soldiers' uniforms were superb.

Foreign dignitaries led the first part of the procession; Nadejda recognized her father in his guard's uniform. Next were Princes Heirs Apparent and Princes of the Blood. The girls recognized Prince Boris, who processed between the prince of Sweden and the prince of Siam. After these dignitaries, the members of the royal family of England and the royal children appeared. Finally, the gold coronation coach appeared, pulled by eight cream-colored horses, and carrying King George V and Queen Mary in their coronation robes. The spectators cheered, wildly enthusiastic.

For Nadejda, the spectacle had a poignant beauty. The coronation ceremonies continued for a second day, when the royal couple assembled at Whitehall with all of their dominion representatives. Therefore, at 8:00 a.m., the girls were installed with reading materials and lunch to await the procession. They saw parade detachments from all the colonies from Canada to Malta, from Africa to Gibraltar, and from Australia to Aden. In addition, they saw Scottish regiments, as well as Irish and English. The maharajahs and the rajahs in their national costumes paraded by; they were "a grand spectacle, brilliant in color, glorious to watch," in Nadejda's view. [68]

In London, Nadejda and her father spent time visiting with friends, including the Thompsons, whom Nadejda dubbed honest and colorless. Their son, Douglas, found Nadejda appealing enough to permit him to accompany her and

Vera to several museum excursions as well as walks in the parks. After this trip, Nadejda and he corresponded. She also had tea with Lady Nicolson, the former ambassadress to St Petersburg. At their residence, she visited with the mischievous "little" Gwen, now fifteen, with whom she had played and taken dance lessons in the Russian capital.

Nadejda also made time for a long visit with her friend, Meriel Buchanan, whose father was now ambassador to Russia. The girls walked together, went shopping at Harrods, and then to Meriel's house at Lowndes Square for more talk and shared secrets. They talked about everything—their families, their writing projects, their thoughts, and ideas. Meriel shared her adventures in flirtations. She was the more daring of the two, and throughout her life, she would carry on a series of frivolous liaisons, relationships of no consequences to her. This was a practice that Nadejda found foreign and alien to her own nature. Although Nadejda, too, enjoyed flirtation, her version was of the more distant and impersonal type—with a stranger in a museum, at a train station, or with a fellow passenger—to while away the time. These flirtations were nothing more than subtle impishness. Meriel tended to allow men to woo her and then tired of them quickly. She seemed as unhappy with her suitors as she was with her parents.

During this visit to London in 1911 Nadejda caught a glimpse of Great Britain at precisely the time when it was to begin its decline. That year, and that coronation ceremony, marked the moment when the empire began the descent that would ultimately lead to its complete disintegration in the late 1940s. Nadejda had the good fortune or perhaps the ill luck to visit England for the first time at the luminal point when the superb past, of omnipotent and omnipresent British power, began to diminish. For the Stancioff witness and for Britons themselves the moment may have been virtually imperceptible however, the change began. English society, the economy, the monarchy and the very government were being shaken up albeit gently but steadily.

After the coronation, the Prince Heir Apparent Boris stopped in Paris. Therefore, the first days of July were spent escorting the prince to official and formal meetings as well as the obligatory rounds of dinners, theater shows, horse races, and even an aviation display. The Stancioffs combined private life with public engagements seamlessly. On a single day in July, Feo and Ivan paid a private visit to Prince Boris at 10:00 a.m. Then at 11:30 a.m. Papa, Nadejda, and Prince Boris left to attend the maneuvers of the Grand Armée motorcycle division. Lunch followed in the prince's honor at the Bourboulons; and in the afternoon, the entire family took an excursion with the prince. They rode in four automobiles—which included a Daimler, a Mercedes, and a Renault—to Fontainebleau. The speed was exciting, and the heir apparent was so thrilled that he drove the Mercedes and the Daimler, in turn. The Stancioffs were perfect professionals and companions.

Although the Stancioffs were called upon to perform their official duties as representatives of their country, they also created a type of surrogate family for the future monarch as they toured France with him, be it Compaiègne and Versailles, or the horticultural estate of the Vilmorin family. He felt comfortable lunching with them in an informal way and carrying on conversations while reclining on the couch in the study at Avenue Kleber. The ceremonial barriers were reduced to the barest minimums. The family still used the formal forms of address, but no more than that. Their familiarity with each other, royalty and childhood playmates, extended to outings and meals, musical evenings with dancing—all in the tradition of their summertime relationships. The prince felt comfortable enough to jump right into that informal atmosphere, and the family obviously made him comfortable enough to do that.

Summer at Les Trois Sources

Following Boris' visit; the family began preparations for their summer retreat to *Les Trois Sources*. Once in Bulgaria, they marveled at their property, the promise of a bountiful harvest from the vineyard, and the fruit trees heavy with fruit. Jasmine and lime trees scented the evening as the family strolled among the pagodas in their garden.[69] A walk by the shore in the moonlight reminded them of the pleasures to come; summer was theirs at last.

This particular summer, they had nine domestic servants in Varna, including a new cook from Constantinople. The gardener, Ivan, and his wife, eldest daughter, and son were the core of the staff, as well as five others. Their cook was delayed due to a quarantine imposed on Constantinople; a cholera outbreak trapped its inhabitants. When the cook finally arrived, Nadejda described him fat and short, an oriental figure with a languid and oily drawl, an Armenian. At first he appeared a good man and a nice person, yet only two days later Nadejda viewed him as a bizarre man but good at his job. She comments that "his character appears excellent."[70]

The Stancioffs were accustomed to employing domestic staff and the entire family was involved in the hiring and retention of employees. As early as 1908, when their eldest child was only fourteen, the parents consulted the children regarding domestic help.[71]

Regarding this particular cook the initial impression was reversed, he displeased his employers when he exhibited "lavish spending, his disorder and his cigarette perpetually in his lips and his Armenian tastes."[72] Dimitri dismissed the cook, who, apparently, was to return to Constantinople very soon. Then equivocating on the decision the Stancioffs reversed themselves and since he did a remarkable job preparing a celebration for the Stancioff's anniversary, his behavior was judged to have improved. The Armenian cook was permitted to stay on. He had, in Nadejda's words, "become appropriate enough and we deign to keep him for now."[73] She also admitted to a fundamental family trait when she noted that "the Stancioff family has always been practical."[74] This was a characteristic that served them well.

Nadejda's duties as an older first-born female child also increased that summer, and she found herself overwhelmed with responsibilities and chores. In her journal, she complained not so much about the work itself as the time it took away from *intellectual work*. As her mother's second in command, among her many chores, she also made curtains for her sister Feo's room; the results were pretty, but she found the chore time consuming.

When the Stancioffs were invited to tea at the palace, the two eldest girls helped to serve as they had in times past; thus, their roles as guests and servitors to their majesties were blurred once more. They were simultaneously public and private personae. Their time in the summer was split among duty, fun, and chores. They had tea with the queen and other Bulgarians at the palace on one day, and they made tomato puree with their Baba and bathed in the sea on the next day.

International Sensationalism

In September, the Russian Black Sea fleet visited Varna and fired thirty-two cannons upon arrival, a salute to the Bulgarian queen. Russian ambassador Nekludoff, accompanied by Dimitri, paid a visit to the palace to arrange for the official festivities. After her official tour of the fleet, the queen invited the Russian officers to the palace for tea. In all, over 100 guests were served. Nadejda and Feo practiced their Russian and flirted with the officers. Then, in a return volley of entertainments, the admiral organized a dance for Varna society on board his flagship the *Rostislav*. According to Nadejda, it was a "beautiful spectacle but the public is too 'public'."[75]

Continuing with receiving-day protocols, the Stancioffs welcomed friends as well as members of the Varna diplomatic community to their home. Generally, these gatherings consisted of tea and musical entertainment. The Stancioffs, when either alone or with their guests, they played musical instruments and danced. A typical day included guests such as Monsignor Simeon, the Bishop of Varna, Mr. Von Visin, and the Russian consul in Varna, neighbors, and friends. The Stancioffs' days were full, returning visits to acquaintances in Varna, keeping up with correspondence, practicing their musical instruments, housework, and walking by the sea. Nadejda, the family's most prolific letter writer, continued to hone her craft, commenting that she wrote "letters enough to strike fear in the hearts of the postal service."[76]

In September, at the inauguration of a statue to Emperor Aleksandûr II in Kiev, Prince Boris witnessed the assassination of Russian Minister Stolypin. A shocking event, Nadejda recorded in her journal details about the assassin, who was "a nihilist Russian Jew named Bagroff. He was a secret police agent charged with protecting the person whom he killed!!!"[77]

Other foreign news included a rise in political tensions due to the Italo-Ottoman clash over Tripoli and the potential for a more widespread conflict. Nadejda's entry for October 2 describes the events:

> The Italian fleet opened fire on Tripoli; the Turks say that they will resist to the last man. All of Europe is agitated and alarmed. The Minister of Foreign Affairs from Sofia phones Papa to beg him to leave for Paris! This news upsets the household, Papa decides to leave tomorrow with Uncle Nic for Sofia; there he will see Ministers Guechoff and Todoroff; from there he leaves for Paris. Tonight we start packing. What an event! We who were so calm in our dear

home! Papa who will leave so quickly, so suddenly, without even knowing
whether he will be able to return and miss the best month in Varna! Ivan must
accompany him . . . tonight we walk together as a family, by the light of the
moon in one of the most beautiful nights . . . serene, limpid, admirable . . . only
regrets.[78]

On his way to Paris, Dimitri visited with the king and the minister of foreign affairs; their conversations served to at least confirm to Stancioff his position of importance in the king's esteem and in the country's roster of essential
diplomats. The family was relieved that at least the Tripoli crisis, despite the fact
that it spoiled their vacation, served to further the patriarch's career, and therefore, was in some way a useful interruption.

Meanwhile the most important task of their stay was ahead, the autumn
grape harvest. They hired peasants from the same village every year—Gagauz
(Christianized Bulgarian Turks) villagers from Kisteritch. The Stancioffs kept a
quantity of the white grape for their own consumption as wine and sold the ex-
cess. The peasants presented an image that reinforced the Orient in Nadejda's
mind. She recorded:

> The departure of the grape pickers at twilight is a ravishing oriental tableau; the
> heavy cart pulled by large black buffaloes, laden with the barrels full of grapes
> and covered with flowers. The group of Turkish peasants in turbans, their hands
> under their red belts, the coming together much less poetic of masters and ser-
> vants of Europe and all with the background of a purely blue sky, soft and
> beautiful.[79]

When Papa was away in Paris, Nadejda replaced him at her mother's side
when the latter returned social visits. The two had lunch at the Von Visins;
Nadejda comments that it was an

> excellent repast in a miniscule dining room. Russian style heat in all the apart-
> ment! We have a good time since our hosts are charming, especially him! . . .
> Von Visines make music together; it is delicious.[80]

Royal Guests and Playmates

The Stancioffs continued their intimate relationship with the royal family that
summer. Their mutual attraction was so strong that the royal family felt no com-
punction about arriving to the Stancioff villa unannounced and behaved as close
and old friends might, free to indulge their whims without the need for formality. They did not stand on decorum or social protocol of any sort; instead it was
an opportunity for the royal family to be spontaneous. The royals felt this family
would understand the gesture for what it was—a royal license to bend the rules
of convention and still elicit proper respect and deference. Therefore, the Stancioffs could anticipate having unexpected guests drop by, but the Bulgarian
royal family was the only one in that category. The rest of their circle observed
the conventions of the day and arranged ahead of time, observed calling hours,

or waited for an invitation. The royal family could of course intrude on the Stancioffs at will.

> Charming surprise this afternoon; the dear little Princesses come to see us in a donkey pulled cart. We receive them with happiness and spend two good hours together; at 5 an English tea in the hall and good conversation. Princess Eudoxie is very intelligent, dignified, noble, and nice. She has the manners of the Queen. Princess Nadejda more a child, is equally nice more "Italian" than her sister is. We were charmed by the visit of the Princesses.[81]

In addition to impromptu visits, the families continued their traditions of reciprocal invitations to each other's summer residences. In November, when the entire royal family was in residence at Euxinograd, the king following customary tradition, invited the Stancioffs to mass at the palace, followed by lunch. Later in the day, they saw the king with three of his children at vespers at the Catholic Church in Varna. A day later, they continued the closeness by participating in another mass at the palace; it was Day of the Dead, November 2. Afterward, the adults and children took walks in the gardens. Maman walked with the king and the children with the princes and princesses.

The king then gave notice that he intended to visit the family that afternoon, so the Stancioffs returned home as quickly as possible to prepare for their tea with the royal family. The Stancioffs rushed to organize food preparations and put the hall and gardens in order—the primary areas where they anticipated their guests would visit. They lit two fires for their august visitor who was, according to Nadejda, "completely charming; he talks to us a lot about dear Papa."[82] The praise King Ferdinand heaped on his subordinate was important to Dimitri's family; they felt a certain pride and redoubled their own devotion to their country and sovereign. Positive reinforcement was effective!

The royal family and the Stancioffs were together on a daily basis over two weeks in November, until it was time for the Stancioffs to begin their journey back to Paris. The Stancioffs were companions, playmates, escorts, entourage, confidants, and sounding boards. Both collectively and individually, the Stancioffs played the roles of ladies- and gentlemen-in-waiting as they formed a general made-to-order suite for the king's household.

Prince Boris spent the most time with the Stancioffs; he visited quite often alone and stayed for long conversations. This was especially touching for the family. The fact that he chose to spend time alone with the Stancioffs and sought them out was a testament to his depth of feeling and a reflection on their ability to put him at ease and to serve as a source of wise council. When they were invited to the palace they could observe the royal family at their habitual pursuits and formulate their impressions.

When attending mass at the palace Nadejda had an opportunity to study the family in another context. She not only reflected on the atmosphere in the palace chapel but also on the demeanor of the royal participants.

> I love these masses that resemble each other so and are so special! The chapel misty; the air hot, heavy with the scent of pine, the priest who silently murmurs

the prayers, the redoubtable personality, loved and venerated of the King, the two Princesses in "navy" dresses and with hair done up tight, the two Princes so thin and distinguished planted on their prie-dieu, the group desperately silent, the tension that floats about the missals in the clenched hands, the jerky prayer of uneasy lips!!![83]

During these days of togetherness, the Stancioff family was brimming with love and devotion for a king who showed them so much attention and showered them with compliments. They experienced his consideration as a special favor. Certainly, the royals were generous with their interest as well as with valuable tokens of their estimation for formal service rendered. Therefore, Prince Boris naturally bestowed an expensive and meaningful gift to Dimitri Stancioff as a thank-you for Dimitri's help during the coronation of King George V in London—a gold enameled cigarette case with a warm inscription.

At least through the eyes of the Stancioffs' eldest child, King Ferdinand was an ideal sovereign:

> We are sad that the King will leave so soon; we love our dear sovereign so, the benevolent friend of our parents, our good protector of all. In addition, he is so special and so profoundly intelligent! Dear King!...Dear Princes we love them too, with respect and tenderness.[84]

When their parents were away, the royal children were sometimes escorted by their teachers and their personal guard, a soldier named Kourtoclieff to the villa. A typical tea included piano playing by Maman; and the group sang some Italian airs as a choir. Feo and Ivan played their string instruments, and the rest of the company danced waltzes, Bostons, and a quadrille. The entertainment was so compelling that the royal company left rather late, and their hosts were enchanted and cognizant of that show of appreciation.

On their penultimate day in Varna, the Stancioffs, in their turn, were invited to the palace to tea; Princess Eudoxie was hostess. The group entertained themselves with games, music, Italian airs, dances, and tableaux vivants.

On their final day, the Stancioffs completed some last-minute packing, which included flowers and rosemary from their garden; they also packed some fruits and Bulgarian dried peppers for their pantry in France.

At noon, Prince Boris paid them a last visit, and they talked for a long time under the Stancioffs' poplar tree. In addition, Nadejda commented, "We will think long time about this pretty and poetic interlude. Good-bye Prince Boris! May God keep you always."[85] The Stancioffs made their last good-byes to all their favorite spots on the property, then headed for the train station, where some Varna friends saw them off.

Returning to Duties

In Sofia, the first order of duty was for Maman to go directly to the cemetery to visit the tomb of her first-born, baby Sasha. Then they proceeded to the Stancioff family home to reunite with their uncle, aunts, and Baba. The feeling of family was so strong that Nadejda commented excitedly about ten Stancioffs gathered under one roof. In addition, while the children were busy with their grandmother, their parents dined at the palace with the king and queen. Maman returned at midnight, and Papa at 3 a.m., after finishing last-minute conversations with his sovereign. Dimitri and King Ferdinand were at a particularly close point in their relationship at this time.

The Stancioffs spent Christmas in Sofia that year. Their family tradition was to buy a tree very close to the holiday, and an equally important ritual was for the parents to decorate the tree together, without the assistance of anyone else in the family. When the family sang Christmas songs and gathered about the tree for the first time, it was a truly exciting and much-anticipated event.

While the parents carried on their custom on the twenty-fourth, the children continued with their normal activities: studying, running errands, and going to confession. At 5 p.m., the extended family came together to celebrate the Christmas tree. Their Uncle Aynard and Stati Panitza were there, as well as the servants. With the radiant tree lit up by a mass of candles as their focal point, the family exchanged gifts, as the pine scent of the tree resin complemented the celebration.

On the twenty-fifth, the family attended mass. Nadejda perceived her mother as lovable and mystical on that Christmas holiday. She had, according to Nadejda, inspired writers and artists. To Nadejda, her mother evoked the eternal Orient:

> She is soft, she is blue; she makes one think of yellow lands dotted with heavy palms of sunshine; of cities so white and clean in the bright ardent light; of the delicate profiles of Madonnas and of the eyes of children . . . and all this mysterious and very veiled.[86]

Her mother was Nadejda's feminine ideal. As she recorded her thoughts in her journals Nadejda chronicled her own maturity to adulthood.

Nadejda was very adamant about keeping her journal on a regular basis. Her entries provide a running commentary on the family's daily pursuits as well as their commonly held views on everything from politics and culture to practical skills like cooking and sewing. She made a point of making year-end summations. At the beginning of every year, she started a new journal with a brief report on where the family resided, the ages of all the children, including herself, and the general state and well-being of their extended family on both her mother's and father's sides. The following entry is typical of her annual ritual to inaugurate her journal:

> January – Paris, 38 Av. Kleber
> One starts writing in a new journal with a certain amount of emotion. 1911 was favorable to us but who knows what is held in store for us in the unfathomable 1912? In addition, despite all the nice wishes of relatives and friends one experiences a fear that is very justified! Good day new confidant of my quill; your predecessor was a charming being, I hope that on your last page I will have nothing but beautiful and nice things to record!!! I am 17 and half, Feo 16 and a half, Ivan 14, Chou will be 11. Feo and I have finished our studies...already a

long time ago last year in June. Ivan in the third year of the Lycée Janson and Chou in 4th year in normal school. Baba is doing very well, thanks be to God. The Tachet, Grenaud, Panitza are all doing very well. Good news from the royal family of Bulgaria. Calm day. Immense correspondence to dispatch.[87]

The family's close relationship with the royal family was reinforced with the arrival of Christmas cards and letters from all the members of the royal family. These were not simply pro forma cards but letters to Anna, Dimitri, and Nadejda. The royal family also sent photographs of themselves as gifts as well as other small tokens of their affection. Nadejda recorded the Stancioff reaction to these tokens: "The smallest memento, which we receive from our sovereigns, fills us always with joy!"[88]

Education and Its Many Forms

After all the holiday celebrations were over, the family returned to its normal routine: the younger children prepared their lessons and attended classes; Maman went on her rounds visiting; Papa attended to his work as a diplomat; and the two eldest went on their various courses. Nadejda and Feo continued their studies by taking language lessons, dance lessons, singing lessons, and attending a history lecture series.

> A course on history; very clear expose on Russia of 1848 and the Crimean War; we come to understand it better and Nicolas I and the different eastern questions of the century. Then they talk to us about the Egyptian question . . . It was very interesting.[89]

The education of the girls continued in this selective fashion. Their involvement with diplomats and their families on a regular basis educated the children in ways which no formal curriculum could duplicate. Nadejda hardly exhibited a sense of superiority in her entries about her privileged position and in her finer understanding of history, politics, and current events. She, instead, felt virtually her entire life as inadequate and less than ideal when compared to her social equals. Her commentary on herself consistently downplayed her talents and abilities; therefore, it is not surprising that on her eighteenth birthday, she evaluated herself in the following manner:

> January 17 1912
> I am 18 today . . . a beautiful age! The age of youth and of 'beginnings' the age which we will doubtless regret so much later! One must already be 'made' from all points of view at 18, and I am far away, very far, so far that it would make one smile. I remain more or less equivocal, alas but one must not confide anything to this, which everyone reads!!![90]

Nadejda and Feo's educations continued contemporaneously with their positions as their father's official helpers. Nadejda, rather presciently wrote, "I become a counselor to the Legation and Feo First Secretary; we help Papa as much as possible! German lesson at 1.30."[91] Feo recalled that they spent evenings in Papa's study filing, translating or decoding documents, preparing letters for his signature or scanning newspapers for "Balkan sensations."[92]

Balkan Neighbors as Friends

Once Bulgaria's independence had been recognized, the most important work in which Dimitri Stancioff was involved during his years in Paris had to do with the negotiations that would lead to a rapprochement between the neighboring Balkan states. This warming of relations among the Balkan neighbors would lead to the decision to launch the First Balkan War. The efforts of the respective leaders of Serbia, Greece, Montenegro, and Bulgaria led to the meeting of the minds that would lead to a unity of purpose, a rare event in the Balkans of that era.

Thus, Milovanovitch, Venizelos, and Gueshov, the prime ministers of their countries, worked for their respective governments to good effect. The Habsburg annexation of Bosnia-Hercegovina in 1908 had galvanized the young Balkan states to take action. They felt an urgency to act out on their territorial aims before the Great Powers divided up the remainder of the Ottoman Empire among themselves. It was not an unrealistic concern, the Eastern Question dominated European diplomacy and its resolution would be on the field of battle.

Small states had to act, since they could not negotiate from a position of inherent weakness. If possession is nine-tenths of the law, then the new allies would legitimize their claims with occupation and control of their intended desiderata. A Balkan League unexpectedly gained the support of Russia, since the perception from St. Petersburg was that any rapprochement among the Balkan states would impede further Habsburg encroachment into the Balkans.

According to his biographer, Ferdinand had the notion to form a Balkan federation as soon as he took on the post of ruler of Bulgaria in 1887.[93] That political cooperation gained a public-relations boost with the opportune celebrations in 1912 of the coming of age of Prince Boris, the heir apparent of Bulgaria.

Dimitri returned to Sofia for the festivities. It was natural to invite all of Bulgaria's neighbors to the celebrations in Sofia. The sovereigns of the formerly antagonistic Balkan states mended fences and strengthened the nascent military alliance under the guise of the very public and innocuous celebration of the Bulgarian prince's birthday.

It was a triumphant event, since all of the monarchs and most of the crown princes or heirs apparent of the neighboring states congregated in Sofia. In addition, the Russian Emperor's envoy, Grand Duke André, who served as proxy godfather, attended, as did all the foreign ambassadors. Prince Boris had a grand birthday celebration, with birthday wishes from all the gathered throng of Balkan and foreign officialdom as well as from Bulgarian officials such as the director of the railways, the president of the Academy of Sciences, heads of the National Bank, and numerous others.

The Stancioffs, minus their father, followed the celebrations from Paris. Nadejda decorated the two pages of her journal entries with oversized exclamation points, a large Cyrillic letter "B" for Boris, with a crown on top of it, stars, and an *Ooora!* (The Bulgarian equivalent of hooray) drawn in the margins.[94]

The grand coming-of-age celebrations of His Royal Highness Prince Boris of Tûrnovo, Prince of Saxe, excited the entire country on February 2 and 3. A twenty-one cannon salute followed by the peal of church bells announced the opening of the official ceremonies in Sofia. Church services preceded military parades, then a lunch at the military school, official felicitations by the assemblage to His Royal Highness, and a dinner in the evening, followed by a reception in the palace. Fireworks capped the evening. Nadejda wrote, "General happiness – a great big dynastic sigh of relief warms the country, the press, and the institutions."[95] Princess Eudoxie wrote a description of the festivities to Nadejda. Apparently, the two Bulgarian Princess' ignored their stepmother's wishes, the queen, and attended the evening reception, wearing dresses of their own choosing. The young princess Eudoxie relished the fact that she irritated the queen. She reported to her playmate in Paris that, while her brother was taking his oath, the queen dabbed, with her handkerchief, at dry cheeks.[96]

On the second day, more official receptions and felicitations culminated in a ball that evening. As a sign of favor, Grand Duke André presented, on behalf of his sovereign Emperor Nicolas II of Russia, a precious gem-encrusted sword. King Ferdinand bestowed the order of Sts. Cyril and Methodius. The Ottoman sultan sent a gift of an Arab mare to Prince Boris.

The year 1912 began auspiciously for the Bulgarian kingdom. The coming-of-age celebrations of Prince Boris raised the hopes of Bulgarians that their country had an increasingly bright future. Neighboring Balkan monarchs seemed to recognize Bulgaria as an equal, Imperial Russia continued her political support, and consequently the king enjoyed a rise in popularity among his subjects.

Notes

1. Nadejda Stancioff, unpublished journal, 2 June 1909, PASF.
2. Muir, *Dimitri Stancioff Patriot and Cosmopolitan.* 125.
3. See descriptions in *Diplomatist's Wife* and Nadejda's unpublished journals.
4. See Nadejda's unpublished journals.
5. Nadejda Stancioff, unpublished journal, 27 September 1908, PASF.
6. Nadejda Stancioff, unpublished journal, 14 December 1908, PASF.
7. Nadejda Stancioff, unpublished journal, 27 December 1908, PASF.
8. Nadejda Stancioff, unpublished journal, 28 January 1909, PASF.
9. Nadejda Stancioff, unpublished journal, 4 March 1909, PASF.
10. Stancioff, *Diplomat and Gardener Memoirs.*
11. Nadejda Stancioff, unpublished journal, 21 February 1909, PASF.
12. Nadejda Stancioff, unpublished journal, 29 June 1909, PASF.
13. Ibid. 16 March 1909.
14. Ibid. 15 June 1909.
15. Ibid. 4 August 1909.
16. Ibid. 14 June 1909.

17. Ibid. 1 November 1909.

18. Ibid. 1 January 1910.

19. Ibid. 2 January 1910.

20. Dimitri Stancioff, unpublished letter, 5/18 August 1908, TsDIA F143 ae. 38, l. 345.

21. Nadejda Stancioff, unpublished journal, 13 February 1910, PASF.

22. Ibid. 20 April 1910.

23. Ibid. 24 March 1910.

24. Ibid. 7 May 1910.

25. Ibid. 14 June 1910.

26. Ibid. 20 June 1910.

27. Ibid.

28. Nadejda Stancioff, unpublished journal, 25 June 1910, PASF.

29. Ibid. 26 June 1910.

30. Ibid. 23 July 1910.

31. Ibid. 28 July 1910.

32. Stancioff, *Diplomat and Gardener Memoirs.*

33. Nadejda Stancioff, unpublished journal, 5 August 1910, PASF.

34. Ibid. 11 August 1910.

35. Ibid. 4 September 1910.

36. Ibid. 5 September 1910.

38. Ibid. 26 September 1910.

39. Stancioff, *Nadejda Memories of Love*, 18.

40. Nadejda Stancioff, unpublished journal, 2 November 1910, PASF.

41. Ibid. 9 November 1910.

42. Ibid. 10 November 1910.

43. Ibid. 12 November 1910.

44. Ibid. 13 December 1910.

45. Ibid. 11 January 1911.

46. Because the 13 day difference between the Slavic Orthodox calendar and the western church and civil calendars meant that the Stancioffs celebrated Bulgarian Christmas on 7 January1911 and New Years' Eve on 13 January 1911. Nadejda Stancioff, unpublished journal, 13 January 1911, PASF.

47. Nadejda Stancioff, unpublished journal, 20 January 1911, PASF.

48. Ibid. 22 January 1911.

49. Ibid. 21 February 1911.

50. Stancioff, *Diplomat and Gardener Memoirs*.110.

51. Nadejda Stancioff, unpublished journal, 11 February 1911, PASF.

52. Nadejda Stancioff, unpublished journal, 10 May 1911, PASF.

53. Lilie Bouton de Fernandez-Azabal, *Romance and Revolutions* (London: Hutchinson & Co., 1937). 90.

54. Ibid.

55. Ibid.

56. Nadejda Stancioff, unpublished journal, 6 May 1911, PASF.

57. Ibid. 25 February1911.

58. Ibid. 24 June 1911.

59. Ibid. 21 March 1914.

60. Nadejda's "women," those about whom she writes in her journals with loving affection and adulation, were a creation of her imagination. She did not express any erotic affection for the women with whom she interacted on a daily basis. Her fantasy realm,

where her idols were arranged in secluded niches accessible only to her, did not overlap with her real life.

61. Nadejda Stancioff, unpublished journal, 27 February 1912.

62. Ibid. 14 February 1912.

63. Ibid. 29 May 1914.

64. Ibid. 6 December 1911.

65. Ibid. 12 December 1911.

66. Fernandez-Azabal, *Romance and Revolutions.*, 97.

67. Nadejda Stancioff, unpublished journal, 12 May 1911, PASF.

68. Ibid. 20-30 June 1911.

69. Ibid. 22 June 1911.

70. Stancioff, Nadejda Memories of Love, 28.

71. Nadejda Stancioff, unpublished journal, 13 August 1911, PASF.

72. "Should we take ...Nicolas to Paris? His trip will be paid (a French servant will not be as good and will be expensive)...the children should give their opinion—they are good judges on domestic help. Tell them Papa asks their opinion." Dimitri Stancioff unpublished letter, 5/18 Aug 1908, F 13 ae. 38 l. 438.

73. Nadejda Stancioff, unpublished journal, 16 August 1911, PASF.

74. Nadejda Stancioff, 21 August 1911, PASF.

75. Ibid. 16 August 1911.

76. Ibid. 4 September 1911.

77. Ibid. 27 September 1911.

78. Ibid. 21 September 1911.

79. Ibid. 2 October 1911.

80. Ibid. 13 October 1911.

81. Ibid. 18 October 1911.

82. Ibid. 31 October 1911.

83. Ibid. 2 November 1911.

84. Ibid. 5 November 1911.

85. Ibid. 6 November 1911.

86. Ibid. 1 November 1911.

87. Ibid. 25 December 1911.

88. Ibid. 1 January 1912.

89. Ibid. 5 January 1912.

90. Ibid. 12 January 1912.

91. Ibid. 17 January 1912.

92. Ibid. 24 January 1912.

93. Stancioff, Nadejda Memories of Love, 34.

94. Constant, *Foxy Ferdinand Tsar of Bulgaria.* 105.

95. Nadejda Stancioff, unpublished journal, 2 February 1912, PASF.

96. Ibid. 3 February 1912.

97. Nadejda Stancioff, unpublished letter, 7 February 1912, Nada VIII, PASF.

4
Wars and More Wars

"The Balkans always has surprises for Europe. Poor Europe!"
Nadejda Stancioff, unpublished journal[1]

Using various convenient, though nonetheless very real, grievances, the kings of the Balkan states prepared to grab by force what the Ottoman State was unwilling to consider granting. The year 1912 was one of geo-political shifts that eventually led to an all-out war on the Balkan Peninsula. Each Balkan kingdom had a list of territorial desiderata, which sometimes complemented, but oftentimes overlapped, those of her neighbors. Unison achieved by a mutual animosity toward the Turks and their historic domination of the Balkans created a cooperative atmosphere. In the details, the devil had his opportunities.

The Interesting Lives of Diplomats

In Paris, as the social season began, the family warmed up to its usual routine. Nadejda and Feo, who attended a dance class for the daughters of the diplomatic corps, were getting ready to attend a ball hosted by the Izvolsky household. The girls were excited and nervous; this would be a very visible, though temporary, outing before Parisian society.

The ball was a splendid success from the Stancioffs' point of view. The girls had the time of their lives and were surrounded by some of the most notable debutants. Attendees included the daughters of the important diplomatic missions from Russia, Germany, Austria, Italy, and others. Nadejda recorded the list of attendees. The daughters of the diplomatic missions' danced cotillions, enjoyed the attention of their escorts, tossed confetti-filled "snow balls," and had an unforgettable evening. While still reflecting on her experiences at the ball, Nadejda recorded the names of the diplomatic corps in Paris, including notable families and their children, and listing only those whom she considered "interesting."

A day later, the Stancioff women attended a performance by Sarah Bernhardt in *Lucretia Borgia* by Victor Hugo. The show had gotten rave reviews, and the Stancioffs joined those who shouted praise. Nadejda found it an incredible spectacle, as she notes in her journal:

> Me, with my Oriental temperament like only things, which are a bit ardent. I prefer summer and autumn to spring and winter. I do not like half-measures but full intensity! I will probably change my opinion in 6 months, but right now, I do not like anything but reds, golds, and purples. I adore adjectives like: raucous, spirited, fiery, shimmering, luminous, bizarre, enigmatic, violent, prophetic, the ensemble lingers in my room like a scarf of fire![2]

Meanwhile, a French-German accord had stirred the political scene in Europe such that the French chamber of deputies was bogged down in heated debates. Maman attended each of those sessions. Nadejda first recorded her mother's observations, and then read the accounts of the sessions in the French newspapers. She ultimately pronounced herself to be in the same camp as her mother; both supported Pichon's position.

> February 8—Maman was at the Senate where she heard a splendid speech by M. S. Pichon, the former Minister of Foreign Affairs... [He] declared that he would not sign the Franco-German accord.

> February 9—Maman returned to the Senate and she heard M. Ribot who refuted the point made by M. Pichon. This evening I read both in Le Temps and I prefer that of Mr. Pichon.

> February 10—Maman returns to the senate to hear the continuation of the discussion, very well attended [by the public]. A fiery dialogue between M. Clemenceau and M. Poincaré.[3]

As a family, the Stancioffs were always interested in current affairs both as a vocation and as an avocation. Anna Stancioff informed herself by listening to these important debates in person. Although she maintained her usual schedule of visits and other engagements as well; for example, six social visits in three hours was not an unusual feat. She obviously believed it important enough to take time out of her busy social schedule to attend several sessions of the Chamber of Deputies.

As a couple, Anna and Dimitri discussed current events with their children. Since their children were in the company of other diplomat's children, the conversations about political events and contentious issues had ready faces to link with countries and their foreign policies. In her journal, Nadejda comments on one of these gatherings:

> We have a big afternoon party for children very gay games, tea, tableaux with costumed personages, and new animated games. Feo and I have a good time

with these young ones. It was a very cosmopolitan group; Italians, Germans, Austrians, Greeks, French, Bulgarians!!! It is so interesting to be the children of diplomats![4]

Did the Stancioff children acknowledge the correlation between being the child of diplomats and having an eternally cosmopolitan view of the world? The family was constantly in the company of a diverse international society; they lived in several countries, studied and spoke several foreign languages, and traveled. They developed notions of how the world should be shaped, and then create expectations of what to look forward to for the rest of their lives. Nadejda recalls Easters past:

> We go over our memories of Easter in Russia; Bulgarian Easters celebrated at Plovdiv near His Majesty the King, Parisian Easters of preceding years. Papa and Maman went to Holy Offices at midnight at Rue Daru [Russian Orthodox Church] a very select group of worshipers then a big, grand, pompous supper at the Russia Embassy. Maman was seated next to the Grand Duke...I would love to go around the world, I am especially attracted to Asia, the Indies,...and Africa of the North.[5]

When her parents and Feo left to go to the wedding of a relative in Brittany and Ivan was away on vacation with his cousins, Nadejda was in full command of the household and took over some of her mother's responsibilities. In addition to assisting in her father's work, she directed the servants; kept Chou focused on her homework, did the usual rounds delivering *cartes de visite*, and even hosted a dinner party at their home for some Bulgarian families. She described the party as "a very gay repast and cordial then bridge, dance, talk, tea and collation at 10:30 p.m. then bridge again, cigars, liqueurs, coffee, and noise. We part at midnight."[6]

King Ferdinand's Royal Jubilee

In mid-July, the family traveled back to Bulgaria. The biggest event of their summer was the king's royal jubilee celebration in Veliko Tûrnovo in August. The entire Stancioff family received an invitation or more precisely a charge from the king to present themselves at Veliko Tûrnovo. Papa was ordered to appear in his guard uniform in Gorna Oriahovitza on August 14. The family was touched by the king's attention to their comfort. They had an entire train car to themselves; their suitcases serving as closets, and they had an improvised washroom. Their service staff included their man, Boyo, and with the conductor, Stavri.

On August 15, the celebrations began. It was 25 years since Prince Ferdinand, now King Ferdinand ascended to the Bulgarian throne in the Old Bulgarian capital of Veliko Tûrnovo. At 6 a.m., a Catholic mass was followed by a parade; the king and queen processed with the princes and princesses. Maman was *grande maîtresse* of the court; and Papa was a member of the civilian suite. The military, with all its generals, was present.

When the assembled company, dignitaries, and guests enjoyed a banquet, the children of both the Stancioff and the royal families managed to find time to socialize briefly. The children visited the sights in the area, and Nadejda appreciated everything: the old churches, the scent of flowers, peppers, the smell of frying oil from the cafes, even the dust. They visited Preobrazhenie monastery and were invited by the *igoumen* (abbot) for coffee in his parlor, which Nadejda describes as

> a little white room with muslin curtains, red divans, and wooden table. In addition, imposing view on the Yantra [river] and Sveta Troitza monastery. We take water, confitures of plums, and black coffee! Maman spent some time here with Prince Ferdinand and his august mother, in this very parlor one can see a photo of our dear Maman![7]

The Stancioff children had an opportunity to learn more about their parents' lives as newlyweds.

The Stancioffs continued with their vacation routines. For the first time that year, Nadejda was called on by the queen to be her Her Highness' lady-in-waiting, and Nadejda comments: "I am happy but a bit nervous. The night is spent in preparation and packing. The queen herself will come to pick me up tomorrow."[8]

Nadejda was installed at the Aladja monastery in Euxinograd in a room of her own, next to the other lady-in-waiting to the queen, Vera Hakanoff. Lunch was at the monastery with the princesses and the entire suite. The group included Messrs. Bourboulon and Furth. When King Ferdinand arrived from Shumen with the princes, they dined as a group. The king tried to put Nadejda at her ease by saying complimentary things about her parents and their villa. Nonetheless, she felt intimidated.

The royal family did not stay together for long. By September, the plans for a war on the Balkans were moving into place. The king departed for another review of his troops; the princes departed as well. By September 30, there were general mobilization appeals to all able-bodied men to leave their households. Nadejda asked permission to return home during those troubled times. Since male servants left their peacetime jobs, life at the villa had to be simplified.

The First Balkan War

This war was a manifestation of the frustrations the Bulgarians, Greeks, and Serbs felt as the power relationships on the continent changed; these relationships seemed consistently to their disadvantage. Their respective Great Power protectors were determined to keep their Balkan protégés in permanently weakened, colonial-like servitude. It was not in Great Power interest to have strong, independent monarchies replace the Ottoman Empire, now in retreat.

The three Balkan states created an alliance, based on secret and public agreements, that aimed to redress some of that unequal treatment by waging war on the Ottoman Empire and claiming territories each state considered part of their national trousseau.

The popular mood in the Balkan states was wildly pro-war. As in other moments of national enthusiasm, fueled by feelings of messianic vision, national life stopped to focus on the impending conflict. Cities filled with people who milled in the streets looking for information. Trains, packed with soldiers covered in flowers, mad with enthusiasm, eager to engage in battle, acclaiming their leaders at the top of their lungs, rushed to the front lines. Veterans colored the streets with a rainbow of uniforms from past wars, adorned with their medals and carrying ancient rifles.

The Bulgarian armies were enormously successful against the Ottomans and managed to come within striking distance of Constantinople, stopping at a well-known defensive construction called the Chataldja line in early November. Their success, however, led to a split among the three Balkan allies and their respective military strategists.

While the value, for all the combatants, of using the occupation of Constantinople as an important negotiating chit was undeniable, the Bulgarian army's rapid advances to that point had been costly. Another major assault would have been dangerous, since supplies and the soldiers' ability to fight effectively, due to fatigue and casualties were reduced. Bulgaria's allies were wary of so successful an ally. Furthermore, the rapid spread of a cholera epidemic was having its impact on both military and even civilian populations. An armistice had already been signed in late November and peace negotiations were to be conducted in London. Had the peace been concluded rapidly and with a minimum of acrimony, the spectacular gains of the war might have survived the process. However, springtime brought renewed unrest in the Balkans which led eventually to renewed hostilities as talks broke down in Britain.

Diplomats in Times of War

During the First Balkan War, Dimitri Stancioff left his post in France and joined the Bulgarian army. His assignments were not so much front-line duty as protocol and dealing with foreign journalists who covered the war. When he saw action, he was recognized with a cross for bravery at the front near Salonika. At one point, he accompanied the Bulgarian princes, in the Rila division, under General Thodoroff, when they marched to Salonika. They did not meet serious resistance.

One of Dimitri's anecdotes, as recorded in his biography, is precious for its illustration of Balkan ingenuity. He witnessed, on more than one occasion, the resourcefulness of the native population who would have a portrait of King Ferdinand displayed in a prominent place in their home but who inevitably hid behind it a portrait of King George of Greece.[9] The natives were prepared to meet and welcome either monarch or his armies! This was not a question of loyalty but of survival, a necessary quality in a citizen of the Balkans.

After Bulgaria declared war on Turkey, in late October 1912 the Stancioffs moved and installed themselves in the capital city in the Stancioff family house on Oborishte Street with Baba, their uncle, and aunts.

During the first days of military engagement, they attended a mass with their sovereigns for the victorious conclusion of the conflict. They prayed not only for the success of the Bulgarian troops but also their allies, the Greeks, the Serbs, and the Montenegrins.

Before the casualty numbers became large, the Stancioff women participated in support activities.[10] They helped the queen make bread on one occasion, and Maman spent an entire day sewing for the army on another. They busied themselves with war work and at the same time persuaded themselves of the rectitude of their cause. Nadejda and her compatriots were convinced that they were on the side of justice and honor. She wrote on October 21, 1912

> ...superb weather... Vitosha stands out proudly in a light that is azure and gold. Papa leaves for the HQ; we are all emotional. We accompany him to the stations;...Sad departure! May god protect him! In addition, we think of all the poor mothers, wives and daughters who have more to complain of than us. ...we admire this war it is noble, a crusade, a fight for an ideal, a fight for a pure, elevated goal: deliverance of our brothers oppressed by the tyranny of the Muslim enemy. Let us glorify the Balkan Cross, the Cross-of the East raised by a Bulgarian hand against the Turkish crescent! Oooora![11]

Nadejda's words reflect a patriotic and nationalistic atmosphere at the time. A function of government propaganda, yellow journalism as well as a feeling of historic injustice pervaded Balkan societies. Her outburst, and others much like it, was common; it called for revenge in pursuit of a just cause. The cause of the Balkan states, was legitimate and sought to reverse a historic disequilibrium. Each Balkan state felt wronged by history and saw the war as a way to redress past injuries.

Wartime Sofia was denuded of all able-bodied men who were either drafted or volunteered for service. Servants left their employers. Even the palace lost the majority of its domestic staff; ministry employees joined the war effort. A lively wartime hub, with troops and civilians from all over the country passing through, Sofia presented a colorful canvas with a wide variety of people in the streets. Nadejda describes the city:

> Here life is very interesting. Sofia offers an animate aspect; to get to Clementine [hospital] I traverse the entire city twice a day; there are many Macedonians. The spectacle is picturesque at the foot of the mosque, the roving merchants, the Schops, the Macedonian peasants in long white veils.[12]

Various interest groups gathered in semi-permanent assemblages around the palace and vied for attention, along with newspaper boys shouting headlines. With at least one-half of the regiments already departed for the front, foreign journalists were the only men entering the city. The mood was not simply martial. The war quickly took on a religious sectarian flavor as propaganda focused on the potential for an epic conflict of the cross against the crescent. Priests blessed the troops in public places; the religious note was prominent.

While both their father and their Uncle Nic were at the front, the family waited for news. The mood in the country was one of suspense. Civilians lived daily in hope that the cost would be bearable while preparing hospitals for casualties.

Censorship prevented the publication of the location of generals and their armies or lists of dead and wounded. The only way the Stancioffs could discover the toll of battle was by the numbers of casualties that began to arrive in Sofia on October 24, 1912.[13] The family found, ultimately, that they could get more news from foreign publications but, of course, with a delay. By the end of the war, the lives of Anna, Nadejda, and Feo, and to a lesser extent, Chou Stancioff revolved around hospital duties and invitations to the palace to spend time with the princesses and the queen.

Patriotic Duty on the Domestic Front

The Stancioff women did their part when they joined the national effort nursing in Sofia. Maman Stancioff headed the hospital run by the French Red Cross, and her two eldest daughters worked as auxiliary nurses in *Clementine*, the Bulgarian hospital. The Stancioff women were fulfilling a patriotic duty, which only strengthened their devotion to the country and its people.[14]

While the queen set about organizing the major Bulgarian hospitals in Plovdiv, Iambol, and Stara Zagora, the Stancioff women remained in the capital and planned their days around their hospital shifts. Nadejda comments on their experiences at the hospital:

> We already love our wounded a lot. My favorite is a poor fellow named Dimitri Kovatcheff; he lost an eye and we have just cut a limb. He is grumpy, capricious, and original and pinches without laughing. Feo likes a certain Vasil and one that we call Kirdjali. The Countess prefers the old invalid Stoyan and Yordan Micheff. I write this for later. We are there until 11 pm waiting for new wounded! They arrive at midnight. Maman received 50; she had more than 150 and seems content with her establishment.[15]

The family shared their experiences at the hospital often. Hospital work was a formative event, especially for the girls, who were in awe of the soldiers. Ecstatic about each incredible victory, and horrified by the suffering of the wounded, the girls worked at what Nadejda termed their "white work." This phrase alluded to a labor beyond the ordinary and mundane chores of women. In fact, they observed ladies of the diplomatic community doing their best to assist at the hospital. Feo witnessed, "...an Italian Countess ...bending gracefully over a patient's bed, her pearl earrings touching the sheets, her gloved hand holding a mug of soup, her dainty muslin cap framing a striking profile."[16] Angels of charity, the Stancioff girls persisted through their inexperience, with goodwill, to the cause of helping the wounded.

The girls' lives were changed in many ways. Their daily schedules, social contacts, and time for rest and relaxation, all revolved around their new duties and a constant hunger for information from the front. For example, they found out where their father was only through a news report, on the Bulgarian princes entrance into Salonika. Since he was attached to the princes, they could happily surmise that he was in Salonika at their side participating in that happy Bulgarian triumph. The family's lives were substantially altered from their peacetime pursuits, as Nadejda notes:

> What a new life we lead now! This charity work, meals disorganized, agitated nights, streaked with dreams, interminable conversations, evenings of reading papers and studying maps! The poor old house at Oborishte keeps everything safe! Baba is well. Aunt Eudoxie takes care of wounded everyday at the Military School.[17]

Nursing offered unexpected rewards; contact with the wounded nurtured the Stancioff women's love for their nation. Maman reported the brave and self-sacrificing words of one soldier who had a foot amputated: "Yes, my leg has got shorter, but Bulgaria is larger now."[18] This kind of heroism in the face of primitive conditions on the battlefield and in the hospitals inspired the Stancioffs to love their country and their compatriots even more. They were no longer far removed from their homeland, living and working in a foreign capital; now they were experiencing the war with their fellow citizens, and they shared in each glorious moment. They did not have to imagine or simulate "Bulgarianess;" they witnessed it every day. It was a time of exhilaration and excitement as well as sadness over the losses, the kinds of emotions that build profound memories.

For Nadejda, now a young lady, wartime experience was formative on many levels; at the very least, her experience showed her, for the first time, the cost that war, victory, and defeat could inflict on one's homeland. She learned how military success and diplomatic victory did not necessarily go hand in hand. She would return often to this point of the historical development of her country in her journal entries and bemoan the soldiers' sacrifices and their suffering.

In the course of their hospital work the sisters encountered death and the attendant feelings of loss, helplessness, and futility. The girls saw the bodies of their favorite patients laid out in the silent chapel; the white pine coffins held the cold, lifeless, lugubrious bodies. Some chrysanthemums adorned the sparse room, but there were no candles; and the odor of decomposing bodies reminded the girls of the immediacy of mortality. Nadejda writes:

> I felt in this glacial visit the horror of the war! I thought of the families of the unfortunates. Mourning because of a murderous bullet, the shot that found its mark on these unfortunates! God recompense them for their devotion and give them an immortal crown.[19]

The nurses suffered for their soldier patients, and their experiences added to their own growing loyalty and patriotism for Bulgaria.

Anna Stancioff, who adopted her husband's homeland as her own, wrote an emotional entry in Nadejda's journal:

> Snow! The war continues, glorious, rapid, stunning. . . . this battle, this fanati-
> cal combat of body-to-body, inspired by so much vengeance and accumulated
> hates! May God make is stop to the glory of Bulgaria![20]

The women, at one point, had to cease their work in the hospitals because a cholera outbreak threatened to reach epidemic proportions.[21] They then focused on domestic support, such as knitting for the army; they also spent more time with the royal children in the palace in Sofia or out at the palace in Vrana.

The war did force one important improvement in the domestic sector, that of public health. The disastrous mismanagement of military and civilian health facilities, which led to the cholera outbreak in 1913, prompted a major reform in the health-care system. The lack of proper sanitation techniques, and mixing the wounded and diseased with the civilian patients and prisoners of war, caused the spread and exacerbation of contagion.[22]

Once they were forced to quit their hospital work, because of fear of infection, the sisters had little to occupy their time. They took walks, ran errands, visited with friends, and waited impatiently for news of the war and, of their father. With her parents busy, Nadejda took on the responsibility of making sure her youngest sister did her homework and studied her lessons for her correspondence course:

> Weather cold and humid. . . Melancholy impressions. . . Bulgarian lesson in the
> morning . . . Maman continues to go to the hospital. We spend the afternoon
> with Hélène Petroff. Big walk . . . it rains softly and our path is long . . . The
> wet fir trees emit their unique aroma; Vitosha is barely visible in the distance;
> there is a vast moist silence full of peace. What a contrast with our thoughts!
> Hélène tells me many things; we have tea at her house with her sisters. . . .
> Calm evening in the study of Uncle Nic.[23]

Wartime life continued with solemn reflections and that unique air of lives lived on the edge of time. When information blackouts and censorship magnified tensions and put life in a state of suspended animation, when one's world could be shattered by the next scrap of news from the front, civilians lived in hope and dread. Nadejda muses:

> Weather cold, somber, humid... We pray for the happy conclusion of the war,
> and for our dear absent one. . . . Feo and I take a long walk with Hélène Petroff;
> we to go to the Hantche . . . we talk a lot touching quickly 1000 varied subjects;
> we cover everything, lectures, Sofia society, Parisian society, the war, philoso-
> phy, criticism, personal opinion. Etc., etc. —We have tea at the Petroffs. . . it is
> cozy and gay. Maman goes to bed early and we very late since we stay with her
> in her room to talk with her, soul to soul, in a night of silence, lethargy.[24]

Bulgarian Prospects for Victory

Dimitri Stancioff was not optimistic about the prospects of a triumphant victory. He and King Ferdinand shared a generally pessimistic outlook when it came to geo-political developments in the Balkans. No agreement or treaty of peace could be fool proof or perfect. They envisioned, or rather feared, an uncertain and possibly disastrous future for Bulgaria. Even at the height of cooperation among the Balkan neighbors and when the king was hosting his son's coming of-age celebrations, the king did not feel relaxed, and he fretted.

When in January 1912, Stancioff congratulated him on the achievement of bringing all the Balkan crown heads together in his capital, King Ferdinand's reply had been laconic: "...pourvu que cela dure [only if it lasts]."[25]

However, by the time of the outbreak of hostilities, the king was antagonistic and openly disparaging of his French courtiers because his view of the prospects of success had become markedly optimistic. At the height of military successes in October/November 1912, Ferdinand wanted—and eventually got—Dimitri Stancioff as far away from him as possible. Dimitri had been advising the precautionary step of sending a delegation to St. Petersburg, Berlin, and Vienna to clarify Bulgarian goals. Anna, by her nationality and her support of Pichon's policies, made herself equally repugnant to the king; he took her political position as a personal affront.

Although no one else at court felt that way, the sarcasm and pure hostility toward the Stancioffs exuded by King Ferdinand was palpable and noted by those who knew him well. The king was interested only in his military successes and strategies for the next assault. He neglected or reviled everything and everyone else in his life—including his children—who opposed his views. [26] He thought nothing of sacrificing individuals or the interests of his country to his very personal ambitions. He perceived Dimitri's insistence on caution, with respect to the Great Powers, as disloyal. Relations were decidedly cool to frigid between the king, Dimitri, and Anna. Only a victorious end on the field of battle softened the king's demeanor.

At court, it was an open secret that the royal children were largely opposed to their father's political positions, and that even his wife, who was a German princess, did not side with his adventurist foreign policies. These personal opinions among Ferdinand's intimates were reserved for private discussions, among themselves, but were never presented before the king, whose spitefulness and mean-spiritedness were legendary. Prince Boris was opposed to his father's military policies and especially Ferdinand's decisions regarding Pichon's government. However, the prince did not appraise his father about his own opinions. Instead, Boris chose to share his opinions with people at court whom he trusted to keep his secrets, like Anna Stancioff and the Comte de Bourboulon. The latter noted the following about the heir apparent:

> Il est étonnamment intelligent mais ne sera pas toujours commode. Il a bon coeur. . . pour vu qu'il le garde!! [He is astonishingly intelligent; however this

may not always be pliable. He has a good heart. . . if he manages to keep it that way.][27]

Ferdinand's children pretended to agree with their father in all things because they were terrified of his reaction if they did otherwise.

The Beauty of Nature

In Sofia, unaware of the tensions between their parents and their sovereign, the Stancioff daughters continued to work for the war effort. When news was vague or negative, they found refuge in nature, taking frequent walks and enjoying the views of mount Vitosha. The peak that dominates Sofia, Cherni Vruh, rises up about 2,290 meters and is an arresting natural landmark; the play of light on its contours is a delight. Majestic and imposing, the peak lends the city an aura of invincibility and nobility and serves to elevate the mood of the city's inhabitants. It abruptly announces the end of the Balkan mountain range and the beginning of the vast plain that sweeps north and east of Sofia. Nadejda reflects that "the beauty of nature makes us forget the meanness of life; Vitosha . . . proudly dominates . . . the light is dusted with gold; it is clear and soft like water."[28]

The Stancioff and the royal families' children continued to entertain each other in the meantime. The following entry, written by Nadejda, is typical of the kind of time they spent together and is illustrative of the nature of their amusements:

> We spend, all three, the afternoon at Vrana with the princesses and we amuse ourselves a lot with the eldest. We return to the palace at 5 and we have a big meal. After, we play charades and tableaux vivants in costume. I cite the two most successful subjects; an audience of Yaver Pasha (prisoner in Sofia) and the peace in London. The latter truly very amusing. The Princess Eudoxie was the Montenegrin, the Princess Nadejda was the Turk, Feo the Serb, Ivan the Bulgarian and me Venizelos![29]

When Maman came down with a recurring case of bronchitis and was forced to spend several days bedridden.[30] The palace sent her flowers from their greenhouses.

By the end of December 1912, with the peace conference under-way in London, the Stancioffs began to think of their return to France, and a life of representing their country. This life also meant restricted movement for young ladies and ordered lives for young gentlemen. Nadejda was already mourning the loss of the freedom she experienced during this wartime interlude. She enjoyed the precious respite in Bulgaria and says:

> I will really miss this life in Sofia a lot. Life that is free, free, free; nice pretty nature, no contact with society; no need to practice any of the manners or habits of society; a nice climate and the healing ambiance! I will cry in the train![31]

The Stancioffs were in Sofia preparing to return to Paris, where Dimitri would resume his post. As their friends paid their farewell visits, conversation inevitably turned to the sophistication of Paris and how much more gilded and enriched their lives would be in the French capital. The royal couple showered the Stancioffs, as they did all their courtiers, with gifts on Christmas.

Papa received a bronze bust of the king, and from the queen, a cigarette holder.[32] Maman received a gold bracelet dotted with rubies from the king, and a blue enamel pendant from the queen. Feo and Nadejda received rings with sapphires and medallions with amethysts surrounding a circle of enamel. Ivan received sapphire cufflinks, and Chouchou a ring with three different-colored stones and a box of chocolates. On their actual day of departure, Anna and Dimitri had lunch with the royal family; the children gathered later.

Peace in London

January 1913 held the promise of peace and tranquility on the Balkan peninsula. The peace negotiations in London offered hope for a resolution of the tension. However, Bulgaria's aspirations regarding the Macedonian territories, with the acquisition of an outlet on the Aegean, dissolved like a mere chimera.

While the Russian government supported a Balkan league and agreed, in principle, to be an arbiter of any territorial disputes among the combatants at the end of the conflict, the Russians did something entirely different. Without supporting what were largely legitimate Bulgarian claims, and disavowing largely spurious Serbian and Greek claims to the Macedonian territories, Russia was singularly responsible for creating the atmosphere of mistrust and recriminations among the former allies that quickly devolved into hostile posturing and finally the Second Balkan War. The Russians, by 1913, had resolved to support the Serbs against the Bulgarians because the former's geo-political interests coincided with theirs. Serbia was naturally anti-Austrian, and that tendency was to Russia's advantage; a stronger, larger Bulgaria, on the other hand, would have impinged on Russian interests in the Black Sea. Furthermore, a larger Bulgaria might have competed for control of the Straits of the Bosphorous and the Dardanelles.

Work in Paris

Back at the Bulgarian legation in Paris in January 1913, the Stancioffs plunged into a host of visits with members of the diplomatic community and acquaintances.[33] The children took up their studies, and their mother her duties. This year was an important one for Nadejda and her parents. Their eldest turned nineteen and came out into society. As a mature adult and a woman of marriageable age, her responsibilities and her options as a member of society grew. Her parents were responsible for the impression she would make on her social equals and the result would reflect back on them as good role models and as equals of their peers.

Nadejda not only had to take up the wardrobe of a grown woman but also pay attention to her manners and duties with respect to making calls, carrying on appropriate conversations, keeping attention to protocol, and undertaking delicate social interactions. She now was obliged to attend all the social functions that were de rigueur for her parents.

Therefore, while she was caught up in the excitement of new fittings with the seamstress responsible for overhauling her wardrobe, she also dreaded the requisite social obligations.[34] In the same week as she and Maman visited her couturier, where she stood for three hours for fittings, she also made her first official visit. She and Maman paid a congratulatory call to M. Raymond Poincaré (1860-1934) on his election to the presidency of the French Republic. Nadejda acknowledged that she was mature for her age and commented on how bothersome, time-consuming, and, finally, expensive the entire coming-out process could be.[35]

As Nadejda's trousseau was being put together, and she chafed at the amount of time it took to be fitted properly but she also took time out to consult a fortuneteller.[36] The seer in question, M. Gerard d'Houville, gave her some enigmatic information about herself and reaffirmed her "oriental nature." The process appealed to her sense of the mysterious and the unknown.[37]

Despite protesting about the hours of fittings Nadejda constantly noted her admiration for the beautifully attired women she saw in her favorite Parisian streets: Rue de Rivoli, Rue de la Paix, and Rue Royal. She enjoyed the pretty shops, the glitter of the elegantly dressed crowds, the women's jewelry, the exotic perfumes that lingered in the air, and the excitement of living in the French capital. She gave a rather detailed and clearly mindful description of women's fashions in Paris in 1913:

> Women's silhouettes are long, narrow, high-spirited, disheveled, ruled by long capes that envelope the body, Russian style blouses which appear vaguely Slav, … shoes are small, not tall; hats are also very small, coquet, twisted, dented, curled up, mocking, but all ornamented with a cigarette, with a panache or a vulgar feather which dominates the entire creation!!! It is very amusing![38]

In addition, while she grudgingly celebrated her coming of age, her brother Ivan experienced his own rite of passage by now being permitted to wear high collars like a proper young man in gymnasium. The children of the Stancioff family were growing up.

Armistice Unravels

By the end of January 1913, the armistice that was to have led to peace was dissolved, and war seemed inevitable. The Bulgarian military leadership was not ready to risk another assault, but the combined weight of King Ferdinand's desire to enter Constantinople as its conqueror, and Prime Minister Gueshov's desire to have that victory at his disposal during the peace negotiations, tipped the balance in favor of continuing hostilities. In late January, with the support of the Serbs, hostilities would recommence.

The Stancioffs prayed for a successful conclusion in favor of their country. Meanwhile, life in Paris continued as usual; they went to see a play by Offenbach and resumed their social schedule.[39] They decried Mardi Gras' celebrations as vulgar, and Nadejda claimed the Stancioffs hated the custom. Instead, they focused on the distant war in which their countrymen fought for what they believed to be a just cause and yearned for success on the battlefield in their righteousness.

From their post in Paris, the Stancioffs balanced joie de vivre with pragmatism. Their confidence and the overwhelming feeling of certainty of a victory inspired the following entry, written by Nadejda: "Monday February 10th it's good to be alive! The war is glorious; the soul of Paris smiles through the eyes of . . . pretty women. . . All passes and we only live once! In addition, life is so very short; [so] let us live!"[40] The Stancioffs reveled in the opportunity a diplomatic status afforded to socialize with the crème de la crème of European society "who," according to Nadejda "[are] very modern, cultured, intelligent, and nice; we are among cosmopolitans. Long live [the] career of diplomats."[41]

The Bulgarians were convinced that success was inevitable, even when French public opinion began to turn against Bulgaria.[42] French newspapers decried the war and Bulgaria's role in it. Dimitri's duties, as a representative of his country, became unpleasant and onerous. Furthermore, the situation was exacerbated by the demands of the Romanians, who now sought territorial concessions from Bulgaria. These types of quid pro quo agreements were not unusual, and although the Romanians had not participated in the conflict, they could demand compensation, reasoning that Bulgaria had managed to extend her frontiers at the expense of the Ottoman Empire. Nadejda describes the family's state of mind at the time:

> She wants Silistra and also Baltchik. . . we wait, the press waits, everyone discusses the events! What will happen, where will 1913 take us? Only God knows; we can do nothing but pray. Papa is overwhelmed with work; he lives between the Ministry, the embassies, and the journalists, working without break, even at night. Laconic and disquieting dispatches arrive. . . we wander among the quarters of old Paris to distract ourselves. We drift about Notre Dame, the Sorbonne, and Luxembourg [gardens]. The Seine flows; twilight leaden.[43]

The troubles for Bulgaria were just beginning in February. As the fighting intensified, her Balkan neighbors began to behave in ways that were contradictory to their positions as allies—or even nominal neutral parties. Furthermore, the situation became even grimmer when it appeared that the Russian Empire supported the Romanians, as did the French. It was a sad situation for a Slav Balkan state when even the power most in a position to support their cause—both politically and culturally was unsupportive.

The position of the Russians on this war in the making was critical to a favorable conclusion for the Bulgarians; the fact that the tsar could not take up the Bulgarian cause offers a glaring example of how poorly conceived Russian foreign policy goals were in 1913. The Russian Empire could not capitalize on the unique opportunity for the close relationship the Russian liberation of Bulgaria had offered in 1878, and now, when the Bulgarians would need "rescuing" once more, Russia decided not to seize the opportunity. Russia had too many other factors to consider in its choice to side against its former protégé. Seemingly feckless, with little regard for the outcome, Russian foreign policy temporized by switching its position at will.

Even in the throes of the evolving crisis, when everyone in the family was harnessed to the accomplishment of Bulgarian national goals, Nadejda could not resist commenting on how fortunate they all were to be engaged in a common goal:

> Very agitated evening, Papa has discovered support for the Romanians and that Russia asks the French to do the same. It's not yet very grave, we are disheartened by our brother Slavs. Everyone for themselves unfortunately! We are all working on transmissions. Life is interesting and we have vibrant part in it. What a choice childhood we have.[44]

She also discusses the family's state of mind during the crisis:

> The talks are not going well . . . Papa spends the afternoon with Count Sczecen Ambassador to Austria. He also saw Ambassador Izvolsky [Russia]. We are all going to a big party to benefit the Bulgarian wounded . . . Mama is surrounded and feted. We play bridge so that we will not think of other things.[45]

Charity Work

The Stancioff daughters and mother took on additional responsibilities by collecting money for a charity—founded by the Bulgarian royal family—to benefit Bulgarian orphans. Nadejda recorded their collection amounts and the names of the most generous donors. This supplemental burden on a family already stretched by their duty as Bulgaria's representatives to the Quai d'Orsay was a pleasurable one. The Stancioffs felt closer to the Coburgs as they worked for a noble charitable initiative. Writing about her charity work, Nadejda describes some of her duties:

> I have a lot of work for the princess' [the charity], I take it seriously, like some kind of secretary; we get gifts from all over France and we already have 4000 Francs without counting the clothes and linens. I respond to each donation, which takes a long time![46]

Nadejda is modest. The family's workload for the charitable donations was a full-time job: "Work after midnight, finish addressing all the letters, included photograph of the princesses to every donor. Deliver to the post office 147 envelopes; all written, folded, sealed, and stamped by my own hands. Does it ever finish?"[47]

Creating an Image

Over the course of their lives, the Stancioffs commissioned a number of portraits of themselves. Each of the children had at least one. Nadejda, by her own account, had at least four portraits of herself painted and also posed for photographs.

In April 1913, she commissioned an interesting photograph, wearing a theatrical Balkan costume she might have imagined Europeans believed typical of the region.[48] Facing the camera's eye, her direct but unapproachable gaze sears into the depths of the lens; with the fierce look of a rebel, her arms, in contrast rest. One arm is at her side, and the other in her lap. Her garments are loose-fitting linens and rough hand-woven fabrics. She has a long striped head covering draped on either side of her shoulders, and there is a curved dagger on her lap; a rough, ornate cross hangs from her neck, and there is a heavy cabochon ring on her left hand. Her right hand is poised over a beaten brass coffee pot, which rests on the small table beside her.

It is a bizarre ensemble for a Bulgarian-French woman who posed in a studio sometime in 1913. This photograph, in composition and timing, is witness to her affinity for the Orient. It is no accident that she created and recorded that image of herself. She felt truly a part of the Orient—the mysterious, dangerous, and enigmatic part of the world that seeped into the eastern parts of Europe and simmered at the periphery of civilization. As the Balkan wars progressed, her self-identification with that part of the world matured. She wrote: "Let us be fatalistic and enigmatic like true Orientals!"[49]

A few years later, she followed her sister Feo to the studio of a female portrait artist, a Miss Darcy. According to Nadejda, Feo was painted in oriental costume and wore a gold robe of Bulgarian muslin; she wore her hair down, and there was a gold ribbon at her temples.

The Stancioffs were obsessed with all things oriental, with the image of the Orient which had much more allure than the tangible incarnation. The Orient of the European imagination was exotic, mysterious, and sensual.[50] The Stancioffs internalized their own orientalization and enjoyed the fact that they somehow belonged to yet at the same time felt alien to that environment, as Nadejda explains:

> I would have loved to have lived in a harem; to be among the odalisques the most beautiful and the most beloved; to sleep on the rich rugs . . . to have long perfumed hair, to inhale the warm scents of rare essences, to be dressed in long veils . . . the blazing hot gazes of the Orient. Le dolce far niente d'Orient.[51]

Exhibiting very Victorian views about harems and the erotic nature of life in the Orient Nadejda and her family gazed to the East while they lived and worked in the West.

Coming of Age in Paris

Nadejda's life vacillated between the existence of a debutante and a teenager not yet of age. Her first coming-out ball took place on March 1, 1913. Preparations were solemn, and when Minister Stancioff, Madame Stancioff, and Mademoiselle Stancioff left for the gala event at 7:30 p.m., Nadejda reported feeling happy and intimidated.[52]

The reception was elegant. All the diplomats wore their uniforms; the women wore sumptuous dresses wafting expensive perfumes; the dinner and the flowers were excellent, in her opinion.[53] She could still describe her coming-out ball while writing about a children's reception at the Kotchoubey's, the Russian ambassador's residence, on the next day. This dichotomy was not lost on her, but she was well adept at bridging and transcending roles. She felt, to a certain extent, the wise, supportive, vigilant elder when she escorted her younger siblings, especially the youngest two, Ivan and Chou, since she had already taken on the responsibility of supervising Chou's homework preparation, and pushed her brother to excel at his scholastic efforts. She also used the tone of a superior adult when she recorded her brother's progress or lack of diligence to his studies.

Although the Serbs declared hostilities against Bulgaria, in Paris, the social engagements were not disturbed by rumors of war. Only an actual outbreak of hostilities would stymie the season. While Nadejda noted the possibility of a war with Serbia and the news of an earthquake in Bulgaria, she still focused on the social life. "In Paris, we have fun constantly! We go out morning and night; in the evening carried away by the whirlwind!"[54] Nadejda observed events and had the uncanny ability to comment sardonically on the whole ensemble "while war looms, disasters, strikes, Paris is awash with social activities."[55]

An Author in Our Midst

Between the two Balkan wars, Nadejda had the pleasure of meeting one of her favorite authors, Maurice Barrès. The French journalist, novelist, nationalist, and occultist who, at the time of their meeting, was also a member of the French Academy of Science, stirred Nadejda's imagination. As an aspiring author, she was completely bowled over by the prospect of meeting him in her very own home. Her opportunity came unexpectedly. Barrès came to the Bulgarian legation to thank the minister plenipotentiary, Dimitri Stancioff, for King Ferdinand's generous donation toward the building of a monument in Versailles.

Barrès, in his capacity as president of the monument committee arrived in person instead of sending a note. Nadejda watched him unobserved from a room adjoining the salon. She was transported with joy when she could hear his "grave voice which evokes the ancient splendors of Toledo."[56] He had a Caesarian profile and a hairdo in the style of Napoleon. She filled the pockets of his overcoat with flower petals as a kind of homage.

Papa, conscious of how much his daughter worshiped the man, invited her to meet Barrès as the interview was ending. Predictably, Nadejda was unnerved and excited to shake the hand of "the eminent author, the leader of the strange philosophy, and the creator of so many wrenching, tormented, and intense works."[57]

Barrès did not disappoint. On the next day she received two of his books; each was inscribed with a personal message. He encouraged her to write; she

sent him one of her essays. Nadejda was emotional as she recorded: "Oh, beati-
tude! I am still full of emotion . . . the god is reading my little works! . . . I was
also presented to Rostand!!!"[58] She then searched for and reread Barrès' latest
"masterpiece."

For his part, Barrès, continued to correspond with the teenager and send
supportive missives. She was flattered by his heartening words, saying: "He
writes elegies to me! Oh, joy, joy, joy! I must cultivate hardworking persever-
ance." They kept in contact until his death in 1923.

Work with Papa

At the age of nineteen, Nadejda was fully incorporated into her father's working
world. She helped him decipher all dispatches from Sofia, write and correct re-
plies, press releases, and all official and personal correspondence, especially
when he was most busy.[59] She was literally indispensable to him; he could not
part with her services. When Maman was asked to Menton as companion to the
Bulgarian princesses for a month in May 1913, it was Feodora who went along
with her mother. Nadejda stayed behind to help their father with his ever-
increasing workload.

Father and daughter had full days, of concentrated work, official visits, and
attendance to obligatory soirées, which also fulfilled an official function, and
occasional excursions to the theatre or a walk in the Bois when time permitted.
Moreover, Nadejda understood that she had "...a very interesting life, work—
pleasure, and nothing in between!"[60] Dictated by the demands of the job, their
daily lives were the result of combined efforts and exertions as well as shared
pleasures.[61]

In spring 1913, the Bulgarian legation in Paris had to contend with rapidly
rising tensions that led to renewed hostilities in the Balkans. When Adrianople
surrendered in March, a second armistice had begun. Nadejda and her father
lived the months of March and April overburdened with negotiations, dispatches, interviews with journalists, and official appointments; they worked late
into the night and sometimes into the next day. While accomplishing the work of
a bona fide assistant to her father, Nadejda also did the work of her mother when
she was absent. She was in charge of the domestic staff; she took care of her
siblings.[62]

In the guise of a diplomat in the making, Nadejda commented on the negotiations of the victorious Bulgarians in April on the disposition of various Balkan territories: "If they give us all that we want, then we will stop our nice war;
but if the Powers make the Bulgarians unhappy, then they will take Chataldja
and enter Constantinople! Ooora!"[63]

Then later, as Bulgarian military triumphs solidified their bargaining posi-
tion, she added: "We will not give you Rodosto but we will agree to the Enos-
Midia line. The king demands that they give him, as a personal gift the island of
Samothrace; this original idea pleases us a lot."[64]

This was Nadejda's life, and it suited her to perfection. It was a cosmopolitan life that included the pleasures of luxury European grand hotels, fine clothes,

the company of intelligent men who discussed politics with her, the indulgence of exotic foods, and above all, the satisfaction of a difficult and demanding job done well.[65]

In this way, Nadejda became a de facto participant in the Bulgarian diplomatic corps, and Feo too, although neither, at the time, held a position that was remunerated. Nonetheless, the sisters fulfilled many duties of a member of the ministry of foreign affairs; they undertook translations, ciphers, and reports for Sofia.

As the sisters worked at their father's side, he, no doubt, made sure to advertise their contributions to his superiors. Thus the Stancioff sisters performed a kind of apprenticeship for a career in diplomacy. Their experiences would endow them with the qualifications needed in the Bulgarian diplomatic corps. Although the sisters did not look forward to a position with the service however they were born into the profession. Most Bulgarians could not hope to have had the education, the facility with so many languages, and, most importantly, the international experiences that, made the girls genuine candidates for a position in any diplomatic service. The Stancioff sisters were natural contenders.

All of the Stancioff children had not only the requisite qualifications of language facility but also the more difficult, but equally important, capability of interacting with aristocrats, who demanded a specific kind of refined handling. The children observed, studied, and imitated their parents' manners and learned everything at their parents' side.

Nadejda was the most likely candidate to enter this world; she was the eldest and, seemingly, most talented in the profession. She was tactful, charming, and intelligent; she knew how to be discreet yet seduce her audience into a sense of self-assurance. Combining guile with directness, she became an adept conversationalist who could woo her listeners with her apparent sincerity.

Her skills included the ability to assess the big picture of power politics in Europe from the perspective of a small impotent power and determine the strengths and weakness of any given situation. When the tide flowed against Bulgaria, as former allies turned antagonistic, the outlook was bleak, as Nadejda notes:

> April 12— Politics is disheartening. . . We are going to have to cede Silistra, . . . It is a piece of the flesh, they are ripping from us a piece of our flag. . . We are not going to have Rodosto. . . These Grandes Impuisants [Great Powerless] are ineffectual; Russia is crazy. Austria isolated. . . We must keep quiet and wait, wait. Our hearts become like the big deserts denuded, pale, and empty; we remain there on our knees in the silence and solitude. . . of those who supplicate by their very resignation.

> April 16— Morning of work . . . Papa has a long interview with Pichon. It is a dark hour. We know many secret things about current politics.

> April 23— The political situation is chaotic black. The Great Powerless tremble at the possibility that Scutari will be taken soon! An evening of work.

April 24— The Serbs and Greeks are causing terrible problems for Bulgarians. They don't want to observe the clauses of her treaties! We expect a war; and this will light the incendiary Russo-Austrian pyre. Serbia is running toward her destruction.

April 26—The Bulgarians claim justifiably the islands of Thassos and Samothrace; I hope they will deign to give them what belongs to them.

April 29—I return home quickly decipher numberless dispatches. Things are getting more complicated over there. We work furiously in all the chancelleries. [We]... slave away day and night.

May 2—The political labyrinth becomes more and more inextricable . . . awaiting fatalistically an imprecise peace.[66]

Although she helped with the family's domestic duties, which any eldest daughter would have done, Nadejda was also a stand-in for her mother outside the home. She became Papa's female escort to all social functions, which were so important in maintaining valuable political networking.[67]

While her mother and Feodora were performing the duties of lady-in-waiting to the Bulgarian queen at Menton, Nadejda took up her mother's other position as "wife" of the Bulgarian minister plenipotentiary—the role of the female counterpart to the male representative of a state. She became her father's female escort to all social functions, which were so important in maintaining valuable political networking; purely social acquaintances often turned into fruitful professional relationships.

This breach into the adult world of duty and responsibility at the public and professional levels is impressive. This title, "wife of the Bulgarian minister plenipotentiary" and its duties were paramount to the success of a diplomat's mission.

An ambassador would not be successful unless his wife possessed impeccable breeding and understood the intricacies of entertaining the social elites in the manner to which they were accustomed.[68]

Nadejda's ability to take over that role from her mother, at a moment's notice, is a clear indication of her talents and abilities to be a member of this particular social milieu. She was supremely capable of playing out that role for herself and, more importantly, for their father and the Bulgarian nation. Her mother had trained her flawlessly. Nadejda Stancioff stepped into the unaccustomed role of minister's consort and fit her mother's shoes admirably. There is no question that had she been less than perfect in fulfilling her role, her father would have kept her at home. Instead, she accompanied her father to all events in her mother's stead. Nadejda describes several soirées she attends in one evening:

May 4— Papa and I go to the grand soirée of the Italian Embassy; it is elegant and interesting. I have a really good time!

May 6—I go this evening with Papa to two nice soirées the first very chic at the Russian embassy, . . . elegance, luxury, jewels, diadems, perfumes, ravishing women, . . . the beautiful Grand Duchess Cyrille and four Grand Dukes! We dance, talk, we feel alive. I observe and study and I philosophize! Second soirée at the palace of the Argentine legation; midnight . . . supper, dance.

May 7—The arrival of His Majesty Alphonze XIII King of Spain. Enthusiasm! . . . I go with . . . Papa to the reception at the Elysée Palace and see the king very well. A brilliant and elegant evening; all the diplomatic corps and the French Academy are there, all the French ministers with their wives.[69]

When Maman and Feo returned from Menton, the household resumed its former arrangement governing the spheres of domestic interest. Although Nadejda comments, "We [dinner guests and the Stancioffs] talk politics; after the meal, the ladies talk down below and the men smoke upstairs bent over maps and plans for the war."[70] Entertaining normally required the observance of rules of decorum for each gender. Nadejda was part of those conversations upstairs when her mother was away, and the invitees to the household were mainly her fathers' colleagues or Bulgarian friends. Once Maman returned then convention dictated that men could smoke and discuss wars; women could retire to the salon to discuss other topics.

Diplomatic Training in the Throes of War

Journal entries about those spring days in 1913 convey the atmosphere of constant activity, the stress of fulfilling duties and obligations, and the occasional distractions of pleasurable outings. Most importantly, Nadejda's training as a diplomat continued at an incredible pace. Work and more work; the father-daughter pair was tireless. The lesson each child absorbed early on was that the family enterprise was a collective effort and that no one could spare individual energies as long as that enterprise required responsibility. In May, the pace of unremitting work continued according to Nadejda's diary entries.

May 13—Formidable amount of work on my return... three reports to compose in English and to copy! I slaved away from 9-12. We will soon sign the preliminary of the peace.

May 14—Morning of work, I write from 9-1! In English, French, Bulgarian! Papa works without a rest. . . . One would say that this is a fratricidal war, but it has been a long time that we have hated each other, we neighbors.

May 16—Basically incessant work and very tiring.

May 17—We talk politics until 2 a.m. and all washed down with ciphered dispatches! I finish my last letter at 1:30! A hot bath and after this feverish day one is so troubled that one cannot sleep . . . We speak of nothing but politics of finance and polemicize.

> May 20—It is good to be alive, sometimes . . . Grand dinner at the Chamber of
> Deputies. I dine between the Prefect of the Seine and Mr. Simond, Editor of
> Echo de Paris.[71]

With few details about the military developments in the Balkans available
in Paris, and news, that seemingly the Serbs and Greeks were taking bold offensive moves against the Bulgarian armies, the Bulgarian community in Paris was
paralyzed with the thought that all might have been in vain.

The lives lost, the sacrifices of the civilian population—all lost. What was
the Bulgarian government thinking? What were the generals doing? How could
this be happening when victory had been in hand? Nadejda muses, "Where are
you heroes of Lule-Burgas and of Kirk Kilisse?" Maman was overwhelmed with
emotion and lost herself in prayer to assuage her feelings of helplessness. Papa
maintained his composure and worked to save Bulgarian honor. Nadejda adds,
"He does not let himself be beaten and does not show us his emotion."[72]

In 1913, during the Second Balkan War, the rapid retreat of Bulgarian armies on all fronts led to depressing thoughts in Paris. The concerns were at
every level: national, professional, and personal. Bulgaria was in the process of
experiencing a horrendous defeat on the very heels of a heady victory months
earlier.

For the blended Bulgarian-French family living in the French capital, the
comparisons to the French military defeats of 1813 were inescapable; this was a
debacle of the same scale. The family discussed the French humiliations of
1813, 1814, and 1870. Seemingly, Bulgaria had reached that same moment of
total ruin.[73] The future appeared black, and the Stancioffs consoled each other
by quoting Musset as Nadejda recorded in her journal: "One must resign oneself, suffer in silence and start anew patiently, solidly without allowing oneself
to feel defeated."[74]

The Bulgarian community in Paris gathered at the legation every night "like
the lambs of a flock in a storm seeking safe haven," according to Nadejda.[75]
They assembled the men upstairs and the women in the salon, sharing scant
pieces of news and consoling each other. Discussions over tea, water, and bis-
cuits turned the legation into an expatriate center in a new sense; it became a
meeting place at a time of national calamity.

The Stancioffs played the role of national symbols of strength and unity. As
they worked making copies of dispatches, translations, writing letters, answering
the telephone, and dealing with the press, they had to show fortitude. Nadejda
received a long letter from Bulgaria, her friend Hélène Petroff wrote of the war,
life at court, the diplomatic community in Sofia and she urged Nadejda to do
what she could with her diplomatic contacts in Paris to help their country. She
also asked Nadejda to write to Meriel Buchanan, and ask the British minister's
daughter, to "stir things up a bit in our favor with Sir George," Meriel's father,
and Britain's representative at St. Petersburg in 1913.[76]

While they had to cope with their own feelings of bitterness, they also had
to play the role of extended national family to the expatriates. They symbolized
the country not only for the French but also for their fellow Bulgarians. They

had to bear up as best they could as their roles evolved from legation functionaries to counselors to grief-stricken Bulgarians.

The Stancioffs spared some thoughts to the possibility of a personal loss. They hoped no harm would befall their home, *Les Trois Sources*, so near the border with Romania. Nadejda thought: What if the Romanian armies reached their property? What would they take from their lovingly put together home? What would become of all the time and memories invested there or what would become of Euxinograd?[77] Nadejda anthropomorphized their villa by the sea in the following musings:

> I am certain that at this moment she [the house]wears an air of suffering, under the greenish paint applied during mobilization . . . with her closed windows . . . the fruits which fall to the ground so that they can better see the sun; the flowers who waft their perfume for themselves alone, and a long maudlin silence!"[78]

The Stancioffs spent hours just waiting for concrete news and making interminable suppositions. They strained their imaginations to grasp what was really happening on the "sunny bloody fields of the orient."[79]

The Second Balkan War

A tragically perfect combination of factors led to the Second Balkan War. Starting with the First Balkan War, the war of 1912 was a success for the combatants; the peace, however, was a complete failure both for the presumed victors and for the supposed losers. Although a peace had been signed in London in May 1913, the actual divisions of territory were not clearly set down at that time so Bulgaria's good military fortune combined with the territorial shrinkage caused by the creation of a new state—Albania—transformed Greece and Serbia into natural allies against Bulgaria.

The Great Powers' insistence that an Albanian state had to be created from the "liberated" Ottoman territories is what disposed the situation against Bulgarian interests in 1913. The forced creation of a new national entity in the Balkans increased tensions among the former allies and allowed the Romanians to declare their desire for territorial compensation, in return for their continued neutrality in the course of events.

The situation might have been salvaged, had the Bulgarian Prime Minister Ivan Evstatiev Gueshov, (1849-1924), had the backing of his king; the latter, however, was in a belligerent mood and sided with those who would continue the pursuit of war. When Gueshov resigned and was replaced by Stoian Danev, the latter initially joined Bulgaria to the belligerents' cause then, when fighting actually began, he reversed himself, too late.

Both Danev and Gueshov came to revise their martial decisions regarding the prosecution of war, however both temporized too late. In June, Gueshov resigned, and in July, he was in Paris briefing Dimitri and Anna Stancioff on the details of the situation in Bulgaria.[80] Gueshov as pessimistic in his vision of Bulgaria's prospects for a fair solution in peace, and his interpretation of the events did nothing to dispel the Stancioffs' own despondent mood.

Ultimately, Bulgaria ended up fighting a Second Balkan War against all her former allies, plus the Romanian armies and the Ottoman armies, who took advantage of the concentration of Bulgarian forces on the western front, primarily aimed at the Greek and Serbian armies, to re-conquer most of the lost territories in Thrace. The Turkish assault included the retaking of Adrianople, an important defensive position. Nadejda exhibits frustration with the turn of events:

> What do the heroes of Lule-Burgas and of Adrianople, who died and are now interned in that black earth, what do they think? The noise of the Turkish invasion must have woken them up; they must have grimaced under the ground and said: 'Why? . . . cowardly Europe . . . did not give us even the Enos-Midia line'?[81]

Thus, the war in the Balkans, which began as a quest for territorial justice for three powers, ended by creating even greater tensions and suspicions and causes for vengeance than before. Danev's resignation in the face of the national disaster was followed by the entry of the Radoslavov-led government, which worked harmoniously with King Ferdinand; both men had the same temperament and outlook when it came to foreign and domestic policy.

Informants

The Stancioffs were disgusted with France's lack of political will in its refusal to support Bulgaria. The family was also disappointed in the unwillingness of the European diplomatic establishment to intervene when they witnessed obvious injustice.

During peace treaty negotiations in August 1913, the Stancioffs finally received some reliable first-hand information from a source they trusted. One of their Panitza cousins, Staty, who served in Thrace and fought the Serbs, visited the family in Paris. He told them of his experiences during his year of fighting in the war, saying, "the army did not want the second war and it had no enthusiasm. . . things were really disorganized."[82]

In the same month, the Stancioffs received a letter from Princess Eudoxie describing the mood in Sofia. The king, addressing his troupes, spoke of past victories and promised vengeance. "Vendetta, a magic word which is the only one that can assuage in these atrocious days!"[83] The Stancioffs in Paris were tortured by two concerns that occupied their worried minds: that the debacle could have been avoided, and that the future might bring fresh troubles. It had been a wet summer in Paris that year, and the precipitation itself seemed sympathetic to the inconsolable Bulgarian expatriates; the drops cried out condolences in a melancholy beat in the words of Nadejda.[84]

Papa, despite his brave exterior, eventually expressed his despondence over the debacle. He felt his five years in Paris had been wasted, saying "We will never forget the cowardice of France in 1913!"[85] Despite his determination to salvage something for his country from the wreckage of war, the outcome—that he could do little to assuage—from Paris in 1913, was a bitter pill.

In early August, the new Romano-Bulgarian borders were decided, and the changes permitted the Romanians to claim the territory between Tutrakan on the Danube and Baltchik on the Black sea.[86] The Stancioffs seethed as Nadejda records: "the despicable Vlachs," "a little people that are pretentious and ridiculous." [87] The Romanians claimed twelve kilometers on the southern part of Baltchik.

The family was so disgusted by the ease with which the Romanians claimed territories they did not have to fight to acquire that the family even enjoyed a private conversation with Chou Chou's former governess. Miss O'Donnell, who was passing through Paris with her Romanian charge, filled the Stancioffs ears with humiliating vignettes about what—in her opinion—the Romanians were really like. This description reassured the Stancioffs' sense of hostility toward the country of "Johnny come latelies, of flashy outlandish people" as Miss O'Donnell put it. Thus, the family enjoyed a conversation with someone who shared their scorn of the "thieving nation."[88]

Treaty of Bucharest

The Treaty of Bucharest, which concluded the Second Balkan War, was a disaster of unprecedented proportions for Bulgaria. So much valuable territory had been lost. The Dobrudja, an arable territory that made the viability of Varna harbor, and therefore successful grain trade, feasible for Bulgaria —was swallowed by Romania.

The Enos-Midia line, the approximate line of advance before the foolhardy decision to attack Constantinople, had it become a Bulgarian border, would have given the Bulgarians not only a convenient outlet to the Aegean but enough hinterland to have unimpeded overland access. The treaty rolled back that economically viable border to an impractical access to Dedeagach, an underdeveloped outlet to the Aegean to which access could be had only by a rail link that inched in and out of Ottoman territories.

Macedonian territories gained in 1912 were also reduced to Pirin Macedonia, and even that was a paltry expansion. In sum, the territories acquired were unusable and had no value as arable land while the vanished territories denoted significant economic losses.

The other disastrous result of the treaty was less difficult to assess immediately but eventually had greater and more profound consequences. Every Bulgarian community that was incorporated into a foreign state would now be subjected to active oppression. Each Balkan state, including Bulgaria, carried out a policy of forced assimilation of its "foreign" populations.[89] This policy included making it a punishable offense to speak one's mother tongue, to worship in one's national church, or to educate the next generation in any of its cultural inheritance.

Each state shouldered the burden of justifying its acquisitions of new territories. The mood of rabid nationalism, which followed the peace, led to an atmosphere of distrust and created a barrier to any future cooperation among the Balkan states. Each had to fear his neighbor, since the next conflict would be one of reckoning.

Bulgarian Politics and Domestic Turmoil

The First and Second Balkan Wars created unforeseeable stressors on a society not yet perfectly unified by a sense of national purpose or a vision of a national destiny. King Ferdinand had a fleeting opportunity, at least from the point of view of the physical proximity of his Bulgarian armies to Constantinople in 1912, to realize his ambition to recreate a greater Bulgarian medieval state. He hoped to reconstitute and echo Byzantium by capturing Constantinople, its capital city.

His vision was so pronounced that he had photographs taken of himself in Byzantine-style court dress. His vision did not correspond with the realities at home or abroad. His frustration with the outcomes of the wars made him obstinate and increasingly inflexible to diplomatic solutions. By the end of the debacle, his country was roiled by internal dissention.

In 1913, Bulgaria's political situation was perilously close to chaotic. The rightist government of Radoslavov had barely gained a majority in parliament, and the November election results were embarrassing for the Radoslavovist party—ninety-seven seats versus one hundred nine opposition seats in the Narodno Sûbranie.[90] With so many Bulgarians voting their displeasure with Radoslavov's party and favoring, instead, agrarian, socialist, nationalist, and even liberal parties, the government faced a precarious domestic situation. It had to produce some tangible proofs of its worth, or the domestic situation would deteriorate. At one point Radoslavov's government was threatened with a military coup. Narodno Sûbranie meetings were punctuated by fistfights and even a threatened pistol volley. The situation was politically untenable, and since the rightist government could not accommodate any one particular political bloc by January 1914, the Narodno Sûbranie was dissolved.

Radoslavov's government regained power in the new election because of disunity among his opponents and because he was able to use the new territories' populations in the voting process to his advantage. By openly buying votes, the government managed to win the next elections. Furthermore, the government was able to use its advantage in other ways; the most significant economic development in this period was the agreement for a substantial loan with German banks.

The Balkan Wars had exhausted the largely agrarian economy, and the Bulgarian government was in desperate need of an infusion of hard capital. A German 500 million gold leva loan caused an up-swell of resentment at home.[91] The stipulations of the loan were not only economically onerous for Bulgaria but also insulted national pride and caused consternation abroad, especially in Russia and France. France had been the original source of the loan, but the Bulgarians had been put off by the French equivocating on the conditions, and the timing of the loan, thereby giving the Germans a perfect entry into the process.

Acceptance of the German loan by no means cemented the relationship between the two countries. Although the Austrians and Germans, who were close allies, hoped for a closer partnership, King Ferdinand was an expert at tantalizing his equals; he seemed to pledge all kinds of cooperation. In the end, he chose to keep Bulgaria neutral when war broke out in 1914 between the Central Powers and the Entente states.

Bulgarian public opinion, although sorely tried by the Russian indifference to their plight during the Second Balkan War was largely antipathetic toward the Germans and Austrians. Bulgarians were even more disillusioned with the Russians' open support of Romania's territorial gains but nonetheless they held a largely favorable opinion of the Russians.

1914

At the end of 1913, during the Christmas and New Year holidays, most of the family was still in Bulgaria. They spent their first winter at *Trois Sources*. Maman was in France taking care of an ailing brother, and the three Stancioff sisters were even more responsible for the domestic order. Each girl wrote on the first page of Nadejda's 1914 journal.[92] The family decorated the Christmas tree together, and when they exchanged gifts, it was in a generosity of spirit and family single-mindedness that was their hallmark.

To usher in the New Year the family attended a ball at the military club in Varna. Nadejda notes that "we flee the sinister year and begin the unknown year with dance and champagne! This golden liquid relaxes the nerves deliciously!"[93]

Toward the end of January, the family packed and began their migration back to Paris, and Nadejda remarks that "Our packing is done, our bags are ready. Because of Maman's absence, I have the annoying responsibility for everything! Papa is very calm and his well-organized brain foresees everything; I do my best also."[94]

When they arrived in Sofia, the Stancioffs visited the site of Aleksandûr's grave to pray, a tradition they maintained every time they left the country. Nadejda writes that "the cemetery is one of the most implacable that I know; no poetry or tenderness... it is a place chosen for the dead and that is all. There is no European cult of the dead here!"[95]

Their plans to depart Sofia by the five o'clock train were upset by an invitation from the palace to dinner. Their departure put off until the next day, they dined with the king and the entire royal family; the king was amiable, and the children were nice hosts.[96] Since the heir apparent's and Princess Nadejda's birthdays, were on January 30, the family also celebrated with them at a lunch party at the palace. Finally, released from their obligations, Papa had one last audience with his sovereign in private. He also met with Radoslavov and sat in at the council of ministers meeting.

When the king left for Plovdiv the next day to pay his respects at his first wife's burial site on the anniversary of her passing, the Stancioffs were sent off with fond words, wishes, and flowers from the royal family.[97]

On their trajectory across Europe, Nadejda noted that she loved the sensation of train travel, which gave her the feeling of heading toward unknown destinations suspended in a timeless capsule. She was amazed at the speed of twentieth-century travel:

> Who would have believed that on Saturday we were in Sofia? . . . after having had that wonderful intimacy with the sea, the wind, the winter, we are very far, far away! The sensation is very strange, truly; I think about the hall at Trois Sources, of the other furniture, of the other books, the other paintings, and what is truly bizarre is that the mentality changes so much with the surroundings.[98]

In Paris Once More

Soon after their arrival in Paris, the family was pleasantly surprised and proud when they learned of the French government's announcement that it would bestow the Gold Medal of Epidemics on Maman in recognition of her services to the Red Cross in Sofia in 1912. In part, the award read: "Madame Stancioff, by seeking to serve the contagious, has fully merited this mark of gratitude." Their Maman was celebrated in her native land, and Nadejda wrote: "All the morning newspapers comment on this news and write elegies to Maman."[99]

Back to their Parisian routine, the Stancioffs kept busy. Papa picked up his duties. Nadejda took up delivering Chou to her lessons, and while she sat in the back of the classroom working on embroidery, Nadejda observed her sister's fellow classmates and made mental notes on their relative merits, both intellectually and as companions to her sister.[100]

Feo and Nadejda took time to attend enriching events, such as a talk given by Sarah Bernhardt. Although awe struck by the power of the "princess of gestures" and "Queen of the Theatre" – titles bestowed on her by the press, Nadejda recorded Bernhardt's outward appearance and practically nothing about the content of her talk.[101] Nadejda was a teenager and as a young woman living in Paris and a member of elite society, she had her eye on trends in clothing. She, her sisters, and her mother critiqued fashions, although they kept their attire to the more conservative palette of styles and colors. Nadejda comments that:

> fashion is not pretty this year: in daytime women wear very tall hats, their suits loose fitting, little shoes with vertiginous heels; plain blouses . . . in the evening, deep necklines. . . . The fashionable hairstyle requires that all the hair be pulled back . . . all this gives women a serene and chaste air. . . fashions are hideous for women: hats are disgraceful too small in the shape of valves, jackets very short, and skirts . . . a nightmare! And . . . disgraceful . . . hobbling the feet, double skirt is too full, all the way to the knees, an abundance of flying folds, complications. . . . Hair in fashion is burnished red; [fashionable] dogs are still greyhounds.[102]

Political Labyrinth

French domestic politics were increasingly chaotic, perhaps in sympathy with women's fashions. While tensions among the Great Powers escalated, the lesser, newer states, like the ones in the Balkans, scrambled to curry favor from their Great Power patrons and find succor in a progressively tense international climate. In 1914, Bulgaria's reputation in Europe, especially in France, had descended to a low point. Her neighbors, Greece, Serbia, and Romania, all had a much more glowing reputation, and their respective European supporters found it easy to gather public and governmental support for their protégés, while Bulgaria languished as a virtual political orphan.

The first decade of the twentieth century had been witness to several narrow escapes. Newspaper headlines proclaimed war scares across Europe. The decades after the Congress of Berlin, in 1878, had hardened the alliance system once manipulated by the German Chancellor Otto von Bismarck. Its contemporary incarnation had turned dangerously brittle; too little flexibility among leaders and followers in the international arena created an atmosphere of fear and distrust among national governments. Sensationalist news reporting and biased journalism did the rest of the work of whipping national public opinion to an irrational and belligerent beat.

Europeans were already partisan in their domestic politics and equally opinionated when considering international allegiances. National honor was part and parcel of an internalized system of behavior that would facilitate the triggering of a general European war. Europeans formulated their political views and their opinions of foreign states as they continued to live their personal lives; reputation and international (or social) rank carried some weight. In 1914, honor and a good name still mattered above all other things in life, and Europeans projected that credo onto their families, friends, and politicians. This state of mind is perfectly illustrated by the political scandal that rocked France in mid-March.

On March 16, 1916, the Stancioffs enjoyed a typical day. Nadejda went to her singing lessons with Maman, then they took a walk in the park, enjoyed the sunny weather, and took care of household chores together.[103] That evening, after returning from his dinner at the Italian embassy, a party in honor of Poincaré, Dimitri, who was please with the event, shared with a bit of sensational gossip.

Mme. Caillaux, the wife of the French minister of finance, had murdered M. Calmette, director of *Le Figaro*, in his office.[104] She wanted to avenge her husband's honor because of a series of negative articles published by *Le Figaro*. Apparently, she walked in the newspaper office at half past six, and gave her card to his secretary, who ushered her into the director's office. There she took out a revolver and shot Calmette several times. The gravely wounded Calmette died later, and Mme. Caillaux spent the night in prison, under arrest for murder. Paris was shocked and a little titillated.

This kind of murder, to assuage honor, was almost comprehensible to polite society and practically expected by the noble elites. When M. Caillaux handed in his resignation, the ensuing governmental crisis, and the discussion in the

French chamber of deputies brought out some of the disorganized and highly partisan nature of the administration and its cabinet members. The sensation of the act and the ensuing trial drew European-wide attention. Europeans understood murder in the name of honor; death was considered just payment for a dishonorable transgression.

Developments à la Famille

The family routine quickened with the advent of spring 1914. Nadejda continued with her singing lessons; she was working on Tosca.[105] Feo was making progress with her Italian lessons. As a pleasurable pastime, the family as a whole would attend the horse races, followed by tea at a fashionable spot like the Carlton Hotel.

That spring there was a religious retreat for the two older sisters; they listened to sermons on duty and free will, on sweetness and humility.[106] Their mother went to a retreat for ladies at the Spanish Chapel in Paris; their father pressed on with his work-related obligations.

The family took their spiritual instruction seriously; introspection, which was called for at these retreats and by their faith in general, had become second nature. Feo was concerned about her soul and how she was preparing for its eternal life. She focused on her interior life according to Nadejda and as the two sisters worked on themselves in order to meet the standards their religious training set down.

When one of the children's aunts died, leaving behind a husband and seven children, the Stancioffs entered mourning, and Nadejda and Feo contemplated the mysteries of life and the fleeting nature of existence. Their separations— their mother was away that week, and their brother, Ivan, was at school in Bulgaria—made the somber reflections even more sobering. Nadejda writes: "I despise myself in these days of mourning. . . . Death is a horrible thing; it is truly the end of everything, the end or the beginning . . . God make it so that I die before all of my [loved ones]."[107]

Perhaps it was the effect of Christian introspection that made Nadejda feel and profess throughout her entire life her belief that she was inadequate, an underachiever. When the family invited a young French woman to tea after the races that spring, Nadejda could not help but set the woman on a pedestal, and remarked that "this young woman speaks four languages, plays the piano exceedingly well, passed her first exam for the baccalaureate and prepares the second, dances like a ballerina, plays the sports that are in vogue, and in addition has a sweet face. A girl well prepared for life."[108]

Nadejda's own achievements appeared less outstanding by her own accounting:

> This evening I am completely stupid; I drew a little, in my life and I abandoned it after a few months; in music I am arrived at [a certain spot] and I have stopped [improving]; I speak two or three languages somewhat well . . . I reason poorly, in effect I am nothing but a mediocrity. My dear writing remains,

but I don't do much with it; it amuses me but I don't get anything out of it! So? Discouragement and worthlessness.[109]

Nadejda remained a life-long skeptic when it came to her own accomplishments, even after she attained professional heights rarely achieved by a woman. She was humble and truly appreciative for all the goodness in her life as her frequent prayers of gratitude offered to God attest. Introspection focused the Stancioffs' efforts to attain greater accomplishments and to value the gifts life had already presented. The special nature of their lives was not lost on the children. They were grateful for their blessings, as Nadejda writes:

> ...what a wonderful life I have! So many resources and a character that is so comfortable for me! . . . The older I get the more I thank God for having a father such as him; what an exquisite nature and how interesting and attractive and original! Maman is perfect. We were happy children.[110]

World War Begins

On June 23, 1914, Nadejda wrote about the usual round of events in Paris: the theatre performances, embassy dances, soirées, teas, afternoon musical performances, and days at the racetrack:

> We fly from one to the other [event] without being able to enjoy the agreeable parts, a very modern logic! . . . at the end of the season we have impressions that are more intense; the women all have the same dresses, we feel we have seen them too much; the music is the same; the petites fours at the long buffet tables are identical every evening; the servants are all listless; only the flowers are radiant and the jewelry marvelous. I know the hair, smiles and dresses of all the women what an annoying routine![111]

The Stancioffs were happily anticipating their annual pilgrimage back to *Trois Sources* and a well-deserved rest. The season was winding down in Paris. After a few more social engagements and a few more horse races, Parisians would retreat to their respective villas to wait out the heat of August. On June 28, 1914, the Stancioffs heard the happy news from Bulgaria; Ivan had passed his baccalaureate with distinction. Nadejda writes:

> Weather hot, sunny, almost oriental. A happy day . . . it is the day of the Grand-Prix race. We are all going to the races, invited to the President's platform. . . . elegant public . . . all of a sudden they let Poincaré and Sczecsen, the Austrian Ambassador know the dreadful news . . . assassination at Sarajevo.[112]

At Longchamps, the news of the tragedy stunned the audience. Nadejda recorded the scene, "The Austrian ambassador, Count Szecsen read the telegram and vanished."[113] As whispered conversations rose above the crowd gathered at the race track, groups of officials parted to allow rushing ministers and ambassadors to leave.

On the next day the Stancioffs were already certain that the assassination of Archduke Franz Ferdinand and his wife, Sophie, was a Serb plot, a sentiment that became commonplace among the leadership of the European powers.[114] With no inkling of how this tragedy could impact their future, the family discussion first revolved around the orphaned children of the assassinated couple and then swirled pleasantly around the fact that the heir apparent to the Austrian throne was married to a Princess of Parma – Zita – which made the Bulgarian princes and princesses nephews and nieces of the future empress of Austria. There could be distinct advantages for Bulgaria in this new circumstance. In Nadejda's words, "The Balkans always has surprises for Europe, Poor Europe!"[115]

Summer in Bulgaria

When the family left for Bulgaria in July, Papa remained behind in Paris. Once back at the villa in Varna, Ivan reunited with his siblings, and the family could enjoy their holiday by the sea.

While the Stancioffs gave themselves over to the summer-time pleasure of swimming and relaxing the aftershocks of the assassination intensified, came closer together, and rose in crescendo. When the Austrian ultimatum was rejected by Serbia, and the two countries broke off relations at the end of July, the questions on Europeans' minds were also on the Stancioffs minds. As Nadejda writes:

> Across all Europe, we think about it and discuss it; little news. . . . War is not yet declared; will Serbia be supported by Russia? What will be the attitudes of the other Balkan states? Bulgaria affirms that she will remain neutral; let us hope that she has the courage to persevere in that direction.[116]

With their father still at his post in Paris and their Uncle Nic chargé d'affaire in Vienna, the Stancioffs had access to Europe's diplomatic community. They observed that Poincaré, the French president was welcomed with enthusiasm at St Petersburg. The president spoke of keeping the peace in Europe and said that, presumably, his Russian counterparts agreed with that point of view. Tsar Nicholas II, Sergei Sazonov (1860-1929), the Russian minister of foreign affairs, and Izvolsky, Russian ambassador to France all sounded pacific intentions.[117]

A general war seemed unthinkable since publicly all parties seemed to want to work for peace. Hope was high that cooler heads would prevail. On Sunday August 2, the Stancioffs received a coded telegram from Dimitri in Paris: "General Conflagration imminent."[118] With a full moon shining on the sea, a perfect summer's eve received that dreadful announcement.

Official comments soon confirmed what their father had warned would transpire. The Stancioffs were stunned, as Nadejda writes:

Europe thinks about war! Humanity is so complicated, and the so-called refined civilization of modern times has not learned much. . . . There is talk of war . . . we discuss these chimeras while stressing that humanity has not changed, that man is still an animal. Who takes pleasure to pounce on another man . . . we recapitulate all the wars of the two last centuries and the number is horrendous! I hope that all of Europe will not just shake its head today.[119]

When the continental Great Powers seemed to rush toward war Nadejda wrote "Later we will call 1914 the year of folly; for now we don't know much and it is very difficult to foresee what will come."[120] While writing about the weather, she could just as easily have been predicting war: "There is a prognostication of a storm in the heaviness of the air."[121]

Vacation After All

The Stancioff family visited with the royal family as they usually did during their summers at Trois Sources and the royal children came to enjoy the cabins and beach as Nadejda recorded:

We install ourselves in front of the cabins with a violin (Ivan) a balalaika (Feo) rabbits, hazelnuts, Fly [their dog] and son, we talk politics, studies, the future... Princess Nadejda leaves at 6:30 before rejoining the Queen at the Sanatorium. Prince Boris remains until 8:00 he is happy to spend time in a house full of friends; he can count on us.[122]

While Papa followed the French government to Bordeaux, since the French feared an attack on Paris, his family enjoyed their time at the shore. A distant relation of their Italian grandmother, Cinzano, was elected Pope Benedict XV just as the war began.

The Reality of War

The declaration of war on Serbia by Austria on July 28 began the mêlée. The first battles between the Central Powers and the Entente Powers were fought in western Europe. European populations in both camps felt a preternatural enthusiasm about the conflict; combatants and civilians looked forward to a brief and decisive conflict. They expected peace by Christmas time, and volunteers rushed to join their armies before the war ended. Patriotism and nationalism enthused populations, while their leaders looked forward to a decisive victory, which would give them license to rearrange some inconvenient borders. So many diplomatic Gordian knots might potentially be cut by a rapid, decisive European war. The disposition of the Ottoman Empire's territories was one of the biggest prizes.

The realities imposed on the field of battle by modern armaments and new battlefield tactics changed the nature of the war. Machine guns, barbed wire, airplanes, and trench warfare slowed the pace of victories to a crawl, and no side could boast of superior advantage on the front. The war that first appeared destined for the life of a shooting star across the firmament became, in a few months, a war that would remain in human consciousness as the conflict that exposed the most perverse and loathsome aspects of humanity's character in a protracted brutal carnage with no precedent.

For the Stancioffs, 1914 and 1915 seemed to promise no change in their lives. Since Bulgaria remained neutral, her diplomats could continue to ply their profession as before. Once they returned to Paris, the family reentered the life of their vocation; despite wartime changes, many of their duties remained the same. Dimitri was engaged in "more talks that are secret" with the French and the Russians, but, for the most part, life continued as before.[123] The family kept track of family members who were at war, mostly French cousins, and followed war news closely. As they had a tremendous amount of information from both public and diplomatic sources on the course of the war, their view of events was fuller than ordinary Europeans; yet still they could not predict the evolution of the conflict.

Red Cross Training

Although they had had some experience with nursing during the Balkan wars Nadejda and Feo took a five-week nursing course with the Red Cross. After they passed a written as well as practical examination, they were ready to join the ranks of nurses in Paris.[124] The girls became members of the hospital run by the Japanese, the Astoria, and they took alternate shifts —Nadejda in the mornings, and Feo in the afternoons.[125] The girls were responsible for a variety of menial duties and occasionally helped with re-bandaging wounds.

Working with a cosmopolitan crew, the girls tended a variety of wounded and worked with nurses of different nationalities. Nadejda describes that "in one room we can observe the following: a wounded Norman, an emaciated Italian, a Negro looked after by Japanese and Bulgarians! An interesting and complex thing is human nature. Different types of people as well as different types of mentality."[126]

Although working in the hospital in Paris was a new occupation, the girls, especially Nadejda, continued to help their father with his work when it was necessary. Their brother's letters, as well as letters from the Count de Bourboulon, who was back in service at the palace in Sofia, kept the family abreast of events in the lives of the royal family. Working in the hospital also kept the girls well informed on the nature of war.

Living and working just miles from the front, the girls were as close as they could get to the war. They heard of gas attacks in the trenches and then received the survivors of those attacks in the hospital. Nadejda writes that:

> The new wounded arrive. . . . They recount their adventures and describe asphyxiating bombs, which the Germans have begun to use. In the 20th century, we fight with chlorine, vitriol, and petrol! Humanity has degenerated by this terrible war, at the same time that it ennobles itself; everyday we read of new horrors and of new heroisms . . . The cynical cruelty of the Germans is dis-

played each day . . . Feo and Chou took soldiers out for a walk in the woods from 2:30 – 4:30![127]

The Stancioffs' lives acquired the stilted rhythms of unique epochs; wartime transformed their worldviews and forced a reexamination of values and principles. As Nadejda wrote in her journal on 27 March 1915,

> I find an enormous difference between the Astoria hospital and the Clementine hospital in 1912; I liked the one in Sofia better. But I was a Bulgarian taking care of Bulgarians, in an atmosphere where victory was certain![128]

While the trials and disappointments of the Balkan Wars had been extreme, the course and outcome of a general European war were to be a different type of ordeal. The Stancioffs had already experienced the uneven course of victory and defeat along with other Bulgarians. They had suffered for their nation and had worked hard to help national goals. This new conflict seemed impossibly cataclysmic.

Notes

1. Nadejda Stancioff, unpublished journal, 25 June 1914, PASF.

2. Ibid. 14 February 1912.

3. Ibid. 8 February 1912.

4. Ibid. 3 March 1912.

5. Ibid. 7 April 1912.

6. Ibid. 10 April 1912.

7. Ibid. 15 August 1912.

8. Ibid. 20 September 1912.

9. Muir, *Dimitri Stancioff Patriot and Cosmopolitan.*

10. See the following for the role of women during wartime. Kate Adie, *Corsets to Camouflage Women and War* (London: Hodder & Stoughton, 2003), Gail Braybon, *Women Workers in the First World War* (London ; New York: Routledge, 1989), Joshua Goldstein, *War and Gender: How Gender Shapes the War System and Vice Versa* (Cambridge: Cambridge University Press, 2001), Margaret Randolph et al. Higonnet, ed., *Behind the Lines Gender and the Two World Wars* (New Haven: Yale University Press, 1987), James Hinton, *Women, Social Leadership, and the Second World War Continuities of Class* (Oxford: Oxford University Press, 2002), Billie Melman, ed., *Borderlines : Genders and Identities in War and Peace, 1870-1930* (New York ; London: Routledge, 1997), Efi Avdela and Angelika Psarra, "Engendering 'Greekness': Women's Emancipation and Irredentist Politics in Nineteenth-Century Greece," *Mediterranean Historical Review* 20, no. 1 (2005), Nancy M. Wingfield and Maria Bucur, *Gender and War in Twentieth-Century Eastern Europe, Indiana-Michigan Series in Russian and East European Studies* (Bloomington: Indiana University Press, 2006).

11. Nadejda Stancioff, unpublished journal, 21 October 1912, PASF.

12. Ibid. 19 November 1912.

13. Ibid. 24 October 1912.

14. Stancioff, Nadejda Memories of Love, 38. Lady Georgina, Meriel Buchanan's mother did the same in St. Petersburg, during the Great War, when she organized a hospital for the Russian wounded. Meriel took up nursing as her contribution to the (Russian) national effort in support of the war effort.

15. Nadejda Stancioff, unpublished journal, 5 November 1912, PASF.

16. Stancioff, *Nadejda Memories of Love*, 38.

17. Nadejda Stancioff, unpublished journal, 15 November 1912, PASF.

18. Stancioff and Muir, *Recollections of a Bulgarian Diplomatist's Wife*. 153.

19. Nadejda Stancioff, unpublished journal, 16 November 1912, PASF.

20. Ibid. 7 November 1912.

21. Ibid. 20 November 1912.

22. Richard Crampton, *Bulgaria 1878-1918: A History*, vol. CXXXVIII, *East European Monographs* (Boulder: Columbia University Press, 1983), 506.

23. Nadejda Stancioff, unpublished journal, 25 November 1912, PASF.

24. Ibid. 8 December 1912.

25. Muir, *Dimitri Stancioff Patriot and Cosmopolitan*. Attributed to Napoleon's mother on the probable success of his reign and cited in Dimitri Stancioff's biography, page145.

26. See de Bourboulon on page 251 and elsewhere.

27. Bourboulon, Ephemerides De Bulgarie.

28. Nadejda Stancioff, unpublished journal, 2 December 1912, PASF.

29. Ibid. 15 December 1912.

30. Ibid. 28 November 1912.

31. Ibid. 19 December 1912.

32. Ibid. 7 January 1913.

33. Ibid. 22 January 1913.

34. Ibid. 27 January 1913.

35. Ibid. 21 February 1913.

36. Ibid. 26 February 1913. "M. Déclassé is nominated Ambassador of France to St Petersburg. In the morning work and piano; lessons, decoding dispatches, writing for Papa. He takes work seriously, works without stopping and has an incredible popularity. Life in Paris is still active, intense, preoccupied, there are some nice exhibitions at the moment. I make Chou work. Maman and Papa dine in town. Feo and I spend the evening at Joyce's house playing bridge and we amused ourselves well. My trousseau is being put together and I spend detestable hours trying on dresses."

37. Ibid. 27 February 1913. "In the evening I bring my letter to…, enveloped in a Bulgarian handkerchief, with my Spanish novel, in one of the Turkish boxes, a Bulgarian necklace, an ancient medallion; all saturated in rose oil, from essence of rose in a narrow flagon from the Orient. It is less complicated than this seems; and charming to imagine."

38. Ibid. 8 February 1913.

39. Ibid. 24 January 1913.

40. Ibid. 11 May 1913.

41. Ibid. 12 April 1913.

42. Ibid. 3 July 1913.

43. Ibid. 14 February 1913.

44. Ibid. 16 February 1913.

45. Ibid. 15 April 1913.

46. Ibid. 27 February 1913.

47. Ibid. 21 April 1913.

48. Stancioff family photo albums. Camden, Maine.

49. Nadejda Stancioff, unpublished journal, 28 February 1913, PASF.

50. Billie Melman, *Women's Orients, English Women and the Middle East, 1718-1918 : Sexuality, Religion, and Work* (London: Macmillan, 1992).

51. Ibid. 25 January 1913. Italian colloquial expression which denotes the unhurried Mediterranean approach to living the good life.

52. Ibid. 1 March 1913.

53. Ibid. 2 March 1913. "I had a very good impression of my first 'out' into the monde; the cosmopolitan and elegant union was interesting and fun. There were pretty visions of women, flowers, gems and waves of capitol perfumes. [On the next day Nadejda records:] Feo, Chou, and I go to a reception for children at the Kotchoubeys'; we have a good time; our three young hostesses, Olly, Alix and Zezi are pretty, intelligent and original, three enchanting flower. They have Russian charm linked with the most Parisian culture."

54. Ibid. 23 June 1913.

55. Ibid. 25 June 1913.

56. Ibid. 2 April 1913.

57. Ibid.

58. Ibid. 7 May 1913.

59. See Nadejda Stancioff journal entries in spring 1913.

60. Nadejda Stancioff, unpublished journal, 17 April 1913, PASF.

61. The following are entries from Nadejda's journal in spring 1913.

March 7— Papa is in his office; we arrange the archives.

March 8— It feels good to be all united [the Bulgarians in Paris] we thank God for all his benedictions [and] pray arduously for the war.

March 11— Long dispatches in the evening. Politics at a standstill, still quite serious. Germany and France attack each other [in the press] with a lot of acrimony.

March 12— No specific information about the war. It is said the Greeks will not be able to take Janina.

March 15— Papa works hard and I help him to the best my ability. I go to a soirée at the Elysée with Papa; it is interesting and pretty.

March 19— Horrible news: the King of Greece is assassinated...Papa and I trembled that the assassin was not a Bulgarian; he was a deranged Socialist Greek. We thank God for having delivered us from that shame!

March 20— Ministerial crisis here...Briand give a speech [at the Chamber of Deputies] that is a work of art.

March 28— Work correspondence, reading newspapers, and [the work of a] private secretary, I write letters all the daylong. Papa and I hold pens, bent over our papers.

March 29— I...work a lot in the morning with Papa who is very preoccupied especially with the sudden intervention of Austria. He's working a lot on a financial article, which will appear tomorrow along with his interview with *le Matin*.

March 31— A very full morning. Worked all morning.... Solemn mass at Russian church in the honor of the fall of Adrianople; it was requested by Papa and the Bulgarian Legation...Papa invited the representatives of our allies; in addition the Russian military attaché. The church is packed; in attendance members of the [diplomatic] colonies and legations Russian, Bulgarian, Serbian, Greek; members of the Patrician aristocracy, friends of our king. The Te Deum is followed by a Requiem.

April 1— I work a lot with Papa. Papa busies himself with a great deal of energy on the question of our indemnity; he doesn't rest for a minute! Evening of writing with Papa. We truly have a formidable amount of work each day.

April 4— Papa talks to me about politics and I listen to him religiously; he is so intelligent and interesting.

62. For example, while her mother and Feo were at Menton, (a fashionable resort on the French Riviera), she helped her father with his work, took care of Ivan when he became sick with stomach flu, supervised Chou with her lessons and found time to manage the household.

63. Nadejda Stancioff, unpublished journal, 5 April 1913, PASF.

64. The following are entries from Nadejda's journal in spring 1913.

April 5— [I] spend morning working paperwork and playing the piano. Papa and Raffalovitch, one of the Russian delegates of the financial commission, consult on indemnity.

April 8—To the horse races with Mme. Raffalovitch; ... we talk about people and Russian things and we hardly look at the horses. She takes me to an elegant tea at Prillon; lots of pretty Americans and pretty flowers. There are lots of dispatches tonight.

65. Nadejda Stancioff, unpublished journal, 10 April 1913, PASF. "I love the cosmopolitan life and the luxury of grand European hotels. Nyky, Papa and I talk about politics and we eat oranges and black olives and we decipher dispatches and as we listen to the falling rain, the melancholy tears of this great world."

66. See entries starting with 12 April 1913. These entries emphasize the rollercoaster ride of their emotions and Bulgaria's fortunes in that critical period.

67. See journal entries on various dates when Maman was away.

68. The following all mention the roles of female spouses in the success of diplomatic missions. Buchanan, *My Mission to Russia, and Other Diplomatic Memories*, Fernandez-Azabal, *Romance and Revolutions*, Hickman, *Daughters of Britannia the Lives and Times of Diplomatic Wives*, Hughes, *The Accidental Diplomat Dilemmas of the Trailing Spouse*, Jeffereys-Jones, *Changing Differences Women and the Shaping of American Foreign Policy, 1917-1994*.

69. See journal entries on 4, 6, and 7 May 1913, PASF.

70. Nadejda Stancioff, unpublished journal, 1 June 1913, PASF.

71. Entries on that critical period see 13 and 14 May 1913 and later.

72. Nadejda Stancioff, unpublished journal, 25 July 1913, PASF.

73. Elena Boianova Statelova, Radoslav Popov, Vasilka Tankova, *Istoriia Na Bûlgarskata Diplomtsiia, 1879-1913* (Sofia: Fondatsiia Otvoreno obshtestvo, 1994).

74. Nadejda Stancioff, unpublished journal, 10 July 1913, PASF.

75. Ibid. 12 July 1913.

76. Helene Stancioff, unpublished letter, 14 July 1913, Nada VIII, PASF.

77. Nadejda Stancioff, unpublished journal, 7 July 1913, PASF.

78. Nadejda Stancioff, unpublished journal, 5 August 1913, PASF.

79. Ibid. 8 July 1913.

80. Ibid. 9 July 1913.

81. Ibid. 11 August 1913.

82. Ibid. 29 August 1913.

83. Ibid. 12 August 1913.

84. Ibid. 18 July 1913.

85. Ibid. 6 August 1913.

86. Ibid. 3 August 1913.

87. See Nadejda's journal entries for 16 January and 3 August 1913, expressions like these are sprinkled throughout her journals.

88. Nadejda Stancioff, unpublished journal, 5 June 1913, PASF.

89. On the Bulgarian government's attempts see Barbara Jelavich, *History of the Balkans*, 2 vols. (Cambridge ; New York: Cambridge University Press, 1983), Zhorzheta

Nazûrska, *Bûlgarskata Dûrzhava I Neinite Maltsinstva 1879-1885* (Sofia: LIK, 1999), Maria Nikolaeva Todorova, *Balkan Identities : Nation and Memory* (Washington Square, N.Y.: New York University Press, 2004), Antonina Zheliazkova, Bozhidar Aleksiev, Zhorzheta Nazûrska, ed., *Miusiulmanskite Obshtnosti Na Balkanite I V Bûlgaria* (Sofia: IMIR, 1997).
90. Crampton, *Bulgaria 1878-1918: A History.*, 429.
91. Ibid. See too Roumen Daskalov and Tsvetan Todorov on the Bulgarian economy.
92. See first page of Nadejda's journal 1914.
93. Nadejda Stancioff, unpublished journal, 9 January 1914, PASF.
94. Ibid. 28 January 1914.
95. Ibid. 29 January 1914.
96. Ibid.
97. Ibid. 30 January 1914.
98. Ibid. 4 February 1914.
99. Ibid. 5 February 1914.
100. Ibid. 10 February 1914.
101. Ibid. 14 February 1914.
102. Ibid. 26 February 1914.
103. Ibid. 16 March 1914.
104. Ibid.
105. Ibid. 24 March 1914.
106. Ibid. 25 March 1914.
107. Ibid. 25 February 1914.
108. Ibid. 2 April 1914.
109. Ibid. 25 March 1914.
110. Ibid. 1 April 1914.
111. Ibid. 23 June 1914.
112. Ibid. 28 June 1914.
113. Stancioff, Nadejda Memories of Love, 41.
114. Nadejda Stancioff, unpublished journal, 29 June 1914, PASF.
115. Ibid. 24 June 1914.
116. Ibid. 27 July 1914.
117. Ibid.
118. Stancioff, Nadejda Memories of Love, 43.
119. Nadejda Stancioff, unpublished journal, 28 and 29 July 1914, PASF.
120. Ibid. 5 August 1914.
121. Ibid. 31 July 1914.
122. Ibid. 10 August 1914.
123. See journal entries 1914-1915.
124. Nadejda Stancioff, unpublished journal, 5 January 1915, PASF.
125. Ibid. 5 February 1915.
126. Ibid. 19 March 1915.
127. Ibid. 26 April 1915.
128. Ibid. 27 March 1915.

Part II:
A Second Generation of Diplomats

5
Growing Up Fast: World War

"Will the tragedy of 1913 begin again? ... we are mourning the victims in advance..."
Nadejda Stancioff, unpublished journal[1]

Deciding to side with the Central Powers in 1915, primarily Germany and Austria-Hungary, against the Entente Powers, France, Great Britain, and Russia, Ferdinand hoped to recoup the humiliations Bulgaria experienced in the Balkan War of 1913. When Dimitri disagreed with his sovereign over the latter's decision to join Germany and the Central Powers in 1915, King Ferdinand was furious. The king sent Stancioff a telegram that read "I did not ask for your opinion."[2] This was a relatively mild rebuke from a king with an acerbic character. Indeed, that reputation was soon proved out because Stancioff received, another, unofficial message—a coarse ad hominem attack: "Vil laquais de la Russie, vous pourrez alors vous faire foutre et vous faire gouverner par un cosaque quelconque qui vous convienne mieux que moi [!][Vile Russian laquais go f___ yourself and be ruled by some Cossak who is more to your liking than me!][3] Ferdinand had equivocated as long as possible: Stancioff and others questioned his decision. He wanted his revenge for the Balkan War debacles, and he would have it.

Bulgaria Enters the War

King Ferdinand was not a foolish or impetuous leader. He understood that remaining neutral during the first year of the European war gained Bulgaria some much needed breathing space. The country would not have benefited in any way by participating on either side of the conflict in 1914. Neutrality permitted the king's government a host of facilitations with respect to keeping domestic political control and nurturing economic stability.

As a neutral power, the Bulgarians took the opportunity to be equally generous with both warring parties, using good will gestures to assuage both sides. Queen Eleanore sent Bulgarian cigarettes to the French, English, Russian, and Austrian wounded.[4]

Neutrality also gave the government the excuse to declare a state of emergency, ban the Narodno Sûbranie, and muzzle authentic opposition presses. The government also signed a defensive pact with the Ottoman Empire soon after the outbreak of the war.

While to outside observers, the Bulgarians were adamant about neutrality, in reality, King Ferdinand constantly shifted his sights on the opportunities posed by various alliances—both with and against each belligerent bloc. Ultimately, what led to the decision to join the Central Powers was not so much an affinity for those particular powers as a clear indication from the Entente, that they would steadfastly support Bulgaria's primary enemies, the neighboring states that had gobbled up so much of Bulgaria's territories: Dobrudja, Macedonia, and Thrace. Recovering the losses of previous conflicts was in Ferdinand's grasp.

Radoslavov's government and the king approached the Germans as early as January 1915 about what possible price could be exacted for Bulgaria's entry into the war on their side. Following the course of the war with keen interest the Bulgarians were seeking an opportunity to advance their policy goals. The Germans were willing to be magnanimous in terms of territorial concessions. However, the Bulgarians watched the progress of the war carefully and held their cards closely. Instead of entering the war on the side of the Germans, in July 1914 the Bulgarians instead extracted a low interest loan from them, just for remaining neutral. At the same time, the Bulgarians negotiated with the Entente for favorable terms of admission into their camp.

The plurality of allies who made up the Entente muddied the secret negotiations and the offer price for Bulgaria's entry into the war on their side. Quite understandably, it was uncomfortable, even risky, to offer the Bulgarians lands which their neighbors already claimed, regardless of the territory's historical provenance. Therefore, the language of these negotiations with the Entente Powers remained somewhat vague; the Central Powers, on the other hand, were quite willing to part with sizeable portions of their enemies' territories in exchange for Bulgaria's participation in their camp.

Ultimately, it was not the generosity of the territorial settlement that made up King Ferdinand and Radoslavov's minds but rather the dramatic victories of the Germans against the Russians in the east. The once mighty Russian empire was routed, and its armies forced into retreat. This dramatic change in the balance of power in Europe seemed to be the future – Ferdinand was convinced the Germans would be victorious in this war.

The other tipping point was the geographic reality of fighting on two fronts. With the Entente Bulgaria would be squeezed by enemy belligerents, while joining with the Central Powers would permit the luxury of fighting on a single front. When the Germans convinced the Turks to concede eastern Thrace to the Bulgarians, the choice was easy.

Finally, and significantly, the Entente Powers' failure to lure Bulgaria to their side was an error in judgment; the Entente's poorly conceived campaign to woo the Bulgarian monarch was a feeble attempt to gain the allegiance of Bulgaria. While the Germans and Austrians understood that they could exploit Ferdinand's weakness for flattery and exorbitant gifts, the French, Russians, and British never attempted to influence him personally but focused instead on the disaffected Bulgarian politicians and their parties. That significant lack of judgment cost the Entente dearly in the game for influence. In September 1915, Bulgaria joined what appeared to be a winning power bloc—the Central Powers.

An Interlude in Rome

On May 29, 1915, Dimitri Stancioff was assigned to the post of Bulgaria's representative to Rome, Italy had already declared war on Austria and Germany and joined the Entente. Leaving Paris was a painful process; the family had enjoyed six years in France, and their relationships with the French government, press, the diplomatic community in general had been exceedingly cordial.

It was a matter of distinct pride to the Stancioffs that when Papa went to deliver his letter of recall to the President of the French Republic, Poincaré the Frenchman informed Dimitri that he had personally interceded on his behalf to Sofia. Asking the Bulgarian government to let Dimitri Stancioff stay on in Paris until the end of the war. This was an extremely flattering and unusual gesture and one that spoke to the high regard with which Dimitri's representation was esteemed in the Quay d'Orsay. As the family prepared for their departure to Rome, with little suspicion of the changes under way in Bulgaria's foreign policies, they prayed for the success of the Entente.

In Rome, amidst unpacking and arranging their new home, the family discussed what possible hints they could garner from rumors and sources in the government about the direction of Bulgaria's foreign policy. Could it change from neutrality to something else? Could the apparent amicable discussions with the Turks on a Bulgarian outlet to the Aegean lead Bulgaria to consider throwing in her lot with the Central Powers? Would Bulgaria consider an alliance with the Germans if the Turks did as well?

The Stancioffs foresaw the inevitability of these moves, or rather felt them before they became fact. Nadejda reflects on these feelings:

> Our government is becoming more and more arbitrary; we are basically governed by two exclusive owners: the King and Radoslavoff! . . . .they do not pay attention to neither the diplomats, nor the heads of the opposition, the Sûbranie is not convened! It is extraordinary. A good and courageous but useless protest of the opposition. . . . at the moment only the Germans advance and are successful![5]

A Terrible Vengeance

King Ferdinand's frustration with the outcome of the First Balkan War, and the ineptitude of the Great Powers to help settle quarrels after the Second Balkan War, were partially instrumental in his ill-conceived decision to join Germany and Austria in 1915. By 1915, he felt he had little choice in the matter, since alliance with Germany would at least undo the harm of the disastrous Second Balkan War.

The Treaty of Bucharest, which ended that Second Balkan War, deprived Bulgaria of all the gains of the first Balkan War. Apocryphal or not, one can imagine that King Ferdinand did indeed declare "Ma vengeance sera terrible! [My vengeance will be terrible!]" in 1913 when that treaty was signed.[6] The decision to join the Central Powers would give Bulgaria finally, the Macedonian territories that the Treaty of San Stefano promised, the Bulgarian armies had occupied, and his subjects so desperately craved. However, not all Bulgarians were convinced that joining the Central Powers was a advantageous option.

Ferdinand's decision to join the Central Powers left the Stancioff family feeling dejected. They were not optimistic about the benefits of engaging in another war on the heels of recent defeats.

> Will the tragedy of 1913 begin again? Everything points to that possibility. ...I still dare to hope, to believe that this mobilization is simply a measure of intimidation, of national pride.. we should at the very least keep quiet and make ourselves invisible. One more time Rumania and Greece show themselves to be more adroit than us.[7]

Bulgaria entered the war in October 1915, with the understanding that she would occupy, immediately, the Macedonian territories promised her; this occupation would primarily entail fighting the Serbs. Bulgaria would also gain a portion of Thrace, which would give her access to the port at Dedeagach and a part of the rest of the territorial spoils once the war was over. At home, neither the Bulgarian population nor most of the opposition parties were in favor of joining in the European war, but the king's will and Radoslavov's intransigence before the Narodno Sûbranie proved an unbreakable combination. Opposition in Bulgaria was widespread despite the fact that the war, in fall 1915, appeared headed to a conclusion favorable to the Central Powers.

Joining the Central Powers had another far-reaching impact on Bulgaria. On the last day of March 1916, as Bulgaria joined the Central Powers in war, the Julian calendar was retired and the new Gregorian calendar erased fourteen days and pushed Bulgaria into April 14th and the western style system.

Living in Limbo

The Stancioffs' stay in Rome was frustratingly brief. When Bulgaria declared itself in the German camp, the Stancioffs had to pack up and move once again in October 1915. Their professional status was unregulated, their father had no new assignment, and so the family searched for a temporary layover point while a European war exacerbated travel plans. They headed for limbo in Switzerland.

The Stancioffs made the best of the situation with skiing, skating, and sledding excursions. Geneva seemed full of spies as well as refuge seekers and Nadejda heard a variety of languages in the streets including Armenian, French, German, Greek, Italian, Romanian, Russian, Serbian, and Turkish. The family felt that the Bulgarian colony was of the "fourth order!" not people to the Stancioffs' tastes.

Although not officially a member of her father's staff, Nadejda diligently continued working for him while in Geneva. She spent long hours gluing newspaper clippings—on subjects of interest such as the progress of the war, articles on notable people—in albums as well as translating and composing letters. She missed her hospital duties. In Paris she had felt a part of a greater war effort nursing, helping with charitable work, entertaining the wounded or helping them write letters home all of which made her feel "proud and tender for humanity." Nadejda wished for those responsibilities again.[8] While forced to remain relatively inactive in Switzerland, she felt distanced from the war and quite guilty about not doing her part to relieve the suffering.

Dimitri did return to Bulgaria to do his part for the war effort while his family remained in Switzerland. The separation was painful for all of them, especially his wife, who felt apprehensive about their professional future. Although Maman arranged it so that her children would continue with a normal daily routine, which included their lessons, she wanted most of all to return to the family's most familiar abode—*Trois Sources*—all together, along with her dear husband. Yet they were aware that the villa's location in a potential war zone would make returning to their home virtually impossible. Yet, returning to the familiar location, all together and safe, had a common appeal in wartime.

Traveling Back to the Orient

By May 1916, the Stancioffs had permission from the Bulgarian government to return to Bulgaria. Nadejda's musings on this odyssey are typical; she professed Switzerland to be "peaceful, antiseptic, honest, and banal" while she perceived their destination as "the Orient, which is always troubled, uncertain, tragic, and savage."[9]

Their trip back to Bulgaria was filled with adventures. First, when they attempted to get their passports from their own embassy in Berne, Bulgarian embassy functionaries held them up. The two men whom Nadejda accused of holding up their paperwork were the second secretary of the legation and the former military attaché to Rome. These two felt the need to use the power of their new positions to avenge "certain little incidents in Rome over the demissionned Stancioffs."[10] Thus, they spent three weeks in Berne, where Papa's contacts in the military, specifically General Taneff, were more helpful. Nadejda comments that "Bulgarian officers have much more integrity than the other citizens of this complex country do," which is an opinion shared by her father.[11] Dimitri often found military men trustworthy and was forever skeptical of the motives of diplomatic representatives and their social group, the aristocratic elites. While the family waited and received a series of contradictory directives, they saw much of the city, found it charming and called it "old German" while they lived in the "ultra modern" Schweizerhof hotel.

When they finally had a clear signal to leave, they prepared themselves for the trip prudently tearing up their French journals, and even disposing of their English books and speaking to each other only in German and Bulgarian.[12] When they attempted to cross into Austria from Switzerland, what followed was a tragi-comedy, a bureaucratic farce.

At the Austrian border they entered a shack which served as the customs station. A uniformed and much-decorated lieutenant with a Dantesque profile, with a prominent bony nose, clouded eyes, and an inflexible jaw took their passports, while his cohorts began inspecting their luggage. The inspection was extremely thorough, including opening umbrellas, going through each compartment of their suitcases, going through their most intimate possessions, even trying on their hats. All these activities took place while the customs agents maintained a running commentary on the quality of the merchandise.

To further the humiliation, each family member had to endure the indignity of disrobing before a matron down to their chemises while she ran her fingers through their hair. This indignity was all borne first with a suppressed fury and then a wild desire to laugh at the absurdity of the situation. Finally, their train departed while they were still trying to put their luggage right. Then, to add insult to injury, the lieutenant announced that they would have to cross not through Austria at all but instead through Zurich into Germany. The family's reactions were predictable, and Nadejda's description is eloquently comical:

> From four corners of the shack we emerge to register our protests and we energetically proclaim, in a German that is half Parisian and half Slav that the President of the Council of Ministers of Bulgaria Radoslavoff, himself had given us the authorization to return to Bulgaria.[13]

This information apparently softened up the menacing lieutenant enough for him to allow them to telegraph Vienna and obtain further proof of their worthiness to travel through Austria. Meanwhile, he ordered the Stancioffs to a hotel for the night. Nadejda's indignation was complete. From the perspective of a nationalist, Nadejda, the Bulgarians had helped their allies against the "oily Serbs," and, therefore, their Austrian-German allies should have shown their gratitude by treating their allies' citizens with more grace.

The hotel *Baren,* they discovered, was more like a military headquarters than a refuge from bureaucratic blunderers. Ironically, their "Torquemada" dined there along with them. In close quarters they could thus eye each other over "war food and detestable bread." The family's meager funds permitted them to order only venison and boiled rhubarb.

In the town of Feldkirch, which Nadejda described as coming right out of the Middle Ages, she observed that the Bulgarian flag and the Turkish flag flew next to each other on public buildings. She could not help but comment that "life is a bizarre thing. Everything changes, everything passes."[14] When the orders permitting them to proceed arrived, signed by the Austrian minister of foreign affairs, their overzealous allies were shamefaced as they waved them on their journey.[15]

In Vienna, the stores were perfectly elegant and of impeccable taste, and the women were dressed in the latest Parisian fashions; and gaiety bubbled in the streets.

Home to Varna

In Bulgaria, on the train ride from Russe to Varna, the family observed war preparations—mainly defense works against Romania and trenches—first hand. Maman and the children arrived to a Varna full of unfamiliar faces, Germans in uniform, military regulations governing the lives of civilians.

The militarization of the country became most obvious when the family reached their final destination. They were compelled to seek the permission of the general in charge of Varna to spend time at their own villa. The city was one of two Bulgarian ports and it had to be scrupulously defended. Varna was a fortified city of high strategic importance with batteries installed on the Galata and Euxinograd points to guard the harbor. The Stancioffs found a German garrison installed in the outskirts of town along the road to their villa.

After they found lodgings in the city, the Stancioffs routinely spent their days working on the gardens of *Les Trois Sources*. They even managed to bend the rules of their modified access to the villa when they had an old friend, an officer stationed at the fort, come for evenings of music and dinner, although they had subdued lighting, and the drapes were pulled shut so that the house would not be visible from the sea.

The Stancioffs enjoyed their beach, built a chicken coop, watered their gardens, and entertained guests on their property. In fact, they were able to nourish themselves almost entirely from their estate; as Nadejda remarks, "Our menus are biblical." Moreover, the family was current on all the news of the war, since the Ministry of Foreign Affairs supplied them with European newspapers.

Since he had been dismissed from his diplomatic post Dimitri had to regulate his status as a male eligible for military service in wartime. He received a "helpful" suggestion from the king—to ask the government for an extension of his "vacation" from the diplomatic service, and apparently, this idea suited the patriarch of the family perfectly.[16] Dimitri served on the Macedonian front, mostly near Kavadartsi, in his capacity as captain of the Royal Horse Guards starting in winder 1916.[17] Later he organized Red Cross and Ambulance work for Allied prisoners in Plovdiv.

Wartime mobilization affected the Stancioffs' ability to keep domestic help; thus, the children were even more occupied on the property than customary. For Nadejda, that work was not overly onerous, since she found that it was necessary to "...be intellectual while one waters, cleans, or while mixing dough, it is what we do, and the combination of tasks is successful!"[18]

Seeking Refuge in Svishtov

At the end of July 1916, the Stancioffs received official notice form General Kantardjieff, Commandant of the Fortress of Varna, that they must leave the villa immediately. The family faced a complex decision about where to go. The rumors of an imminent conflict with Romania led them to turn to the king for advice. His reply gave them options between Svishtov, Sofia, and inner city Varna.[19] The king was also thoughtful enough to ask the authorities in charge of Varna to assist the family if they chose to depart.

The Stancioffs chose to head for Svishtov, Papa's hometown. There they would have the advantage of being close to family and would be able to supplement their food provisions with the produce of some family properties in the area. However, they risked displacement yet again if hostilities broke out between the Bulgarians and Romanians. In addition, the location was prone to malarial outbreaks. Nonetheless, despite dire warnings to the contrary by their local friends, they chose to leave for the town on the Danube.

Their entourage left Varna with four horses, two pigs, four chickens, and four servants (Kosta, Mara, Ivane, and Gerassime). They traveled in "a patriarchal manner" according to Nadejda, and passed the time managing the servants, the baggage, and the animals. "We decidedly do not have a talent for simplifying life!"[20]

While in this form of internal exile, they continued to oversee their properties. For example, while in Svishtov the family made excursions to an inn which they owned outside the village of Belina, which their father rented out, then to their vineyard at Stklen. The inn was now an officers' club for the Austrians. War eventually visited Bulgarian territories.

The Stancioffs were in Svishtov when Romania declared war on Austria at the end of August and began to bombard first Austrian vessels leaving Russe, and then Bulgarian territory. The family heard the first cannon on August 29 at 3 p.m. while drinking their coffee. According to Nadejda, the family was nonplussed: "We are neither astonished nor surprised nor alarmed, but very interested….Papa goes to the Commandant, Ivan with friends to the port "to see" we women continue to play our music….I feel as indifferent as the Danube."[21] Perhaps the expectation of the outbreak of hostilities with Romania prepared the Stancioffs better than ordinary citizens for a military assault.

A day later, however, after they saw the trajectory of the projectiles from one of their windows, they joined the mass exodus of Svishtov residents. Where would the Stancioffs go next? Resolution arrived via a telegram from the king. Ferdinand ordered them to go live in Plovdiv while giving authorization to use his palace.[22]

That strange "order" saved them the effort and expense of finding a suitable residence in time of war. They were logically grateful. Nadejda called the order an unexpected solution and "proof" of the king's "good will." The family was delighted to live in the "quaint oriental town." They would receive the royal treatment, travel in style and comfort with their own train car, and live in the king's residence. They must have discussed their prospective new home with some relish. Maman had spent a great deal of time there and had happy memories of her stays with the king, Princesses Clementine, and Marie-Louise, while Feo, and Nadejda had spent Holy Week there in 1907.

Surviving in Wartime

The palace in Plovdiv was a Bulgarian Revival house that once belonged to Madame Petroff-Chomakoff (lady-in-waiting to the queen); it had a little garden and a large courtyard, and most of the house was enclosed by a high wall. The family brought with them three servants: The palace servants would augment their staff: a steward, Dimitri, and a guard, Nicolas.

The Stancioffs' internal exile—from October 1916 to July 1918—was made comfortable by the fact that they had the use of the entire residence, the garden, and access to all the fruits and vegetables grown there. The palace garden had a guard, a little old man, three Albanian workers, and a few prisoners. Therefore, although they were not at their home, the Stancioffs felt nearly as safe, secure, and provided for as they would have in their villa on the Black Sea. They could enjoy strawberries for breakfast and decorate their home with bouquets of roses.

The city was cosmopolitan, with not only Bulgarians but also Armenians, Greeks, Jews, and Turks. It had numerous orthodox churches, a synagogue, mosques and three public gardens. According to Nadejda, there were so many minarets rising up to the sky that when viewed from a distance, the city appeared to be all Muslim. She later compared Constantinople to Plovdiv. Feo wrote that the "Thracian retreat" was a happy time for her sister.[23]

The royal residence was on one of the seven hills of Plovdiv in one of the oldest parts of town. This section of town contained rough-hewn stone-paved streets with improbably steep ascents and descents that offered commanding views of the city. It was the kind of picturesque, Old World feel that appealed to Nadejda's sense of the exotic, the Orient.

Nadejda listed several notable edifices in their neighborhood: St. Constantine Church; the Cathedral Sveta Bogoroditsa; the Greek school and orphanage; St. Dimitri; the chapel, St. Petka, and the metropolitan church, Sveta Marina. The houses and buildings in this area, virtually all surrounded with high stone walls, lent the neighborhood an air of mystery and a hint of possible intrigue. The neighborhood recalled the Orient, the world where western civilization and the rules of conduct among people were different from Europe. This view was one that had come to dominate European concepts of the nether regions of the continent. An imagined place and culture, the European perception of the Orient as a region of deception, languor, and savagery made it enigmatic.

The Orient of Nadejda's imagination was everything other Europeans believed it to be. It was a place where men dominated and ruled and women were submissive and prized for their decorative qualities.[24] While she recognized that she was not one of those cadres of submissive, objectified women she also let her imagination play with the possibilities of pretending.

Gender roles in Europe and the Orient were in transition during the war years. However, overall, women were relegated to the domestic sphere while their men roamed from home in the public sphere not much different than in the east of Nadejda's imagination.

Throughout Europe women who considered themselves as a rank above the working classes opened themselves up for criticism for being bold and out of their "place" for working out of the home, even if by virtue of their talents, they performed certain socially acceptable occupations such as teaching or nursing. Although women had proven that they were capable of leaving the domestic sphere for the public realm, and performing capably, social convention expected that they would remain at home. The men of the family, who often chose to continue to perceive women as weaker, even less competent, than men, regulated their lives. In any event, women continued to be more prized for their qualities as objects of affection or private enjoyment and for their gifts as practitioners of the fine arts: singing, playing musical instruments, painting, and politely and adeptly conversing.

Rationing and Shortages

The war put an incredible strain on the economic infrastructure of Bulgaria. Already weakened by two successive wars, the country was unprepared and ill-equipped to handle another wartime crisis. Radoslavov's government managed to survive the war primarily due to the resolution of virtually all Bulgarian territorial desiderata in the country's favor. Also until mid-1917, the victories of the Central Powers seemed to augur a certain peace.

However, war profiteering, especially in foodstuffs, at first aggravated, then made dire by German and Austrian pillaging of the food supplies in the form of exports for their constituencies, led to significant unrest. Riots, demonstrations, mass protests spread throughout Bulgaria and increased in seriousness through 1918. The civilian population was starving, a fact that the government seemed to ignore.

Soldiers began to rebel at the front because of the suffering of their loved ones at home. Even their Allies' better-supplied and -equipped regiments caused friction at the front, as Bulgarian soldiers observed the generous food rations and the better defensive and offensive preparedness of their fellows in arms.[25] The German and Austrian soldiers even had better equipment to build trenches, and, therefore, experienced a higher survival rate.

In Plovdiv, the Stancioffs also began to feel the pinch of the war-time shortages. The rise in prices of the most common commodities appeared outrageous. Nadejda remarks that

> Wheat is rare and bad, epicerie horribly expensive; butter, cheese, oil, and fat are almost completely missing. We have only meat and vegetables in abundance. Salt and sugar are worth their weight in gold! We no longer make jams, what a disaster for the women of the Orient![26]

Over the course of their stay in the royal residence, the pressures of the war-time economy, and their inability to travel far from the city created some foreseeable stressors. Although they continued to relish their comfortable and beautiful abode and access to the royal garden, the wear and tear of everyday life forced even Nadejda to become disheartened with the care it took to supply the material elements of everyday life. In exasperation, she complained in her journal:

> The bother of having to busy oneself with a trio of servants who are ingrates, unreasonable and vulgar like their race...Oh beauty, nature, the arts, gardens, museums, statues, fountains, perfumes, come to my aid and chase the phantoms of crates of sugar, gasoline cans, bags of rice and basins of butter. Gas virtually impossible to find. Soap precious like gold with an exorbitant price! No wine to buy; fruits extremely expensive. Meat, vegetables, fish are the only affordable commodities. Bread is rationed; sometimes the bakeries have none to sell.[27]

Wartime rationing was the purview of the government body called the Directorate for Economic and Social Welfare. Run by a former general whose subordinates were also military men, the directorate dealt with the domestic issues in a time of war. Its powers were extensive and stretched from the agrarian and industrial sectors' production and distribution quotas to wage and price controls. Because of its actions, especially during the last year of the war, Bulgaria averted the worst suffering.

The fluctuation of the bread ration alone illustrated the wartime crises in Bulgaria and at the front. While in spring 1917, bread rations were set to 500 grams per person per day, with exceptions for workers in heavy industry and soldiers at 800 grams and 1000 grams, respectively, the situation one year later was radically different.

In April 1918, bread was not only rationed at smaller quantities, but now the rich would receive less and pay more—300 grams for them and 400 grams for the poor. Soon after that order, rations were reduced again to 200 grams for the rich, 250 grams for the poor, while soldiers and heavy laborers received the same ration—400 grams per day.[28]

Despite strict controls and some truly creative and energetic innovations on the part of the directorate, industrial output during the war managed only 65 percent of the output of the same industries in 1912.[29] As the war dragged on, the effectiveness of the directorate declined, especially when it came to grain requisitions. Bulgarian peasants reacted the same way their Russian counterparts would react to collectivization a decade later; they hid, destroyed their surpluses, and, in the end, produced only enough for personal consumption.

By late 1916, meat and butter were unavailable, and other essentials had become prohibitively expensive. The Stancioffs obtained supplies such as rice, tea, and coffee through Papa's friends. Nadejda writes, "I do not know what would have become of us without the talents and activities of Papa."[30]

The Stancioffs' information on the progress of the war came from their father's military contacts and Bulgarian censored media; the latter was nearly useless, and the western media, which arrived very late or not at all, was little better.

Alone in the evenings, they read old issues of *Revue de Paris* and *Revues des Deux-Mondes*, as well as works on Byzantine history and novels. They also had illustrated papers in English, French, Italian, and German. Nadejda continued to supervise her youngest sister's studies as she had done in Paris. In addition, her father had rented a piano; playing music in the evenings helped the family regain some of the feeling of home and reintroduced some of the beauty missing in their lives.

Meanwhile, Ivan was accepted into the fleet and assigned to serve as a sailor in the coastal battery next to *Les Trois Sources*. Since her brother would have the opportunity to sleep at home in his own bed and have Kosta, their servant, as a kind of orderly or protector, it occurred to Nadejda that her brother's assignment had "the feel of a military service of a member of the royal house!"[31] This kind of privileged treatment was a boon of their station.

Ivan's service segued into a training course for Reserve Officer School in Kniazhevo. He soon left his comfortable assignment for an experiences in the barracks. His account of that life echoed the universal experiences in Europe and elsewhere of death by the dread influenza pandemic or "so-called" Spanish flu, rather than a bullet. He reported attending so many of those funerals for his comrades that, along with firing the customary salute over the graves, the eating of the traditional boiled wheat sprinkled with a cinnamon cross was so frequent that it made the scent forever a morbid association for him.[32]

Ivan's last contact with King Ferdinand happened by chance when Ivan served as honor guard to the king of Bavaria during the latter's visit to Bulgaria in the last weeks of the war. King Ferdinand acknowledged Ivan's presence by making the malocchio sign at him, the Italian hand gesture that wards off the evil eye.[33]

Ivan eventually did serve with the retreating Bulgarian army in an artillery regiment on the Macedonian front and had a narrow escape when his unit was dispersed by enemy fire. His return to Sofia was forestalled by the Radomir Rebellion, the so called *Voinishko vûstanie* or Soldiers' rebellion. A brief army rebellion at the end of the war, when conditions on the front and domestically led to extreme hardship and frustration among the troops, who rebelled in September 1918. Eventually, Ivan found his way home via the familiar mountain paths over Vitosha.

Russian Revolution

While living in internal exile and facing increasing difficulties acquiring the most essential commodities, the Stancioffs received the news of revolution in the Russian Empire.

The family read about the ordeals of Russia at first without much alarm but then, riveted by the revolutionary events, their nonchalance developed into dismay. When the imperial *ukaz* (decree) suspended the Duma in Russia, Nadejda observed that the move was "bad, very bad and a dangerous example for France and England."[34]

The news out of Russia was confusing, but the imminent collapse of the system was real. The Stancioffs' sympathies were a reflection of the family's social standing and class-based point of view. Nadejda writes "Out of tradition, respect, love of the past and a hatred for the system of democracy I mourn this fall of Russian imperialism. The abdication of the Emperor is the most nerve-racking thing of the century; it is a shame for the Entente."[35]

Nadejda had extremely fond memories of her childhood in Russia and she referred to them often. She practiced a form of nostalgia that was both nourishing and selective in its emphasis; she loved the language, the people, and her memories.

At times, her musings had the quality of a Russian expatriate reminiscing solemnly about the good old days—when recollections of moonlit sleigh rides and miles of birch forest and summer vacations at dachas in the country were shining memories of an invented, perfect Russian world. That world held suspended the goodness of the Russian peasant, the idyllic village life, the benevolent Russian Orthodox Church, and paternalistic Russian nobles in its sphere.

Nadejda's memories and her perceptions of life in St. Petersburg, of vacations at "their" dacha at Tarkhovka, the Gulf of Finland, were idealized mementos of her life in Russia. These memories of her childhood years were as precious as those of any child holding on to shreds of early memory as a comforting blanket of one's own history. Musing about her childhood memories, Nadejda wrote:

> [When I am sick] I immediately revisit the Bulgarian veil, which we put on the lamp when I had influenza in Russia. As I tossed and turned, I would fix my gaze on that curtained lamp for entire hours; I would create a story, the pleats would become ravines and the folds, mountains, and I would recount the histories of the Chinese and the Hindus. One of my numerous memories, of my dear childhood in my unforgettable Petrograd![36]

Throughout her life, Nadejda followed the developments in Russia with more than casual interest because of her attachment to the people and the land. The Russian Revolution was as difficult for her to bear as it was for many Russians. She saw it as an event that swept away the essence of Russia and replaced it with features that were ugly, brutal, and meaningless.

The structure of the established class system, in Russia and the rest of Europe, had preserved a certain order in life around which the *haute bourgeoisie* like the Stancioffs could build their lives. The removal of that structure signaled the end of the Old World and the creation of a new paradigm. Her family had not been critics of Russian autocracy; they accepted the order as divinely ordained; therefore, they feared the change of the order in which they believed. The Stancioffs predicted that nothing good could emerge from what they viewed as the new, destructive, revolutionary force.

An Ugly Century

On March 16, 1917, in Petrograd, people with ladders began to remove imperial emblems from public buildings and stores and burned or threw the emblems into the canals. The dismantling of imperium was literal. It was as though the past was disintegrating and all the Stancioffs' happy memories of Russia disappeared along with it. As Nadejda states, "The ugliness of the century is affirmed with the unfolding of events in this so-called democracy."[37] As though to confirm their rank and social standing Nadejda recorded the family's collective disdain of the process by writing, "...all this reeks of the factory, strikes, worker things that are base and black. No more prestige or beauty."[38]

The theme of linking prestige with beauty is a constant in Nadejda's journal entries. In fact, the entire family was overwhelmingly affected by objects of beauty: in nature, in art, in an elegant human form, in a witty phrase, and in all things elevated and refined. Common and low were things of the other, baser classes, according to Nadejda. The worker state in the making was shaping up into the very idea their life and social milieu rejected. Rank evoked privilege, and prestige accompanied rank; no worker culture could compare to the fine and noble world of the elites from the Stancioffs' perspective.

Worker Culture on the Move

When in late March rumors of possible worker revolutions in England made headlines, the Stancioffs' distress built up to a frightened crescendo. The possibility that the royal family of Russia, or for that matter, all royal families of Europe, might be demoted to "mere mortals" was inconceivable. As the Russian Empire appeared to dissolve in their lifetime, the Stancioffs had to consider how this dissolution would ultimately affect their future. It was clear from the reports that the army was disorganized and Russian generals and ambassadors based abroad had submitted to the new government.

The family's disillusionment with this degeneration of the world they considered noble and eternal was complete. Nadejda remarks that "All this is ugly, low and revolting... We bitterly pity the imperial family."[39] If the great Russian Empire could be brought to this state, and even Great Britain had similar concerns over worker unrest, what could this bode for lesser monarchies?

The Bolsheviks imprisoned the imperial family in Peter and Paul Fortress, and Nadejda opined that this action presaged a revolution in the style of 1789. She was prescient about the possibilities of bloodshed with the change of the caste system in Russia.

When she learned of the exile of the imperial family to Tobolsk, Nadejda blamed the English for not taking any action to prevent the Romanovs' further suffering. It is not clear what she would have had had them do.

Months later, when the Stancioffs learned the details of the executions of the Russian imperial family and other members of their extended family from the papers, their reaction was predictable. "No need for commentary!" Nadejda wrote. "Horror, immense pity, a painful stupor; Oh XXth century! How could

Wilson not impede these infamies, by any means possible, instead of occupying himself with these utopian idealistic projects? [Wilson's fourteen points as preconditions for armistice]"[40]

The Threat of Bolshevism

The next concern for Bulgarians was how this insidious ideology could or would affect their homeland. As the Bolsheviks neared Odessa, chaos reigned in the Russian city. Receiving such news, the family understood that they were witness to a new age but could not quite grasp the gravity of the change. Therefore, they were outraged at the inaction of the Americans, as well as the British, who were technically on Russian soil but who could not or would not do anything to intervene directly in imperial Russia's disintegration.

Would none of the larger powers help their fellow Great Power Russia out of this unthinkable horror? Would they not at least lift a finger to help? Did they not anticipate the inherent danger of what allowing this worker-inspired, base, and egalitarian doctrine would do to their own internal order?

As the workers' parties were growing more influential, the French ambassador had to leave the country because he could not negotiate with the new political power, and the English ambassador, Sir George Buchanan—the father of Nadejda's friend, Meriel—was recalled by his Foreign Office. Finally, the revolutionary government replaced the Imperial Russian Ambassador to France, Izvolsky.

These were all men who were part of the Stancioffs' social circle, on a professional and personal level; their demotions were evidence of the degradation of what was once the well ordered world of the aristocratic elites in Europe. This, a worker state, then was modernity and its consequences.

The Stancioffs abhorred the revolution. They believed as Nadejda wrote: "A revolution brings only ugly things; democracy has never had panache."[41] The American declaration of war on Germany, although rather late, did not evoke praise for that particular American democratic system! Panache, pomp, ceremony, and rank mattered to the Stancioffs. The elites, the Stancioffs among them, built the structure and framework of their lives on these kinds of values and principles. To see them eradicated, or in any way threatened, was a direct menace to their value system which embraced monarchy and conservatism; the religious establishment and patriarchy as key components.

Nursing and Other Occupations

When Nadejda and Feo found nursing prospects, they were happy to return to the "dear 'white work' near our heroes."[42] The hospital in Plovdiv, run by an Armenian mission that included French and Armenian sisters, had 350 beds. In September 1917, a German doctor replaced the Armenian doctor.

The hospital had few provisions. According to Nadejda, it had no instruments and no medicines, and the rooms were furnished like barracks. At the end of their first day on the job, the Stancioff sisters exchanged impressions. Since they had had the experiences of working at the Clementine Hospital in 1912 in Sofia and the Japanese Hospital in 1915 in Paris, they had a great deal of background against which to compare this nursing experience. The Plovdiv hospital was lacking in virtually everything except *esprit de corps*.[43]

The medical personnel were a bit disoriented not only because of the stark surroundings but also because of the communication gap. The composition of the staff created quite a tower of Babel, since most did not share a common language. In fact, Nadejda claimed that the hospital walls reverberated with the sounds of at least 12 languages: Armenian, Bulgarian, English, French, German, Greek, Italian, Latin, Romanian, Russian, Serbian, and Turkish.

Therefore, it was not extraordinary that a Bulgarian medical student who helped the surgeon knew only French; and another student assistant knew some German; the two Bulgarian sisters only spoke their native tongue, and the Armenian sister could speak one-half dozen in addition to Bulgarian. The Stancioff sisters were "the modest cement" of the hospital, in their own estimation.

Furthermore, Nadejda noted that while this mismatched crew was hobbled together, they were caretakers of wounded who were mostly "good Bulgarian peasants some of whom speak only Turkish!"[44] The hospital was a microcosm of the vanishing Ottoman legacy of multi-nationalism. The future would usher in a new type of world order—dedicated to championing the rights of nation-states, the development of homogeneous populations of like nationals—under one government. In another decade, this kind of multicultural, multiethnic reality would become a rarity as Europeans convinced themselves that multiethnic states were one of the root causes of the War to End All Wars.

The Stancioffs' involvement with their volunteer work in the hospital included preparing gifts for all the wounded of all the hospitals of Plovdiv. Dimitri was in charge of this project in his capacity as director of the prisoner of war camps in southern Bulgaria. For Christmas 1917, the gifts included a "...pretty handkerchief in red, tobacco, rolling papers, post cards," and the women of the family were in charge of wrapping 2000 packets.[45] They did this work in their spare time.

Feo helped to organize a Christmas party at the hospital. The party was a kind of variety show with singing, recitations, *tableaux vivants*, and national dances. Ivan and Feo played viola and piano; Chou danced the *rûtchenitsa*—a dance performed while the dancers hold hands and move rhythmically in a single line to the music—with three other nurses, and four soldiers in national costumes.

As the casualties mounted and the war dragged into yet another year, Nadejda privately and publicly exalted the dead. Through their brutally won glory, she, too, felt herself elevated to a superior plane as their nurse. She saw and felt the aura of glory, the mystique of dying for a national cause in war. She enjoyed the heady feeling of those splendid months when Bulgaria was victorious in the first Balkan War, and the future seemed bright.

On a short visit to Sofia, she relived the days when Bulgaria was triumphant and when being a nurse to soldiers who fought in a victorious army held a special cachet; she wrote:

Clementine hospital, I return to the sick rooms where we all worked in 1912; our few months of true national glory! The aureole, unblemished! We enjoyed it too little. We were young, the people young, and the victory fresh! Those were heady months.[46]

Uncomfortable Cosmopolitanism

The Stancioffs experienced all the ambivalent feelings of cosmopolitans from two distinct family cultures and histories. Their Bulgarian and French roots were at war with each other, and they felt torn. Nadejda recorded: "divided loyalties seemed to be our fate as we heard of our favorite French cousin's death on the battlefields of Champagne."[47] The waste and suffering caused by the war disgusted them.

The inner conflict regarding the war was difficult to overcome for the family, since they sympathized with both sides. They could not, in good consciousness, cheer one side over the other. However, they noted each Bulgarian military victory with pride. Furthermore, the general shock a civilian was bound to feel, when confronted with the results of martial combat, was a frequent topic at home.

With no prospects for an end, the war seemed to drag on and the iniquities perpetrated by both sides were a genuine horror. For example, when Paris was bombed in October 1916, the Stancioffs were appalled at not only the casualties but also the reach of war. This type of warfare was a new experience for European civilian populations, who expected localized military campaigns fought only between armies. Traditionally, civilian casualties had been an aberration rather than the norm in battle. The twentieth century, however, was ushering in a new, ugly era.

The Stancioffs' estrangement from the king, who could not bear to have the family within close proximity, compounded their apprehension. Ferdinand reviled the family because he understood how their divided loyalties would affect their position *vis-à-vis* Bulgaria's alliances. The Stancioffs felt slighted by the distance that the king put between himself and the family during the war.

The Stancioffs feared the future. In fact, they felt the pain and disillusionment of the national situation as a uniquely personal dilemma. The children were collectively indignant for their father for what they perceived as a lack of gratitude or compensation for years of loyal service to the state and to the king. They were critical of the politics involved in the diplomatic corps. The family viewed their situation as unjust punishment for Dimitri's reasonable opposition to the king's foreign policies. Dimitri had professionally sound reasons for his anti-German stance; he was not just remaining loyal to his wife's natal country.

Despite the estrangement the king did intercede on their behalf once again. By Ferdinand's order, on October 1, 1916, Dimitri Stancioff assumed the post of officer in liaison with the second Division of Thrace, based in Plovdiv. He was a lieutenant, a reservist in the Regiment of the Guard; thus his position as a sort of aide-de-camp for General Kovatchevich suited him well. The post permitted him to live at home and still serve his country, which made his family very happy. He was involved mainly with charitable work such as assisting the wounded and the prisoners.

Culture and Patriotism

Culturally, the family was "west" European not simply because of their mother's Savoyard French and Italian roots but because they, as diplomats, had experienced and preferred the culture of France and Britain to Bulgaria's. Their family cultural preference was a question of taste and inclination that no amount of patriotism could erase.

The family reached out to the prisoners of war and not only visited the soldiers in their camps but invited some of the officers to spend time at their home simulating a feeling of normalcy for the British and French prisoners of war, (POWs). Feo remarks that "For a few hours we could be young together."[48] While Nadejda frankly admits to her journal that she "prefer[red] practicing the language of Shakespeare with an English officer who . . . [was] a prisoner" she preferred it to the "guttural idiom of the Teutons!"[49]

However, the Stancioffs' position on French and British culture was neither unique nor an aberration; most of the "civilized" world had been schooled to adopt it too. Years of political and economic dominance had assured the above-mentioned countries a central place in at least the cultural history of the world. The Stancioffs simply experienced a double dose of favoritism for the French.

While she cheered Bulgarian victories in the war, listed the numbers of POWS, captured arms, and even noted the capturing of a Russian flag, which she acknowledged as a psychological victory, Nadejda continued to bemoan the fact that France, Russia, and Bulgaria had to be enemies in this war.[50] It was a cruel irony to her on many levels.

She understood the incongruity of POWs of the Great Powers held captive by what she termed "a tribe of Slavo-Mongols."[51] As a Bulgarian, who owed a debt of gratitude to the Russians, she recorded a bittersweet image of Russian POWs working to build pontoon bridges to cross the Danube not far from the site of the greatest Russian victory over the Ottomans in the 1877-1878 Russo-Turkish war of the liberation of her country.

As a good Bulgarian, she saved her most vociferous language for the Romanians. In graphically anti-Romanian entries, she practically shouted on December 7, 1916: "Glorious and unforgettable date—Bulgarian armies enter Bucharest . . . the pretentious and vain capital of a people who are parvenus . . . Oh perfidious Rumania . . . this is the law of revenge and of rehabilitation."[52] Bad blood between the two countries was the result of numerous martial and diplomatic episodes and conflicts over the years. Those battles embittered relations between the two countries to the point where there was little hope of cooperation even in peacetime.

Ordinary Days

By June 19, 1918 they were back to the routine of "ordinary day[s]." Feo and Nadejda returned to the hospital, where there was a heavy workload. The wounded arrived from Zanthie and Gumurdjina, and there were cases of malaria as well.

Working during a suffocating heat wave, the sisters would come home from work in the hospital taking care of the wounded, then make rose petal preserves in the afternoon, keeping up the rhythm of storing and preserving food for the winter.[53]

Nadejda reveled in the July heat; she imagined summer as a tigress guarding Plovdiv in a close embrace. Describing the heat, Nadejda says that she loved to feel "the heat on my eyes, on my eyelashes; it touches me like the tender hand and never wounds me."[54] The house was cool in the mornings, but after 1 p.m., the heat became increasingly insupportable; it did not begin to cool off until midnight. These were her favorite days of summer, when heat, bright light, flowers, fruits, and various perfumes all blended to create a balm for the soul and an *oriental* setting for her life. She was in her element then; when the heat was at its peak, she described it as a delicious bath for the nerves; that offered a type of escape from thinking about the war.

In order to distract his family from wartime life and its bleaker aspects, Papa organized escapes in the form of short outings for his family. They visited the valley of roses in Kazanlûk; another time they took a trip to Kamenitsa and its thermal springs. Next to a hand drawn map of their route to the valley of the roses, with the approximate distances and some topographic features, Nadejda included a quote from F. Kanitz book, *Bulgaria and the Balkans*.[55] In addition to noting the different appellations of the plant, she pointed out that it takes 3,200 kilograms of rose petals to make 1 kilogram of oil.

When they shared their impressions of one of their trips in the Bulgarian countryside the Stancioff sisters exhibited interest in the features of their homeland as much as any involved tourist to a new destination.[56] They exhibited polite interest, as a foreigner might. As the family traveled, their parents kept up a running commentary, their memories linked with particular points of interest; of the arrival of the king in Bulgaria, of the court, and of the character of Comte de Bourboulon.

On a brief visit to Sofia with her father that July, Nadejda's impressions were not complimentary. "This chic Sofia is bothersome, pretentious, and a little ridiculous. Living here would displease me; I only like Vitosha and the roads that lead to it. God keep me from the banal life of Sofia!"[57] Bulgaria's capital city did not meet with her well-traveled expectations.

When sharing a bedroom with her grandmother, Nadejda, waxing nostalgic for the days when she and her sisters had shared the same room during the 1912 war, wrote: "We laughed a lot in it! .. A time when the minor feelings appeared to be profound. The war was marvelous; the future seemed magnificent..."in contrast to the darkness that lingered over the Bulgarian horizon in 1918.[58]

On another outing, the family paid a visit to hot sulfurous baths in Kamenitsa; they traveled to the baths in carriages drawn by ponies. On the way back they passed through Batak and Peshtera. Their excursions included historical sites as well as sites of natural beauty. The Stancioff parents continued to educate their brood.

In some villages the Stancioffs saw Pomatsi (Bulgarian Muslims), and Nadejda noted their unique attire as well as the singular pleasures of being a tourist:

> Travel always engenders something bizarre; it is the only movement when the present has value because there is never a past and perhaps not a future. ... During the course of a trip the present takes on an enormous importance; we are attached to it in desperation! In addition, we tell ourselves so much in one hour and when at home so many hours for the same thing![59]

Throughout the summer, the Stancioffs kept up a campaign of letters and telegrams to the military officials in Varna, asking permission to spend the summer at *Trois Sources*. There seems to have been quite a bit of strategizing on this issue in the family circle: think, discuss, hesitate, and wait.

While they waited, the family worked in the heat of summer—in the hospital, in the prisoner-of-war camp, making preserves, and waiting for an affirmative response on the subject of a move back to Varna.

Believing that the stock negative response they received for reasons of military security was false, Nadejda wrote: "We understand that there must be another explanation, which we do not want to acknowledge."[60] Her mother's reaction was to be despondent while her father proposed to try another source—perhaps the king.

On the king's birthday, which fell on the Feast of the Assumption, in mid-August, the sovereign celebrated in Tûrnovo. The event was an annual ceremony with the princes, their entourages, all the ministers, all the generals and the royal suite. This time the Stancioffs were not invited. The family was bitter. As Nadejda writes: "the true friends, those who surrounded the young sovereign, for 30 years have been forgotten. Nothing astonishes people who have seen a lot!"[61] However, as fate would have it, Papa was passing through Tûrnovo train station on that very day and managed, in his own inimitable way, to mark the day by congratulating his king by lifting his hat in a salute from the station![62]

Papa brought back figs from Varna and so the women set to making fig preserves under the direction of a Greek woman from the neighborhood. Toward the end of August, the women had progressed to plum marmalade. They cooked as many Bulgarians still do, over an open fire in their courtyard. Nadejda claimed to have liked the work of constant stirring of the viscous, dark mass. To her, it seemed that "the weeks pass[ed] like meteors," while they worked in the hospital, made provisions for the winter, cooked, and took walks.[63]

Orient

At the beginning of the 20th century, the region refered to as the Orient began somewhere in Serbia, or even just east of Vienna and swept through the Balkan Peninsula, crept into the Anatolian Peninsula, and beyond. The exact location of the Orient in the mind of Europeans fluctuated first in relation to the rise and subsequent fall of the Ottoman Turks and later with the nascent national states that arose as the empire receded from Europe. For the Stancioffs, and most Europeans, their homeland was part of the inscrutable Orient. It is interesting that Nadejda reveled in what the Stancioffs considered an essential part of their ancestral heritage—that they belonged to a place of mystery, menace, cruelty, and beauty. The savage Orient of Nadejda's musings and the image, which her European contemporaries projected onto the Balkans, was authentic. The perception of what was then considered the Near East as an uncivilized, distant place, firmly rooted in ancient traditions and one that refused to come forward into the modern age, was the basis of prejudices that guided Europeans' attitudes toward those lands and peoples.

Furthermore, being relegated to the Orient colored the populations' in question own perceptions of their inadequacies or at the very least of their impenetrably setback manners. Bulgarians, for example, compared themselves to the "civilized" West Europeans and found themselves lacking in high culture, in mature political systems, stable economies. In other words, the Balkan peoples were painfully aware of their status as young nations still shaping their features as states among the established European powers. Amongst themselves, these relative newcomers to Europe were brutally harsh about each other's shortcomings. Abroad they felt ashamed and hesitant about their "obvious" failings.

Nadejda placed Bulgaria firmly in the Orient and used that notion to spin imaginary tales of "visions of white towns, arcades, veiled women, and strangest jewels!"[64] Her Orient included Africa, which she called her quintessential Orient. She perceived the Orient as a place of mystery, beauty but at the same time dangerous, a stereotypical European perception prevalent in the 19th and 20th centuries.[65]

While living in Plovdiv, the Bulgarian town which most resembled Nadejda's Orient because of its architecture and multiethnic population, she created fictional scenarios about her own life to feed her imagination. Spending internal exile in that historic city encouraged the development of her notions of the Orient—its people and its nature. Such skewed descriptions abound in her journals about herself and those who mattered in her life. These flights of fancy projected her perceptions on her native land as aberrant as compared to European nations and it an unusual way, apart. She employed "imaginative demonology" to exoticize Bulgaria and to tacitly exoticize herself.[66] She internalized orientalism and did not perceive it as contradictory to her essentially elite status in society.

The Stancioffs' socio-cultural background led them to understand the world to be structured based on concepts of political, cultural, and social superiority and inferiority. From their perspective western Europe represented the pinnacle of superiority. Belonging to the Orient, even as a flirtation of the imagination, gave the Stancioffs a device for rationalizing some of the differences they exhibited as a family when juxtaposed to western cultural elites. They also employed the device of the Orientalist, placing themselves outside the Orient while casting themselves in the roles of interpreters of the mysterious Other for their western elite associates.

For Nadejda that family-held view of living in the Orient was fodder for creative fiction. For example, when the family moved to Svishtov in the summer 1916, she had typed a two-page short story about an Arab and his family. Traveling along with their horses, servants, and possessions, including fowl and provisions, they stopped in an oasis to rest their caravan. In this pseudo-biographical essay, her father became an Arab chief, and the family his entourage. Together they were nomads venturing from place to place with their goods and livestock. She writes, "And it is here that we, eternal nomads, are come to plant our tents for a few weeks or long months!"[67]

Perhaps the nomadic imagery in Nadejda's story was apt for a family of diplomats who too were destined for a life of wandering and rootlessness. She continued the oriental imagery in her journal with descriptions of Svishtov. The city apparently was not much to look at during the day but when the setting sun cast a special light on narrow streets and houses, the ambience transformed it into a Tunis or Smyrna or Bursa, with all the appropriate accoutrements of Oriental cities Nadejda had visited only in her imagination.

Nadejda's view of the world incorporated some deep-seated beliefs about national character and temperaments. It was natural, therefore, for her to write that "every race has its habits and its particularities; I find the people and the countries of the Orient more interesting than those of the Midi. The Arab is more profound than the Italian, the Hindu than the Toulouse. The Muslim religion makes the chasm even more unbreachable."[68] She was not alone in these beliefs; her family had similar perceptions as did their European contemporaries. The orientalisation of the non-European world made the identification of Europeaness simpler for Europeans. Furthermore, it served to separate the comprehensible, therefore acceptable, world from the other, incomprehensible, alien, oriental setting.

1918

Joining the Germans during the war had come with certain territorial benefits for Bulgaria. Lands lost or taken at the conclusion of the Second Balkan War were reclaimed. The country recovered, for a tantalizing interlude, Macedonian territories divided between Greece and Serbia, its outlet to the Aegean via Dedeagach, and Dobrudja, taken by Romania.

The loss of the Great War was a catastrophe of even greater proportions for the Bulgarians than for their German co-belligerents. The human costs and the territorial losses of the two Balkan Wars created a deep scar in the Bulgarian psyche. Their fresh losses in this European wide war, compounded by the great humiliations at the conclusion of the Second Balkan War, generated a crescendo of anger at the government.

The population heaped their collective dismay and frustration on their government and especially their king. His was an already tainted reign. He had led his subjects to believe that the First Balkan War would win them not only territories they had dreamed of possessing since 1878 but also Constantinople the ancient city that was once part of Bulgaria's former cultural glory.

The final blow, that of being once more on the losing side led to a profound disillusionment that translated into a upsurge of riots, anti-war protests among civilians, desertions, mutinies, and finally a substantial rebellion in the army in the last year of the war. A band of Bulgarian troops attempted to march on Sofia in a bid to carry out a military coup d'état in 1918. That act was the ultimate expression of revulsion to the policies of the pro-German, authoritarian government that had linked the country with the Central Powers in an unsuccessful alliance. The Radomir Rebellion signaled to the state that only a profound change of course could quiet down a nation in turmoil. King Ferdinand abdicated the throne. He left the country to live in exile on his properties in Hungary.

A New King, a New Leader

The abdication led to two new domestic developments: the ascension to the throne of Ferdinand's son, King Boris III, at the age of 24, and the emergence of Aleksandûr Stamboliiski, (1879-1923), as prime minister. Stamboliiski was an outspoken Agrarian Party member who King Ferdinand had jailed in 1915 for his anti-war opinions. Stamboliiski and his party emerged as the leaders of a humbled Bulgaria.

The Bulgarian Agrarian National Union (BANU) was a party with a radical platform, and its leader, Stamboliiski, was a man with unique vision and a seemingly inexhaustible stamina with which to implement his dream of a true peasant state.

Aleksandûr Stamboliiski was born to peasant parents and as a politician was a self-made man. He had been educated for a time in Germany. However, his primary life experience had been as a land owner and farmer rather than a politician. His experiences as a member and eventually leader of his party, gave him first-hand opportunities to take stock of the plight of large numbers of common peasants whose lot had changed little from that of their parents or even grandparents.

International Political Changes

In the early twentieth century, the Bulgarian agrarian economy floundered through periods of blooms and withers while the government did nothing to relieve the suffering of the largely agricultural population. The new party in power set out to create an agrarian state that would focus on peasants and their needs. This policy would also necessitate the dispossession, in certain cases, of the moneyed minority who had managed to accumulate wealth and considerable holdings of arable land.

The well-to-do—the few economic elites that existed in Bulgaria—had a great deal to fear when the government fell into the hands of BANU, especially after the 1920 elections. At that time, the Agrarians managed a majority in the Narodno Sûbranie. Stamboliiski behaved as though he had a comfortable mandate to put his plans for an agrarian utopia into place. His often abrasive and sometimes punitive measures against his political opponents and his social "betters" created a growing cadre of enemies. He was a controversial political leader in Bulgaria.

In the tradition of politics as usual, when the Agrarians swept into office, they swept out all of their predecessors since no party would abide having other party loyalists in their midst. The result was a predictable disorganization and a general deficiency in competence, not simply because of lack of on-the-job experience but, in many cases, due to an absence of political experience of any sort. Party stalwarts overran the governmental bureaucracy. Their agenda was similar to their predecessors: feed at the government trough at national expense and with a complete disregard for the costs of incompetence and corruption.

There were few men of conviction and principle such as Stamboliiski. He had a native intelligence and zeal for the job of reforming his country that was unparalleled among his contemporaries. He had a genuine desire to level the economic playing field for Bulgaria's peasants and a plan for how to put it all into action. Like a man with an exact focused vision, he insisted on being in the center of every branch of government and involved in all decision-making with respect to domestic policies and in foreign policies.

He traveled a great deal in order to meet personally with European heads of state. He wanted to make important political contacts and cement good relations so that Bulgarian foreign policy could flourish. Stamboliiski also traveled widely to study agrarian practices in other states, to borrow from their best ideas, and to bring them back home to his people. He never tired of meeting with prime ministers, kings and queens, factory managers and farmers, shepherds and livestock breeders. He was diligent and he made sure that everyone who worked with him worked as tirelessly for the cause of a better, more prosperous Bulgaria.

Occupied Varna

When Ferdinand abdicated in favor of his son, Boris, the war was finally over for Bulgaria, and a new chapter in her history could begin. A coalition government included the Agrarians, the Narrows (who would become the Bulgarian Communist Party led by Dimitûr Blagoev), the Broad Socialists, and the Democrats.

The former government had plunged the country into war for the promised gains of Bulgarian Thrace, Macedonia and Dobrudja. Instead its allies' demands for supplies and support, followed by the victors' occupation, had ravaged the country. Occupied Bulgaria was reduced to her August 1914 borders, losing its outlet to the Aegean Sea, possibly the most devastating of all the country's territorial losses.

The atmosphere in Varna, indeed all of Bulgaria, had changed. From a proud junior partner of her allies, Bulgaria was now an occupied, defeated nation. Foreign troops occupied Varna. Toward the end of the war the Stancioffs returned to a changed city. They had been divorced from involvement with the government and were adrift both professionally and as citizens of a state in the last months of a devastating war.

Dimitri and Ivan found peacetime occupations. Ivan became a liaison officer with the English forces in Varna, a kind of aide-de-camp to the British general in charge of the city and the British troops of occupation. He joined the 228 Brigade for a year and accompanied them when they traveled to Constanza to relieve the Bulgarian First Army, which still occupied the region.[69] Dimitri once again found employment at the Ministry of Foreign Affairs in Sofia and worked on preparing for foreign delegations' visits to the country.

For civilians in Bulgaria life was resuming some semblance of normalcy. For the Stancioffs, this meant, among other signs of familiarity, access to their own subscriptions to foreign publications; they were reading *Tattler*, *Sketch* and similar types of illustrated society magazines. They also read on international political developments, a the subject most popular among Bulgarians was the peace process.

Following the armistice, plans for the peace conference in Versailles began to dominate family discussions about the future of Bulgaria and what would be their own fate. Signs of modernity crept into their consciousness. Their readings revealed the changes in social mores, which seemed to loosen up almost immediately upon the end of hostilities. The Stancioffs were scandalized as Nadejda notes:

> We amuse ourselves at London even more than at Paris. We live to amuse ourselves with a speed that is historic, we have already forgotten the war and its pains and we have no worry of the sad heritage, which she will leave to humanity; jealousies, envy; cupidity, the spirit of vengeance and hate etc. The women undress at will![70]

Shocked and disgusted they dug further into their well of beautiful images to obliterate the ugliness of the twentieth century, which they found repulsive.

Thus, instead of acknowledging the breaking of conventional rules, they focused more on reports in French newspapers describing visitors to Paris such as the Belgian sovereigns; the English king and his sons; the Italian king and his son; the American President Woodrow Wilson and his wife; Venizelos, the Greek leader; and Nikola Pašić, the Serb leader.[71] The exuberance for all things gay in the press stunned the Stancioffs. The peace process had hardly begun. They understood that the peace would bring fresh agonies to their homeland, and they feared for the future of Bulgaria. Nadejda, knowing that the victorious allies would extract a terrible price from the losers, writes: "They have too much humiliation to avenge—this is what makes them all so bitter and so difficult".[72]

Coping with Shortages

In Varna, they were fully engaged in their customary pursuits at home. Nadejda viewed it as a return to their old "…feudal life of chatelaines of yesteryear, except that we have few serfs and valets at our command!"[73] They reconnected with the cycle of planting and harvesting, which secured most of their food. Their material life improved considerably in terms of foodstuff provisions. Nadejda credited her father's practical purchases and Ivan's English rations for their relatively comfortable circumstances. They had wood, and their domestic service ran smoothly.

In January 1919, they slaughtered the pig they had been feeding for this purpose, with the help of the head of the Euxinograd servants, who oversaw the butchering. Feo was in charge of supervising the slaughter. As Nadejda remarks, the "three sisters at Three Springs" directed everything.[74] The royal family also lent a helping hand when it came time to plant, since the Stancioffs had permission from King Boris to take plants, grains, and seeds from Euxinograd for their own beds.[75]

Wartime inflation and shortages still affected the Stancioffs' household budget, since there were some things they could not furnish themselves. When they hired a mason to fix some parts of the foundation of the house, Nadejda was outraged by his rates. She writes "I note, for my children! That we pay this worker 30 francs /day, a sign of the times!"[76] She also listed what she considered "fantastic prices" for basic commodities such as "fish caught under our windows" and potatoes.[77] Since much of their money was in foreign accounts, the Stancioffs were accustomed to quoting prices in foreign currency—in this case, French francs.

They were fortunate in many ways, although they had to economize on wood and conserve heat by lighting fires in only two rooms, since that winter was bitterly cold. In February, Nadejda recorded 6 degrees Centigrade with a very strong wind. The Stancioffs were conscious of all those unfortunates without roofs over their heads in that brutal winter, which was a significant portion of the population of Europe.

Food and fuel supplies were critically low for the exhausted Bulgarian economy. Shortages forced the government to keep a tight watch on private food supplies. The Varna Commission, charged with making an inventory of the bags of wheat of all the inhabitants, visited the Stancioffs that winter. The Ministry of Commerce still kept track of the quantity of its citizens' grain as it had during the war.

The harvest of 1918 for Bulgaria was the most disastrous of the first quarter of the twentieth century and had there been no strict government control over the distribution of grain, the country would have starved. After 1918, government control of the distribution and purchasing of wheat for domestic as well as export markets became commonplace. The Agrarian government that took charge following the peace settlement continued the economic policies of its predecessor.

Difficult Situations

The presence of the English troops changed the appearance of Varna. Military occupation perpetuated an abnormal civilian life. General Gay, the commander in chief of the occupation forces behaved, in Nadejda's estimation, as a viceroy. English trucks jarred the roads to the villa; their motorcycles criss-crossed the large streets of the city center, and officers explored the surrounding countryside on horseback. Varna filled with uniforms: Bulgarian, English, and Italian. There were foreign sailors, too, including French and Americans. Traffic was mostly mechanized with virtually no donkey-pulled carts or horses, since many draft animals were either killed or injured during the war.

Because of the family's linguistic abilities and military connections, the officers of the English occupying forces welcomed the Stancioff men into their social circles. Thus, it was perfectly natural that the officers invited the entire family to the military club for a New Year's Eve Party in 1918.[78] The Bulgarians wished for conquerors and conquered to work together in peace and to manage to erase the bitter memories of the war. The Stancioffs spent a good part of the evening with Colonel Stuart, an English officer, who, according to Nadejda, was "full of delicacy, of tact and who understands difficult situations."[79] Things seemed a bit brighter.

Despite feeling displaced in their own domain, the Stancioffs hosted many receptions at their villa by the sea. Their doors were open to a string of officers, mostly English, some French and Italian, but Bulgarians too. Their guests showed their appreciation for the hospitality in a myriad of ways but most commonly by sharing whatever rare commodities they could offer a cosmopolitan family at a time of rationing. The officers brought books, chocolates, and tea.

The family formed close ties with some of the occupying English. When one of Nadejda's favorites, Colonel Stuart, announced that his regiment was reassigned to occupy Baltchik, she was sad about the departure.[80] She valued the charming and tactful presence of the colonel. She also understood that wartime friendships were inherently more precious and comforting than they were in times of peace. The regiment, affectionately referred to as the "Ox and Bux," whose officers had been frequent guests at *Trois Sources,* moved out.

When, first a French Colonial Division and then by a Brigade of Italians replaced the British, Nadejda saw her representatives of civilization depart. She had felt safe in their care and would not feel the same sense of security in the hands of the Italians. As she noted wryly in her journal, "the films . . . [would] change at cinema Trois Sources!"[81]

Nadejda was an Anglophile despite her French-Bulgarian roots. Her pro-English attitude emerges in her journal entries, in which she notes her love of the sound of English accents. She also envied them their ability to travel. Finally, she was impressed by their military might, as she records, "O masters of the world! Ave! O Balkan misery and painful contrast!"[82]

She loved English global dominance as much as she hated the precarious position of her defeated homeland. She jokes about it when describing the physical features of an English military choir. In a journal entry on January 22,

1919, she notes their ubiquitous ruddy cheeks and the fact that they never had dark circles under their eyes, something she attributed to long nights of uninterrupted sleep![83] This remark could only be an allusion to her perception of their domination of the world; those in positions of complete control lose no sleep, while those who are subject to their master's whims display dark shadows under their eyes, a sure sign of their powerlessness.

The Stancioffs did play a covert role during the occupation despite their good relations with the various armies of occupation. Since the Bulgarian Army had to be demobilized, Ivan, still in his capacity as a soldier, as well as his family, were drawn into the deceptive task of hiding weapons. They hid, in plain sight, thousands of army rifles, two machine guns, the sights of the battery next door to their property. They packed all of them in big cases disguised by oriental rugs insouciantly displayed in their drawing room. The entire family felt the thrill of patriotic one-upsmanship when they entertained Marshal Franchet d'Esperey, member of the Disarmament Commission, in the presence of the very arms he was charged to collect.[84]

A Stancioff Back in Sofia

By February 1919, Dimitri returned to work in Sofia. He left in a railroad carriage which the Ministry of Foreign Affairs had reserved especially for him. From the capital he supplied his family with extra foreign newspapers as well as a running commentary, via his letters, on the various foreign dignitaries who passed through Sofia on inspection tours of the country.

The first such official was the English Catholic Cardinal Archbishop of Westminster Francis Bourne, who made a stop in Bulgaria on his return from a voyage to the Holy Land. The opportunity of serving as host to visiting dignitaries allowed Nadejda's father some infrequent but much appreciated trips back to Varna when the itinerary permitted. In March, he accompanied French General Chrétien on a tour of Bulgaria, and they scheduled a stop in Varna, which included a visit to *Trois Sources*.

The Stancioffs spared no effort or expense for the general; they prepared a bountiful reception in their great hall, with a large fire and festive decorations– almond and *drenka* (wild berry) branches in bloom.[85] General Chrétien appreciated talking with Nadejda's mother, a native speaker of French. Not only were the Stancioffs playing a visible role in international company and having an impact on international relations but also felt they were central and crucial to its success.

The next visit of a similar nature was even more exciting since Papa was to stay overnight in their home. He was accompanying Baron Alliotti, the High Commissioner of Italy, to Sofia. The family's hospitality extended to offering the baron Nadejda's room rather than the smaller guest room.[86] The family took the extraordinary step of inviting a German chef to do the cooking. All these effusive preparations were in recognition of a much older relationship; the Stancioffs had made the baron's acquaintance during their years in St. Petersburg. He had a reputation of being a very intelligent man as well as a good diplomat.

Now in his special capacities as High Commissioner, it was doubly important to make him welcome.

Part of Baron Alliotti's welcome included an excursion to what later became the standard points of interest for foreign dignitaries: Euxinograd and the Sanatorium. The group had tea upon their return from sightseeing, followed by a walk in their garden and along the beach. The family treated the commissioner as they would have treated an honored family friend.[87] Maintaining professional contacts, especially in uncertain times, was essential for lifelong diplomats like the Stancioffs. Therefore, the long workday continued when at eight o'clock, they hosted a large dinner party with two new guests, the commercial representatives from Italy.

Economic negotiations between Italy and Bulgaria had progressed slowly. The purpose of Alliotti's visit was to spark the talks afresh. The next day, after running errands with their guest in town, the Stancioffs stopped in the woods to pick violets with which they decorated his hat![88] The family managed to incorporate a familiar and soft touch into their associations with professional as well as family acquaintances Thus, business and pleasure mingled without deleterious effects to either enterprise.

The Paris Peace Conference

The evolving story of the Peace Conference in Paris was riveting for the family. The first French newspapers they received in the second week of January were so completely devoted to President Wilson's visit to Paris that the Stancioffs declared the abundance of details ridiculous. The newspapers had all the particulars on the opening of the conference with texts of the discussions, amusing descriptions of the personalities, and biting commentaries that Nadejda considered quite spiteful, calling them "ridiculous" exposés on "little ministers of little countries."[89] She was referring to descriptions of Ion Brătianu (1864-1927), Nicola Pašić (1845-1926), and Eleutherios Venizelos (1864-1936), the representatives of Romania, Serbia, and Greece respectively.

The Stancioffs also kept abreast of news on the lives of royalty. Thus, when Grand Duchess Adelaide of Luxemburg abdicated in favor of her sister because of her engagement to Prince Felix of Parma, the family discussed it. Their mother had noble ancestors, after all, and the children were a part of that vast society of European royalty.

The European news also kept them well aware of the menace posed by anarchists, Bolsheviks, and Socialists. In February 1919, an anarchist wounded French prime minister Georges Clemenceau, (1841-1929), in the street. Similar distressing acts perpetrated by other anarchists, the communist rule of Béla Kun, (1886-1938), in Hungary, and the increasing number of Bolshevik victories in the Russian civil war, all focused attention on the possibility of an enduring overthrow of the old order. The Stancioffs were shocked, along with the rest of their peers, at the possibility of an upset of historic proportions all over Europe.

At Easter, the officers from the Bulgarian garrison came by to wish M. and Mme. Stancioff a happy holiday. The men even danced outside for the Stancioffs Nadejda could not help but notice the difference between Bulgarian dances and music and that of the Italians, which she had witnessed on the Italian ship in the harbor. The differences served to reinforce her worldview. Westerners and Orientals were worlds apart temperamentally, culturally, and of course, politically. She noted that the tarantella was a happy, carefree affair, while the *horo* (the Bulgarian folk dance) was a "rhythmic procession" she went on to say that "instead of forgetting while dancing the sadnesses of life, one has more time to think about them more deeply!"[90]

Music affected Nadejda intensely, and she noted it in her journals on many occasions. Good music was a type of release and an escape for her; therefore, she often sought out acquaintances with superior musical talent. Invited to the modest apartment of a Bulgarian family, the Bechkoffs, in Varna, the Stancioffs found the décor and furnishings below their family's standards, but the music was magical. Enthralled to hear real music, Brahms and Grieg, they savored the respite from reality. Nadejda writes, "To listen to a bit of harmony, to forget and to forget oneself, to enter into a marvelous intangible world and to console the senses ... I think of beautiful things, immutable and sacred."[91]

The Unintelligible Future

By late spring 1919, the family discussed whom the government might choose for the Bulgarian delegation to the peace negotiations in France. Although Papa would have been one of the candidates under consideration, the Stancioffs had no illusions; the political situation in the country was unsettled. The Agrarian Party, BANU, had managed to hobble together a coalition government, and each political party vied for its share of influence in the administration. These facts politicized the selection of delegates.

Up until the very last moment, the family was unaware whether they would be included in or excluded from the group of delegates. Initially, of course, the possibility of being on the list was real only for Papa. Nadejda was included among the candidates, perhaps, as an afterthought but certainly at the insistence of her father. Therefore, when on May 17, Nadejda and her father boarded a ministry train car bound for Sofia, neither of them suspected what lay in store.

Nadejda accompanied her father only because he wished it. She and her father did not imagine that they would be separated from the rest of the family and attached to the Bulgarian peace delegation at Neuilly, where they would spend an agonizing four months waiting for the conclusion of the peace. Their send-off at the station in Varna was celebratory, as their family and some English officers entered the train car for a parting toast of vermouth.[92] The furnishings, which were luxurious enough for the English to admire, made Nadejda proud.

The train pulled away after midnight. Nadejda and her father dined, played bridge, and enjoyed a "night of luxury and calm on real beds."[93] Although she regretted leaving most of her family behind, she was glad to be with her father.

At times like these, she forced herself to focus even more than usual on her family and brought herself to a prayer-like state by enumerating her family's individual and collective virtues. She found comfort in evoking their various positive character traits in times of both happiness and sorrow. This evocation served as a prevailing mantra throughout her life. Evoking their many talents acted as a form of validation for her and served to confirm the value and worth of her family in her estimation. She needed to be actively cognizant and thankful for what she considered God's gifts to her as a reference point.

The Stancioffs made a practice of reminding one another of their good fortunes and of their faith that God watches over them and cares for them. Conscious of their privileged lives, the parents and later the children, came to appreciate their good fortune and take a comfortable future for granted. They constantly worked to assure that professionally and personally, they would be able to choose from the best possible options. Above all, they placed their trust in God to grace their lives with goodness. Reflecting on her life, Nadejda writes:

> I think of the tangible past, of the incoherent future; of the noble character of Maman, of the incomparable qualities of the heart, energy, sprit of Papa, of the perfection of my three siblings so handsome, so different, so noble of the many consolations which life offers me, my indulgent life, to me who is so little worthy, to have so much treasure and to live with the Elect.[94]

At the Ministry of Foreign Affairs

In Sofia that spring, Dimitri began work as soon as he stepped off the train. He met with a General Baird at the station and had a brief interview with him there. Dimitri continued his work as official representative and guide for the government to foreign visitors of note. When Mr. Charles Crane passed through Sofia, the Bulgarians took special care with him since he was a friend of President Wilson.

In 1919, Nadejda's impression of the capital had not improved over previous reactions. She remained disdainful.[95] In Sofia, rumors were plentiful regarding who would take part in the Bulgarian peace delegation to Paris. The decision was highly politicized, since politics and political parties were recreating themselves in the postwar period. There was a great deal of uncertainty about which party would have the most influence on decisions of national importance.

The tension mounted as the Bulgarians prepared for a dictated peace. Bulgarian diplomats were nervous about the interminable delays in Paris, and their anxiety rose as they witnessed the treatment of Germany and Austria. There was no question the treaty would be harsh; waiting for the details was difficult.

Nadejda was working for the Ministry of Foreign Affairs under the direction of her father who hired her as his assistant. He entrusted her with work for which he thought her competent. Thus, on May 22, she accompanied him to the ministry, where an Italian officer, the aide-de-camp of Alliotti, dictated "the first official dispatch on the questions of Bulgaria" to her.[96]

She continued with this kind of work, primarily clerical, for her father during the length of their entire stay in Sofia, and she enjoyed it. She adored her father so much that the intimacy of the work, which she dubbed an "intellectual tête a tête," was the biggest attraction of her stay in Sofia.

Nadejda also kept up a voluminous correspondence with her family back in Varna. With her duties to her father, her correspondence, attendance at dinners, soirées, and teas, Nadejda was extremely busy. She had no time to be bored or to be boring. In many respects, this time in Sofia would presage her years in the diplomatic service as a full-fledged participant. No longer a passive observe, she witnessed, now as a young woman, the actuality of how exclusive the field of diplomacy was. Now old enough to be invited to dinners and participate in diplomatic discussions she could assess the world more critically.

Not only were the representatives of different countries the members of elite classes, but they were also almost exclusively male. Nadejda reveled in being the single female in august male company. "I am always the only one of my sex at these Entente gatherings, which amuses me a lot!"[97] Since she could now be included in these exclusive groups the sensation was exhilarating.

She also longed to belong, to be a national of an Entente country, to be with the victors and not the vanquished. When on another occasion, the Belgian high commissioner in Bulgaria invited her to dinner, she was the only woman among a group of Frenchmen, among whom she discovered a relative of her mother's. She was elated, enjoyed the conversations, and mused "...O Entente, if only circumstances were different."[98]

Long Live the King

In Sofia, Nadejda ran into two English officers whom she had met in Varna and to whom she referred as her older brothers: officers Savage and Harris. They were on leave, and she and her father took them to churches, museums, and to Boyana to see the church, driven in a Ministry of War automobile. She recorded enjoying the sensation of speed and wind, the "white smile of Savage and the soft eyes of Billy."[99] She took pleasure in their company, flirted with them, and brought them along everywhere with her, even to a party thrown by the Gueshovs, who were one of the prominent Bulgarian families in the capital, where, according to Nadejda, the invitees were all the "bright young things" of Sofia.

On May 24, Saints' Cyril and Methodius Day in Bulgaria, and a national holiday, the Stancioffs took the Englishmen to watch the celebrations. From their position near the parade pavilion, they observed the king's arrival. He appeared, with little pomp, and stood close enough to their party to recognize her father with a salute. That public manifestation of affection acted as a balm for the Stancioffs, whose estrangement from the royal family dated from King Ferdinand's decision to join the Germans in the war. Nadejda described King Boris in detail:

> It is the first time that I see him in his capacity as sovereign, the child who played with us at *Trois Sources* and at Euxinograd. He has not changed one bit, he is still very thin, too slight, and his color is so pale. His expression has changed; I got a glimpse of his face at rest and it was very hard, with something at once fatal and implacable; one feels that he expects nothing handed to him; when he smiles the impression changes. It ... gives him an air of a child who is confident and gay; and the smile is the natural one that I know, it seems aston-

ishing now. ... His dignity and his aristocratic bearing make a big impression on Harris. (I noticed that he still has his nervous habit to bite his lower lip which gives one the impression that he is trying to suppress a smile that might be out of place.)[100]

A small group of socialists used this national holiday as an opportunity to demonstrate against the regime; they chanted "Down with the King" and "Down with the army," and they were promptly roughed up by the crowd.[101] The crowd then cheered, "Long live the King" and "Long live the army." Since the fear of socialist revolution was reasonable, Nadejda was glad to record Bulgarians' anti-Bolshevik sentiments. She was relieved as a Bulgarian citizen and as a member of her social milieu. Life in her homeland would remain the same, as it once had been in Russia, her home as a child.

Trepidation

In the second week of June, the Bulgarians had to submit a list of the Bulgarian delegates who would attend the Paris peace process. The Stancioffs were pessimistic about the future of Bulgaria and their own professional prospects; Nadejda comments that "... everything is going badly, everything has been bad, everything will be bad, and these people have no future...I have no confidence at all in the historic future of these poor infantile people [she refers to Bulgaria]."[102]

Nadejda and her father were disheartened in a number of ways, since the formation of the delegation was a signal for a final, chaotic competition among the political parties for influence. Thus, personal merit or seniority was not considerations in the selection process. "The hours are heavy and nerves stretched taut..."Nadejda wrote, discouraged by the petty domestic politics.[103] She could not understand why her father put so many hours of work into the ministry when he was not compensated, either financially or in any other way.

Nadejda, Published Author

In the meantime, while Nadejda continued to work for her father she wrote an article on the contemporary parallels between the Paris peace process and the Congress of Vienna in 1815. She was published for the first time on June 19, 1919 in *L'Echo de Bulgarie,* a Bulgarian newspaper published in French so that it could have an international distribution. This comparison occurred to many observers and negotiators that year. The similarities between the two peace conferences were inescapable: the short century between two European-wide conflicts; the sense of remaking the future of the world; and the complete condensation of power into the hands of a mere handful of men.[104]

Meanwhile, Nadejda Stancioff was still a young woman, at 25, in Sofia society. Therefore, at a tea arranged by the municipality of Sofia for Italian officers, she along with other young women, acted as hostesses serving tea, ice cream, and desserts.[105] There was an orchestra, dancing, and Nadejda's first encounter with fame. According to her,

...all the ministers and politicians talk to me about my articles and seek me out
from among the youth of Sofia, as a woman of letters and even a political person with a big great future! A type of irony! I begin to have fervent admirers
among young people who write as I do, for example Petko Petkoff, one or two
detractors, which is even more amusing – and a chain of female admirers, with
Helen and the Guechoffs in the lead.[106]

She was pleased with her notoriety and indeed the praise was not frivolous.
Her uncle by marriage, Grigori Natchevich expressed the strong desire to put her
prodigious talents to the use of their homeland's renaissance in a letter to
Dimitri:

Will she use this learning and her talent of hers . . . ? [Will she] dedicate wholeheartedly her talents and qualities to the rebirth [of our country], the civilizing of our
sexe faible . . . as in the elites of France not the Bolsheviks. By her family background and by her education Miss Stancioff is seemingly ready to order for that kind
of role.[107]

For her part Nadejda experienced the next generation (she felt much older
than they did) as decadent and artificial. The youth of her acquaintance had no
spontaneity or originality: "Young men . . . are a bit ridiculous; young girls . . .
are futile, empty and . . . not at all interesting."[108] The few Bulgarians whom she
judged to be worthy of note, such as the Petroff-Chomakoffs, a Bulgarian family
of notables, she believed were "people who alone know things which make life
worth living. I think that this family is unique of its type in Sofia."[109] Although
she enjoyed the pleasures inherent in her status as a diplomat's daughter and as
member of the upper class, she deplored the vulgarity and "futility" of Sofia
youth.
      Living in Sofia allowed her frequent contacts with representatives of the
Entente. It reminded her of her past life in St. Petersburg, Paris, and Rome. At a
dinner party for the representatives of the Entente, Nadejda felt in her element.
She was deliciously titillated by the contrasts of her existence in postwar Bulgaria. She writes:

I am between Baron Alliotti and General Mombelli, Mr. Charlotte between
Miss Vassileva and General Baird . . . conversation on the royal family of Italy
with General Mombelli. All the representatives of the Entente seem well disposed toward our country and are very nice . . . a beautiful European evening in
sum! The pleasure of having a dinner, which we did not order, cosmopolitan
neighbors, a pretty dress, flowers about one! Papa was also in his element, the
diplomatic world. I enjoyed the benefits of civilization immensely! Tomorrow
ragout of spinach and a bouillon of vegetables and bread ration etc. O, contrast!
But these are doubtless the contrasts, which give life its spice! But I certainly
love life more and more, its dangers, and its pleasures![110]

One of her duties in Sofia for the Ministry of Foreign Affairs was to translate
into English the speech that Bulgarian Prime Minister Theodore Theodoroff

would give at the peace conference. She admired the speech as relatively well composed, adroit, and noble.

The Bulgarian delegation roster, when finally published, included the Stancioff name. Each delegate would have five councilors attached to them. Dimitri Stancioff would attend the conference in the capacity of "private counselor and head of the cabinet of the president of the council."[111] When Theodoroff, the president of the council, took Stancioff on board, his decision was personal and practical; Dimitri Stancioff was a gifted and an experienced negotiator and he was a hard worker. There was a vague possibility of Nadejda going to Paris as a private secretary to her father and to Theodoroff. These important decisions seemed to be made somewhat haphazardly.

The time between the pronouncement of the list of delegates and the time of departure was a matter of days. Father and daughter telegraphed the rest of the family in Varna about their new plans. An emotional time, the importance of the mission weighed on them and more importantly, the prolonged separation was especially difficult for the close-knit family.

King Boris III Exchanges Confidences

Before they left, the king invited Dimitri and Nadejda to the royal residence at Vrana. Although he had spent the time following his father's abdication without his family—his siblings had left the country along with his father—Boris, now King of Bulgaria, was his old, companionable self. Boris greeted his visitors and spoke with them as though they had just parted company.[112] It seemed as though the war years separating the two families vanished. Nadejda was astonished that he called her "Nada" as before, and that she did not blunder, but called him "Sire" and "Your Majesty" as was appropriate to his new role. They talked about current events, and Nadejda and he "exchanged confidences" as before. She felt they were as close as when they were children. Nadejda comments on their close bond, the years had not severed:

> We exchange [confidences] sure of understanding one another, given the similarity of our points of view, we who knew each other so well as children and who have always had very close ties, despite the circumstances, the differences ... We always knew how to understand each other with half spoken words and to grasp the nuances in passing ... [he has] in politics, pessimism but lots of good sense, and enough confidence in the affection of his people.[113]

She left enchanted with their interview; she was touched by and as devoted to Boris as ever; the king even picked flowers from his greenhouse for her with his own hands. She perceived him as eminently sensible and yet human as well He was not cold and unapproachable as was the royalty she knew from her many experiences abroad.

King Boris' humility and lack of pretense as a monarch perennially surprised the Stancioffs. Each time they witnessed him doing something, which they considered beneath his station, they noted it in amazement. Other Bulgarians were surprised by it too.

The king often drove himself to and from Sofia when in residence at Vrana. On the occasions when he did use a chauffer, Boris preferred to sit next to his driver and not in isolation in the back seat. This behavior was unlike any that the status-conscious Stancioffs or Sofia society could comprehend. Bulgarian elites did find it charming and endearing but nonetheless, déclassé and not a little strange. It seemed Bulgaria's monarch was a real populist. Many of his closest advisors commented on this behavior.

King Boris was thoughtful and compassionate and had fully adopted his kingdom's people and their culture in his heart; he felt Bulgarian. On the other hand, as a descendent of multiple royal dynasties, he had been brought up to rule. He created boundaries between himself and his court as necessary. He could breech the walls to reach out to individuals. Boris often showed his humanity in small and large gestures, such as stopping on a country road to give an elderly peasant woman a lift to her home or convincing the train driver to give the monarch a turn at the controls.

Nadejda Stancioff Bulgarian Delegate

Nadejda was excited and a bit overwhelmed by her impending trip. She was profoundly sad not to be able to see the rest of her family before departure. In her journal, she described the entourage and their journey in detail.

The journey of the Bulgarian delegation to Paris launched the hopes and prayers of millions of fellow citizens who placed their trust in the assemblages of elected representatives and their cadre of experts and secretaries to do their utmost. They numbered fifty, and their circuitous route, planned by the French Military Mission in Bulgaria, directed their train north via the Iskur valley toward Romania, Hungary, Yugoslavia, Italy, Switzerland and, finally, France. They left Sofia at 11 a.m., with no ceremony and in almost complete silence, apart from the benediction of two priests, lending an impressionable muteness to the event.[114] In Bulgaria, dignitaries at every local stop greeted the train after it left the capital. Nadejda experienced those stops as Stations of the Cross on the road to Golgotha.

The almost complete absence of women in the crowds gave the scene a more somber tone, according to Nadejda. The delegates and their secretaries formed a large group of Bulgarians from different political parties. On this journey, they had an opportunity to take measure of each other, to exchange views, and to argue principles. "Everyone observes one another while pretending not to, the Bulgarian way, without letting anything get by them of the smallest detail."[115]

By the second day on the train, Nadejda reported that the relations among the members of the delegation were becoming very amicable and that "the most diverse mentalities come in close contact in the narrow corridors."[116] The group played animated games of bridge using suitcases as improvised card tables. The journey served to cement the diverse personalities into a Bulgarian national front.

The four ministers, who represented very different political parties, sat about one of the commonplace dining tables in a dining car suffused with the odors of cooking oil and other travel-related scents. In such close quarters, their patriotism overcame political differences, and they began to craft unexpected bonds. Their solidarity, however, would be tested in the weeks ahead in Neuilly.

Peace of Paris – the Balkan Conundrum

When the armistice began in November 1918, neither peace nor tranquility was assured for the continent generally, and for the Balkans specifically. The relative calm of the western parts of the continent contrasted sharply with the disorder and continuation of conflict in the east. The Russians were fighting a civil war; the Greeks and Turks had differences that were settled only in 1922, after another war; the Italians and Yugoslavs disagreed violently over the territorial settlement; the Romanians and Hungarians fought. In sum, the Peace of Paris negotiations began, but the real settlement took years to resolve, if one believes that there was resolution.

The peace process after World War I was a continuation of a system that had been the standard modus of operation for the Great Powers. Despite a change in the players small states could not hope for a different environment than one in which the Great Powers dictated the peace.

The Russian Empire was out of the system, since the rest of the Europeans did not recognize the Bolshevik state. Germany was no longer a member of the club, and Austria-Hungary simply dissolved. With the addition of the United States—a new player whose entry into the war had been one of the decisive factors that ended the conflict—the Great Power configuration changed even more.

The peace of 1919 was the creation primarily of France, Great Britain, Italy, and the United States of America, with the Italians a considerably weaker and less able partner in the mix. It was, in fact, Georges Clemenceau and Woodrow Wilson, (1856-1924), who, by their own contentious squabbling during the peace negotiations in 1919, led the way to the final settlement. Lloyd George, (1863-1945), played or posed the role of temporizing agent for balance.

In the end, although the three leaders agreed to the peace treaty, they were all attacked in both the foreign and their domestic press for giving away too much: too much territory, too many concessions, too much on principle.

Another aspect of the process, which narrowed the field of options for the negotiators, was the secret wartime treaties used to lure signatories into the conflict with the promise of territorial concessions. These treaties tended to be quite embarrassing, especially for the Great Powers, who now had to own up to their duplicitous stance when the high-minded principles, especially the one of self-determination, contrasted smartly with the rapacious agreements bargained during wartime. Idealism, in contrast to pragmatic negotiations in war, made for a tricky landscape for the peacemakers as they worked to recreate the European balance of power.

The introduction of communist propaganda, and the rise of socialist parties throughout the continent, spurred the powers to create a solid settlement that would prevent the spread of movements dangerous to the status quo. As the two remaining powers of the original pre-war five however, France and Britain had very different visions of what would constitute a durable peace, and their disunity proved the undoing of the peace almost before it began.

While the British foreign office worked to establish a balance of power that would keep France from becoming the predominant power on the continent, the French goals would impede that initiative. Clemenceau wished to create in Europe a defensive line of friendly nations that would serve as a buffer between France and her former enemies. In the end, these policies empowered two lucky Balkan winners at Paris, Romania and Yugoslavia. Their good fortune led to the establishment of an imperfect peace settlement, especially for their Bulgarian neighbor.

The Balkan region was a puzzle for the peacemakers in Paris. For most Europeans, the area was an undistinguishable jumble of states and peoples—all mysterious, all incomprehensible, all fairly alike in their inscrutability and, above all, uniformly dangerous to the stability of the continent. For those who bothered to study the region, and there were precious few, the Balkan states represented mere geographic objectives over which the Great Powers had come close to blows on numerous occasions.

The debate over the Balkans reduced Austro-Hungarian and Russian diplomatic negotiations to the equivalent of growls and snarls. In the past, the contention over the area led Germany to distract her ally, Austria-Hungary, in order to prevent the latter from starting an all-out war with imperial Russia. The Great War itself had been sparked by the assassination of the Archduke Franz Ferdinand in Sarajevo by a Serb nationalist in a moment when Germany had neglected to distract her ally.

The Ottoman Power Vacuum

A series of wars of independence fought by different Balkan national groups had rolled the Ottomans back from the area over the preceding decades. Ottoman presence on the European continent was reduced to a mere few hundred square miles on the tip of the Balkan Peninsula in Eastern Thrace. Constantinople, the city, was still the Ottomans' capital, but virtually all their territory was in Asia Minor and beyond.

The legacy of hundreds of years of Ottoman rule in the Balkans had left visible and invisible traces. Architecture, music, dress, manners and cuisine, were all a unique blend of East and West. This admixture of cultures also included generous doses of corruption, political intrigue, and a general atmosphere of distrust of figures of authority and lack of openness toward other ethnic groups. This reticence, to engage in what Europeans would have characterized as their own straightforward, law-bound ways, was a stumbling block to a variety of negotiations both domestic and foreign.

Finally, the Ottoman legacy left minorities in its wake: Armenians, Greeks, Jews, and Turks, in Bulgaria's case. These groups, too, added a complexity to the state's negotiations of policies which outsiders could not grasp. Just as a receding glacier leaves boulders of inchoate size and shape and color, so did the retreating Ottoman state leave an admixture of ethnic diversity and a territorial incoherence that thwarted even well-intended peacemakers.

For the Great Powers, comprehending the needs of the people from the Balkans was complicated by the fact that they persisted in perpetuating the atmosphere that had precipitated the Great War. Each of the Great Powers in Paris continued to play the role of patron to lesser client states. With the power camps now rearranged based on the war-time alliances, Bulgaria was one of the lesser powers left out of that type of arrangement. Other lesser powers used this advantage and played their cards to accentuate whichever aspect of their geography or other national feature would evoke the most favorable response from their patron.

Both the Romanians and Greeks presented themselves as apart from the mass of barbarous and enigmatic other. The Romanians claimed descent from the Romans—a claim that was intended to raise them above and beyond the Ottoman cultural stain. They were the darlings of the French. The Greeks used their Classical Greek past as a touchstone to affirm their status of greatness and superior cultural importance. They exploited the preponderance of Hellenophilia among European educated elites to distance themselves from the Ottoman association. The British championed the Greeks.

Both Balkan states represented themselves as superior to their neighbors, and by virtue of their cultural superiority, closer to Europe and farther from the undesirable oriental neighborhood. The other nations—Serbs, Croats, Slovenes, and Albanians—could separate themselves from the less prescient Bulgarians simply by contrasting their loyalty to the Allies with their antipathy for the German alliance.

The nature of these games led to a fierce competition among the Balkan states to capture the attention of a Great Power patron and translate it into tangible gains in territories and reparations. Their neighbors would counter by presenting competing claims for the same commodities. This tactic inspired a rivalry to bring forward every case of historical precedent to claim some superior status of importance. Thus, each Balkan state used the geographic dimensions of its greatest and oldest medieval incarnation to justify contradictory and often spurious claims for territorial settlement in Paris. The Bulgarians were denied that luxury, however.

President Wilson's idealism, illustrated in his Fourteen Points, which so appealed to both the victors and vanquished, formed the nucleus of a disaster in the making. While each state issued territorial demands based on historically anchored greatness, they then used quite confused, sometimes deliberately misleading, maps to make their case for ethnic, political, economic, cultural, religious, and any other form of self-determination they could invent. Despite armies of "experts" which each delegation brought along to Paris, the main peacemakers had little real specific knowledge.

Lloyd George was notoriously poorly informed about the map of Europe and the Middle East.[117] The combination of ignorance or plain disregard for the fate of the Balkans on the part of the Great Powers led to a peace settlement that rewarded without regard to the offense given to others; a settlement that punished with no regard to the consequences of a well of resentment that filled at the signing of the peace treaties. The French felt no need to look too closely into the fate of the Balkan states once they secured a buffer of friendly central European countries and the eternal gratitude of the Romanians.

The French, represented by Georges Clemenceau, insisted on the erection of a line of buffer states as part of their future security needs. Their insistence on exact reparations for all damages the Germans inflicted (a figure whose provenance would be impossible to ascertain) and their desire to compensate themselves through the acquisition of German colonial holdings, led the way to a peace which was at best a compromise and at worst an ignorant, clumsy, shortsighted endeavor.

The creation of the new state that began as the Kingdom of the Serbs, Croats, and Slovenes and ended as Yugoslavia suited French security interests and did not threaten the security of any other Great Power; the Russians could not voice an opinion on the process since they were no longer part of the Great Power club.

However, that new entity sucked into its very core a mass of resentment from all its neighbors for the territories and captive minority populations it eventually encompassed. Contentment with an all-too-generous settlement for the victors blinded those victors to the many seeds of revenge sown in the process establishing peace.

The new kingdom took from every one of its neighbors, Albania, Bulgaria, Greece, Romania, Hungary, Austria, and Italy. Even the Romanians, who should have been more than satisfied with their peace settlement, were resentful of those parts of the Banat the Serbs claimed. Serbia became the torso around the patched together Frankenstein body of Yugoslavia. It lived as an aberrant organism, repudiated by its neighbors and reviled by them as a parvenu and monster. Greece was the only neighbor that was willing to overlook minor territorial squabbles and extend a friendly hand to the new state; that albeit was a weak salute.

Stamboliiski and the New Bulgaria

For the Bulgarians, the future seemed bleak, but with a simple faith in Wilson's promises, especially of self-determination, they went to the peace expecting some just solution.

Stamboliiski was a realist and pragmatist. He and his party, BANU, would force Bulgarians to reassess their vision of the nation and their expectations of the political path that Bulgaria should take in the near future. The peasant-led party would focus on domestic reforms and a vision of a country guided by the needs of its farmers rather than its urban bourgeoisie. This paradigm shift in the government included all those who labored with their physical powers, but vehemently excluded intellectuals and the rising middle class, who had a different vision.

In at least one matter, Stamboliiski was contradictory, he supported the monarchy and her king. In King Boris, the "kinglet," as he referred to him, Stamboliiski saw a monarch whom he admired and with whom he could work. For his own reasons, Stamboliiski came to love Bulgaria's king as his own children and said as much in public.[118]

Bulgaria experienced a real class revolution when the Agrarians came to power. The radical nature of their rise to power, the callous and rough treatment of their political opponents, and their obvious disregard for any interests but those of the peasants, exposed them to criticism and eventually real discontentment at home. These party agenda won Stamboliiski and his party significant political opposition.

With his first appearance on the international horizon at the Peace of Paris in 1919, Stamboliiski had a directly opposite effect on foreign observers than he had at home. Abroad, he was perceived as a man of vision, a great statesman who was capable in domestic policy. He was viewed as a valuable colleague among world leaders and as a man who did not shirk in his duties to create political stability in the Balkans. He insisted on fulfilling all the stipulations of the treaty of Neuilly, in the interests of European peace which was a laudable effort in the chaotic post war period.

Stamboliiski's vehemently anti-communist stance won him admirers abroad, and his willingness to subsume many of Bulgaria's national territorial ambitions in the name of international cooperation and good neighborliness made him a curious celebrity. Thus, outside the country, he was celebrated as a new breed of statesman who practiced bold, modern reforms.

Abroad, Bulgaria became an interesting experiment in green party control; a state governed primarily by the interests of its agricultural laborers. What would this new political ideology augur for the future? The political spectrum in the early twentieth century was still narrowly focused on monarchy and some type of representative or consultative legislature. Single party control which championed the rights of farmers and other laborers seemed a novel idea that could evoke a more sinister platform—communism.

New ideologies had begun to emerge in the breach made by the war. The most famous and eventually, the longest-lived ideology was the Bolsheviks' call for communism in Russia. However, communists and socialists were pushing for reform and change across the continent, sometimes with bloody results and civil strife. For Bulgaria the case of a single party with peasant interests as its goal was unique. The Agrarians came to power peacefully and seemed to have no desire but to focus on internal reforms and remain at peace with their neighbors. Europeans did not know what to make of this political entity. The Bulgarian Agrarian party seemed very close to a communistic system of government because it espoused even distribution of land, government support for agricultural production, compulsory service for the state, aimed at young people.

The Bulgarian Delegation

The Bulgarian delegation approached the peace process with trepidation but also with a large amount of unfounded optimism. The delegation had a faith that Woodrow Wilson's Fourteen Points would be applied to their case on an equal basis with all others, a faith that self-determination especially would secure Bulgaria the territories that were mostly populated by Bulgarians. While the Allies continued to see the Bulgarians as traitors and as the "minions of the Hun," the Bulgarians seemed to believe that changes in the politics of the country would be sufficient to win the sympathetic ear of the Big Three, especially Woodrow Wilson. They felt that the abdication of Ferdinand and the rise of their new Agrarian led government were ample evidence of the country's earnest desire to change its foreign policy direction. However, the Agrarians did not take control of the country and most importantly neutralize the communists until after they signed the Peace of Neuilly.

It is highly probable that the Bulgarians approached the conference with President Poincaré's beautiful and eloquent quote from his inaugural speech—given in January before the assembled negotiators in Paris—resonating in their heads: "In you hands you hold the honor of the world."[119] For the Bulgarians honor would not be salvaged.

The negotiations were flawed, and the first few months of the peace conference, long before the Bulgarians arrived in Paris, cemented Bulgaria's fate. No one who could have made a difference in Paris cared that Bulgaria was undergoing a dramatic change in domestic political control.

When the fate of tens of thousands of people was decided by the intransigence of one or another policy maker, many decisions at Paris were based on whim not on fact or certain knowledge. Under these conditions the peace settlement of Bulgaria could have little chance of getting a fair agreement. Bulgaria would be punished for her entry into the war on the losing side as severely as the primary culprits, Germany and Austria-Hungary. Turkey's fate would have been just as severe had it not been for the military resistance movement that led to a revocation of the Treaty of Sévres and the negotiation of a new treaty, the Treaty of Lausanne in 1923, which became Turkey's peace settlement.

The complicated and protracted peace process accomplished a great deal of damage. Regardless of how eloquent her pleas, Bulgaria would not get a fair hearing at Paris. From the very beginning, in January 1919, the Big Three—Clemenceau, Wilson, and Lloyd George—started on the wrong foot tussling over the official language of the conference. Ultimately they agreed to give French and English equal weight. Then they feuded over the number of representatives of each allied state—a tricky issue once Britain introduced the initiative to allow her colonies a vote. In this way, the Big Three whiled away the first weeks of the conference.

Ultimately, the power struggles among the allies led to the bungling of peace settlements and inefficiencies in calculating boundaries, reparation payments, and other peace accords which changed the prospects of millions of people on several continents. As Nadejda noted in an uncharacteristic understatement that the conference was inchoate. The peace makers turned out to be just as delusional as the peace breakers about what the Peace of Paris would create for their collective futures.

Notes

1. Nadejda Stancioff, unpublished journal, 23 September 1915, PASF.

2. Unpublished copy of telegram from King Ferdinand to Dimitri Stancioff in DS II, PASF.

3. Stancioff, *Diplomat and Gardener Memoirs*. 25. Ivan Stancioff has a slightly different version than this quote, which is in the form of a typed transcription of the original telegram sent June 23, 1913 and kept in PASF file DS II.

4. Nadejda Stancioff, unpublished journal, 17 February 1915, PASF.
"Her Majesty, the Queen sent 50,000 Bulgarian cigarettes for the French wounded; their distribution is confided to Count J. de Castellane. She has also sent cases of cigarettes to the English wounded Russians and Austrians; it is neutral charity."

5. Ibid. 2 September 1915.

6. Buchanan, *My Mission to Russia, and Other Diplomatic Memories*. 148.

7. Nadejda Stancioff, unpublished journal, 23 September 1915, PASF.

8. Ibid. 17 March 1916.

9. Ibid. 18 June 1916.

10. Ibid. It is not clear what these might have been, possibly some kind of personal vendetta for a professional reprimand.

11. Ibid.

12. Nadejda Stancioff, unpublished journal, 2 June 1916, PASF. Chronology is a bit confused as Nadejda wrote her notes on their trip home to Varna.

13. Ibid.

14. Ibid. 4 June 1916.

15. Stancioff, Nadejda Memories of Love.

16. Nadejda Stancioff, unpublished journal, 13 July 1916, PASF.

17. Muir, *Dimitri Stancioff Patriot and Cosmopolitan*.

18. Nadejda Stancioff, unpublished journal, 18 July 1916, PASF.

19. Nadejda Stancioff, unpublished journal, 29 July 1916, PASF.

20. Ibid. 2 August 1916.

21. Ibid. 29 August 1916.

22. Ibid. 5 September 1916.

23. Stancioff, Nadejda Memories of Love.

24. The sources for these kinds of attitudes are many. See Melman, *Women's Orients, English Women and the Middle East, 1718-1918 : Sexuality, Religion, and Work,* Edward W. Said, *Orientalism*, 1st Vintage Books ed. (New York: Vintage Books, 1979).

25. R. J. Crampton, *A Concise History of Bulgaria*, Second ed. (Cambridge: Cambridge University Press, 2005).

26. Nadejda Stancioff, unpublished journal, 28 September 1916, PASF.

27. "Here the prices of commodities: bag of flour 75-100f – 1 Kilo of oil 12-16 f, sugar very rare 1.30 f in Sofia, 1.80 here, fresh butter 10-12f/Kilo; tapioca 5f the Kilo." In Nadejda Stancioff, unpublished journal, 16 October 1916, PASF.

28. Crampton, *Bulgaria 1878-1918: A History*, 501.

29. Ibid. 503.

30. Nadejda Stancioff, unpublished journal, 30 November 1916, PASF.
31. Ibid. 28 April 1917.
32. Stancioff, *Diplomat and Gardener Memoirs*, 30.
33. Ibid. 31.
34. Nadejda Stancioff, unpublished journal, 15 March 1917, PASF.
35. Ibid. 19 March 1917.
36. Ibid. 24 February 1916.
37. Ibid. 16 March 1917.
38. Ibid.
39. Ibid. 25 March 1917.
40. Ibid. 13 March 1919.
41. Ibid. 21 May 1917. Nadejda wrote an honest appraisal of the political changes in her world as the revolution unfolded in March. The Stancioffs were not democrats but supporters of the conservative order. "Out of tradition, respect, love of the past and a hatred for the system of democracy I morn this fall of Russian imperialism." See Nadejda's journal 17 March 1917, PASF.
42. Ibid. 19 August 1917.
43. Ibid.
44. Ibid. 20 July 1917.
45. Ibid. 19 December 1917.
46. Ibid. 12 June 1917.
47. He died on September 25, 1918. Stancioff, Nadejda Memories of Love, 50.
48. Ibid. 52. See too, Nadejda Stancioff, unpublished journal several references at beginning of 1919.
49. Nadejda Stancioff, unpublished journal, 20 October 1917, PASF.
50. Ibid. 26 April 1916.
51. Ibid. 20 October 1916.
52. Ibid. 7 December 1916.
53. Ibid. 30 May 1917.
54. Ibid. 16 August 1917.
55. Ibid. 15 June 1917.
56. Stancioff, Nadejda Memories of Love, 52 .
57. Ibid. Nadejda Stancioff, unpublished journal, 3 July 1917, PASF.
58. Ibid. 5 July 1917.
59. Ibid. 23 June 1917.
60. Ibid. 25 June 1917.
61. Ibid. 15 August 1917.
62. Ibid.
63. Ibid. 22 August 1917.
64. Ibid. 19 July 1917.
65. Said, *Orientalism*. Nadejda Stancioff's views on what constituted the Orient and who was an oriental march in lock-step with contemporary perceptions of what Said calls "a formidable scholarly corpus [of British and French projections of] Oriental despotism, Oriental splendor, cruelty, sensuality." 4.
66. Ibid.26.
67. Nadejda Stancioff, unpublished journal, 10 August 1917, PASF.
68. Ibid. 27 September 1917. The essentialization of the traits of peoples and nations was common in the period and developed under strong German influence of the *Volkspsykologie*. See K. Daskalova's article "Bulgarian Women in Movements, Laws, Discourses (1840s-1940s)." *Bulgarian Historical Review* 1-2

(1999): 180-96.

69. Stancioff, *Diplomat and Gardener Memoirs,* 33-34.

70. Nadejda Stancioff, unpublished journal, 12 February 1919, PASF.

71. Ibid. 15 January 1919.

72. Ibid.

73. Ibid. 27 February 1919.

74. Ibid. 27 January 1919.

75. Ibid.

76. Ibid. 2 May 1919.

77. Ibid. Meat of muton15-20 francs [f]/ k; beef 12-15 f, butter 50-55; fat 50f; nuts 18; dry fruits 15 f; prunes 18 f; ...workers [in the vineyards] 15-20 f/ day with meals. Table wine 18 f/k. Where are we headed!! [She moaned that] fish caught under our windows sells for 7-8 f/k and potatoes for 4-6 f/k. In Nadejda Stancioff, unpublished journal, 2 May 1919, PASF.

78. Ibid. 1 January 1919.

79. Ibid. 31 December 1919.

80. No romantic relationship or feeling on Nadejda's part is in evidence. Although on 3 January 1919 Nadejda described the colonel in the following way in her journal: Col Stuart: he has a seductive physique: very thin with beautiful hands, a very agreeable voice, nice eyes and a smile which is quite captivating.

81. Ibid. 13 April 1919.

82. Ibid. 24 January 1919

83. Ibid. 22 January 1919.

84. Stancioff, *Diplomat and Gardener Memoirs,* 34.

85. Nadejda Stancioff, unpublished journal, 19 March 1919, PASF.

86. Ibid.

87. Ibid. 21 March 1919.

88. Ibid. 2 April 1919.

89. Ibid. 28 February 1919.

90. Ibid. 22 April 1919. Essentializing peoples based on preconceived, European notions of national characteristics was commonplace in the Stancioffs' world.

91. Ibid. 27 March 1919.

92. Ibid. 17 May 1919.

93. Ibid.

94. Ibid.

95. Ibid. 18 May 1919. [The city was] "very modern, a coquette, elegant enough, sunny with gardens. One feels or gets an impression of pitiful size, of mediocrity" [and] "... no art, no taste, and no originality!"

96. Ibid. 22 May 1919.

97. Ibid. 7 June 1919.

98. Ibid. 16 June 1919.

99. Ibid. 23 May 1919.

100. Ibid. 24 May 1919.

101. Ibid.

102. Ibid. 6 June 1919.

103. Ibid. 14 June 1919.

104. Harold Nicolson, among others, mentioned the very same idea in his *Peacemaking.*

105. Nadejda Stancioff, unpublished journal, 4 July 1919, PASF.

106. Ibid. 8 July 1919.

107. Ibid. 3 July 1919. See typescript of original letter in DS V, PASF.
108. Ibid. 25 May 1919.
109. Ibid. 25 June 1919.
110. Ibid. 25 May 1919.
111. Ibid. 13 July 1919.
112. Ibid. 15 July 1919.
113. Ibid.
114. Ibid. 21 July 1919.
115. Ibid. 22 July 1919.
116. Ibid.
117. Margaret MacMillan, *Paris 1919* (New York: Random House, 2001).
118. Nadejda Stancioff, unpublished letter, 11 May 1922, Nada II, PASF.
119. Nadejda Stancioff, unpublished journal, 28 February 1919, PASF.

6
The Disillusionments of Peacetime

"Hope and Constancy! Always!"
Nadejda Stancioff, unpublished journal[1]

When the Bulgarians arrived in Paris, the head of the French military mission, Colonel Henri, as well as other dignitaries from the peace conference and city representatives, greeted the Bulgarian delegation at the train station. It was a somber hello. A convoy of cars drove the Bulgarians to Neuilly-sur-Seine and the Château de Madrid, which was to be their home for the duration of the process (the Hungarian delegation would also occupy the Madrid when their turn came at the peace talks in 1920).

Nadejda found that ride from the station especially painful, since she felt connected to the Entente states by "blood, culture, tastes, and ideas, strong friendships and via English, French, and Russian pasts."[2] She felt the cortege resembled a Roman triumph; the victorious parades of prisoners of war and booty assembled for Roman generals. Their cavalcade passed before Notre Dame, the Académie Française, the Louvre, and the Place de la Concorde, via the Champs-Elysées. The avenue was flanked by rows of captured German canons, armored vehicles, and shells. Decorations aflutter festooned city streets still celebrating the victory. It was indeed a parade of the vanquished before their masters. Until the peace treaty was signed the Bulgarians remained enemy combatants, rejected by the European community, and treated with hostility.

Bulgarian Delegates under Confinement

The French hosts installed the Bulgarian delegates at the chateau in a state of permanent house arrest. They could not visit Paris under any circumstances. They could only run errands in Neuilly and take walks in the Bois de Boulogne when accompanied by inspectors from the *Sûreté* (police), put at the Bulgarians' disposal for that purpose. The Bulgarians' humiliation was absolute. They were forbidden to have visitors, and so on one occasion, Nadejda actually conspired to meet her Uncle Aynard at church, and then proceeded to scandalize their fellow worshipers by talking through the service![3]

The original restrictions on the Bulgarian delegation during their confinement were relaxed over time due to the easy-going nature of their French guards to the point that on her name day, September 30, Nadejda and her father were able to go to a popular patisserie for tea and gateaux unaccompanied. Subsequently their French liaison officer was reprimanded. The Bulgarian delegates could not elude the stigma of being the representatives of enemy combatants.

Once settled in their quarters, the wait for the Bulgarian delegation seemed interminable. Smaller Balkan "victor" powers had had their day at the Peace Conference, in spring 1919, while the "loser" powers—especially the small ally of the Central Powers, Bulgaria—were kept waiting for weeks at the Château de Madrid. The Bulgarian's stay would be costly. The delegation had to pay 2,500 francs for the rent of the furniture; each individual was responsible for the cost of his or her meals, which was 40 francs per day. Settling into their rooms and the new routine, the stratification that distinguished the delegates in their professional lives was projected onto their accommodations. Thus, the delegate ministers had their own dining room, as did the French liaison group, while the rest ate in a spacious dining room with three large tables.

Nadejda made herself at home as best she could.[4] She decorated her room with two Rossetti engravings pinned to the wall and photos of her family on the fireplace mantle. She also had a large quantity of books, work-related papers, and newspaper clippings, and, as a final touch, the Bulgarian tricolor attached to the bed post. She wrote home: "this is a strange experience, captivity in the comfort of a luxury establishment, supervision by French and British officers, escorts of security agents . . . Papa often asks me to accompany him to the Russian church in the Rue Daru, where the singing is beautiful . . . only Russians can sing with such pathos and cry to Heaven."[5].

The atmosphere in France was hostile toward the Bulgarians. The French press ridiculed and maligned the Bulgarian delegation Nadejda bemoaned the rabid anti-Bulgarian tone of the publications; "It is horrible to be able to analyze and understand everything French and to be at the same time a barbarian from the Balkans!"[6] She also found it intolerable, as did the other Bulgarians that their neighbors and rivals in the Balkans had relatively good press in France and were able to use that to their advantage in the peace negotiations. The Bulgarians resented the benign and warm reception Romania, Greece, and Serbia received in Paris, while were treated with utmost suspicion and animosity. This considerable disadvantage was something Nadejda would not be able to contend with, and it would become an increasingly bitter reality for her and the other Bulgarian delegates.

It was an era when newspapers printed all sorts of ephemera about the personal lives of politicians; much of it yellow journalism intent on swaying public opinion about current political issues. For example, the French newspapers noticed the fact that the Bulgarian delegation had stopped at Lausanne for twenty-four hours. Journalists, anxious to entertain their readers, wrote that the Bulgarian delegation had felt a need to go clothes shopping in order to refresh their wardrobes![7]

In addition to this kind of ephemeral reporting, some newspapers published biographies of members of the delegation, which were largely erroneous and malevolent. In fact, French newspapers published a fictional interview with Dimitri Stancioff. Because he was the only delegate who had a positive reputation in France, he was given good press with favorable comments on his career, on his Francophilia, and on his marriage to a Frenchwoman.

Nadejda found her name listed in the newspapers along with the rest of the delegation. This reportage was an exciting first in her life.[8] She was proud, despite the generally poor reception of the Bulgarian delegation as a whole. The *New York Herald* listed her as "young woman, the private secretary of the First Delegate."[9]

In the Château de Madrid, Dimitri established three rooms as offices. The entire delegation had to contend with doing a lot of their work in their bedrooms, since the building was simply too small to have designated rooms for every function. The former palace of François I, the chateau, in more recent times, had become a favorite rendezvous spot for Parisians. The Bulgarian delegation lived in isolation and at the same time on display, as Nadejda observes: "The [French] crowd passes by and we sometimes hear, amusing commentaries! No hate but a type of commiseration on along the lines of 'the poor Buggers'!"[10]

Nadejda worked in the diplomatic section—specifically under Minister Theodoroff and her father. She also had to read all the English newspapers and write all the English translations along with Vladimir Tsanoff , who had studied in the United States.[11] She saw her father in his characteristic environment and noted wryly, that they lived in "paper, ink, books, dictation, statistics, and archives!"[12]

Their virtual prisoner status restricted the Bulgarian delegation's daily routine. If there were no escorts available, the Bulgarians had to be content with stretching their legs in the chateau yard "like caged lions" as Nadejda quipped. She was enormously busy from the very beginning. Theodoroff worked tirelessly which meant she did, too.

The delegation had had ample time to come together as a unified cadre since their slow train journey from Bulgaria. They traveled through the southern tier of Europe, made a stop at Lausanne, where the Bulgarian community came out to greet them, and then north to Paris.

The delegation had begun as a rather slapdash construction. Most delegates were representatives of the Bulgarian interest groups, members of the various religious groups and major political parties; a delegation that would represent to Europe the newer, friendlier people of Bulgaria.

Believing that the rights of minorities were an important priority promised by the principled language of the peacemakers, the Bulgarians created a miniature representative body of the country's largest ethnic and religious minorities as part of their delegation. Small in number, the delegation nonetheless included a member of every major religion: Bulgarian Orthodox, Catholicism, Protestant-ism, Judaism, and Islam. Nadejda was included in the special committee on mi-norities since she was the only Catholic in the delegation. There was also one Jew; one Muslim who was Turkish and two Protestants, a husband and wife pair. These improvisations apparently added a certain Slavic charm to the dele-gation considered by Nadejda as endearing in contrast to methodical, German precision![13]

It was in this haphazard and casual atmosphere where friendships devel-oped. Nadejda grew to enjoy the camaraderie of some of the members of her delegation. Ianko Sakazoff, (Minister of Commerce) in fine Socialist form, ad-dressed her in the familiar and called to her in the hallways, "Ey, Nadejda, de-voike, kak si?" (Hey, Nadejda, girl, how are you doing?)[14] Stamboliiski became increasingly sociable and funny and advised her to shorten her skirts to coincide with the latest Paris fashions.

Members of all the largest political parties had representatives in Paris: Narodniaks (People's Party, a conservative group organized in 1894), Agrarians (Bulgarian Agrarian National Union, BANU, principally concerned with peasant welfare organized in 1899), and Socialists (Bulgarian Social Democratic Party organized in 1892). Hosts of representatives were diplomats; many of whom were complete novices to the international atmosphere and politics in general. Several had never left the country of their origin.

Bulgarians were on the threshold of an entirely new era, and their experi-ence, both the delegates and those at home, of the Paris Peace would be tem-pered by the complete overthrow of those who had marched the country into war. The introduction of a peasant government, led by a larger than life party leader, offered hope that the mistakes of the past would not be repeated. The Bulgarians' instruction in the new century began at Paris.

Men of a Certain Age

Nadejda had an opportunity to study her compatriots over the course of their forced proximity, and she noted that Minister Sakazoff was an interesting man with a charming taste for beautiful things.[15] She also noted, with some surprise, that despite his Socialist affiliation, he was refined and elegant, and the most reserved of the ministers. He broke the stereotype of gruff, unpolished, wild-eyed subversive—the kind of label her contemporaries readily applied to anyone who represented a challenge to the established social and economic order.

This was the beginning of Nadejda's own education with respect to the op-position political parties. She got along very well with Stefan Panaretoff, (1853-1931), who was minister plenipotentiary to the United States of America. He was, in Nadejda's estimation, charming, erudite, and a good patriot, with a mod-erate point of view.[16] He was also a quick study of the shifting diplomatic envi-ronment. She admired him and found him an easy conversationalist. This as-sessment was typical for Nadejda, who recognized quite young that she preferred older, well-educated, knowledgeable men to the younger, frivolous types. In fact, she comments that she was happy surrounded mostly by these capable men rather than their wives and daughters:

> I prefer to pass free time with men of a certain age. It is very interesting to live, without women, with men chosen from among the most educated and the most capable of an entire nation; I visit with the experts with pleasure, and they instruct me every evening, while I speak with them about various subjects... The men of my country have always been infinitely more interesting from all points of view than the women; if I think, even for one instant, of having in the place of my companions their spouses, their daughters, their sisters I tremble with dread . . . I made the same observation at the POW camp in Plovdiv.[17]

Her views about other women are not an exception. Most of the educated women of her time, who were not gender sensitive, would have written the same. They were not at all surprised at the circumstances that dictated women's and men's roles and behaviors.

Living in close quarters, with the predominantly male Bulgarian delegation was comfortable for the young woman who preferred older intelligent men. Nadejda painted a convincing portrait of the chaotic and sometimes absurd goings-on at the chateau. Thus on a given day, in her father's bedroom—a room cluttered with paper files, toiletries, family photos and newspapers which also served as an office—the following scene could be played out. Her father would dictate corrections to a letter, while Theodoroff would supervise. At the same time, a tailor and a shirt maker from Rue Royale would measure her father for custom-made clothes. To add to the confusion, Colonel Henri, their French liaison at the conference, would walk in with a communication from the conference.

The delegates' lives were certainly hectic and unpredictable at times. They experienced technical difficulties at the chateau. At one point, there was no central heating; on another occasion, as Nadejda describes, the electricity expired:

> I have an image in Papa's study etched in my brain: Theodoroff seated on the big table, adding some phrases to his note on the evacuation of Thrace, Papa leaning over toward him to help by the light of a candle we bought for ourselves in Russe for the trip. It is an unexpected and pathetic tableau.[18]

She worked hard on a variety of communications to the peace conference, but she always felt that no matter the amount of effort, the results would inevitably lead to naught. She repeated that conviction frequently in her letters home. Possibly the entire delegation felt the same.

When she and another secretary worked on translating a résumé of Bulgarian politics since 1912 into French, a labor that was difficult and long which took them into the early hours of the morning, she felt the effort, like all her previous efforts at the conference, was destined to be stillborn. The Bulgarian delegates worked for the satisfaction of knowing that their labor "produced an excellent impression at the conference and 60 copies would be printed." [19] Then Nadejda had the additional privilege of translating the same document into English.

The pace of their work quickened right before a courier was due to leave for Bulgaria. She noted that on the days leading up to that date, she read fifteen newspapers and was responsible, along with her normal duties, for working on the disposition of Thrace to such an intense degree that she was now an expert on the statistics and could navigate all the *kazas* and *sandjaks* (districts and counties). Once the courier left, the diplomatic laborers would allow themselves a distraction as reward for their hard work.

A Feminine Regret

On one of these pleasure excursions, Nadejda experienced the double embarrassment that only an intelligent, fashion-conscious woman could experience. While they were at the Pre Catelan, a pleasure park in Paris, Mrs. Vesnić, the wife of the Serbian minister, saw and publicly commented on Nadejda's attire. Not only did Nadejda feel humiliated that Serbia had the upper hand in those days of diplomatic crisis, but she knew that she was not dressed in her finest. Members of her own delegation had prodded her to shorten her skirts in keeping with modern styles. She, of course, understood the frivolity of her humiliation and remarked on it in her journal:

> The entire Balkan question from the superficial aspect is crystallized here! With a hateful voice of a woman, she [Mrs. Vesnić] shouts: [in English] 'look, there's the Stancioff girl' I look ostentatiously toward Paris. The daughter, 'Where? No! Yes, it is! And here! Of all things!' I laughed a long time with the only regret—a very feminine one—of having on a dress that is out of fashion, before women who are dressed so chic![20]

In the face of public embarrassment, she modernized her wardrobe. She later claimed that she shortened all her dresses in order to please Madame Theodoroff!

Nadejda felt the pain of Bulgaria's defeated status personally. In Paris, she saw people with whom she had socialized on an equal basis before the war but with whom she now felt awkward and ill at ease, since, for the most part, their countries had fought as enemies. She experienced their interpersonal relations as uneven, based on the outcome of the war, as she notes in her journal:

> O, Elena [Tittoni]! O, Nadejda—who were equal in peace and who are no longer in war and victory! Her father has hands full of glory and mine carried nothing but bitterness and disillusionment today, she has luxury, a Rolls-Royce and I the company of the flic [cop] Mercadier![21]

She consoled herself with the thought that at least her experiences were now more novel than those of the victors. Overall, she found the fashions of Parisian society women ugly and too revealing. She opined, along with her family, that since the war, vulgarity had crept into the Paris they had known and loved.

Nostalgic for Freedom

In August, Parisians usually retreated to their vacation spots and the city remained populated by those held prisoner by their occupations. Those remaining in the hot dusty capital had few amusements and, in the case of Nadejda, much to regret. At mid-month, it was a tropical 30 degrees Celsius in Paris, and Nadejda noted several watersheds in the diplomatic world including the:

> death of the great diplomat Aleksandûr Izvolsky in a clinic in Paris;—the Bolsheviks appear the victor everywhere in Russia, Kolchak and Denikin's armies are retreating, in Petrograd famine and death. It is the 20th century! Tomorrow election in Bulgaria![22]

Meanwhile the delegates spent time shopping and sending their finds back home to their families. Wartime had left stores depleted in Bulgaria, and all the delegates, including the ministers, were eager to stock up on the necessities and luxuries Parisian shopping offered at Bon Marché and the Galleries LaFayette.

Nadejda was with Aleksandûr Stamboliiski when he took his first metro ride on one of these excursions in September. In fact, virtually every outing they took was to go shopping. Nadejda joked that the French *flics* (French slang for cop) were very happy to give the Bulgarians leave to go out because they spent so much money in their municipality!

Frivolity did not mask the building tension, however. Everyday that brought them closer to the final version of the treaty increased the Bulgarian delegates' stress levels. The future of their country was being wrought in gilded French halls, and the Bulgarians were overwhelmed with the burden of the final product, which would be ultimately out of their control. Nadejda describes her feelings about the future with irony:

> Tonight I feel nostalgic for freedom, youth, and the pleasures of life. After the peace, I will enter a Cook agency . . . and have myself sent to Palestine. On the days when the public is not allowed in the ruins I will find a sarcophagus and lie in it in a corner where iris and jasmine grow and I will forget the past![23]

In August, the delegation had a collective photograph taken in the courtyard of the Madrid, which they had come to know so well.[24] The "caged lions" displayed themselves for the camera. A somber photograph lends a view on the faces of those Bulgarians who would be primary witnesses to the last sad chapter in the national debacle. The delegation is arranged in four rather haphazard rows, with the most important members seated in rattan lawn chairs in the front of the group and the lower ranking using the veranda portion of the chateau as a pedestal.

The photograph, which became rather well-known in Bulgaria, found its way into general history books and is readily recognizable by those who love history. Only two women are included in the group of delegates, secretaries, experts, translators, historians, economists, politicians, and diplomats.

Nadejda is directly in the center back row. Her placement in this photograph speaks volumes of her role at the conference. She made certain to use the opportunity to create her external persona as recorded by the camera's lens. Posing for posterity, in a world controlled by patriarchs, she carved out a niche unique to her character and still sustained a strong voice. She is the only one wearing a bright white top therefore attracting the viewer's attention. By placing herself at the center and choosing that particular item of clothing she intentionally focused the observer's eye on the lone bright spot in that dark group.

The other female in the group is hardly noticeable and blends in well with the crowd of men because she, like the men brandished dark suits. The other subjects of the photograph wear dark ties accentuated only by their starched white shirts and stiff shirt collars. In their faces and by their hairstyles, facial hair, or its complete lack they run the gamut of dated and up to date looks. There are those who face the camera defiantly, those who gaze in curiosity, some who choose to look away, and others who confound the lens with their own lens of pince-nez. As a group, the assemblage epitomizes the era—not yet completely modern and not yet entirely rid of the past.

Denizens of the Orient

When it was the Bulgarians' turn at the peace conference, the tone was somber in the chateau. The French newspapers sounded a harsh note when most of their articles pronounced the terms of the peace treaty too temperate. However, Nadejda and the delegates plodded on with their work because in some sense it was a relief to come to the end, to get it over with, and to move on with their future as individuals and as a nation.

When the majority of delegates headed home to submit the preliminary treaty to the government, the send-off was a scene closely resembling the departure of a caravan laden with provisions and setting off on a long, arid journey. Nadejda describes piles of many crates, boxes, and large suitcases, "the bundles of komitadjis, [irregular Ottoman militias from 19th century Balkan history], floral decorated boxes of the large stores full of apples, packages of top quality stuff wrapped in cloth, umbrellas knotted with ribbons and even a brand new violin!"[25]

Then, to lend the scene an added dimension of complexity and humor, the delegates jockeyed for seats in the cars, which were reserved for the more important members; the others got berths on the bus. In the end, Nadejda and her father boarded the bus "in order to set a good example." However, the comic scene did not end there, since the vehicle had a mechanical failure. The travelers ended up taking the metro to the train station instead.[26] Meanwhile, their French handlers were frantic for the group to be on time for their train.

The routine at the chateau changed substantially after the departure of most of the delegation. According to Nadejda, the Madrid acquired the feel of a bed-and-breakfast establishment; workloads normalized, routines relaxed, and the remaining delegates were not as crowded.[27] Eating together at the small communal table allowed the twelve more intimacy than the strictly segregated arrangements that had kept the group divided according to rank. Mikhail Sarafoff and Venelin Ganeff, Minister of Justice and Minister Plenipotentiary-retired, were left in charge. The junior staff considered the two kindly, ineffectual, and too nice and dubbed them "Madame" and "Miss."

During these more relaxed days, Nadejda spent time with the young men in the group. She went shopping, chatted, and shared theories with them. These discussions continued into the night. Evenings of political discussion in smoke-filled rooms with cherry brandy and other refreshments became the norm. Those nights were relaxing and fun and were the only diversions the Bulgarians had. Nadejda finally felt she was living the life of a student, which she never had the opportunity to enjoy.

Her favorite of the young men was "Stoyan A. Petroff the Narcissus of the Delegation." He had served in the cavalry during the war, distinguished himself and received three medals: and had brought his collection of photos with him.[28] His military bearing attracted her. Their relationship included some flirtation but it remained platonic; Nadejda viewed Stoyan as a brother. They became good friends.

Stoyan astonished her because of his surprising font of knowledge and because he liked all things Anglo-Saxon, very much as she did. As she notes, they both admired "...sport, the color green-blue-gray, horses, and the army!"[29] He also had a very high opinion of himself and was not very ambitious. In this regard, he reminded Nadejda of her own brother Ivan! Petroff was also handsome, strong, with powerful shoulders and a broad chest; and he maintained his physique by exercising with dumbbells at every opportunity.

In addition to all these characteristics, Stoyan was an extremely talented draughtsman, and he gave her some of his sketches.[30] During one of their parties in her father's room, Nadejda went to the bathroom to redo her hair, and Stoyan followed her. He watched her from the doorway as she prolonged the moment by doing her hair in a variety of ways to tease him. She recorded the scene mentally. She sat on the edge of the bathtub playing with her hair, while he leaned against the doorway looking on with a cigarette between his lips.

When father and daughter entertained in their rooms, they served the menu of transients: strong drinks, fruits, and nuts.[31] They heated grog in a water bath on the fire and served it in an odd assortment of cups and glasses over slices of lemon. It was important to them to celebrate the moments when they could congregate in fun and enjoy their freedom from work. The atmosphere was light-hearted and frivolous. Stoyan would bar the door to Nadejda each time she had to pass back and forth between the adjoining rooms, and she would tug on his ear as a form of playful protest.

She enjoyed having so many men dote on her; it was sheer vanity. Nadejda's felt pride in triumphs other than successfully completed work. When she went to the Café de la Paix to have ice cream, she recorded the event as special.[32] This was not the reaction of a neophyte to the wonders of Paris. It was rather the impact of the novel experience of being alone with so many men. She had lived fixed in the orbit of her family for so long that the half-step toward freedom, an inconsequential outing to a café, was new and exciting. For the first time in her life she felt a woman admired for her feminine charms and merits. Since she now also had an accomplished record as a valuable Foreign Service functionary the combination of acknowledged competence and flattery for her feminine charms had an influence on her. A group whose opinion mattered admired her as a woman and appreciated her talents as a professional. This was a rare experience for any of her female contemporaries.

In many ways, the delegation experienced a makeshift life, since they had to make do with so few of the accoutrements of living in comfort and style. Yet they had to maintain certain social conventions that dictated their interpersonal relations.

Disappointment

In the early fall 1919 the fate of Bulgaria still seemed to float on optimistic hopes. Newspapers published articles that Thrace might become autonomous under the control of the yet-to-be-formed League of Nations while James Bourchier, journalist and champion of Bulgaria, continued to press for Bulgaria's goals through his steadfast support in his articles published in the *Times*. Perhaps the outcome of the peace might not be so very harsh; the Bulgarians lived in hope.

Nonetheless, when the delegates were summoned to pick up the preliminary peace in October, they spent hours in morose conversation and contemplation of their collective future. Nadejda describes that day:

> We amble in silence in the courtyard of the Madrid; everyone has a grave demeanor—I will not forget this day, full of brutal contrasts which end with a conversation for an hour with an Italian officer, standing in the corridor and then one hour at Mrs. Theodoroff, she in a blue peignoir, me in a yellow blouse with a carnation in my broche; while Papa and Theodoroff reread the famous speech that I had already translated into English in the shadow of Vitosha – what times![33]

The Bulgarians worked feverishly through October, trying to find ways to mitigate the blows that would result from the punitive clauses of the peace. At one point Nadejda recorded her speculations:

> What is the weather like these days? Where are we? What hour is it? What time is it? Are we asleep or awake? Do we greet each other with a hello? I would not be able to answer any of these questions. I no longer have the time or the energy nor are there limits or conventions. We live in work, for work, by work. . . . today . . . I managed to translate the entirety of the 35 pages of translation all by hand! I bring my last pages to Minkoff at 2:15 a.m. he is in his jacket, no tie, slippers with a fire in the fireplace, a bottle of wine, bread and cheese tranquilly resolved to stay up all night since he has to review my work, and then correct the first versions from the printer! [34]

The war had devastated personal lives at so many levels. Men fought, were wounded, and died. An entire generation of women lost the opportunity to marry because so many men of marriageable age perished, a consequence of war that was difficult to measure.[35]

On November 24, 1919, three days before Stamboliiski signed the Peace Treaty of Neuilly, Nadejda heard of the death of her friend Douglas Thompson, the Englishman whom she had met during Easter holidays in 1911. With this episode, she effectively joined the ranks of the women of her generation who would not marry. Indeed, had she not found a mate late in life, Nadejda would have been one of those who never married since she found so few men of marriageable age appealing.

Her friendship with Douglas had blossomed into something more and he was now gone. Their relationship may have developed into marriage but his death changed everything. He had died while part of an English armistice mission attached to Denikin's armies. One of the White forces that had attempted to wrest Russia from the Bolsheviks during that country's civil war.

He was buried in a little English cemetery in Ekaterinodar. Nadejda remembered him as "good, young, gay; he loved life, he loved me as well...we understood each other."[36] She wrote a letter of condolence to his father remembering to him "dear and noble Douglas."

Douglas Thomson and Nadejda Stancioff had corresponded for years; he had last written her when stationed in Salonika, in January 1918, but they had not been able to see each other then. As she reread his letters, she remembered him as spontaneous and charming and as someone who loved her. She allowed herself to mourn him against the backdrop of mounting Bulgarian agony over the signing of a dictated peace. Nadejda had hoped that someday she and Douglas might make each other happy.

No Justice for the Defeated

When the peace conference representatives refused the Bulgarians' requests to amend any clauses of the peace treaty—neither the territorial nor the military clauses—the delegates were despondent and angry. Nadejda says "We are staggered, petrified, crushed. Theodoroff suffers in his entire being; Papa is overwhelmed; the youth [of the delegation] full of pain but also of *rage*."[37]

The Bulgarians found out through an Italian officer that the American and Italian commissions to the peace conference had defended Bulgarian interests in regards to Tzaribrod. In fact, they had made even stronger and more reasonable arguments for the Bulgarian position on all of the contested regions. However, France and England had rejected those arguments categorically. Nadejda concludes, "So, we owe our treaty to France and England only!"[38] It was a crushing realization for the Bulgarians that there was "no justice or equity for the defeated."[39]

Nadejda read the treaty in detail and found that its conditions infringed on the rights of peoples. This was not the settlement promised in President Wilson's Fourteen Points. The delegates to Paris had to put their faith in the hard work, patience, and endurance of the Bulgarian people. The Stancioffs believed that a viable agrarian state could take Bulgaria out of any political, territorial, or economic loss, Stamboliiski and members of his party obviously shared that opinion. Based on the premise that if the Bulgarian government focused on educating, supplying, and helping their farmers the economy would thrive. The political and economic uncertainties of the times called for radical changes in domestic course and the Agrarian party was ready for the challenge.

The Peace Treaty of Neuilly-sur-Seine

The day of the signature of the Bulgarian treaty of peace was November 27, 1919. Nadejda witnessed the signing and recorded the event as follows:

> Rainy gray and cold. We leave in successive batches for the Neuilly town hall, in different cars. I arrive in good time and I am present for the arrival of a large part of the signatories: Polk, Sir Eyre Crowe, Clemenceau, Nardieu, Klotz, Venizelos, Romanos, and Cambon. Neither Serbs nor Rumanians; the staircases full of people; many elegantly dressed on lookers even in the room itself. A beautiful room; austere green table; a little table isolated for signatures At 10.35 Stamboliiski and Papa enter everyone in attendance rises. Clemenceau declares the sessions open and invites the Bulgarian delegation to sign the treaty; Stamboliiski advances with a resolute step, signs without trembling, returns to his place and follows the ceremonies calmly. Papa lists the signatories that defile before him. Meanwhile I talk with Bourboulon and Bousquet who are seated behind me! In addition, I make interesting studies looking at these famous heads. The animated and brilliant eyes of Clemenceau, the large red face of Tardier; the intelligent and well-proportioned figure of Klotz, the marble profile of Polk, the evocative face with red hair of the English delegate, the triumphant immobile and at the same time eloquent one of Venizelos, the astonishing head of a Balkan Cyclops of Stamboliiski, the beautiful and sad profile of Papa and his eyes full of thoughts, which I do not understand very well.

> Fast ceremony; Clemenceau declares the séance over and we are at peace- signatories, secretaries and assistants descend the grand staircase – I see Alliotti, nod to Romanos, study Madame Marconi and Baroness Alliotti; we return drained. – Exchange of autographs among the members of the Bulgarian mission and the officers of the Liaison group... we furnish each close to 100 signatures since we are obliged to give them to the flics and the personnel, from noon on liberty! All visits are authorized. – Dinner pleasant with pleasantries; we assuage our feeling despite everything by saying at least it is finished![40]

With the Treaty of Neuilly, Bulgaria lost all the territories she had gained by joining the Central Powers and more. The country was forced to limit its armed forces to a 20,000 volunteer force and was denied an air force. Reparations were tallied at 2,250 million gold francs. Reparations in the form of livestock were also part of the terms of the peace as well as coal shipments to the Serbs were slated for the next five years.[41]

The losses of men, draft animals, and actual farm acreage had a significant negative impact on the ability of Bulgaria to feed itself. The loss of southern Dobrudja was an especially difficult blow to the economy, as this fertile territory produced almost a fifth of the country's total agricultural production.[42]

Temporary blockades set up by the allied military commission in occupation of the country stymied trade. The movement of raw materials essential to industry was stopped. The losses to an industrially backward, labor-intensive agricultural economy were devastating.

Peace signaled a new set of trials for Bulgarians as those from the now reoccupied Bulgarian territories chose to return to the homeland. Thus, the housing and feeding of those populations added to the already impoverished state's burdens. In addition to these refugees, the Bulgarian state had to contend with caring for large numbers of White Russian and other refugees. These refugees included approximately 30,000 White Russian soldiers and over 20,000 Armenian refugees, survivors of the Armenian genocide perpetrated by the Ottoman Turks.[43] Both populations were destitute and in need of the necessities of life: food, shelter, work.

Diplomats Once More

In Paris, the lives of the Bulgarian delegates took on a more normal rhythm once they were no longer enemies of the Entente. Now they were free to receive visitors and to visit Paris. It was a completely new France. Just as Colonel Henri made a point of officiously shaking hands with every single delegate upon their return from the signing as a show of his welcome to these now accepted members of the European community, so did the rest of the country.

When the Bulgarians left the Château de Madrid the delegation split into two parts, one headed to the Avenue Kleber legation building to reestablish a Bulgarian diplomatic presence in Paris and the rest to an apartment on Avenue Emile Deschanel.

Nadejda and her father lodged separately for the sake of Mrs. Loloff, Stamboliiski's secretary. As a lone woman conventional propriety required that a second female had to be lodged on the premises to "keep up appearances." Therefore, Nadejda lived in the apartment with her, Stamboliiski, and two other male functionaries.

Nadejda described it as a bizarre life when, on one day, she could hear Stamboliiski in the room next to hers rattling his wash basin and spitting into his handkerchief and then the next day sit down to breakfast with him when he appeared "very neat, shaved, red, gay, making jokes on love."[44] She went shopping with him one afternoon in the superstore Printemps, where he bought items as incongruous as a fur collar and an imitation Persian carpet. She found him to be an agreeable companion; he was well informed and an intelligent conversationalist.[45]

Touring the War Devastated Sites

In December, the Bulgarians from the legation toured of the devastated sites of Northeast France, including visits to Soissions and Reims. They traveled in two cars loaned to them by the French ministry in charge of the devastated areas. At La Ferte-Milon, they began to see evidence of the recent conflict: destroyed houses, broken windows, woods with mutilated trees, and trenches. They saw cemeteries for soldiers from each of the allied countries. These cemeteries contained white wooden crosses and high palisades or shrubbery as walls.

Although the roads they traveled were passable, they observed large tracts of mud and the trenches that POWs filled with rocks and gravel. The French had put German prisoners of war to work. Nadejda observes that these POWs wore "horrid spinach green government issue uniforms, which [were so lamentable that] they made one's teeth ache."[46] Nadejda recognized the power of the half-ruined Reims cathedral, she thought it should be left in its devastated state, as a monument to the ruination of warfare.

As they examined the war-inflicted damage, Nadejda and her father felt even more humiliated for having fought with the Germans. While the unspeakable devastation crushed the Bulgarians Nadejda chose to record Lord Hay's caricature of English stiff upper lip attitudes: "...oh well, this sort of thing is bound to happen; it is all in the game, you see, during the war."[47] He was referring to the waste of the country and her distraught denizens.

Reims, the city, was on its way to recovery. There were little shops lit up among the ruins and a considerable amount of foot traffic, but the overall impact of the scene was one of utter ruination. Nadejda, at one point, commented that she felt she was going through a country of ghosts, that she was living in a strange and terrible fairy tale.

Stamboliiski was apparently so awestruck by the devastation that he preferred to wander among the ruins mute and alone. He is credited with the following pronouncement: "Three days in the land of the dead and they have made me forget my three years in prison."[48] He understood the gravity of the devastation and was prepared to face the future undeterred by those who criticized him for having signed what was an extremely punitive, unforgiving peace treaty. Bulgaria had fought with the Germans and, by association, was as responsible for the ruin as her ally. The price for choosing that road was dear.

On their way back to Paris, the entourage passed through Roubaix, Lille, and finally Amiens. They were able to see the various levels of damage and reconstruction and note that the process of recovery was slow and painful. The trip had the intended effect on the Bulgarians; they returned to Paris exhausted, both physically and morally. Nadejda comments on the journey: "Paris at 10.30, 310 kilometers today 840 kilometers in 3 days (in the land of the dead alas) bed, mental fatigue, which does not permit me sleep, I fall asleep very late."[49]

Back to Rome

Soon after that visit to the battle sites, most of the Bulgarians left Paris for other duties. Stamboliiski, Dimitri, and Nadejda headed for Rome. Nadejda's return to Rome was joyful; she had missed her favorite city. Over four years had passed since the Stancioffs had been in Rome. On their first day Nadejda chafed at having to translate for her chief while on an automobile tour of the city, since the task interfered with her complete enjoyment of the experience.

From 1919 until she left the diplomatic service in 1923, the man with whom Nadejda worked most closely, after her father, was the Bulgarian Prime Minister Aleksandûr Stamboliiski. The Agrarian Party had come to power in Bulgaria after the devastating losses of the Great War, and Stamboliiski's leadership, although unorthodox and nontraditional at times, eased the country into recovery and stability.

Stamboliiski was a controversial figure, and Nadejda's descriptions of him and his manner support the points made by his biographers: he was brusque and unaffected. Much of how he operated was not found in any protocol manual.[50] It is telling of his perceptions of women that he observed to her—in a voice of admiration, perhaps even awe—that she did not behave like a woman and that she did not know how to flirt like a woman. He also obliquely mentioned that it was unfortunate that she was not a man. Nadejda accepted these as compliments.

Nadejda's skill as a diplomat derived not so much from work experience but from life experience.[51] Both of her parents prepared her for a life that not only taught her to negotiate the fine points of treaties but also to receive guests who were often members of royalty.

Stamboliiski himself noted the seminal influence of Nadejda's mother on all her children. He referred to Anna as "that woman who makes her life work like a train on rails! No derailments...she keeps her husband safe and sound, the children, and the husbands-in-law to come too..." [52]

A Child and a Genius

The relationship between Nadejda and Stamboliiski seems to have been a type of mutual admiration society, but both were quite earnest about the goals they hoped to achieve for Bulgaria. When she became, a little later, the Bulgarian prime minister's private interpreter and secretary, she skillfully avoided awkward moments and even diplomatic blunders by toning down his rather abrasive and undiplomatic verbiage in her interpretation of his conversations with other heads of state. She coached him on etiquette and on certain occasions saw him as her charge, despite their age and gender differences and the discrepancy in their official capacities. She wrote to her family:

> ...nothing would astonish me about Stame [Aleksandûr Stamboliiski], at one moment a child and the next a genius. (Yes, very simply and I am not joking.) He dazzles me sometimes with that immense intelligence! He is disconcerting and I understand him.[53]

Nadejda and her family saw in Aleksandûr Stamboliiski an uncut diamond. He was someone whom they believed they could shape, polish, and school. Their very paternalistic and somewhat arrogant attitude toward Stamboliiski was one that emerged from members of Bulgaria's nascent nobility at the turn of the century. As Nadejda writes, "If Stame could have or would have had a mentor...near him...he would become a great man."[54]

Despite Stamboliiski's shortcomings, father and daughter chose to work with the prime minister and supported his vision for Bulgaria. Dimitri Stancioff admired him while he was well aware of his shortcomings. He reveled at Stamboliiski's native talents and wished to give him all the benefit of his efforts. In a letter to his family Dimitri made his feeling of esteem clear:

> This self-made man is astonishing . . . where did he learn this sense of gratitude! Of respect ... In his youth he was not likely to acquire this trait—he used to tell me that his relatives used to chase him from the house when he forgot to bring back his sheep and cattle—and all of a sudden he has an elegance of his thoughts which we thought so often as crude . . . does Stame feel that need—and call us . . . this Stame deserves so much—to be criticized as well as admired—how those extremes come full circle constantly in this world! The yeses and the nos are always so close one to the other—in all that we do.[55]

Nadejda's relationship with Stamboliiski only strengthened with their increased proximity and collaboration. They worked so closely that eventually his absence evoked distress on the part of Nadejda: "my Tribune [Stamboliiski] has been gone for seven days I have positively missed him! "Momiche?"[Girl?] "Ida!" [Coming!] A single tear rolls from my darkened eyes!"[56]

She respected him enough to work per his instructions. However she was also experienced enough to forestall potential diplomatic disasters when as a talented interpreter, on more than one occasion, she saved her prime minister from making verbal gaffes. In fact, commentators noted that while he spoke briefly, her translations tended to be considerably longer than his monologues! She modified and softened his tone and added her own brand of diplomatic savoir-faire.

Nadejda and Stamboliiski worked well together, and they had fun together as well. She described an outing in Paris to Petit Trianon, Marie Antoinette's playground, with Stamboliiski. There, the two of them raced to the top of a long staircase. The image of the Agrarian minister running after his secretary and translator on the staircase of one of the palaces on the grounds of Versailles is priceless. She recorded that he arrived after her, "enormous, breathless, red, and gay."[57]

In Stamboliiski's ideas, the Stancioffs saw the potential for positive change for their homeland. They did not, like so many others of their milieu, work against him. Nadejda enjoyed the prime minister's company, his willingness to carry on conversations and personal observations about a range of topics, from treaty negotiations to interpersonal relationships. According to Nadejda he spoke "with a lot of spirit." She says "He is a very interesting man, very unexpected. I really like him very much and I have a lot of confidence in him, if Bulgaria only will let him work in peace."[58]

Unique Friendships

On this occasion in Rome, Nadejda had the luxury of time and the status of an official representative of her country with which to observe the Eternal City. She also had the pleasure of spending many hours with her old friend, Meriel Buchanan, whose father was then the English ambassador to Italy. They had not seen each other in eight years. They were now both grown women, Nadejda was twenty-five and Meriel was about the same age, but with very divergent tastes.

Nadejda was much more the conservative than Meriel, who had the advantage, as Nadejda perceived, of not only beautiful clothes and position, but also a much more liberal attitude toward her relationships with men. They were confidantes for each other. However Nadejda was the kind of friend who helped one to get dressed for special occasions but did not join in the merry making. For example, when Meriel was preparing to join revelries to which she had invited her friend, Nadejda demurred.

Although the party was in the same hotel in which Nadejda was a guest, Nadejda allowed herself to sit at a distance in the salon adjoining the dance hall, catching glimpses of her friend but not participating in the fun. A social event, which seemed focused on simply bringing together young people, with looser rules of social interaction was indecorous. She perceived modern courting styles to be unseemly.[59] When she observed that dancers were dancing so closely that they resembled one figure from a distance. In the subdued light she could discern gloveless male hands resting, moist and pink, on bare female shoulders, on the dance floor of her hotel; she was shocked at the impropriety. In addition, Nadejda automatically perceived herself as superior to those revelers, since she believed to have a more developed intellect than all the dancers on the floor put together! She was a serious girl who sat in the corner, away from the dancers and wrote letters to people like Noel Buxton, Member of Parliament, (MP).

She and Meriel were reacquainted in Rome, and the relationship grew stronger with more frequent contact. Lady Georgina Buchanan, Meriel's mother, had been diagnosed with cancer and suffered, despite morphine injections. Meriel was despondent. Nadejda attempted to cheer her up.

Meriel and others of Nadejda's acquaintance knew that Nadejda was good with descriptions and creative make believe. On one occasion when Meriel was sick, she requested that Nadejda entertain her as Scheherazade had her sultan: "Draw one of your word-pictures of the East for me Slave-girl darling!"[60] The pair used pet names to address each other and Nadejda was alternately Snake Girl, Golden Eyed Princess, and Slave-girl.[61]

Nadejda described the scene in Meriel's sitting room that evening in detail, and then added, "after Rome I have all of England in one vision" in reference to Meriel lounging in her boudoir.[62] Then Nadejda accommodated her friend and sat at her feet in the shadows, like a good little slave, and told Meriel a story of love and flowers and fountains.

It was clear that the young women had different mores. Meriel talked to Nadejda of her latest flirtation, while Nadejda would rhapsodize about Rome. Meriel could not believe that Rome was Nadejda's only love.

Once when an admirer made his attentions known to her, Nadejda's response was to tell of her own approach to romance and games of the heart. She was not going to lead him on, as Meriel would have, just for the fun of it. "I do not like anything about him or of him! If I were Meriel...I would allow him to court me despite everything if only for the novelty of the thing, but I am not Meriel except in the passion for writing!"[63]

Nadejda was an unusual woman according to then contemporary norms. Not expected to work among men, women were expected to prove their status as the frivolous, less intellectual other by playing the part of flirtatious "lightweight." Flirtatious seductions were part of the game of male-female interaction at every level of society. Nadejda refused to participate in this expected manner. Based on Nadejda's letters to her family, she was very capable of flirtation, although this was a side of her Stamboliiski did not notice. She enjoyed the game a great deal because she knew when to settle down to business. Her type of flirtations were generally "safe," as she models in the following passage:

> [I] go to the St Laurent-in-Lucina church to see the Guido Reni. I am alone in the old sanctuary with a young Englishman who is holding a Baedeker; he is very handsome, I am for once perfectly dressed and we look at each other, then we look at the suffering Christ and we forget ourselves—We see each other again outside in the light and we smile at each other and then we flee.[64]

She felt that it was acceptable since the flirtation was so much a game of the intellect and not words and deeds. Once, she was rudely awakened to the undesirable possibilities of flirting with a stranger. On a train, she flirted with a man sitting opposite her, and when the train passed into a tunnel, she suddenly felt a hand on her knee. She was outraged and raised a fuss about the incident.[65] The twentieth century was creeping steadily along. In that one incident, Nadejda had to be aware of the progress and emerging modernity in the relations between men and women.

As a conservative, modern attitudes regarding the equalization of the sexes, and especially sexuality, revolted her. One of the women in the group of Bulgarians who arrived later confided her beliefs on free love and other types of behavior Nadejda considered immoral; Nadejda was embarrassed for her gender and disgusted, even crushed, by the ugliness that kind of behavior represented.[66]

She also was privy to a variety of lewd anecdotes about the new leader of Bulgaria and her superior, Aleksandûr Stamboliiski. The stories were all in poor taste and shocking. Stamboliiski was an enigma to her, but early in their acquaintance, she developed a playful relationship with him. She describes him in the following passage from her journal:

> My chief is very gay; we talk like two comrades, he gives a better impression the better one gets to know him. He has very primitive sides as well as very advanced ideas; he has read Tolstoy and Marcel Proust; he is a mixture of the most heterogeneous elements—he has a completely paternalistic attitude toward the "little" King Boris. . . . tells us anecdotes including the story of his father and the daughter of the Bey, the relations of his father with King Boris.[67]

In Rome, they learned more about each other. With each revelation, the relationship between Aleksandûr Stamboliiski and Nadejda Stancioff strengthened. Nadejda became the trusted professional on whom he could rely to carry out his orders, even when he was absent. Nadejda came to appreciate his critical mind and his native intelligence, and in this manner became a great admirer of his. She comments on his confidences: "He talks to me about his life in prison; he studied the psyches of the prisoners. The difference in the mentality of an assassin and that of a thief etc. It is interesting and new for me."[68]

Busman's Holiday

For a Christmas present and as a reward for all her hard work in Neuilly, her father took Nadejda on a dream trip to Naples to see the ruins of Pompeii and the island of Capri. They arrived in Naples in time to go to Christmas Eve mass. At St. Lucia "church of the poor," they observed women without hats, painted statues dressed in real clothes of silk and velvet, and very eloquent priests.

During her ideal vacation with her father, Nadejda and Dimitri were with two other couples on a tour booked through the Cook travel agency; she imagined that the waiter would think them a married couple on their honeymoon![69] The age difference did not seem to be an obstacle. She quickly gave up her status as a young person when she and her father watched the "young people" dance. She did not participate, nor did she feel excluded.

She was very aware of the sacrifices he had made to please her with the trip, that she was overwhelmed with gratitude toward her father. He did not like traveling, change, or anything unexpected, and yet he did all this for her. Feeling special in the aura of this extraordinary man was its own reward.

Nadejda had loved working at the peace conference, since there she had the option to spend her time talking about something other than "cooking, gossip, and fashions," although she wryly remarked that her effort produced as few results as if she had spent the time on more feminine pursuits.[70] Her biggest joy was in spending most of the year with the "noblest being, the most interesting and the most special that exists"—her father.

Back in Rome, they shared more time together, since she had little work to keep her busy, and there was less pressure on him. Her days were wonderfully relaxed. She worked two hours in the morning, and then took a walk to meet her father at a restaurant. After dining, she took an hour's walk with him toured Rome by herself then capped the day with a visit to Meriel. Finally, she would go home to work some hours in the evening.

In her favorite city Nadejda fantasized that she and Ivan would invite their younger sisters to dinner at a fine Italian restaurant, where, wearing their best clothes, they would revel in each other's company while their parents looked on approvingly from a table near by.[71] She missed her family and mused in this letter to them that her life had been rather bizarre since her departure from Bulgaria in spring 1919. She now wore fashionable clothes, men admired her and paid her compliments, she dined regularly with important personages and their spouses and she regretted that the rest of her family could not join her in the fun.

In Rome, because of their family ties to the Pope via their Cinzano relatives, the Stancioffs received an invitation to the Pope's mass at the Vatican.[72] It was a rare honor. Nadejda immediately recapitulated the other time her family had been so honored—the day they had all left the city on October 10, 1915. This time she dressed in black with her grandmother Grenaud's (née Cinzano) veil over her pulled back hair. Her father dressed in black with a white tie.

The Pope's chapel was a square room completely covered in red damask and contained numerous religious relics. The Pope entered exactly at 7 a.m., with a small procession of acolytes, his valet, and two bodyguards. His voice, which emphasized the Ts in Latin, was the only sound they heard. She was a devout Catholic and was extremely moved to receive Holy Communion from the hands of the successor of St. Peter. This was a perfect crown to her Roman experience.

Varna in 1920

In February 1920, the Stancioffs left Rome to return home. It was a long and circuitous journey first by train to Brindisi, and then by ship through the Bosphorous, and finally to Varna. They disembarked in Constantinople, still an occupied city, when a group of officers representing England, Italy, France, and the United States conducted passport control. There Dimitri and Nadejda visited the major sights in the city, plus the Bulgarian church, hospital, and school. They noted the congested streets full of natives, soldiers from all over the world, and Russian refugees. Their voyage engendered a heightened sense of excitement. They traveled only by daylight, since there were floating mines adrift in the Black Sea. Two ships had been recently sunk by inadvertently bumping into mines at night.

When they finally arrived in Varna, they heard Russian spoken all over. The Russian refugees spilling into Bulgaria to seek safe haven had already established schools, a newspaper, and opened restaurants. Some remained in the city, and others used it as a transfer point to more distant ports. The Stancioffs were sad to see the survivors of the Russia they had once known throng Varna streets.

Much of the bittersweet joy of being reunited with old friends and acquaintances from the their St. Petersburg days turned to dismay. Repeatedly, the Stancioffs were astonished at the inability or unwillingness of so many members of the Russian elites to acclimate to their changed circumstances. They were impractical in the extreme and could not bring themselves to adapt to performing simple chores such as cooking for themselves. They also persisted in expecting first-class treatment from the rest of humanity.[73] In this regard the Stancioffs were perfectly comfortable. Their adaptation to changed circumstances had been tested countless times in recent years and they found the inflexibility of the Russian titled, those few who managed to escape with their lives, astounding.

The British army of occupation in Bulgaria was under the direction of General Ross of Cromarty for whom Ivan had become liaison officer. Highland regiments were plentiful in the streets and guarded the ports and ships. Most of the ships were transports of refugees from Bolshevik-controlled Russia.

Nadejda plunged into the routine of life at *Trois Sources*, a life measured with visits, teas, and soirées interspersed with chores around the property. She also reestablished some of the weakened links to her siblings by joining in what she called "juvenile frivolity."

When Maman and Papa were both away, the children would gather in their mother's bedroom, play dress-up games, and mess about with each other's hair.[74] Their brother was the principal hairdresser and they even dressed him up as a girl, giggling until they ached, eating preserves out of a jar, and going to sleep exhausted in the early morning hours. Nadejda admitted to herself that their company made her feel young again, in contrast to her time spent with all the old fuddy-duddies in Neuilly. Some Russian refugees served as domestic help that summer, and the siblings had an opportunity to practice their Russian.

Homeland Reexamined

Too soon, Dimitri and Nadejda returned to work in Sofia, and she experienced what world travelers often experience once they return home from sophisticated foreign locations. When confronted with the familiar and not-so-cosmopolitan scene of their well-known environment, they chafe at the differences. They resent the dull, unsophisticated ways of their homeland and feel choked by the triteness of it all. Nadejda and her siblings had experienced much by the time they actually had the opportunity to live in their homeland. As children of diplomats who had lived in St. Petersburg, Paris, London, and Rome and who had traveled to elite resorts in Europe, they had acquired the expectation that their lives would continue to be as sophisticated, varied, and cosmopolitan as they had been during childhood.

Moreover, while they lived in their villa *Trois Sources,* they were able to create that cosmopolitan society around them by inviting a variety of officers from the occupying forces and Bulgarian armies, visiting foreign guests, and the few cultured Bulgarians of their acquaintance. Soirées, teas, and dinners at their home were occasions to recreate the same kind of atmosphere of intellectual and cultural high points they had experienced in foreign capitals.

However, for the most part, they experienced their forced stay in Bulgaria during and after the war as an onerous burden. Nadejda was cruel in her observations of the capital, the Bulgarian elites, high-society in Bulgaria:

> If one could choose not to be a Bulgarian and not have any relationships or ties to unpleasing compatriots except for the country and its beauties. There are no exceptions! At the moment and it is horrible to say, but outside of my father, two relatives and two friends I do not like anyone else in Sofia! . . . Poor dear exquisite and nice Bulgaria with common, lying, odious inhabitants![75]

These kinds of outbursts do not indicate some deep-seated antipathy towards all things Bulgarian. Nadejda made a distinction—as did the entire family—between the "right sort of acquaintance" such as the Petroff-Chomakoffs and those who were completely unacceptable on many grounds. In other words, the Stancioffs found members of their social class acceptable, Bulgarians who believed in the same values and traditions and who could be relied upon to have the same worldview. The family performed their duties to the nation as a sacred task, not to be confused with an emotional or intellectual connection to "the [Bulgarian] race."

Traditional Pursuits

The summer of 1920 was extremely hot; at one point, the temperature rose to 39 degrees Celsius in the shade. Nadejda reported being perpetually drenched in her clothes and feeling pursued by the heat indoors and outdoors. Although she also spent a lot of time playing tennis in this heat, she found Sofia oppressive.

At one point, the Stancioffs—Dimitri, his siblings, Baba, and Nadejda— took an excursion to Gorna Bania to indulge in a daylong ritual of bathing in the hot mineral baths, Anna and the other children were in Varna.[76] After a luxuriously long soak, the family met together at a "poetic spot" and ate a picnic lunch on a meadow. At 4 p.m., already losing the feeling of freshness the good long soak had imparted, Nadejda opted to jump into the cold water of a nearby mountain stream; the glacial water and the coffee and watermelon afterward all made for a "patriarchal day, oriental, and calm."

In mid-August, Nadejda returned to *Trois Sources* to celebrate her parents' anniversary; her father had to stay behind to work. As was their habit, the entire family participated in the celebration. The children created a special throne of flowers for their mother and presented gifts and tokens of their boundless love for their parents.

A couple of days after Nadejda arrived, King Boris invited the entire family to lunch at the summer palace in Varna. Excited and a little anxious about the event, they dressed in their finest outfits. The king was in a simple suit of white, and according to Nadejda, was gay and sweet. Lunch included the officers of his suite, who must have been quite a sight Nadejda comments that they were "fat, cropped in white, resembling plump, bleating sheep!"[77]

At the end of the afternoon, the king drove the Stancioffs home personally in his own car.[78]

Fall 1920 Tour of Europe

At the end of summer, Papa joined his family, and they spent some memorable days and nights with guests from many parts of Europe and Bulgaria. They felt happy and blessed. When Papa returned to Sofia, almost immediately, he began to write home about the proposed trip Prime Minister Aleksandûr Stamboliiski would take abroad in October. Dimitri had good cause to believe that he would be chosen to accompany Stamboliiski in some diplomatic capacity. An ideal reassignment would have been a diplomatic post in one of the capitals in Europe; England would have been most preferred. Just as promptly, Dimitri warned Nadejda that she should expect to accompany him.

On September 22, the news was affirmative and decisive; Papa would be traveling as Stamboliiski's principal advisor and Nadejda as his secretary-interpreter. They would visit London, Paris, Brussels, Prague, and the Balkan capitals. Stamboliiski was intent on using the trip to introduce the *new Bulgaria* to Europe by personally interacting with heads of state and showing them literally that he and his government were honest and sincere about reentering the European fold after the war.

The new leader of Bulgaria was certain that once Europe was convinced that Bulgaria was a new country, with a new political organization, with a new direction in diplomacy, other countries would be receptive to the state. Stamboliiski was carrying a message to Europe: "Instead of the gun and the cannon we have slogans of peace, for friendly neighborly relations..."[79]

For the Stancioffs the venture offered a golden opportunity. Could Nadejda use this trip as a springboard to reinsert Papa into the diplomatic service in his previous rank? Stamboliiski had evinced a predilection for the Stancioff father and daughter pair and since Nadejda had spent the most time in his company and the two got on well, she would have been the one to have some influence over him.

Nadejda felt ill at ease about leaving the rest of her family, since it would be once again she who would leave to travel while her mother and siblings remained behind. Her mother was adamant about not spending yet one more winter in Varna and insisted that her other children needed civilization and change. All their hopes rested on the possibility of Dimitri being reappointed as Bulgaria's representative and extricating them all from the provinces and from Bulgaria in general Nadejda held the key to that appointment.

Preparing to leave Varna and the only house, she ever considered home, Nadejda was excited and sorrowful at once. She adored her life but mourned the separation from her family. She also remembered her French cousin Lele who was a casualty of the war on the battlefields of Champagne:

> Anniversary of the death of Lele; as every year, we go to mass, which is particularly moving today in view of all these departures. He will always be for me the young archangel on the blue horizon and I am sure he is well placed among the other saints in armor. I begin to pack for my trip without enthusiasm . . . will I return soon to Trois Sources or will I be gone for years? Still a mystery. So how much to I pack for how long? And I still manage to laugh naturally with Boulot [Ivan] and Djam-Lang [Feo] when actually I want to scream to them in tears all my love, my confusion, my respect! I pack, take down, and take things apart while thinking of my life (which I egotistically love) since the armistice, of that of Papa, of our travels. Of Neuilly, Rome, Naples![80]

Her mother accompanied Nadejda to Sofia in order to see her husband once more before he left for yet another trip of indefinite duration. There were joyous sendoffs for the Stancioffs, father and daughter. At one such evening, the toast was for them to get the posting in London.[81]

The day of her father's departure Nadejda described a chaotic scene in the house. Her father was at the ministries and various legations all day. Dimitri had the responsibility of traveling ahead of the main party; he had no time to pack, and the women took care of that for him. He was called to the palace at 7 p.m. when his train was leaving at 10 p.m. He rushed home after that interview to go over his accounts. In the process, he lost his keys, dined, received a man from his bank, found his keys, and gave the women thousands of pieces of advice. All this at one and the same time according to Nadejda!

On the day of Nadejda's departure with Aleksandûr Stamboliiski and his entourage, the scene was officious and pompous. Her uncle Nic and Maman accompanied her to the station where it seems all the Bulgarian ministers, diplomatic representatives of foreign countries, and the chief of police, the mayor, generals, as well as her friends had gathered.[82] Stamboliiski arrived at the last minute, dressed in mismatched clothes and a floppy hat. He had time to talk to Maman and then the train pulled away, as Nadejda began another adventure in her career as a diplomat, secretary, interpreter, translator, and shopping and fashion consultant.

A Friendship with the Prime Minister

Aleksandûr Stamboliiski was well aware of the effort Bulgaria would have to make in order to find a sympathetic ear anywhere on the European continent. His 1920 fall tour included stops in the major European capitals. As he chose to take Dimitri Stancioff as his principal advisor and Nadejda Stancioff as his secretary interpreter, this foray solidified the position of the father-daughter pair as indispensable to Bulgaria's foreign service and, in particular, to Aleksandûr Stamboliiski.

Despite every effort to breach the English position on the terms of the peace treaty with Winston Churchill (1874-1965), Eyre Crowe (1864-1925), Lord Birkenhead (1872-1930), Lord Curzon (1854-1925), Lloyd George, the Bulgarians received the same polite refusal and redirection to the Greeks. The small Bulgarian mission visited agricultural sites like Lord Carnarvon's Home Farm and Piggeries and took tours of local factories and farms in Birmingham, Manchester, Liverpool, and Glasgow. Nadejda describes the experience:

> ...working hard. Mad rush from one place to another with varied forms of the following program: long meals with confused reciprocal explanations of Balkan politics and labor in England . . . visits paid to ploughing machines, endless inspections of . . . factories . . . to the sound of machines grinding away their strength and the hoarse explanations of polite and expectant English guides; I have come to understand the fascination of boilers, elevators and especially furnaces and the terrible beauty of smoldering iron.[83]

Nadejda interpreted all these conversations, Stamboliiski's speeches, and even jovially sexist remarks. After a polite refusal to reconsider the restrictions on Bulgaria's army and hearing Bulgaria's equally polite request for a mandate over Adrianople Lloyd George asked "Do women have the vote in Bulgaria?" The answer via Nadejda's translation was "No, thank God!" when they all three broke into laughter.[84] Despite the back slapping attitude and old boy conviviality with the British Stamboliiski did eventually grant some Bulgarian women the vote.

In Prague, while discussing agricultural trade conventions with Czech foreign minister Edvard Beneš (prime minister 1921-22, president 1935-1948), Stamboliiski came down with a fever, and Nadejda played nursemaid, making his bed, preparing gargles, and administering compresses to his brow.[85] They spent this forced leisure time conversing on history, love, psychology, and the development of political states. In Warsaw, they negotiated with Prince Sapieha, the Polish foreign minister, in Bucharest with Queen Marie (1875-1973)—all to lay the groundwork for solid friendly relations. By December 1920, it seemed the Stancioff team had secured the position the entire family dreamed of— another legation posting, in London.

Besides projecting the friendly face of a new Bulgaria Aleksandûr Stamboliiski's visit sought to reassure Europeans that Bulgaria had turned a new leaf and was willing to look forward and not backward. He proclaimed that Bulgaria would not seek any territorial revision and that she only sought to have Article 48 of the Treaty of Neuilly applied—the all-important access to the Aegean Sea.

He further cemented his rhetoric by pressing the League of Nations at every opportunity to enforce its vigilance and protection over the Macedonian territories and the Bulgarian minority's rights. In order to underscore this benign path, Stamboliiski pursued a single-minded policy to establish good relations with Yugoslavia, a decision that was a tough political choice between a stable foreign policy at the expense of domestic tensions and unrest.

Since this policy led to protests and violence at home from the pro-Macedonian factions among his population, achieving a rapprochement with Yugoslavia escalated domestic violence and added scores of enemies to a growing list of BANU opponents. The Internal Macedonian Revolutionary Organization (IMRO) was active and continued to build support as Stamboliiski put his words into action. That opposition factor would weigh heavily against him and his government in the coming years.

Notes

1. Nadejda Stancioff, unpublished journal, 18 September 1913, PASF.
2. Ibid. 26 July 1919, PASF.
3. Ibid. 15 November 1919.
4. Ibid. 30 September 1919.
5. Stancioff, Nadejda Memories of Love, 56-57.
6. Nadejda Stancioff, unpublished journal, 26 July 1919, PASF.
7. Ibid. 27 July 1919.
8. Ibid.
9. Ibid.
10. Ibid.
11. Tsanoff had studied at Drew Seminary in New York City.
12. Nadejda Stancioff, unpublished journal, 28 July 1919, PASF.
13. Ibid. 29 July 1919.
14. Ibid. 10 August 1919.
15. Ibid.
16. Ibid. 30 July 1919.
17. Ibid. 5 August 1919.
18. Ibid. 20 October 1919.

19. Ibid. 3 September 1919.

20. Ibid. 13 August 1919.

21. Ibid.

22. Ibid. 16 August 1919.

23. Ibid. 23 August 1919.

24. 1919 Neuilly photograph, PASF.

25. Nadejda Stancioff, unpublished journal, 20 October 1919, PASF.

26. Ibid.

27. Ibid. 21 September 1919.

28. Ibid. 29 September 1919.

29. Ibid.

30. Ibid. 4 October 1919.

31. Ibid. 18 October 1919.

32. Ibid. 3 September 1919.

33. Ibid. 17 September 1919.

34. Ibid. 21 October 1919.

35. Wingfield and Bucur, *Gender and War in Twentieth-Century Eastern Europe.* The literature on the impact of war on women and the female population in general is growing. *Gender and War* is a recent and valuable addition.

36. Nadejda Stancioff, unpublished journal, 24 October 1919, PASF.

37. Ibid. 3 November 1919.

38. Ibid.

39. Ibid.

40. Ibid. 27 November 1919.

41. Crampton, *Bulgaria 1878-1918: A History*, 471.

42. Ibid. 482-483

43. Doncho Daskalov, *Biialata Emigratsiia V Bûlgariia*, 1. izd. ed. (Sofia: UI Sv. Kl. Okhridski, 1997), Mari A. Firkatian, "Armenian Émigré Communities in Bulgaria," *Balkanistica* 9 (1996).

44. Nadejda Stancioff, unpublished journal, 1 December 1919, PASF.

45. Ibid.

46. Ibid. 2 December 1919.

47. Ibid.

48. Muir, *Dimitri Stancioff Patriot and Cosmopolitan*, 217.

49. Nadejda Stancioff, unpublished journal, 4 December 1919, PASF.

50. Bell, John D. *Peasants in Power Alexander Stamboliski and the Bulgarian Agrarian National Union 1899-1923.* Princeton: Princeton University Press, 1977. Dimov, N., Y. Zarchev and B. Vulov eds. *A. Stamboliiski izbrani proizvedeniia.* Sofia: BAN, 1980. Khristo Khristov et. al., eds. *Aleksandûr Stamboliiski : zhivot, delo, zaveti.* Sofia: BAN, 1980.

51. Nadejda Stancioff to family from Lausanne, unpublished letter, 7 January 1923, PASF. "I received the letter of Mouzily [pet name for her sister] with perfumes, press cuttings, details which I have been awaiting since last year. [On her relationship with her father]: he has a certain respect for me since the world press has provisionally adopted me, instead of scolding me, he laughed and declared to me that basically life is worth the pain of living it!..on your knees and thank God for what is and confide to Him that which is to come and that is all! I have simplified my life—brutally or not, but I enjoy the results. ...I find my sisters everywhere, naturally, in all I see, all I look at, read, and hear that is beautiful......Harold [Nicolson] gave Papa the new version of the Dedeagach scheme, see attached. It is confidential only for Queensgate [Bulgarian legation address

in London] for the moment; it could be changed. ...study it as a family and give your opinions, be frank. "

52. Nadejda Stancioff, unpublished letter, 21 September 1922, p. 3b, Nada II, PASF.

53. Nadejda Stancioff, unpublished letter, 19 September 1921, Nada I, PASF.

54. Dimitri Stancioff to Nadejda, unpublished letter 5 July 1922, p.5, Nada IX, PASF.

55. Ibid.

56. Nadejda Stancioff, unpublished letter, 22 December 1922, Nada II, PASF.

57. Nadejda Stancioff, unpublished journal, 23 November 1919, PASF.

58. Nadejda Stancioff, unpublished journal, 8 December 1919, PASF.

59. Nadejda Stancioff, unpublished letter, 15 December 1919, Nada I, PASF. Nadejda witnessed the shocking change in decorum between men and women.

60. Nadejda Stancioff, unpublished journal, 6 January 1920, PASF.

61. Stancioff, *Nadejda Memories of Love,* 23.

62. Nadejda Stancioff, unpublished journal, 18 December 1919, PASF.

63. Ibid. 16 January 1920.

64. Ibid. 15 January 1920.

65. Interview with Johnny Stancioff July 8 2001.

66. See Ann Taylor Allen's "Feminism, Social Science, and the Meanings of Modernity: The Debate on the Origin of the Family in Europe : And the United States, 1860–1914." *American Historical Review* 104, no. 4 (1999).

67. Nadejda Stancioff, unpublished journal, 11 December 1919, PASF.

68. Ibid.

69. Ibid. 27 December 1919.

70. Ibid. 26 August 1919.

71. Nadejda Stancioff to family, unpublished letter, 15 December 1919, Nada, PASF. The letter is five, double-sided, 8x10 inch pages long. In it she admits to loving to discuss statistics and travel itineraries as much as the weather. An attempt at levity but quite truthful.

72. Nadejda Stancioff, unpublished journal, 18 January 1920, PASF.

73. Stancioff, *Diplomat and Gardener Memoirs*, 37-38.

74. Both Ivan and Nadejda mention these kinds of escapes.

75. Nadejda Stancioff, unpublished journal, 20 July 1920, PASF.

76. Nadejda Stancioff, unpublished journal, 23 June 1917, PASF.

77. Nadejda Stancioff, unpublished journal, 20 August 1920, PASF.

78. Nadejda Stancioff, unpublished journal 24 August 1920, PASF. Nadejda recorded that Feo was joyful. There is merely a whisper of evidence in the family archive on the possibility that King Boris and Feo were romantically interested in each other. This is one such instance. A couple of days later Nadejda called the Euxinograd beach, "the beach of lost illusions;" this was perhaps her way of noting the definitive end to speculation about a possible match between King Boris and her sister Feo. The rumors that the Bulgarian king had romantic feelings for one of the Stancioff sisters were part of the international gossip mill. Nadejda reported in a letter to her family from Lausanne in January 1923 that "Mme. Bristol, sic, told me the 'all of Constantinople knows that if King Boris is not getting married, it is because he is in love with one of the three Stancioffs, and that apparently he spends his summers in a boat, bobbing on the waves of Euxinograd, with the one who has captured his affections.'" See Nadejda Stancioff, unpublished letter, 7 January 1923, Nada III, PASF.

79. Stamboliski, *Aleksandr Stamboliski Snimiki ot edin zhivot*, Sofia: Dûrzhavna Pechatnitsa, 1934, 23.

80. Nadejda Stancioff, unpublished journal, 25 September 1920, PASF.

81. Ibid. 29 September 1920.

82. Ibid. 30 September 1920.

83, Muir, *Dimitri Stancioff Patriot and Cosmopolitan*, 225-226.

84. Ibid. 228.

85. Nadejda Stancioff to family, unpublished letter, 22 December 1920, Nada I, PASF. She was already writing home to tell her family that Stame had plans to send them to London, presumably Dimitri would be getting the post of minister to the court of St. James. Stamboliiski already had complete confidence in father and daughter and expected the rest of the family to be just as talented and looked to the future for their incorporation into Bulgaria's diplomatic service.

7
International Kid to First Woman Diplomat

"It is annoying to have a brain! ...but I burn with ambition, adore life more than ever, and savor my position with frenzy."
Nadejda Stancioff, unpublished letter[1]

After Stamboliiski's successful tour in fall 1920 it appeared that, the family had found a secure future for two of its members and by association for the entire family. Dimitri's appointment as minister plenipotentiary to London and Nadejda's appointment as a delegate to the conferences in the early 1920s were practically simultaneous engagements. The family was thrilled and not a little relieved since the decisions had come after some delay and their financial situation had grown meager.

The Post Paris Conferences

The post Paris conferences, which were held primarily in Switzerland and Italy, reaffirmed the dominance of the Great Powers over the lesser states. The conferences were charged with negotiating the finer points left unresolved at Paris. Under circumstances which became increasing complicated as the negotiations dragged on for months, and then years, these conferences did not achieve their stated goals.

Whether in scenic Switzerland or on the Italian Riviera, the delegates, lodged in fine hotels, would debate points by day at conference tables. Then later that evening, while sitting across from one another at the hotel dinner table or at elegant soirées, the delegates would continuing the verbal sparring into the night, either flirting and teasing, grumbling or growling at each other as was appropriate. [2]

The goals of the conferences seemed clear-cut at the beginning, but as circumstances and actors changed, so did the outcomes. The sloppy precedent of Paris spilled over into these negotiations and the results would be just as detrimental to the stability and constructive recovery of the entire continent.

The delegates were aware how flawed the process was from the start; Bolshevik Russia was not invited to participate, and Germany was not recognized diplomatically until 1922. Although diplomats and their experts understood it was important to include all the members of the European continental family, the gathered multitude could not bring themselves to act on that knowledge. Instead, the negotiators and the journalists who reported on their proceedings continued the charade of evenhanded dealings. Newspapers, the source that informed the reading public across the globe featured sympathetic stories of how the proceeding were carried out with the best interest of the greatest number of people involved.

The creation and structure of the League of Nations is a prime example of the nebulous nature of the proceedings. With an assembly composed of a single representative of each member state and a council of five permanent Great Powers and a secretariat located in Geneva the League fell short of all expectations; neither an effective arbiter of disputes nor an effective peace keeper.

Borders and Maps

In 1920, the map of Europe and the Middle East was carved into some tenuous boundaries, which represented the realization of self-determination mixed with *realpolitik*. On the continent, loser and winner states worked on finalizing the disposition of territories left in dispute by the peace treaties signed in Paris.

German territories remained in limbo as negotiations dragged on. The discussions about how the territories would be turned over to their new masters were punctuated by lengthy theoretical and philosophical debates. The new states around the Baltic Sea were wary of their former master, Russia. The decision to create the "Polish Corridor" to the port of Danzig/Gdańsk was under discussion; the future of the port of Memel was also debated. There were territories earmarked for plebiscites in Central Europe along with areas slated for internationalization. Allied forces still in occupied Russian territories, and as the rebirth of the Baltic States presaged, the territories of the former Austro-Hungarian Empire, too, were destined to become the basis of new polities. The map of Europe was reconfigured, and several new states were created where the former multiethnic empire once ruled.

In each case of territorial shift, compromises made to moderate one or another obstacle ultimately proved to contradict the principles of Wilson's Fourteen Points which were the basis of the armistice of November 11, 1918. There were few satisfied participants even among the winners.

In the Middle East, the dissolution of another multi-ethnic empire permitted the Great Power winners to place their mark on territorial mandates. With an eye to reaping the economic and strategic rewards each piece of territory seemed to offer, the powers staked their claims to the body of the former Ottoman Empire.

These arrangements led to the demands of the British over the territory that would be named Iraq; the lands controlled by France which formed the future states of Lebanon and Syria; the territories under British mandate known originally as Transjordan, and Palestine; an Italian zone of influence in Anatolia; lands claimed by Greece in southwestern coastal Anatolia—once known as Ionia; and the vast expanse of the Arabian Peninsula which would coalesce into various Muslim states—the largest known as Saudi Arabia. Over the next decade, in some cases within very few years, these territories would be transformed into something resembling permanent entities either still under mandate or free of Great Power oversight.

At Genoa

In 1920, it appeared that the Great Powers were still in control of the situation. Just one and one-half year later, the circumstances had changed dramatically. Great Britain and France grew distant and could not agree on even minor issues. When Lloyd George convened a general conference at Genoa in April 1922 and invited all the nations to participate, the rift among the former staunch allies became very public. Raymond Poincaré refused to attend in person and the Americans sent only an observer rather than an official representative.

Nonetheless, the Genoa Economic Conference was one of the last in the tradition of European family gatherings where delegates would convene in scenic and luxurious locales to conduct business. Dimitri Stancioff had misgivings right away about the possibility of getting the delegates' work accomplished in a locale that boasted an azure port, sparkling waters, and bright blue skies; he would have chosen Hanover or Liverpool instead.[3] As customary, however, most real business was conducted in private meetings and behind closed doors.

In fact, the Treaty of Rapallo, a treaty of cooperation between the Germans and Russians, was the only tangible result of the Genoa Conference. The treaty, which was the product of secret negotiations, protected each excluded state from the other signatory by promising to maintain their neutrality in case of third party attack. Lloyd George found his power waning as he failed to bring Russia back into the European fold or to get the delegates to approve a general treaty of nonaggression.

Great Britain, resigned to dealing with a Bolshevik state in Russia, had not given up hope of a substantial revision in the disposition of the territories on the extreme southeast of the Balkan Peninsula. The primary interests of Great Britain lay in the revision of the clauses governing free access to the Black Sea. In some ways, free access for Britain would have negated the establishment of a hostile state in Russia, since the British would have been able to blockade the Russian fleet in the Black Sea.

Allied control of Thrace and Constantinople, for a time, seemed to assure the British Foreign Office that a solution favorable to their goals was within reach. What had been called the Eastern Question for over a century seemed to be on the verge of resolution in 1920. The Ottoman Empire was in disarray as the sultan was powerless, forced to concede territories to the rapacious Great

Powers by the stipulations of the Treaty of Sèvres. The Great Powers were left in occupation of Syria, Egypt, Mesopotamia and other territories which were placed "under the protection."

The peace treaty—Neuilly—had crushed the Bulgarian state. However, the decision over the outlet to the Aegean and the fate of southern Dobrudja had yet to be determined. Article 48 of the Peace Treaty promised Bulgaria an outlet to the sea. The prolonged negotiations about Article 48, which were ultimately a dead letter, evolved over the course of the early 1920s. The process and unsatisfactory result was the calamity that most damaged Bulgaria's future after 1919.

Dimitri and Nadejda spent 1920-1923 shuttling between London and the cities of the subsequent conferences. They negotiated, through both official and personal diplomacy, the exact details of the peace settlements left unclear at Paris. As the representatives of the signatories of the Paris peace treaties gathered to hammer out the details left unresolved in Paris, however, conflict in the Balkans and the neighboring regions of Russia and Asia Minor continued to affect the proceedings.

For the Bulgarians, the territorial decisions in their favor would have facilitated the development of an economically viable state. Despite the harsh reparations, the return of southern Dobrudja and gaining unimpeded access to the Aegean with a viable port would have created economic opportunities and nurtured a brighter economic future.

The dissolution of the Ottoman Empire, a consequence of the war, and the creation of a Turkish Republic were ultimately to Bulgaria's disadvantage. Bulgarian diplomats eyed the evolving situation in Asia Minor first with concern, then with some hope to see a solution favorable to their interests. The outcome would prove to be a surprise of monumental proportions. From London, and periodically at Lausanne, the Bulgarian minister plenipotentiary and Bulgarian female first secretary worked on finding a solution to Bulgaria's weak position at the international negotiating table.[4]

Minister Plenipotentiary to the Court of St. James

The years 1919-1923 witnessed the peak of professional accomplishments for the Stancioffs. Nadejda and Papa were chosen as assistants to first Minister Theodoroff and then Minister Aleksandûr Stamboliiski. Their collective talents were indispensable to Stamboliiski, and since their personalities were compatible, the Stancioffs and the Agrarian prime minister worked well together as colleagues. Dimitri was rewarded, at last, with a capstone appointment to London. As Bulgarian minister plenipotentiary to the Court of St. James, he could work off the remainder of his career at the most prestigious post in his profession. The family was ecstatic to be so prominently placed in a coveted posting in Great Britain.

The Stancioffs had had a rough time of it during the war and immediately after. As they had been employed by the previous regime, especially King Ferdinand, their professional prospects, vis-à-vis the Agrarian Party, were tenuous. However, their unstinting labors during the Neuilly peace process in 1919 and their performance and assistance to Stamboliiski's mission in the fall 1920 produced positive results, the appointment of Dimitri Stancioff to London. Dimitri had left France very well respected in 1915 and had been a constructive force at the Peace Conference. His reputation as a stolid professional made him a perfect candidate for the job. He and Anna made an effective team as they worked to repair war-ravaged relationships. They knew how to entertain members of British society. Furthermore, Dimitri joined some important clubs which he frequented in order to foster relations with important British men: St. James's, Wellington, and Cavalry.

Dimitri and Nadejda's new appointment to London also helped to ease the family's financial burdens, which accumulated over several years of underemployment. Because of their new positions, the Stancioff family moved across the continent once more. This time their family life would be disrupted by frequent absences and changes of residence, due to work related assignments that required frequent travel. Yet now they were fully immersed in the stream of significant foreign policy work.

The year 1920 was a watershed for professional success. They had been successful in arranging their professional futures as Anna had admonished Dimitri in 1919: "...bear in mind that you should be a little egotistical and don't work all the time for a hollow policy [foreign] which almost always despises your services. Everyone makes certain to arrange themselves to their own advantage."[5]

Despite the steady income at London, the family had to make do with a limited Legation staff: a butler, a footman, and a cook. They also had to revive their somewhat dated wardrobes. According to Ivan, his sisters arrived in London wearing old-fashioned black hose when the fashion dictated flesh colored stockings. He, for his part, had been wearing his father's hand-me-downs. In addition, the legation at Queen's Gate was furnished with their own stored furniture retrieved from Rome. Ivan spent little time in London; in 1921, he began to study law at the University of Fribourg, Switzerland.[6]

Parental Virtues

The obvious diplomatic virtues of Bulgaria's new minister plenipotentiary to Great Britain aside Dimitri Stancioff was the idealized *père de famille*, as both "hard-working provider" and as a "model of parental virtue."[7] He worked conscientiously to be the best possible diplomat and the ideal role model of paternal qualities. If any criticism was leveled at him by his adoring family, it was that he worked much too hard and that he should take better care of himself by working less diligently.

Internalizing his role as provider Dimitri wrote: "The material aspect... in my view earning money – bread for one's children is solely the job of the Father!!"[8] He did indeed work to his utmost to fulfill his public and private roles as admirably as humanly possible. This type of diligence was one of the reasons for his appointment to London.

Dimitri Stancioff understood the duties of a diplomat to include delicate negotiations with the representatives of other countries as well as meticulous information gathering from governmental sources, from official and unofficial conversations. Ciphered telegrams to the Bulgarian ministry of foreign affairs and to the prime minister included full reports of his efforts to advance Bulgarian foreign policy goals and his assessments of evolving situations or crises. His diplomacy was careful; he paid attention to detail and took into consideration the historical precedents.

Dimitri was also mindful of his host country's sensibilities. Press releases issued by foreign diplomats were frowned upon by the British foreign office and the Bulgarian legation in London was circumspect when it came to making official statements to the press. He received sincere praise from every level of the British government for his discretion and careful diplomatic manner. A traditional diplomat, he believed in patience—slow and deliberate negotiations over hasty military resolutions.

The World's First Woman Diplomat

In these same years, Nadejda's career soared. She was now a delegate at the post Paris peace conferences. Although she had participated in the peace process at Neuilly in 1919, her appointment had been rather opportunistic since she was useful to the delegation and there were precious few Bulgarians, male or female, who had her talents.

However, during the subsequent years, 1920-1923, Nadejda participated in negotiations and the formulation of conventions and in her capacity as her nation's first female diplomatic representative, she attained celebrity. Because there were so few prominent women in international political life, Alexandra Kolontai of the Soviet Union is perhaps the best known example of a woman in diplomacy, Nadejda's career was intriguing to the general public. She was a role model of her gender in the 1920s and she gave interviews to those who wanted to learn more about what kind of woman would take on such an unusual duty. She gave the impression that she was indeed unique in her role as a lone female diplomat and she relished the opportunity to shine while promoting her country to the general European public.

Her celebrity grew rapidly because of her gender, her youth, beauty, her family background and not in the least because of her position as a representative of her country. Feo reported home "Nada was very successful at the session...she is always completely involved in her career...receiving constant homage and the admiration that she inspires, [Frijdhof] Nansen and [Louis-Morris] Bompard are tender."[9]

Despite her popularity, Nadejda Stancioff still managed to keep her composure and tactful reserve. She was by nature a self-composed person. Many factors coalesced to present her as unique and exotic. She represented a Balkan country where political assassinations were still in the headlines, a country whose immediate historical past was the stuff of orientalist fantasy, the kind of disorder the western public preferred to visualize as a backdrop to life in the "East."

The Balkans as "a powder keg," as "the stormy petrels of Europe" were phrases commonly used by journalists who were keen to sensationalize the news from the region.[10] Nadejda was the daughter of French and Bulgarian aristocracy, the playmate of princes and princesses, a friend to a king, exceptionally gifted in languages, and a talented wit; she also possessed a beauty and physical grace that typified the female ideal of the age. How could she not be popular? She was a woman of the times and beyond; the combination of these traits made her even more enticing to the media and the public.

Journalists sought her out for interviews. Her photograph appeared in European and American newspapers. Female, young, beautiful, and modestly articulate, her talents as an interpreter and her behind the scenes work as a negotiator put her in the public eye. Her turns at various podia created a stir. She was "the International Kid" as well as "the First Woman Diplomat," "Miss Machiavelli" and according to an American paper "The Girl Who Would Not Marry."[11]

Not only did journalists whose jobs were, after all, to create sensational copy pursue her, Nadejda Stancioff's name was mentioned in memoirs and books of the time.[12] She sought out intelligent and influential men with whom to exchange ideas on the future of the world and political philosophy in general, and they found in her a deep thinker with an engaging intellect. She used her fame to her advantage by cultivating journalists as friends; she became close for a while with Percival Landon of the *Daily Telegraph, Daily Chronicle,* and John Walter of the *Times.*[13] They could be useful to a diplomat who wished to have a cause publicized in the press. Stories about her provided journalists with an ideal story, with all the elements, that could draw the public's attention.

The contrast of a mere "girl" among all those mustached, be-spectacled, suited men was perfect copy for the newspapers. Admired and appreciated by luminaries of the 1920s, not surprisingly Nadejda lapped up all the praise with glee. Letters to her family were full of anecdotes and "You won't believe what so-and-so said/did" kinds of commentary; she also included the flowing description of her busy life:

> I adore the life of Conferences, of families like ours, compliments from diplomats, absent bosses, the trips, the returns, the experiences and I thank, re-thank, and re-thank God—not well enough perhaps, but I never forget that one possesses quite many things that others do not![14]

She was thrilled and still, in her own inimitable way, at times awed by her own celebrity.

Her natural tendency to be self-deprecating saved her from becoming an intolerable bore to her acquaintances. In addition, through all the publicity, she continued to work rather than to stint her labors. Her workload was prodigious not only because she took on much but also because she was competent. Nadejda, describing her work ethic, says:

> I work from 8.45 to midnight with interruptions to eat, sleep, do battle at the Conference with Ulysses [Venizelos] and son of Ulysses [Harold Nicolson], read the papers to my chief and give a quick glance at the incomparable Alps of Savoy.[15]

Sometimes she was seconded to delegates not of her foreign service because her facility with six languages made her a rare asset, even at an international gathering of exalted caliber. She performed these tasks of translating for foreign delegations in addition to her duties as writer of reports, recorder of proceedings of meetings, and reporter of negotiations that were filed with the Ministry of Foreign Affairs office in Sofia on a regular basis.

Meanwhile, when in London, in addition to her work-related duties, Nadejda began participating and eventually contributing to British nongovernmental organizations that focused on promoting the welfare of certain favored parts of the Balkans—particularly Macedonia, Thrace, or the Dobrudja issues.

She joined the Balkan Committee and the Near East Association. She made the acquaintance of those individuals who would later on become synonymous with a sector of the British public who championed Bulgaria's causes. She became a speaker at their meetings and discussed the post Great War problems with notables like Noel Buxton, (1864-1948), Lord Newton, (1857-1942), Sir Edward Boyle, (1883-1967), Lady Grogan, (1906-1945), and historian A.J.P. Taylor, (1906-1990).[16] In London, she also found time to add to her social contacts. She met "the last Muir with his sister Lady Hamilton and his brother-in-law the general Sir Ian Hamilton who…knows and admires Bulgaria, was in Sofia…Muir seemed to me to be related to so much of Scottish nobility!"[17]

By 1920, as both Nadejda and Dimitri participated in the conferences in their respective capacities, occasionally Nadejda would sit in for her father in London while Feo, still Papa's unofficial assistant, and he were at Lausanne.

The Stancioffs believed the successes for Bulgarian diplomacy to come, were due to their combined efforts—as Nadejda wrote, on their "…incessant work…conversations, interviews, rendezvous, trips, and letters."[18] The younger siblings were being groomed by their father and eldest sister for possible posts in the diplomatic service, especially Ivan. The family envisioned that other family members could take advantage of the opportunities within their reach.

Notoriety Has its Advantages

Nadejda was catapulted deliberately into the public eye when Stamboliiski appointed her first secretary to the Bulgarian legation in Washington, D.C. in 1921. Nadejda's appointment was a great publicity boon for Bulgaria; both she and the prime minister were well aware of the fact and used the opportunity for publicity to advantage.[19] They did a credible job of presenting their homeland as a small peasant nation in which equality of the sexes prevailed; they described the population as hard-working and honest laborers. Through the very symbolic and path-breaking appointment of a woman to an important diplomatic post, Stamboliiski and Nadejda enhanced the international prestige of Bulgaria.[20]

Stamboliiski had often quipped to her that he considered her a "muzhko momiche" or "male girl" because she seemed all business and chose not to behave in ways in which he had come to expect her gender to comport themselves in public.[21] She did not flirt, she did not choose to adorn herself in the latest fashions, and she was unusually capable in her position.

The appointment was visionary in many ways. As early as 1921, the Great War and its impact on Europe were causing political pundits to observe that perhaps if women been the diplomats in 1914 the war might not have occurred. Nadejda's appointment played well in that atmosphere. Stamboliiski asked her to go to Washington to, according to her, in a letter to her family, "work, propagandize, and 'wake-up' Panaretoff [the Bulgarian minister in Washington, D.C.]."[22]

Her family was unabashedly proud of her, as her father's congratulatory letter attests:

> Is Nadejda my son who enters the career world!? . . . it is not my dream—to see my beloved Nadejda enter in the—struggle for life—I dreamed for her a marriage . . . but this should not diminish my legitimate pride in Nadejda—of Maman and mine—to have and to be able to put to the service of our poor country such a serious and brilliant capacity![23]

Her role was only second to the minister plenipotentiary thus she would be in charge of all secret correspondence between Sofia and the minister, maintaining that vital archive and subsequent correspondence, managing the chancellery of the legation. The first secretary along with the minister, had access to safe combinations and keys to vaults that held sensitive documents and would be responsible for the security of all communications to and from the ministry of foreign affairs in Bulgaria. In addition to those duties, the first secretary was equally responsible, with the bursar, for accounting matters and keeping office expenses under control.

Under the Agrarian Party, budgeting for everything from heating, electricity, and office supplies and even matches was an extremely important consideration for every Bulgarian legation. Finally, when the minister was absent, the first secretary had to be his second in all legation matters and, therefore, kept the ministerial obligations as well as regular contact with the local press via official press releases. It was a serious responsibility and so Dimitri could write with satisfaction:

> With intelligent charm—the persistence (à la Dimitri Stancioff) that she possesses, the knowledge of real politics – her encyclopedic education . . . she is destined to render the most eminent service to her country . . . And all this with no Lycée, no University—nothing but what is gained under the continuous spiritual guidance . . . of a mother, who herself is a descendant of Richelieu and Cavour.[24]

Family pride was further inflated when, on an official visit, the Prince of Wales congratulated Dimitri Stancioff on Nadejda's achievement: "I know of your daughter," the prince said, "she is the Diplomat Woman, I admire her, it is all so very interesting but why is she going to America, she must remain here in London, it would be much better for England!"[25] Dimitri reported the exchange to the family and recorded the conversation for Nadejda.

Breaking the "Glass Ceiling"

This appointment caused a sensation on both sides of the Atlantic Ocean and Nadejda was called upon to comment on the subject of women in diplomacy not only after the public announcement but also throughout her life.[26] She became a rarity and a curiosity for the public as well as for the diplomatic community. Her colleagues were intrigued; some were put off by the appointment. All the attention inspired her to work even harder at the task.[27]

She declared that women are born diplomats that men can only learn what comes naturally to a woman: intuition.[28] It is possible that Stamboliiski encouraged her in her feminist views because he was a feminist in his unique way. Although they conversed about many topics over the years, Nadejda and Stamboliiski often discussed gender differences. His liberal views on women and their power appealed to Nadejda, and she made public her views, which were similar to his, on many occasions.[29]

Her appointment and its notoriety permitted her to expound on the role of women in diplomacy while giving a favorable impression of progressive Bulgaria. In a lengthy interview for the Vote, 16 February 1923, a publication of the Women's Freedom League, she is reported to have said "Sex in my country is no handicap to official positions, as Bulgarian women enjoy a greater measure of equality with men than in many of the bigger countries."[30]

She believed that women had an innate sense of practicality that would give them an advantage in the world of diplomacy. She felt comfortable enough to insist, as early as February 1923 that conferences, such as Lausanne, were useless.[31] Instead of convening conferences, which were costly in terms of time and money, she believed that the diplomats and their staffs should work harder and the League of Nations be apportioned more power.[32] She believed women's special contributions to diplomacy would lead to a diminution in warfare since, in her words, "Women hate war so much that . . . those with the necessary authority will use all their weight against it in diplomatic negotiations."[33]

Since the Vote was the organ of the Women's Freedom League, whose purpose was emblazoned on its masthead, Nadejda also commented on Command Paper No. 1244. This official regulatory document of the Foreign Office included a clause which excluded women from "any branch of or posts in the Civil Service ...[and from] all posts in the Diplomatic and the Consular Service etc."[34] She and the readers of the Vote felt it was unjust.

When the Evening News, which also published a lengthy conversation with Mlle. Stancioff, she claimed to be interested in applying "the human touch into diplomatic life" and "studying the conditions of life for women, methods in the schools and hospital improvements" when she began her post in the United States. [35] Traditionally, female spouses of diplomatic representatives pursued this kind of work, in other words, "women's work." When swimming in uncharted waters, she was uncertain about which role best suited her as a pioneer in the field of international diplomacy. She had to consider how to present herself as a feminine or masculine person, a diplomat who tackled soft issues or hard facts, someone who inquired into the state of hospitals or geo-political developments.

When her appointment became public, Nadejda carried out another coup by publishing an article on *Women in Diplomacy*.[36] Although elated by the notoriety of her new title, in her private correspondence, she was at first ambivalent about the post and at times even hostile to the idea. In letters to her family, she expressed an acute awareness of the tragedy of being an intelligent woman in a man's world. She wrote, "It is annoying to have a brain! ...but I burn with ambition, adore life more than ever, and savor my position with frenzy."[37] She was ready to challenge the masculine domain of the public sphere of diplomacy and expand the role of women in an institution that traditionally excluded the participation of her gender.

Nadejda's major trepidation about her appointment to Washington D.C. was being separated from her family. The Stancioffs were unusually close and her greatest regret, whenever she traveled, was separation from her loved ones. She had a special relationship with her sister Feo. The two had been close as the following expert illustrates:

> Everything that the pen of [Feo] produces is so well written. You are the big love of your old [sis] and I love you and I enfold in my embrace your dear hair, your dear eyes, your little charming nose, your lily [white] neck, your flower-like hands, your marble shoulders, your heart, all that your old sister idolizes. She, who is not worthy of what you write about her [Nadejda].[38]

Nadejda never tired of expressing her admiration for Feo as superior to her older sister in all ways: intelligence, beauty, and talents.

The eldest sister had resigned herself to living on meager wages for the rest of her life. In her letters home, she painted warm and humorous images of her visions of her future visits with her family. She imagined that when the family would gather on holidays, her siblings would be surrounded by their spouses and broods; she, the spinster aunt, graying but wise, would be wearing the same frocks and hats and would be dispensing her worldly knowledge to her nieces and nephews.

Lone Female Diplomat

In Bulgaria's diplomatic service, the procedures for appointments or advancements of any sort were somewhat fluid, despite strict hiring and promotion standards. Nadejda's letters to her family emphasized the importance of personal connections and influence. Thus, she could boast "I will arrange my future to my benefit," and in fact, she did.[39]

She was cognizant and sometimes resentful of how easily men were appointed to the service. Despite their incompetence or unwillingness of some men to do the their work, female appointees, who had to work much harder to keep entry-level positions, such as cipher clerk or typist and who worked without hope of advancement. Nadejda comments on the fact that sloth among her colleagues was annoying: "Yesterday I went out between two and six in the evening with Papa after having written work letters all day. No one is doing anything outside the usual group of about six people out of 17 – We are 17!"[40] She was a diligent worker, and since she was in the minority, the fact that not all her male colleagues did the same rankled.[41]

In Bulgaria, women who wanted to gain entry in the diplomatic service at a professional level were stymied by gender prejudice as well as the strangle-hold party appointments had on the process. Thus, Nadejda Stancioff's achievement and position inspired others to try entering the service. However, jealousies and competitiveness among the few female candidates created friction.

In the diplomatic corps, women were marginalized, and Nadejda Stancioff's position(s) in particular, were limited by gender prejudices. Sometimes the prejudice emanated from other women; one woman intimated that "...all Sofia disapproves of [Nadejda's] nomination!" This same woman was also unabashed when she approached Stamboliiski for a job similar to Nadejda by declaring "I *too* speak four languages and I am *also* well brought up!" Nadejda found the woman cheeky.[42]

Compared with the number of women in journalism, the arts, or even the medical and the juridical professions, there were few women in diplomacy or politics in any country.[43] Nadejda Stancioff and her family used her unique status to their advantage by using her notoriety to further their professional careers; her father's and later her brother's careers were sustained by her influence. The Stancioffs did not shy away from the kind of after hours diplomacy that still defined the profession. In this world, personal connections could bolster one's career; who offered one tea and with whom one danced could have more power and meaning than an official memorandum.

This close knit family worked seamlessly together; the women instructed each other on dress appropriate for captivating male delegates' attention and compliments necessary for capturing the sympathies of their wives and consorts. As Feo reported home, the women in the family were constantly looking for opportunities to enhance their own and their family member's power, "Nada had on the new hat that night that I bought for her with great difficulty. Little, velour thing—it looks good on her but it is very modest."[44] Nadejda was notoriously slow to upgrade her wardrobe because she had no patience with the process of fittings and had to be coaxed and cajoled to update her look; her family conspired to help her along.

Nadejda was not a maverick who openly advocated forwarding women's rights or interests. Yet by example and by her penchant for role reversal, she played the part of pioneer in the field of diplomacy. Other women would ultimately fight for the equal treatment of their gender in the work place and in other spheres. Nonetheless, Nadejda could and did enjoy her unique position of lone female diplomat among so many male representatives, "the pleasure of seeing myself greeted by four Ambassadors, illustrious Ministers and cordial secretaries; the little games, little tricks, the Indo-European family tea where four Englishmen offer me bread and butter."[45] She perceived her special status as normal, she, like other successful women of her era, was "gender blind." Believing that any talented woman could advance professionally, Nadejda failed to acknowledge publicly that her family network had a large part to play in her professional accomplishments.[46]

The few contemporary women who did achieve international acclaim in the diplomatic arena were the Bolshevik revolutionary Alexandra Kollontai who eventually became an ambassador for her country in Norway, Sweden, Mexico and one Norwegian ambassador as well as a Hungarian counterpart.[47] Nadejda stood out and reveled in her virtually solitary status at international conferences, as she writes:

> No one has noticed Lady Curzon! He [Lord Curzon] treats me like a colleague! The . . . British are charming, Duca is more than intimate, the Bolshies respectful, the French are honey, and Ismet is loukum [sweet desert]. . . Garoni rises when I pass by. My personal international position is stupefying. . . [48]

On the whole, female contemporaries who did manage to enter exclusively male domains did so through family connections.[49]

Nadejda was one of the pioneers among professional women in the 1910s and 1920s, but she did not enter that realm because of her convictions about women's equality but rather as a way to realize her personal ambitions and the goals of her family's economic security.

Some women took pride in another woman's accomplishment. For example, in a letter to Nadejda, a male acquaintance from the peace conferences wrote, "My wife tells me to convey to you that she too adds her compliments to mine. She salutes your name with enthusiasm, as a friend and as a woman....P.S. I will inform my daughter of this development."[50] Nadejda was a role model, albeit a *sui generis* prototype. Just as women who broke with tradition and traveled the world alone as journalists or artists inspired her, she inspired others.[51] In her values and attitudes she was closer to another prominent Bulgarian woman from the interwar period—Fani Popova-Mutafova—a successful female writer.[52]

When speaking in public, Nadejda stressed the importance of women's roles in furthering social and economic equality among the genders. She was conscious of Bulgarian feminist movements and women's societies that pushed for equality and parity in the work force but she chose not participate.[53] She and Stamboliiski had discussed the future of women's suffrage in Bulgaria, and he was considering giving married women with children and widows the privilege because he believed their life-experience would make them thoughtful voters. Married and widowed Bulgarian women finally could vote in the January 1937 elections. Although even then, they had the privilege but not the obligation to vote, for Bulgarian men voting was compulsory.

Power Broker and Big Sister

Nadejda's professional standing and her prestige among her colleagues was so high that she could use her accumulated power to secure her father's position at the Court of St. James and find work for her brother. Writing to Feo, Nadejda makes the comment that "Papa could have the position of Ivan [League of Nations] that would be better [should he at some point wish to change jobs]. I could live in Geneva with Mama and you [Feo]."[54] As an influential and important government functionary, Nadejda could now manipulate and regulate the professional future of the men in her family. For example, she also writes to the family in London saying that:

> Baker . . . asked me if I wanted to enter the League; I answered by retelling Ivan's story and in being cognizant of his candidature would offer myself for odd jobs and maybe in the future. When I see Baker, again I will ask him to ask Lord Rob to drop the right word in the right place for Ivan.[55]

In this particular instance and many others, Nadejda was ready to forego a prestigious position with the newly formed League of Nations for her brother, Ivan. She willingly relegated herself to "odd jobs."[56] Moreover, on another occasion she voices concern for Ivan's future:

> The "home atmosphere" [the Bulgarian domestic political climate] is super-charged with electricity. Conclusion: that Ivan find himself a position at Boyle's: that Feo help arrange this; an unanticipated development even at 10 quid a month to start. . . . I am not writing to Ivan; send him an extract of this letter![57]

Nadejda directed the entire family in this project of securing work for her brother and hoped to control the outcome with her careful plans. While taking on the Herculean work expected by her immediate and distant superiors, she concurrently worked just as diligently to assure her brother an appropriate job after he graduated from law school in Fribourg. She was intimately involved in his course of studies, his rapport with his professors, and his relationship with the family who boarded him in Switzerland. She reminded Ivan to be especially vigilant about his connection with a particular professor whose beneficence would be critical when he began to look for work.

Nadejda was a person who could be equally involved in detailed negotiations of economic treaties as about the equally delicate business of negotiating interpersonal protocols. In fact all the women in the Stancioff family were. They were each other's closest friends and their friendship informed their professional success. The Stancioff women persisted in behaving, regardless of the professional opportunities available to them, as though they could count on being dependent on the men in their lives. Although they participated in the production of wealth for the family as a whole, they still believed that men create the wealth of the world and hence they permitted an inequality in labor and benefits to permeate their lives.

Nadejda reported that she had it on good authority—from the permanent Swiss representative to the Secretariat at the League of Nations—that Ivan's candidacy could have a chance and wrote home to the family that she "wanted to 'put' Ivan in the League of Nations." She went on to say that "every state has the right to one if not several functionaries at the League . . . therefore silence, prudence, discretion."[58] In skewed roles, the daughter directed her mother on precisely how to proceed and controlled the entire enterprise from a distance.

As an employed professional woman, Nadejda wrote for example that she will take the initiative and approach Ivan's professors about writing letters of recommendation, not Ivan himself. Then she proceeded to direct her mother on what to do next. "Mama, should, in her best French write to Gen. Ross [and two others named]...in the following vein..."[59] She then specified the kind of language that was required, the forms of address for the three different ranks of individuals and she underscored that a copy of the letter Papa had written to Sir Eric [the one ultimately responsible for the hiring] had to be included. Then she gave detailed instructions to her mother:

> Attention! The letter should be typed on good paper from the Legation . . . don't change anything in the letter since I already talked to Sir Eric . . . For me who knows the English, Sir Eric gave the impression that this is almost a sure thing but the recommendations from high places can only make an even better impression . . . Ivan should start with 1300 F Swiss/month (a lot more than me in London) . . . even if Papa is dismissed from London there will be one man at Geneva for starters . . . Silence, hopes and above all write the aspiring one to pass his exams and to bless his father . . . and that Feo and Chou get married.[60]

In addition, as though it were not enough that she direct her brother's future, Nadejda added the last directive to her sisters—to get married! Not because she felt they needed the reminder but because she foresaw specific futures for them as productive wives of diplomats. Nadejda expected that she would remain unmarried, possibly because of her age, but not her sisters. She was adamant in prodding her sisters to marry well, since remaining single had a certain stigma which she was ready to face.[61] She often wrote reminders to her sisters, instructing them about the kind of man they should marry.[62]

For the Stancioffs the world of diplomacy was the world in which they were most comfortable. Anna and her husband had grown close while he developed his career and she served the royal family.[63] They created the cooperative family unit, which became the epitome of Stancioff collaborative life for generations. The women negotiated a place that neither compromised nor endangered their core values as women, Catholics, or as members of a family unit. The family's interest became the women's interests as they measured their successes by the success of the family collective.

The family was extremely close, they felt lost without each other, and the children were all devoted to their mother and in awe and admiration of their father. Even when she found no time to write home, Nadejda assured her mother that she had not forgotten her.

This does not mean that I do not think of you 15 times per hour with infinite fil-ial, respectful tenderness . . . I do not have one minute not for writing a private letter, not for one word in my journal, nor to look at the view, not even to think of an analysis of the times.[64]

Nadejda was an instrument of her family's needs and will. Her family knew of each decision of hers and participated in the formulation of her career plans. Moreover, she in turn shaped her career plans with the family's best interests in mind.[65]

Nadejda's correspondence home carried a constant theme of family coop-eration in work and a solidarity among family members, which included steady efforts to represent themselves well before their professional superiors, espe-cially the prime minister of Bulgaria. Nadejda complimented and assured her father about the reception of his work, as in the following passages: "...your re-ports are remarkable... Stame [Stamboliiski] appears very satisfied...I will put in later for your eventual sabbatical."[66]

In addition, on another occasion, Nadejda gave more praise and support to the entire family "[I read] your excellent creation in the Daily Telegraph...I see that you use my private dispatches and English 'initiatives'. I love your efforts, I approve the results, and I make everyone appreciate them here."[67] By sustaining each other with praise and advertising their hard work to their chief, the Stan-cioffs kept themselves visible and appreciated.

Finally, Nadejda used her professional clout to help the careers of friends too. She nudged along Stoyan Petroff Chomakoff's career, a family friend, in the diplomatic service, by speaking well of him to Stamboliiski. Then she had the satisfaction of hearing that her good word had an impact, Stoyan was posted to London as first secretary.[68]

Perfecting Communication

So as not to lose their special closeness as a family, the Stancioffs wrote each other often and in copious amounts. Father and daughter were the most prolific correspondents, and their letters created sweeping portraits of the meetings and assemblages of delegates in Lausanne, Geneva, and Genoa. Most of the family correspondence was replete with expressions of affection and a reiteration of their longing to be together. The primary language of communication in letters and in person was French. However, when emphasis of a particular point would be more concise in another language, they used terms and entire phrases in sec-ond, third and even fourth languages in the same letter.

In their private correspondence, they kept each other abreast of develop-ments on diplomatic questions and informed each other on their superior's mood, particularly with respect to their work on various projects. Commenting on her father's reports, Nadejda writes that "The *Chief* often tells me his admira-tion of your work."[69]

In fact, their communications took on a largely work related tone when they included summaries of newspaper articles regarding issues relevant to Bulgarian interests. They sent notes to each other on what information to feed journalists sympathetic to the Bulgarian point of view.

Newspaper reports were one way that all interested parties, the states and their representatives, could publicize their respective positions regarding diplomatic negotiations. When a daily newspaper published privileged information on closed-door negotiations, the revealing article had the salutary effect of assuaging feelings of injustice toward more powerful countries, illicit newspaper reports became the refuge of politically weaker states.

Therefore the Stancioffs clipped and sent each other articles on the question of a Bulgarian outlet to the Aegean Sea when, for example, the *Petit Parisien,* a French newspaper, published M. Venizelos' or Greece's point of view by quoting him on the issue: "Why does Bulgaria want a port ...it already has Burgas and Varna. Poland, Hungary, Czechoslovakia don't have ports..."[70] Or when the London *Times* reported on 23 November 1922 M. Stamboliiski's presentation at the Conference at Lausanne on Bulgarian claims to an outlet "...with a clarity which earned the commendation of Lord Curzon..."[71] Or when Ismet Pasha (1884-1973), the Turkish representative at Lausanne addressed the Commission on Territorial and Military questions he "claimed for Turkey the frontiers of 1913 and demanded a plebiscite in Western Thrace..."[72]

As newspapers produced their product, as the article clippings streamed across the continent between the Stancioffs, the family worked in unison to coordinate their efforts. With these communications, sending them, reading them, and creating them, the Stancioffs underscored triumphs and defeats and kept each other feeling supported in their work efforts. Furthermore, their work-related family correspondence carried on with their family tradition of well-coordinated public and private endeavors. They did nothing as individuals or as a group without the rest of the family's awareness.

When necessary, Nadejda took on the task of chastising her younger siblings about their inability to be discreet about their political preferences regarding Bulgarian domestic politics. As members of the government's diplomatic service the Stancioffs were tacit supporters of the party in power; however, not all the Stancioffs were uniformly supportive of the Agrarian Party. Both Chou and Ivan were openly anti-BANU.

When Stamboliiski conveyed to Nadejda that he had heard that "Ivancho talks against us," Nadejda addressed a castigating passage to Chou in a letter home: "Papa and I have only loaned ourselves to Stame and it would be *shameful* on *your* part or on the part of *Ivan* to be vile Bulgarians . . . How I want London to last another two years for us at least . . . stop making your stupid ignorant children's feelings known."[73] This kind of outburst was unusual for Nadejda however the matter was critically delicate. She and Dimitri put in much effort to be indispensable in their positions so that they could secure future employment for not only themselves but also members of the family.

Father and daughter castigated the offenders. Nadejda and Dimitri were aware that there existed powerful forces within BANU who wished to oust them in favor of party loyalists. An indiscreet anti-party position on the part of any member of the family could be used to tarnish all of them and oust them all from their positions. Therefore, Nadejda admonished Chou, who was about to arrive for a visit in Lausanne,

> not one imprudent word or inopportune, you could destroy the patient work of Petron [a pet name for their father] and me, since the armistice. You must never speak without reflecting first! Spend time with my colleagues as little as possible and you must obey me at all times!"[74]

The Stancioffs were able to take advantage of Nadejda's close association to the prime minister to endorse her candidacy for promotion to first secretary. Her rapport with Stamboliiski permitted Nadejda to assure a comfortable appointment for her father at the Court of St. James until he was ready to retire.[75]

They were a good team, and at one point, when Stamboliiski was forced to return to Sofia to plunge into internal affairs, Nadejda missed him. "I am undone by the departure of Stam [Stancioff family shorthand for Stamboliiski]. I cipher and still write letters, look at this room where he had been such a long time; think of this final week from the point of view of a slave of my own free will [when I would] rise at 5.30 ...and him, all the time primitive and in a manner touching...I cry still, I will never forget [our] times [together]...[our] last lunch."[76]

Nadejda's guileless affection permitted her to ask for a delay of her departure for the new position as first secretary to the Bulgarian legation in Washington, D.C. for almost two years by convincing Stamboliiski of her utility to him in Europe. In this way, by remaining near the prime minister, she exerted pressure as necessary to keep her father's career from stalling.[77] Successful in maintaining family professional success, the Stancioff's diplomatic efforts were not so consistently fruitful at the negotiations swirling around them.

Losers at the Negotiating Table

The delegates of a handful of powers carried on the delicate work regarding decisions about territorial dispositions. The final (in)decisions created some uneven settlements. In the Balkans, Bulgaria and Turkey, loser states who were not members of the Great Power clique faced dictated settlements. Forced to reform their nations, ideally on the constitutional monarchy model the Great Powers espoused, the loser states stumbled into the twentieth century with the winners.

The Bulgarian ordeal was extremely harsh most of all because the country, exhausted by previous conflicts, economically disorganized, and unprepared to achieve an economic miracle necessary to success, was forced into an impossible situation. The Big Three—Clemenceau, Lloyd George, and Woodrow Wilson—were ignorant of the state of Bulgaria' internal affairs. Meanwhile, Bulgaria's Balkan neighbors kept up a constant propaganda campaign to sway the peacemakers to view the Bulgarians as still belligerent and able to field a sizeable military force. Quite the opposite was true. Nevertheless, lack of information and a dogged reliance on the intelligence of states that had everything to gain from Bulgaria's prostrate status dominated at the Paris Peace Conference and beyond.

The Bulgarian state's domestic situation did little to contribute toward positive improvements or changes at home. The government had no tools with which to develop its economy and, hence, its provenance, since the political system gave opposition forces the opportunity to stymie government reform.

A small number of educated, experienced elites played a decisive role in the country's political future in 1919.[78] At the same time, the sheer backwardness of the state kept powerless the vast majority of the population—the peasants. Lack of basic education, an imperfect health care system, and grinding poverty prevented the majority of Bulgaria's population from participation in government or from showing their support of government policy that was aimed at furthering their interests. Both individuals and the national government were deeply in debt in 1919; this debt was a burden the Bulgarian economy could not support.

Corrupt politics and self-serving policies of parties in power perpetuated a system of impoverishment in the Balkan states. The culture of corruption the Balkans inherited from their long association with the Ottoman Empire was a difficult habit to break. This habit affected the direction of economic or political change significantly, since the already bankrupt states felt the lack of effective leadership that much more.

Modernization in the Balkans introduced the drive to acquire all the accoutrements of western advanced societies. However, transportation networks, universities, libraries, hospitals, theaters, and modern armies all cost a significant amount. Building urban centers that emulated European cities, especially capital cities, strained nascent economies and drained a poor tax base beyond endurance. The cycle of national insolvency, heavy taxation, and penury on a personal level led to an inexorable development of domestic crises which accelerated over the course of the 1920s.[79]

Although the Bulgarians had little choice but to make a go of becoming players on the world economic scene, they were poorly prepared for a competitive market; they had minimal resources, a poor geographic location, and no viable transportation links. The lack of any industrial development created a situation in which neither domestic nor foreign capital could be induced to invest in the country. Even more damaging was the fact that since Bulgaria was poor in raw materials; foreign investors saw little to interest them. Most well-to-do Bulgarians had little or no experience running an industrial enterprise, and their educated sons preferred to look for jobs in government rather than in industry or agriculture. Meanwhile, a party with an
Agrarian-focused agenda controlled the country; and the question of equitable land distribution was a primary domestic goal for BANU.

Therefore, a just territorial settlement, one that could make the fragile economy viable, became the foreign policy goal for the Ministry of Foreign Affairs. For the Bulgarian state, the primary injustice and greatest error the peace conference committed was the denial of Western Thrace. Although the population there was not necessarily majority Bulgarian, the free and unimpeded access to a port—Dedeagatch—on the Aegean Sea would have been an essential boon to the development of Bulgarian foreign trade. Instead, Greece was awarded the territory; Bulgaria was promised access but no direct ownership of the hinterland. Ultimately, the question of access to the Aegean was unresolved, since Bulgaria refused to accept a compromise and instead chose to leave the question open.

To the north, the issue of regaining the southern Dobrudja, a region that was given to Romania for no logical reason and in which a Bulgarian plurality lived, also remained unresolved until 1940. These circumstances created an opportunity for foreign expertise and capital to make inroads into Bulgarian economic and political life a condition that ultimately served alien goals rather than improving Bulgaria's domestic economic situation. The political standoff in Asia Minor in 1919 and the moribund Treaty of Sèvres led to an irresolute situation. The Ottoman Empire had disintegrated however the unresolved status of its territories on the Anatolian Peninsula led to war.

Greco-Turkish War

The Treaty of Sèvres of October 1920 was the dictated peace produced by the Paris peace negotiations for the Ottoman Empire. The territorial settlements admitted Turkish rights to the city of Constantinople and some European hinterland as well as Anatolia. However, the Ottoman Empire's other territories in Mesopotamia, Palestine, Syria, and Lebanon were taken over as Mandates by Great Britain or France. The Greeks, who had landed in Asia Minor in 1919, were permitted by treaty to occupy Smyrna and the surrounding countryside for five years; thereafter, a plebiscite would decide the city's future. Britain had wished to encourage the Greeks to help dismember the Ottoman Empire, but according to Dimitri, "the English . . . [could not] . . . be Machiavellian," and thus failed.[80]

However, Turkish army officers ably led by Mustafa Kemal, later known as Ataturk, directed a nationalist revolt against the weakened sultan and his government. This revolt, together with the Greek occupation, precipitated the Greco-Turkish War of 1921–22. Ataturk's policy of nation-building created a republic based on perceived threats from the powers and on the Young Turk's self-image as a modern leader of a republican Turkish-Muslim national state.

Peace negotiations at Lausanne eventually collapsed because of diplomatic Turkish intransigence; as Turkish armies scored victories in Anatolia, so did her diplomats in Switzerland. The delegates were amused to observe Ismet Pasha, the principle Turkish negotiator spar with Greek President Venizelos. They speculated on how much of Ismet's witty repartee he planned while rowing, by himself, on the lake. They made small wagers on whose temper would reward them with a vociferous outburst on the following day.

In the fall of 1922, as the debacle in Asia Minor unfolded Bulgaria could still hope for some say in her prospects. The issue of the disposition of Thrace became a lightning rod for the respective territorial ambitions of the Balkan states. The Turks, still in a relatively weak position in 1922, sued for a compromise. The proposal for a solution more favorable to the Bulgarian position, on the port, and a plebiscite for western Thrace were considered.

Meanwhile, each of the other Balkan states voiced notes in keeping with their own national tune; for or against a Thracian plebiscite and the granting of a port for Bulgaria, dependent on their own geographic locations and interests. Naturally, the Greeks wanted to keep as much of European Turkey for themselves as possible, while the Serbs and Romanians sounded conciliatory notes on the port issue. However, Bulgaria's Balkan neighbors were clear that they wished to keep as much territory out of Bulgarian control as possible. Once these concerns showed the complexity of the issues at hand, Lord Curzon, head of the Commission on Territorial and Military Questions, remanded the decision regarding the disposition of those territories to a sub-commission.

The implied threat of a reversal of the territorial settlement of the Treaty of Bucharest in 1913, which concluded the Second Balkan War, did not serve to repair the rift between all the Balkan states. Bulgaria's neighbors preferred to keep their territorial acquisitions without considering the consequences of a resurgent Muslim state at their gates. Ultimately, the opportunity for a unified Balkan bloc to counter Turkish claims did not materialize at Lausanne. The opportunity lost there had greater repercussions in the interwar years.

Crisis in the Balkans

As negotiations dragged on and the Greek hold on Asia Minor loosened Dimitri believed that Bulgaria could be invited to participate in a future conference on the final resolution of the Eastern Question. Information Dimitri gathered led him to believe and hope that the mood and policy direction of the British foreign office was experiencing a shift. Dimitri reassured what must have been a skeptical audience back in Sofia by writing, "Sir William Tyrrell—who replaces Sir Eyre Crowe—and controls practically the Ministry of Foreign Affairs—during the illness of Lord Curzon . . . I am acquainted with him since 1908 when he was the right hand man of Minister Edward Grey."[81]

His conversations with Tyrrell gave Dimitri cause for optimism. He related a synopsis of the exchange between him and Tyrell to Sofia: "You say that there will be a conference to resolve the Eastern Question . . . must not all the interested parties be heard? . . . Bulgaria is a Balkan state . . . do you not find it just that the Bulgarians should be heard?"[82] Dimitri believed that Bulgarians might participate in a gathering of interested parties at a potential conference that would finally to put to rest the Eastern Question. He believed that no other solution could prepare a viable decision; Bulgaria had to be included.

The Bulgarians, as well as others who had put their faith in the English to be fair, were disappointed. Although no state could be purely altruistic, the English were actually devious. Not above using a crass religious argument to shore up their own policy goals, they played the creed trump card. Dimitri reported to Sofia: "The atmosphere in England is changing—it is not Grecophile—but is turning into . . . Christianophilia against Islam . . . or in other words: national egoism (Constantinople, the Straits, and Mesopotamia) rules."[83] Dimitri understood that all diplomacy, no matter how noble-sounding, was ultimately a fig leaf used to disguise self-serving politics; he also understood, however, that hope was part of the game. Lloyd George's foreign office appeared to be preparing a counterattack against the Turkish nationalists. Therefore the Bulgarians hoped for a reversal in their fortunes.

At one point during the crisis, the English proclaimed themselves as saviors of Christian Bulgarians once in the nineteenth century and their potential saviors once more in the twentieth century. If the Sèvres Treaty were ratified, Western Thrace would go to the Greeks. However, a revised treaty might permit liberation of the territory and its declaration as an autonomous—or even international—territory open for use to everyone.

At that particular point, the foreign office interpreted any position that seemed to favor the Turkish stance as Turkophile, which translated into anti-Lloyd Georgism. How could a Bulgarian people, after experiencing the regime of Abdul Hamid, be Turkophile? The Bulgarians were dancing a very delicate *pas de deux*. The insistence of Prime Minister Gladstone to avenge what became known the world over as the "Bulgarian Atrocities" in 1876, gave the Eastern Question, according to Dimitri, the "character of a sectarian struggle of a fight between Christianity and the barbarism of Islam!"[84] Therefore the Bulgarian position could not, in 1922, be in any way favorable to the Turks for those historic reasons. This perspective was incomprehensible to the British foreign office under Lloyd George's direction and ably illustrates that the British were not above using the blandishments of sectarian solidarity when convenient.

The English had a blemished record too; they had not abided wholly by their principles during the Russo-Turkish war in 1878, as Stancioff pointed out to Tyrell. Political interests and principled behavior did not often coincide. Geopolitical realities still pushed the Bulgarians in the pro-Turkish camp over the issue of unimpeded access to the Aegean.

Dimitri anticipated some of the disaster of the Greek military rout in Asia Minor when he reminded his superior that: "the Eastern Question has always remained the most important and thorniest problem of European politics!"[85] Furthermore, he understood that at the core, the English held one longstanding goal above all others: free access to the Straits. Once, this goal meant control over the Ottoman state; now it meant an advantageous division of the former empire's territories. Britain's interests came first; therefore, the economic well-being of any regional state paled in comparison to the strategic importance of the Straits to a seaborne power like Great Britain. Dimitri recounted the historical record to Sofia to emphasize his grasp of the situation:

> England in the days of Palmerston, insisted that the Ottoman Empire must be preserved . . . but this did not impede her from taking Egypt and Cyprus and making gains in Sudan! . . . there have been projects on dividing Muslim lands since the 13th century![86]

With discretion, Bulgaria could still be incorporated into the Great Power system of lesser powers acting as barriers against the undesirable eastern threats of bolshevism and nascent Turkish/Muslim resurgence. Dimitri was sanguine; his report to Stamboliiski noted that the foreign office was considering, unofficially, Bulgarian presence and input on a host of issues still to be resolved.

Dimitri writes to Sofia that "The Great Powers know that if we, Bulgarians, want we could be a fence, a barrier with the Romanians against Russian Bolshevism!"[87] He advised patience and prudence. His advice was sound, it was just what the French desired, what the British thought they needed, and what could appeal in an atmosphere of paranoia. However, many voices and forces shaped the future of Europe.

Diplomats Amuse Themselves

Based in London, in his capacity as minister plenipotentiary, Dimitri directed a stream of commentary toward Sofia on developments in Asia Minor. In a ciphered telegram he sent September 19, 1922 Dimitri, with Nadejda's input, laid out the Eastern Question to Stamboliiski. Mustafa Kemal's military successes and the possibility that nationalist Turkish forces could breech the "neutral zone" occupied by allied troops, forced Lloyd George to consider the practicality of a new war. It was portrayed as "a new crusade in the XXth Century!" according to Dimitri.[88] British newspapers even began to mention a list of potential allies in such a scenario. When Kemal declared that he had no intention of entering Thrace or Constantinople, Lloyd George's public threats seemed to have hit their mark.

However, the British domestic situation, according to Dimitri's report, would not have permitted another military adventure. Agitation by the Workers' Party, the decline of the English stock exchange, and the complications in Mesopotamia and India had put the British in an awkward position. The Bulgarian minister plenipotentiary at London understood that the domestic dilemmas writ large—in England and the colonies—would sway public opinion, and hence the foreign office, even as the English leader Lloyd George did not.

Therefore, the issue of whither Thrace seemed, according to Dimitri, too "far from their [British] shores" to consider with any focus. Nonetheless, the Bulgarians proposed an autonomous Thrace, and Dimitri pressed the point to his foreign-office contacts. He insisted that the solution was obvious to orientals, meaning those from the region, but not to those who had "neither studied the geography nor those who [were] unfamiliar with the ethnic situation," such as the English.[89]

Bulgarian diplomacy kept the issue of Thrace alive, hoping against hope that a solution favorable to Bulgaria could yet be salvaged from the situation. Meanwhile, Bulgarian diplomacy's efforts on this resolution were countered by other Balkan representatives, who reminded the British that historically, as in 1885, an autonomous Rumelia had been incorporated outright into the Bulgarian state. Hence, the precedent predetermined the future of an autonomous Thrace.

It was an uphill battle for the Bulgarians. The Bulgarians' faith in the British government to succeed against the Turks was largely one of a drowning man's faith in the bit of straw. Lloyd George's miscalculation was something else entirely; his mistaken belief that the British government could lead its people in another military campaign was so misguided that it ultimately led to his political downfall.

Nadejda recorded a Lord Curzon's declaration at Lausanne at the end of the
year, in December 1922, she relayed it to her family:

> 'We are all agreed; all finished all perfect, all jolly (sorry!) End of Straits dis-
> cussion!' We Balkans took the punches and await the shocks to come! The
> Powers pretend to arrange the last details with private conversations with Ismet
> at George Nathaniel's . . . who spent two hours with him yesterday!!![90]

The Bulgarian representatives felt once again excluded and on the periphery,
indeed Nadejda placed her country in the same camp as the Russians because
the Bulgarians were so marginalized at the conference.

In fact, the Bulgarians made every effort, approached every state with any
power over the decisions at Lausanne. Nadejda writes that the:

> French are furious against us because of the stupid reparations have blocked
> their brain. The Italians give nothing for nothing and ask us to assure them in
> advance that we will construct a port! The English at least bother to prepare a
> new plan for us...Bompard [said]: "it is necessary to convince the English."
> Harold [said]: "look here, the French say Article 48 does not mention a territo-
> rial outlet. Try and get round Poincaré." Philosophy of life: poor powerless![91]

The Bulgarians experienced these meetings as a constant jostling for position
and understood that they would be bounced back and forth between the powers
on any modifications. They sought to make a weak position potent by official
and personal diplomacy; working in Switzerland or England, they felt that there
was a modest chance of success. Nadejda could report:

> I chatted like an ambassadress with Ganoni who completely forgot Mme Bom-
> pard
> . . . when I attacked Duca who then neglected the charms of . . . Mrs. Child . . .
> I amused myself royally. There was not a secretary of my 'class' invited! . . . I
> told English and French alike that if they opened my heart they would find the
> name Dedeagatch written there . . . I spoke of Turin in Italian with Ganoni and
> say sayonara to the Japanese who were startled to hear . . . doytassimaste! . . .
> later after having conquered all the young French I danced with the English
> fleet . . . I suddenly saw Barrere behind a curtain, who was looking at my an-
> kles![92]

Despite the lighthearted tone, the Bulgarians were aware of the inadequacy
of their negotiating position. The delegates, powerful and powerless, all had
their own frustrations at the conference and some produced rather memorable
aphorisms.[93] Chicherin on the League of Nations called it "organized powerlessness." Neykoff created a definition of Lausanne: "the conference of adjourn-
ments." An anonymous wit expressed cogently the general sentiment on
Venizelos, and the Greek and the English dreams in Anatolia, with the remark:
"He had one gesture to make, that of Pilate! He did not make it...and wanting to
gain Ionia lost Attica."[94]

Diplomats exhibited the lighter side of diplomacy in the verbal puns they tossed back and forth to relieve stress and boredom. The international language of diplomacy, French, served their purposes. The Stancioffs recorded the diplomatic witticisms of the day, such as, "*Ah, la defaite grecque? Honni soit Kemal y pense,*" (Shamed be he who thinks evil of it. Kemal, sounds in French similar to: qui mal) but churned out thoughtful communiqués to their superiors in Sofia.[95]

For the Bulgarians, the English favoritism of the Greeks, as expressed most clearly by Harold Nicolson's efforts on their behalf, was a bitter pill. The Stancioffs perceived Nicolson as sooner Venizelos' secretary than Lord Curzon's man. Still they took heart when occasionally an article in an English newspaper supported a solution favorable to Bulgarian interests. When the *Times* reported the fact that if Greece offered Bulgaria trading access to the port of Kavala as well as Dedeagatch in return for territorial concessions in Macedonia then something akin to the Balkan League of 1912 could once again take form, Nadejda scribbled across the clipping "da vidim [Let's wait and see]."[96] Perhaps the English would help with this solution to the problem Nadejda thought. Nadejda used the press to her advantage; journalists, in turn, asked her to give them advance notice of newsworthy items.

Once, when interviewed on her position as a female diplomat, Nadejda used an anecdote from the recent conference to illustrate the frustration of the Bulgarian position. Interpreting for Stamboliiski, she managed to devise a system of scribbled notes to him along with her whispered translations of the proceedings as the Greek president Venizelos made a speech. Stamboliiski's uncannily quick reaction to the negative tone of the speech led Lord Curzon to protest that her abilities as an interpreter could not possibly have been so rapid and accurate. She cleverly replied: "Such a memory is not only possible but natural for us where Greeks are concerned."[97]

The conferences of the 1920s underscored Bulgarians' position of powerlessness on virtually every issue. Despite their positive attitude about what could be accomplished, the Stancioffs had to recognize the inevitable reality, as Nadejda remarks: "We go to sleep enlightened once more by the knowledge of being useless! Tension. . . . interviews, private, mediation from America; a sort of optimism."[98]

Diplomacy required skill and delicacy in verbal expression. The Stancioffs were perceptive negotiators armed with few bargaining chips; with the turn of a phrase, however, they could put off diplomatic adversaries. They sparred with the best in the world of diplomacy. Nadejda and her father delighted in being able to thrust and parry with diplomats of high repute who were powerful negotiators at the conferences but poor at repartee after hours. Nadejda writes:

> I adore these conferences, this hall, where an only woman, I am struck to the patrician back of Petrone [her father], where I hear the bloody answers of George Nathaniel [Curzon]; where I observe each mute jeer of Chicherin [Soviet representative]; the unique smile of Ukraine [Rakovski]; the false hysteria of Ulysses [Venizelos]; the . . . contestable charm of the Mamalig [Romanian]

Foreign Office; the grecophile maneuvers who make me clench with rage at my colleague Harold [Nicolson]; the amicable gestures of my English friends.[99]

Working as a team with the meager devices of skillful negotiations at their disposal, the Stancioffs, at one point, used Harold Nicolson's obvious Greek bias against him. They conspired to have him leak the news of the Bulgarian plan on Dedeagatch to the press by giving the plan to him for review. Nadejda advised Feo that the translations she sent with a packet of some Turkish documents would serve Bulgaria's cause best if the Stancioffs gave them to sympathetic Englishmen like Arnold Toynbee and Conwell-Evans, on behalf of Stamboliiski. She added that the family should also give the translations to Harold as a "good will gesture," which would expose the plan to the Press not directly, "but indirectly" Nadejda winked.[100]

As the situation in Anatolia began to become static, the French were finally exerting pressure on the Turks to settle, and the economic goals of the Great Powers came into sharper focus. Mosul was important to the Great Powers because of the oil reserves and because the Berlin to Baghdad railroad had taken on more relevance as a link from the lands irrigated by the Euphrates River to the center of Europe.

Meanwhile the Territorial Commission considered Curzon's proposal for a "Mosul League;" the details concerning the Ruhr, Memel as well as Dedeagatch were still on the table at Lausanne. However, as the Turkish position strengthened, the British seemed to weaken, the British appeared to lose faith in their own ability to exert their will.

The foreign office seemed to falter as Nadejda recorded her conversation with Child over cigarettes after dinner one night: "Look here, you can help, do you see the Turks? We want peace."[101] The Bulgarians were willing to "help" but their position was weak.

During the first two days in February, Nadejda writes "...interview with Ismet alone. I cry, he listens...Papa visits Ismet." Then on February 3, she adds: "The Turks are playing [it] close to the vest."[102]

By February 1923, the British prospects in Anatolia had diminished to a pitiful degree. Since the Americans were rapidly withdrawing from European affairs, and the French were focused elsewhere, the British found themselves in an increasingly untenable position. Nadejda had an opportunity to act as intermediary. Lord Curzon, whom, she found to be "in a devil of a mess" and Ismet Pasha needed a go between they could trust.[103] Lord Curzon and Nadejda spent hours talking in private, and Nadejda was brutally frank with the British Lord; she could not have envisioned being so frank under normal circumstances. Addressing Curzon, Nadejda said:

This is what comes of flirting with the Iliad and listening to the boys around you. You have got to make concessions; you have got to drop the Greeks. And other things. He asked me to see the Pasha before tomorrow's 11 o'clock session. To tell him his part (of his will but also of his powerlessness)...I enjoyed it [the conversation] as I would have enjoyed a rendezvous with a lover.[104]

Nadejda then followed through on her promise and saw Ismet Pasha the next day; he, in turn, promised to see Lord Curzon in private. The Treaty of Lausanne followed soon after.

Treaty of Sèvres Crumbles

The situation in Asia Minor ultimately led to the nullification of the articles of the Treaty of Sèvres due to Ataturk's forces entering the territories occupied by the Greek armies in fall 1922. The Turks took Smyrna in early September when Ataturk's significant victories against the retreating Greek forces permitted him to acquire abandoned munitions and trucks.

The Greek rout led to a strengthening of the Turkish nationalist position so that the Turks could now negotiate with the Great Powers for a return of European territories by granting—already lost—territories in Mesopotamia!

In this manner, the Treaty of Sèvres proved an impotent document and eventually the Turks were able to extract a much different Treaty of Lausanne in 1923. They recouped nearly all their lost territories in Asia Minor proper as well as Thrace, and they were never burdened by reparations payments or the requirements to limit their military to a size commensurate with a defensive posture. Most of the credit for this tremendous coup belongs to Ismet Pasha; he almost single-handedly manipulated the conference to commit to a treaty that was overwhelmingly in Turkey's favor.

Ismet Pasha accomplished this feat in a clever way. The delegates to Lausanne began their work at the end of November 1922. When the treaty was ready for signature at the end of January 1923, Ismet Pasha slyly refused to sign, thereby negating the document. Forced to reconvene, the conference, this time under the guidance of Sir Horace Rumbold rather than the intransigent Lord Curzon, managed to come up with a treaty more to the Turk's liking. That document was approved at end of July 1923.

The final product of the negotiations with the Turks, the 1923 Treaty of Lausanne, changed the map of Anatolia and Thrace once more with terms that were much more favorable to the Turks than the unenforceable Treaty of Sèvres. The Greeks' failure to enlarge their territories at the expense of the Ottoman Empire led to the rearrangement of the Balkan and Asia Minor map. A revision that finally dashed Bulgarian hopes.

Domestic British Politics in the 1920s

The election of David Lloyd George (1918) brought the Liberal Party to dominance in British politics, confirmed the unity the British felt during the war, and, in a real sense, reiterated the population's patriotism. Lloyd George was touted as "the man who won the war," and his constituents had full confidence that he would handle the peace equally well. The results of that election served to support the feeling—or perhaps the desire to believe—that the country was returning to normalcy.

The British public wanted to believe that the domestic socioeconomic disruptions caused by the conditions of war would revert to their previous familiar forms, specifically the British class system. The government relied on the capitalist system to negotiate economic storms and to enact reforms. These reforms stabilized the social dislocation and kept the industrial, capitalist elements content with the changes. Instituted by a party that believed it had the support of the population behind them, however, the reforms led to some unforeseen and negative results.

The loss of markets abroad and the significant ballooning of the national debt impacted the British economy. Lloyd George found himself embattled on several fronts, even by Liberals Members of Parliament (MPs), on his policies concerning free trade; he faced even more vehement opposition to his Irish policies. From 1919 to 1921, the British government conducted a war with the Irish Republican Army whose bloody clashes horrified the public and aroused controversy.

While Lloyd George worked in Paris on the Versailles peace process, at home his failing domestic policies served to alter the political establishment's judgments of his foreign policies, especially the shape of the peace. It became obvious that he aimed to place Britain in an overseer position once again as arbiter and controller of foreign lands. War weariness turned into a drive to rein in British responsibilities abroad, and for his own reasons Lloyd George did not notice the shift in his support base.

The political disillusionment which finally booted him out of office was the crisis over the territorial disposition of the former Ottoman territories. A muddled situation that was primarily his responsibility Lloyd George's decision to support the Greeks against the Turks in Anatolia led to his downfall. When Lloyd George began to intimate that war was imminent and that Britain would shore up the Greek armies against Ataturk's forces in support of the Greek territorial claims and to control the Straits his promises led to an up swell of opposition that toppled Lloyd George's coalition government in October 1922.

A Brutal Murder

When Aleksandûr Stamboliiski was assassinated in June 1923, the repercussions on Bulgaria were severe. The Agrarian Party's callous form of control over all political opponents and especially members of the Internal Macedonian Revolutionary Organization (IMRO) were responsible for the assassination. Disagreements and feuds within IMRO had frequently spilled onto Sofia streets and led to public disorder, work stoppages, and grisly murders. Bulgarians who either wished to incorporate Macedonia into Bulgaria or to create an independent state and all other positions in between had turned the country into a field of battle. The change over of political power after Stamboliiski's assassination did little to alter the domestic climate of violent disorder. By the mid-1930s hundreds of Bulgarian citizens had been murdered due to factional aggression and there seemed no end to the violence.

During his tenure, Stamboliiski had failed to create unity and solid support for his policies, even within his own party; and he alienated his political opponents and their supporters. In the months leading up to his murder, he had focused his opponents' anger by signing the Niš Convention, which promised Bulgarian and Yugoslav cooperation in suppressing terrorists—the Macedonian nationalists who disrupted both countries' internal equilibrium.

The agreement aimed to suppress Macedonian extremists, censor their press, restrict their organizations, and arrest their leaders; these restrictions evoked predictable outrage. White-hot hatred of the Agrarian government, and especially its leader, coalesced the opposition. Oblivious of the agreement's effects or perhaps uncaring about them, Stamboliiski also purged his own cabinet of political dissenters that spring. Finally, his oppression of the Wrangel White Russian officers in Bulgaria provided an additional cadre of disgruntled, well-trained, and organized men to his list of enemies.[105] His assassination was the dénouement of those combined angers.

The coup d'état was the result of the coalition of virtually every irritated political group in Bulgaria, with the exclusion of the Communists. Military officers, foreign and national, IMRO and other right-wing disaffected elements came together to overthrow the Agrarians and retake what they perceived as the sinking ship of state. The coup's conspirators' relationship with the king was strained at best.

The plot to murder and overthrow the prime minister was nearly stymied by the unexpected visit of King Boris and his sisters to Stamboliiski's home village, Slavovitsa. The royal group brought fruits and vegetables from Euxinograd on their way to Sofia.[106] The visit typified the kind of relationship King Boris developed with people he liked: easy, warm, and unceremonious. After the royal family left, the coup conspirators could proceed with their plans.

The coup on June 9th was so efficient that by the time news of the event became public, the plotters and their compatriots were in control of Bulgaria and set out to control her diplomatic service. Bulgarian diplomats abroad heard the horrible news from foreign journalists calling their legations for comment. Nadejda, reacting to the news, writes to her father in Switzerland: "Why write what I think! . . . Secretaries have little importance in this kind of situation. They must simply keep their mouths shut and work."[107]

In London, Nadejda was nominally in control of the Bulgarian legation while her father was at Lausanne. Confused about whose directives to follow, she chose to be discreet and revealed none of her ignorance to the press while fending off incessant telephone calls. She tells Dimitri her strategy, "obey only Sofia, that is Kalphoff, we haven't answered Daskaloff."[108]

After the assassination, she relied on her philosophical nature to moderate the pain, and she considered handing in her resignation. Writing to Dimitri, Nadejda says:

But I am asking you seriously whether I should not resign? . . . it is a gesture worthy of me for Stame. Besides they will surely have the idea of discharging me if the esteem of the King does not let me retain the position for a bit! . . . I am so disgusted with my own people—for the moment! Quelle kasha [What a mess]![109]

Reaction to a Political Murder

Ivan had been en route to Bulgaria when the coup took place. He witnessed the turn over of power. Apart from some peasant insurrections and repressions of BANU party members by the military, life in Bulgaria seemed to sail smoothly along with the transition of power. Maman and Chou joined him soon after, and they spent the summer at *Les Trois Sources*. Although showing sympathy for the Agrarians was not in fashion, Papa was clear he would not hide his support for Stamboliiski and wrote to Nadejda:

> Requiescat in pace [rest in peace]...he asked nothing of us—we will keep our grati-
> tude, be very sincere—his portrait will remain on my desk. . . . . The future was not
> for him—as it is not for us. If there are faults—he expiated them—and after his
> tragic death—Honni soit qui mal y pense [Shamed be he who thinks evil of him.]![110]

Dimitri was shocked but philosophical as well when he shared with his family a dear memory of Princess Marie Louise, King Ferdinand's first wife and the mother of Ferdinand's children. Dimitri records that "Marie Louise wrote once on my blotting sheet: You cannot undo that which will happen."[111] The Stancioffs would have to be content with that sad truth and look ahead to their inscrutable futures.

Friends wrote the Stancioffs wishing to express their sympathy and offer some comfort to the family that lost both their professional footing and, with Stamboliiski's murder, a friend. An Irish woman writing to Feo comforted her with the following words:

> I am glad to hear . . . that you do not think the change of government bad for
> your country. All the newspapers differ slightly in opinion and your judgment
> is trustworthy, of course, we Irish sympathize with you, Stambolisky was the
> Micael Collins of Bulgaria.[112]

Nadejda received affectionate and warm notes from friends, one of whom was eloquently emotional and reserved at once. Ms. Wood, a British friend, wrote of her reticence to comfort Nadejda in person, yet expressed her feelings in writing:

> When you laughed like the Japanese telling their sorrows . . . and said Stam-
> boliiski did not make a gap in your daily life and religiously noted all the hu-
> morous touches in the late events, I wonder if you know I longed to hug
> you...[113]

Nadejda kept up that front of equanimity with everyone including her family when she assured them that she felt tremendous sangfroid toward the coup d'état. She calmed her father by telling him not to worry about trying to find her a job; she says "I was touched by what you wrote about me to Sofia but don't bother yourself more on the subject. I am resting very nicely for the moment and will begin to look for work sometime in the future."[114]

Her contacts among journalists paid off and she was offered jobs, which she turned down, including a job as a reporter with the *Times*. One journalist friend offered to write an article to support her and her father in their positions by using the new regime's own words against them.

Nadejda eventually gave up her position in the Bulgarian diplomatic service because she tacitly understood that she was not welcome by Stamboliiski's usurpers and because she personally could not conceive of working closely with another prime minister. Her personal relationship with Aleksandûr Stamboliiski had been a large part of the reward of her positions. When she resigned from the diplomatic service, Nadejda took up temporary assignments as an occasional correspondent for various publications. Although she sporadically published in Bulgarian newspapers, journalism was an entirely new venture for her. At the encouragement of a journalist acquaintance who wrote for the *Observer*, she wrote articles for the *Contemporary Review* and the *Correspondent* —the latter in French.[115]

Ivan still wished to join Bulgaria's diplomatic service in some capacity. He had not supported the Agrarian Party while Stamboliiski was in power and was willing to work for the new regime. His mother was thoroughly against the plan and wanted Ivan to stay away from government service. Imagining a more stable and remunerative occupation for her only son, she wrote to her husband voicing her opinions and concerns:

> This boy would do well to find his way in business not in politics of this country and he should not get his future mixed with that of Bulgarian statesmen. I put them all in the same sack, as usual. What consideration is there for them abroad!? I understand your [this addressed to Dimitri] desire to no longer represent them [Dimitri was considering resigning his position].[116]

Dimitri was happy to withdraw from the diplomatic service at this point in his life. He was close to retirement, and more importantly, he did not wish to represent the new right-wing group that had gained control of the country. He finished his work at the conferences in Switzerland and by 1924 was prepared to retire. When he resigned, he wrote a letter to the British Prime Minister James Ramsay Macdonald, saying "Circumstances independent of any personal desire have led me to retire from my Diplomatic Career of 37 years."[117] His departure was portrayed by more than one English newspaper as a resignation motivated by political considerations—by his unwillingness to serve the Agrarian's usurpers as well as the Agrarians' resentment of his service and the pressure they placed on him to leave office.

Life after Diplomacy

After her resignation from the Bulgarian diplomatic service in 1923, Nadejda, at twenty-eight, had to reacquaint herself with her previous life, the life of a mere member of a diplomatic family, which in London was not without its attractions. Her father did not resign his post until mid-1924. She and her sisters were presented at court where, wearing formal gowns, they curtsied to the royal couple. Nada, Feo, and Chou participated in the richness of the diplomatic community's social life, and they continued to attend balls and to entertain friends at home. Nadejda kept busy with social engagements as well as some intellectual pursuits.

For Nadejda, life in her professional retirement still included public talks on the Balkans and Bulgaria. One of her talks, on February 3, 1924, to a general meeting of the Near East and Middle East Association, was summarized by the *Observer*. The brief column on her talk applauded "Bulgaria for its advocate, Europe for its citizen, and a diplomat for his daughter."[118]

Nadejda found these kinds of events stimulating, and she especially enjoyed the company of older educated men with whom she could discuss "serious topics." Since she was quite young, she enjoyed spending free time not in the company of girls her own age—and eschewed conversations on fashions and hairstyles or the latest gossip; she preferred, instead, deep conversations—on topics such as art, politics, and literature—with men whose perspective and life experience she valued. Her sister Feo noted that by the 1920s Nadejda had a "special group of friends, mostly older than herself, with whom she felt utterly at her ease, declaring the intelligent men in the United Kingdom were ideal companions."[119]

Nadejda, for example, recorded the following conversation with Lord Curzon as a moment of pure personal bliss:

> A flowery conversation on the books of Strachey; Nelson; R.L. Stevenson; the Indies; the American woman; Lassa; Tibet; how one should hang paintings; the British Museum; Manet; the National Gallery . . . Degas; the problems with the Louvre; Barrere; should or should they not include the faults of great men in their biographies; English furniture . . . Anglo Saxon orators; feminism; more of the same. And he knew each name, date, author, and painting.[120]

Like her father, the acquaintances she sought out were men of his generation or slightly younger who were educated, well-traveled, and deep thinkers. She visited the British historian, Professor George Peabody Gooch, (1873-1968), with whom she spent happy hours discussing books and talking politics. That acquaintance led to a fruitful collaboration when she was published in the *Contemporary Review,* he was the journal's editor 1911-1960. She met and was befriended by H.G. Wells, (1866-1946), author, historian, and socialist, who invited her to his house in the country for conversations. Noel Buxton , MP, traveler, and author, who reputedly knew every village in Macedonia, also invited her to his home to inspect his gardens and for more conversations. During these visits her hosts would have expected to be rewarded with the presence of an engaging intellect in an attractive body. Nadejda Stancioff had a circle of admirers throughout her lifetime.

Family Marriages

One of those admirers was an older man whom she met at Claridge's, at a dinner party organized by his stepchildren. In 1923, she was twenty-nine and he was in his mid-fifties. Lord Kay seemed shy, and she did not seem to notice him, or at least not to notice that he had taken special note of her. His family however, conspired to get them together as much as possible once his romantic interest became obvious. That fall, the Stancioffs were invited to social events at the Muir sister's home, Jean Hamilton, wife of General Sir Ian Hamilton.

By December, Feo and Nadejda were invited to a Hunt Ball in Northamptonshire as guests of Kay Muir at Whilton Lodge. He had invited them to take part in a weekend of hunting and merriment—amusements that were part of his world. The house, although primarily a hunting lodge, was well appointed with a library, Italian furnishings, impressive paintings, and fresh-cut flowers; and his guests were the right sort. They could dance elegantly, hunt and shoot expertly, and when in conversation, they talked about "things that mattered."[121]

That weekend invitation was a not-too-veiled endeavor to have Nadejda experiences the kind of life she could expect if she would consider Kay Muir as her husband. He was a member of the Peerage; he had a substantial fortune; he was a member of the Royal Company of Arehers, the King's Bodyguard for Scotland; all this, plus a loving heart.

Their courtship was extremely brief. When he first approached her with his proposal of marriage, she was flustered. Her response was conditional on religious difficulties being righted; he was not a Catholic.[122] Lord Kay courted Nadejda in the fall of 1923. By the end of January 1924, he called for her at the Bulgarian legation and proposed marriage, presenting Nadejda with a diamond and ruby bracelet as a symbol of his devotion.[123] By all accounts their courtship was whimsical and uniquely their own. For example, in February, he sent her a gift of the first salmon caught on his property at the start of fishing season, he was an avid hunter and a fisherman.

They married on March 17, 1924 in a small, private ceremony performed at Brompton Oratory, the Stancioff family parish church in London, followed by a celebratory breakfast. The event, reported in several newspapers, featured photos of the bride and groom and their guests. The early-morning ceremony was markedly understated, as was the couple's attire: a brown frock with matching hat with a sable wrap for the bride, and a blue suit for the groom. Nadejda forswore a white dress for something much more practical. Her bouquet was daffodils interspersed with violets, again, a rather startling choice for a bride. The groom pinned a shamrock to his lapel in commemoration of the holiday. They left after breakfast for a honeymoon in Rome, Nadejda's favorite city.

When interviewed by the *Dundee Advertiser* about her recent marriage, Nadejda, now Lady Muir, was quoted as saying "except for a Bulgarian I would marry no other man but a Scotsman or an Englishman. My admiration for all things British is only equaled by my pride in acquiring the nationality."[124] Although exaggerating for effect, Nadejda was being truthful.

Soon after her marriage to Sir Kay, Nadejda Stancioff Muir wrote a jubilant letter to her parents. It is a letter full of longing for her home and the family circle, altered now by not only her own marriage but also the favorable matches of her brother, Ivan and sister, Chou. Lady Muir made an informative remark about the way in which the Stancioff family cooperated for their mutual and individual successes how they fortified and supported each other in the professional and personal arenas:

> People will think that we are "lucky"! But they do not know that it is all due to the courage, work, and the admirable lives of our parents, that it is the reward of the virtuous lives of Stan and Anci. The three—Nada—Ivan —Chou— profited with modern audacity from the work of their parents and Feo![125]

This quote and similar accolades throughout the family correspondence illustrate the Stancioffs' consciousness as a cooperative unit. This is why months after she had married and had forsaken her diplomatic career, Nadejda continued to attribute her success, and that of her siblings, to the efforts of her parents and to the cooperative labors of the entire family, especially Feo who remained unmarried. They had all participated in the process of selecting, evaluating, and marrying their respective spouses.

She felt torn by her loyalties to her parents, especially her father, and wrote in November 1924 that "there is always a price to pay!"[126] For her parents, especially her father, the departure of their eldest daughter from the family was extremely painful. However, Papa wrote her a tender letter in which he expressed, half in French and half in English, all the joy a parent could express for a happily married child. "I do not accept the words of John Milton—the Paradise—it will not be lost for me, I will find it when I am with you and Kay."[127]

Nadejda and Kay's marriage proved happy and enduring. Nadejda wrote to her family, describing her marriage: "It is honest, with no surprises, no flames! How I am grateful to God for everything—a superb home; charming relatives; marvelous husband; the first country in the world as a fatherland; a flattering and gracious title"[128] This is a sincere expression of Nadejda's lifelong gratitude for the blessings in her life and a true expression of her practicality.[129] She blended into Kay's life as much as her character and personality permitted. For example, she allowed him to convince her to become a fisherman and made him proud when on a single day in September 1925 she caught a 12 pound salmon and a trout.[130]

Her marriage evoked an interesting journalistic piece from her friend, Clare Sheridan (1885-1970), journalist, sculptor, and world traveler, who could not decide whether the marriage was a decision one could applaud without reservation.[131] In her article for the *New York World* Sheridan bemoaned the fact that so few women were able and capable to be successful as professionals as Nadejda had been and that their loss to marriage was disappointing, at the very least.[132] This commentary is perceptive, since so many of Nadejda's acquaintance had the same misgivings, including the groom's family. A close friend of Jean Hamilton, Lord Kay's sister, wrote after her meeting with Nadejda, that she, Nellie Sellar, was sure that "[Nadejda was] a rare creature...[with] that sense of the

elemental feminine, and of intellectual force kept in the background by instinc-
tive womanliness, ... [which] belong[s] to the Slav race."[133] Despite her original
misgivings, Sellar reported that Nadejda was a "pearl of great price." Most of
Lord Kay's friends and family could not reconcile the woman who had been a
diplomat and the only female to address the League of Nations with the relatively mundane persona of a wife albeit to a Scottish Baronet. Some urged her to
take up a career as an MP as a way to segue into a similarly engaged occupation
as her previous career in diplomacy. Ultimately Nadejda blended herself artfully
into her husband's way of life.[134]

In 1924, Chou married a Dutchman, Felix Guepin, whom she met in London. Felix, when he was hired by Royal Dutch Shell, took her and their family to
live on location in Holland, France and eventually the United States—San Fran-
cisco, and later New York. They had two daughters, one of whom was physically and mentally challenged her entire life due to a botched delivery.

One year later, Ivan married Marion Mitchell, (1903-1994). She was the
only child of an American couple, an heiress. They were an odd couple who
nonetheless managed to create an enduring relationship. When he met her in
1923 in London, she was a free thinker who had some novel ideas about relationships, especially marriage. Once Ivan made his intentions clear, she tried to
persuade him that they did not require the sanctification of marriage to have a
successful relationship. However, his Catholic upbringing prevailed. In the end,
she willing converted to Catholicism and became an ideal wife, companion, and
mother.

Marion and Ivan produced seven children together and their family became
an even more complex reflection of the traditions begun by the senior Stancioffs. When Ivan joined the Bulgarian diplomatic service, soon after they married, the cycle of nomadic, cosmopolitan life for at least one branch of the Stancioff clan continued. For a time, their lives paralleled the diplomatic rhythms of
Ivan's childhood. The couple folded themselves into that life, seemingly with
little effort.

Notes

1. Nadejda Stancioff, unpublished letter, 25 January 1923, Nada III, PASF.

2. Nadejda Stancioff, unpublished letter, 8 April 1922, Nada I, PASF. From Nervi Nadejda wrote home: "This conference cannot be successful [she mentions the confusion and inefficiency of preparations, bad train connections etc.] In order to have results...should have chosen Liverpool or better yet Hanover."

3. Muir, *Dimitri Stancioff Patriot and Cosmopolitan*, 245-46.

4. Nadejda was appointed personally by Stamboliiski as first secretary to the Bulgarian legation to Washington D.C., the position second only to the Bulgarian minister who represented his country to a foreign state. She used the title and publicized herself as the first women diplomat even though she never actually went to the United States!

5. Anna de Grenaud to Dimitri Stancioff, unpublished letter, 6 October 1919, DSF IV, PASF.

6. Stancioff, *Diplomat and Gardener Memoirs,* 40.

7. Fuchs, "Introduction to the Forum on the Changing Faces of Parenthood"

8. Dimitri Stancioff to Nadejda Stancioff, unpublished letter, 6 July 1922, Nada IX, PASF.

9. Feodora Stancioff to family, unpublished letter, 24 November 1922, Feo IV, PASF.

10. According to the American Heritage Dictionary a stormy petrel is one who brings discord or appears at the onset of trouble.

11. *Minneapolis Sunday Tribune* 5 November 1922.

12. Fernandez-Azabal, *Romance and Revolutions.* Buchanan, *My Mission to Russia, and Other Diplomatic Memories,* Meriel Buchanan, *Diplomacy and Foreign Courts* (London,: Hutchinson, 1928). Maurice Barrès collected documentation for his memoirs which included the admiring letters Nadejda sent him when she was a young ardent fan of his work. Feo Stancioff also lists the following authors who mentioned her sister: Henri Bordeaux in his *La vie est un sport*, he was at the Genoa Conference, Lilian Mower in her *Journalist's Wife*, Harold Nicolson in his *Curzon, the Last Phase*.

13. Landon (1869-1927) was a rather accomplished man who could boast to have been a playwright, author, barrister as well as journalist.

14. Nadejda Stancioff to family, unpublished letter, 22 December 1922, Nada I, PASF.

15. Ibid. 9 December 1922.

16. All these people were sympathetic to Bulgaria's national aims. Each had considerable influence in public or government circles or both. Boyle was a distinguished military man who eventually received the Victoria Cross. Lord Newton was a British diplomat, a Conservative member of parliament. Taylor was possibly the most widely known English historian in the twentieth century. Buxton was a member of parliament who supported Bulgarian and Armenian causes; he wrote travel books on the Balkans and the Ottoman territories; he was founder of the Balkan Committee. See Ivan Ilchev, ed., *Noel I Charls Bukston Misiia Na Balkanite* (Sofia: Kliment Ohridski, 1987). It is possible Noel Buxton was interested romantically in Nadejda according to an oblique reference in this memoir.

17. This is the first mention of the man and the family into which she would marry in 1924. Nadejda scribbled home, at the end of the description, *da gi niamame!* [let's not have any of these.]

18. Nadejda Stancioff to family from Nervi, unpublished letter, 11 May 1922, Nada II, PASF.

19. See unpublished letters in PASF, Nada wrote this in several letters to her family.

20. Jill Steans, *Gender and International Relations* (Cambridge: Polity Press, 1998).

21. Nadejda admitted to this in more than one interview. The *Daily Graphic* August 29, 1922. "I look upon you as a boy...you don't know how to flirt, you never look at a man in the proper way, you can keep secrets..." In the same piece she described herself in the following way: "If I were alone on a desert island, I could cook, sew, and write an article. My hobby is literature, and I love riding."

22. Nadejda Stancioff to family, unpublished letter, 21 September 1922, Nada II, PASF.

23. Dimitri Stancioff to family, unpublished letter, 6 July 1922, Nada IX, PASF.

24. See letters to Nadejda in the 1920s, Nada IX, PASF.

25. Dimitri Stancioff, unpublished letter, 6 November 1922, DSF, PASF. Dimitri's hand written memento is scribbled across the original typewritten note confirming his appointment with the Prince of Wales on November 6, 1922.

26. Just a few of the publications where the appointment was mentioned: In England: *The Evening News Sunday Post, Daily Mail, Daily Chronicle, Pall Mall Gazette, Daily Express, Daily Graphic, Evening Standard.* In the United States: *The Minneapolis Sunday Tribune, The Evening Star – Washington D.C., The Public Ledger – Philadelphia, The Christian Science Monitor.* In France: *Petit Parisien, Le Temps,* and others.

27. Press release for *Daily Dispatch* 1922.

28. Ibid. and elsewhere.

29. Quoted in John D. Bell, *Peasants in Power Alexander Stamboliski and the Bulgarian Agrarian National Union, 1899-1923* (Princeton: Princeton University Press, 1977), 156. "As a rule the more loving and passionate individual becomes subject to the less loving and passionate one. Usually the man becomes subject because he is more impulsive. The woman, although weaker physically and intellectually, knows her heart and thus can wield power.... No important political event ever takes place without a woman. They bend even strong statesmen to their will."

30. *The Vote* 16 February1923, XXIV No.695, p. 50.

31. *The Vote* was the organ of the Women's Freedom League whose objective was getting women the Parliamentary vote in Great Britain and the right to be elected to public offices in general and to promote equal rights and opportunities among the sexes.

32. *The Vote* 16 February 1923. p. 50.

33. There is substantial evidence of a traditional bias in favor of women as pacifists and men as violent or martially inclined. There is of course a considerable body of literature on this subject but I would like to point out an example Joshua Goldstein made in his *War and Gender: How Gender Shapes the War System and Vice Versa,* (Cambridge: Cambridge University Press, 2001) He quotes Madeline Albright, an undisputable example of a "hawk" statesman urging the admission of "greater numbers of women as ambassadors and as managers at the UN" as a way to address the need for "practical solutions."

34. Ibid.

35. *Evening News* 17 June 1922, *Women as Diplomats.*

36. See drafts of article by Nadejda Muir Stancioff, written sometime in 1931, file Diplomacy as a Career for Women, PASF. A personal friend, W.A. Coates wrote a letter of congratulations and noted: "Yours is an early step in the right direction and I wish that you will be eminently successful...if by your acumen, integrity, and righteous dealing you help to restore your beloved and glorious country to its proper status and power in Europe...I have such a faith in good women—so needed now..." Both the abovemen-

tioned article and an article published by the Vote in 16 February 1923, "Women in Diplomacy," list women involved in diplomacy in the twentieth century: "Lady Surma B'Mar Shimum, plenipotentiary of Assyria [sic] to London; Miss Clotilde Luise, attache to the Uruguayan Legation in Brussels; Miss Henrietta Hoegh, first secretary to the Norwegian legation in Mexico in 1914, Miss Lucille Atcherson, 4th secretary to the American embassy in Paris in 1922-1923; Miss Nadejda Stancioff appointed to the Bulgarian diplomatic service in 1922; Madame Kollontai, appointed Soviet representative to Norway in 1922, later to Mexico and subsequently to Sweden, Frau R. Schwimmer, Hungarian minister at Berne in 1918; Mrs. Ruth Bryan Owen, minister for the United States in Denmark, May 1930."

37. Nadejda Stancioff to family, unpublished letter, 25 January 1923, Nada II, PASF.

38. Nadejda Stancioff to family from Geneva, unpublished letter, 21 September 1922, Nada I, PASF.

39. Nadejda Stancioff to family, unpublished letter, 27 September 1922, Nada II, PASF.

40. Nadejda Stancioff to family, unpublished letter, 12 September 1921, Nada II, PASF.

41. There is a growing body of work on Bulgarian and East European Women's movements that support some of Nadejda's experiences and lend a broader context to the environment in which she functioned. See Krassimira Daskalova, "Bulgarian Women's Movement (1850s-1940s)," *Networks and Debates in post-communist countries in the 19th and 20th centuries* (2006). Zhorzheta Nazûrska, *Universitetskoto Obrazovanie I Bûlgarskite Zheni, 1879-1944* (Sofia: BAN, 2003).

42. Nadejda Stancioff to family, unpublished letter, 14 November 1922, Nada I, PASF.

43. Nazûrska, *Universitetskoto Obrazovanie i Bûlgarskite Zheni, 1879-1944*. Krasimira Daskalova, "The Women's Movement in Bulgaria in a Life Story," *Women's History Review* 13, no. 1 (2004).

44. Feodora Stancioff to family, unpublished letter, 6 December 1922, Feo IV, PASF.

45. Nadejda Stancioff to family, unpublished letter, 22 December 1922, Nada I, PASF.

46. Comment by Krassimira Daskalova who pointed out to me that even Simone de Beauvoir exhibited the same weakness as Nadejda Stancioff, gender blindness, a characteristic shared by successful women.

47. Offen, *European Feminisms 1700-1950*.

48. Nadejda Stancioff to family, unpublished letter, 9 December 1922, Nada I, PASF.

49. Jalland, *Women, Marriage and Politics 1860-1914*. For example, Helen and Mary Gladstone and Gwendolen Lady Cecil became their respective fathers' (William Gladstone and the Marquis of Salisbury became prime ministers of Great Britain) private secretaries when their fathers became prime ministers. Coincidentally the abovementioned women also either wrote or co-wrote their fathers' biographies, something that Nadejda and Feodora Stancioff also undertook. See too Krassimira Daskalova, "The Politics of a Discipline: Women Historians in Twentieth Century Bulgaria," *Storia della Storiografia* 46 (2004).

50. M. Bompard, unpublished letter, 16 July 1922, Nada III, PASF. Letters to Nadejda on the occasion of her appointment to First Secretary are effusively congratulatory. A female correspondent, E. Garrett wrote on 15 July 1922: "...I rejoice too that Bulgaria

has been the first to appoint a woman diplomat. Women everywhere will be pleased."
Leland Buxton wrote on 14 July 1922: "For yourself it is...a stepping stone to higher
things, but in any case it is a unique distinction and one conspicuously well deserved. For
Bulgaria it is good propaganda..."

51. Muir, *Dimitri Stancioff Patriot and Cosmopolitan,* 262-263.

52. Krassimira Daskalova, "A Life in History: Fani Popova-Mutafova," *Gender and
History* 14, no. 2 (2002).

53. The Bulgarian Women's Union, founded in 1901, was responsible for forcing
changes in Bulgarian labor laws that gave women teachers' equal pay with men and did
away with rules that prohibited married female teachers from working, among other reforming measures. The organization developed a wide following and had its own publication, *Zhenski glas,* or *Women's Voice.* Daskalova, "Bulgarian Women's Movement
(1850s-1940s)."See transcript of Nada talk *Women's Life and Social Work in the Balkan
Countries* 1930s to the League of Nations Union.

54. Nadejda Stancioff, unpublished letter to family from London. [no complete date
Samedi 21 VII London, Dear Lausanners], Nada IV, PASF. Emphasis is mine.

55. Ibid.

56. Tovrov, "Mother-Child Relations among Russian Nobility." Tovrov stresses the
context of family life is important when outside observers want to understand the meaning of the relationships. She discovered that "the Russian noble family was held to be
more than the sum of its parts." A key element of this structure was the assumption that
self-sacrifice for the general family good would be expected and performed as a way of
avoiding shame while measuring up to socially accepted norms. I would add that in this
case self-sacrifice, on the part of the daughters became emblematic of how they functioned as a family unit throughout their lives. Krassimira Daskalova also asserts that self-
abnegation was the norm for a 'good mother' in Bulgaria.

57. Nadejda Stancioff, unpublished letter to family, from Sofia to London, 31 October 1922, Nada III, PASF.

58. Nadejda Stancioff, unpublished letter to family, from Lausanne, 12 January
1923, Nada IV and DS V, PASF.

59. Ibid.

60. Ibid.

61. Jalland, *Women, Marriage and Politics 1860-1914,* and elsewhere.

62. Nadejda Stancioff, unpublished letter to family, 9 December 1922, Nada III,
PASF. See also a letter 30 September 1922. "Make an effort to marry . . . to whichever
diplomat, but with a good career and eligible for future conferences. Me, I'll be there, I'll
be behind the journalists. Alternatively . . . Chouchou must marry an Ambassador and
arrange her salon! Feo must marry a young Bulgarian diplomat and make his career."

63. Petersen, *Family, Love, and Work in the Lives of Victorian Gentlewomen.* However, unlike the Victorians the Stancioffs parents did not grow distant from their children
but in fact drew them into the unique relationship between a husband and a wife.

64. Nadejda Stancioff, unpublished letter to family, 9 December 1922, Nada I,
PASF.

65. Nadejda Stancioff, unpublished letter to family from Lausanne, 21 January1922,
Nada III, PASF. On Ivan's career: "Thanks to Feo for her excellent detailed letter and the
snippets precious on Ivan's dossier which I am returning to you now. It should be carefully preserved by Maman..., the words of Sir Eric, at the end of his letter mean that he
will nominate Ivan to the first vacancy. (especially after he receives the letters of Bourgeois, Imperiali, Ross and Nansen.) Read Rappard's letter: Papa thinks he will bring Ivan
in person to meet him in Geneva on Thursday. What an angel of a father!....I am pleased

that you go out a bit into the world and approve the diplomatic sortie ...these are the kinds of relations which must be cultivated; it is more useful and ...I am sending my good wishes for the success of your dinner, which you will describe to me!" Nadejda includes a detailed description of her outfit at fancy dinner and another woman's comment: "I see you've just got that from Paris!"

66. Nadejda Stancioff, unpublished letter to family, 24 September 1922, Nada III, PASF.

67. Nadejda Stancioff, unpublished letter to family, 27 September 1922, Nada III, PASF.

68. Nadejda Stancioff, unpublished letter to family, 31 October 1922, Nada I, PASF.

69. Nadejda Stancioff, unpublished letter to family, 10 October 1922, Nada I, PASF, Nada I, letter, 1919-1922.

70. *Petit Parisiene.*

71. *Times*, 23 November 1922, *Bulgarian Outlet.*

72. *Times*, 23 November 1922, *Turkey's Demands—Ismet's Speech.*

73. Nadejda Stancioff, unpublished letter from Lausanne to family, 14 November 1922, Nada I, PASF.

74. Ibid.

75. Nadejda Stancioff, unpublished letter from Prague to family, 22 December 1920, Nada I, PASF. "Pray with me that we accomplish at last the nomination to that post for which P and I have worked and finally to conquer it – our new life will be happy and easy. This will resemble a dream of lunching and dining together, normally and to see each other well dressed and to feel surrounded by true friends and not liars!" In an earlier letter she made an allusion to the trials they have endured as a family for all of them to be secure and for Nada and her father to be at their current status in Rome. "it is certain that for us to be here and to be where we are ...[she refers to the status of the postings] we had to endure a great deal and many less agreeable hours, but *enfin*, we are arrived." See 15 December 1919, Nada I, PASF unpublished letter from Rome.

76. Nadejda Stancioff, unpublished letter fragment to family from Lausanne, [date unclear 15 December? 1922], Nada IV and DS V, PASF.

77. Nadejda Stancioff, unpublished letter, 27 September 1922, Nada III, PASF.

78. There are a number of works, both general histories and memoir literature that address this period. Ilcho Ivanov Dimitrov, *Kniazût, Konstitutsiata I Narodût*, 2. izd. ed. (Akademichno izd-vo "Prof. Marin Drinov", 2001), Neæikov, *Zavchera I Vchera : Skitsi Ot Minaloto.*

79. See volume one of Daskalov, *Bûlgarskoto Obshtestvo 1878-1939.* See too Martin Ivanov's, *Politicheskite igri s vûnshniia dulg. Bûlgarski siuzheti na stonpanski krizi i vûzhod, 1929-1934.* (Sofia: Zlatiu Boiadzhiev, 2001).

80. Dimitri Stancioff, report numbers 1188 and 1197 to Bulgarian ministry of foreign affairs from London, 10 September 1922, BIA F 13 ae 40 l 15.

81. Dimitri Stancioff, report to Bulgarian ministry of foreign affairs from London, 16 September 1922, BIA F 13 ae 40 l 20-30.

82. Ibid.

83. Ibid.

84. Ibid.

85. Ibid.

86. Ibid. 10 September 1922, BIA F 13 ae 40 l 17.

87. Ibid. [possibly l.24] [possible date 16 September 1922]

88. Ibid. report number 2046 19 September 1922, BIA F 13 ae 40 l 20.

89. Ibid. l 29.

90. Nadejda Stancioff, unpublished letter, 22 December 1922, Nada IV, PASF.

91. Ibid.

92. Ibid.

93. 3 pages handwritten by Nadejda, Nada Miscellaneous File, PASF.

94. Ibid. In addition to these Nadejda recorded what she labeled Sentences of Lausanne: *"Veni-Vidi-Vinci"* by Lord Curzon, "Lose all hope ye who enter here" by Bompard, "Inanity of Conferences!" by Barrère, "the future, the future is mine!" by Ismet Pasha, "Might is right" by Nicolson, a British Delegate, "So much individual effort, so little collective results!" by MacClure, a British Delegate and many others.

95. Ibid.

96. *Times*, 23 November 1922, *Turks' Demands at Lausanne.*

97. *Evening News* , 12 February, 1923, *Girl's Side-Lights on Lausanne.*

98. Nadejda Stancioff, unpublished letter, 10 June 1923, Nada III, PASF.

99. Nadejda Stancioff, unpublished letter, 22 December 1922, Nada III, PASF.

100. Nadejda Stancioff, unpublished letter, 27 September 1922, Nada III, PASF.

101. Nadejda Stancioff, unpublished letter, 22 December 1922, Nada III, PASF.

102. Nadejda Stancioff, unpublished letter, 2 February 1923, Nada III, PASF.

103. Ibid.

104. Ibid.

105. The remains of General Wrangel's army (1878-1928), who had fought in the Russian civil war, had found refuge in Bulgaria. There were approximately 30,000 of them in the country and they found a sympathetic constituency among Bulgarian military men. Both groups were unhappy with restrictions on the size and equipment of armies. The Paris Peace had stipulated a drastic reduction in the size of Bulgaria's military and the kind of armaments the army could stockpile. Career military officers especially, suffered the consequences. Daskalov, *Biialata Emigratsiia V Bûlgariia,* Karl Schlogel, *Der Grosse Exodus. Die Russische Emigration Und Ihre Zentren 1917 Bis 1941* (Munich: C.A.Beck, 1994).

106. Stefan Gruev, *Korona Ot Trûni Tsaruvaneto Na Boris III 1918-1943* (Sofia: Bûlgarski Pisatel, 1991).

107. Nadejda Stancioff, unpublished letter, 15 June 1923, Nada III, PASF.

108. Nadejda Stancioff, unpublished letter, 15 June 1923, second letter Friday night 10 p.m., Nada III, PASF.

109. Nadejda Stancioff, unpublished letter, 15 June 1923, Nada III, PASF.

110. Dimitri Stancioff, unpublished letter to Nadejda, 16 June 1923, Nada V, PASF.

111. Ibid. The handwritten phrase is difficult to read, my translation, therefore is imprecise. My approximation is the following transcription: *"Du kannst nicht ungeschen machen, was geschehen soll."*

112. Nesta [last name unclear] to Nadejda, unpublished letter, 22 June 1923, Nada V, PASF.

113. Ms. Wood, unpublished letter, 12 June 1923, Nada V, PASF.

114. Nadejda Stancioff, unpublished letter, 6 July 1923, Nada V, PASF.

115. *Contemporary Review* was a venerable publication established in 1866, which published articles by writers from all over the world with "first hand knowledge of their subject."

116. Anna Stancioff, unpublished letter to Dimitri, 19 August, 1923, DSF, PASF.

117. Dimitri Stancioff, unpublished letter, BIA, F 13 ae 40, 1 58.

118. *Observer* 3 February 1924.

119. Stancioff, Nadejda Memories of Love, 66.

120. Nadejda Stancioff, unpublished letter, 25 January 1923, Nada IV + DS V, PASF.

121. Stancioff, Nadejda Memories of Love, 72.

122. Ibid.

123. Nadejda Stancioff, unpublished journal, 29 January 1954, PASF.

124. *Dundee Advertiser*, 18 March 1924, "Raised on Scottish Porridge." The piece played up the fact that she had been raised by a Scottish governess.

125. Nadejda Stancioff, unpublished letter, 3 November 1924, Nada VI, PASF.

126. Ibid. 3.

127. Dimitri Stancioff, unpublished letter, 1 December 1924, Nada IX, PASF.

128. Nadejda Stancioff, unpublished letter, 3 November 1924, Nada VI, PASF.

129. In May 1925 she wrote on her relationship with Kay once more. "Kay seems to adore me more and more and we live an idilic life of love, living metaphorically in a prairie of enameled flowers of the field, where the singing birds [described] in the verses of Shelly and Keats, sing in flowering bowers, in the lands of the north!" See Nadejda Stancioff, unpublished letter, 5 May 1925, TsDIA F143K a.e. 19 l. 24.

130. Nadejda Stancioff, unpublished letter, 22 September 1925, TsDIA F143K a.e. 19 l. 30.

131. Nadejda Stancioff, unpublished letter, 25 October 1922, Nada II, PASF. When Nadejda was in Sofia, with Stamboliiski, Clare Sheridan visited Bulgaria on her way back from Russia, where she had just made busts of Trotsky and Lenin. Nadejda was in charge of showing her around in an official car. Sheridan traveled widely and was affiliated, at that time, with the *New York World*. Their acquaintance in 1922 blossomed into a lifelong friendship.

132. As quoted by Feo Stancioff in her manuscript, Memories of Love, 75-76.

133. Ibid. 73-74.

134. A testament to her true feelings for him Nadejda thought about him and missed him long after he passed on. When her mother celebrated her ninety-third birthday Nadejda wrote in her journal, on 29 January 1954, "wish, darling Kay, that I had looked after you as well as Feo has tended her [Maman];…God knows best; but I 'yearn' for you sometimes and wish I had done better in so many, many ways."

8
Admirable English

"One of the most a public-spirited and intelligent women in Scotland"
Bulletin, Scottish newspaper[1]

Nadejda Stancioff Muir began married life fully expecting to be a member of the English elites, who ruled most of the world through their colonial empire. Wealth accumulated in colonial enterprises enhanced their lives and extended their power well beyond the British Isles. Her husband amassed his wealth from tea production, owned estates in Kenya, had business interests in Glasgow, and invested in rubber plantations in the dominions. Lady Muir went on to lead a remarkable life for a Bulgarian-French "mongrel" (her own self-deprecating descriptor) transplanted to the Scottish highlands.[2] Yet her life would have been quite unremarkable if she had been born in England and raised and raised to become an English lady.

Elite English Lifestyles

As a member of the English elites, Nadejda was likely to entertain guests for parties and weekends at her residences. Golfing, playing tennis, hunting parties, and dinner parties were part of the typical activities. Hosting dinner at Claridge's or cocktails at the Renaleagh Club when in London was the done thing to do if one had money and position.[3]

Being a member of the elites of English society meant being admitted to an exclusive social club that observed and guided the preoccupations of its members. Nadejda describes a typical day in her life:

> We took a walk in the park, ended up at Claridge's, at 11:30 we gave a lunch at Wellington Club to friends of Kay, passed the afternoon at Renaleagh just the

two of us but not alone for long . . . at 8:30 we gave a dinner at Claridge's . . .
we had the little salon and the first dancing room . . . a brilliant soiree.[4]

In a letter, some eighteen months after her marriage, Nada (Nadejda often
signed her letters to her family with this abbreviated form of her full name) described her new abode, Blair Drummond and its surroundings to her family back
in Bulgaria in meticulous detail—the gardens, weather, flora, and fauna.[5]

She gave them an indication of how busy she was with obligations to entertain. A tennis party for eighty-five of their local acquaintances was just one example of the kind of social gatherings she planned; she also prepared grand
events with the Peerage invited. Nadejda kept her family current on the details
of these events and even described which rooms she planned to assign to which
guest. As the one ultimately responsible for keeping the estate running, she had
to work with inventories, purchases, lists of chores, and renovations. "The English are ambulatory calendars!" was her observation, as she became one of the
English.[6]

In married life, Nadejda sought to blend into her husband's society as seamlessly as possible; by all accounts, she managed her duties beautifully. At the
same time, she tried to maintain her close ties to her natal family. Despite the
distances that separated the two families, the Muirs made a ritual of an annual
pilgrimage to *Les Trois Sources* for an extended stay virtually every spring.

Reciprocally, Dimitri, Anna, and Feo visited Scotland and stayed with
Nadejda at Blair Drummond at least once a year and, at times, more frequently.
Nadejda prepared a study especially equipped with desks and the newest lighting fixtures, a heater, and file cabinets for her father.[7] Her parents eventually
acquired an apartment in London.

Nadejda's married siblings visited with their spouses when possible. In this
way, Nadejda managed to blend her new husband into her natal family and to
incorporate him into the Stancioff circle while still performing her duties as
Lady Muir. The need for continuous contact with her parents and siblings made
her a conscientious correspondent; thus the Stancioffs' close bonds stood the
tests of distance, time, and, eventually, wartime separations.

Interwar Britain

In the 1920s, after Lloyd George's ignominious exit from British politics, the
country experienced a period of economic and cultural revival. Great Britain
could still claim to control approximately one quarter of the world. Its capital
was a modern city, and major financial center. London, although dirty and over-
crowded, could boast 4 million inhabitants.

The lives of the upper and middle classes continued to prosper and changed
little in the interwar period. Most professional households still employed a
chauffeur, at least two maids, and a cook. The rapidly rising cost of hired help,
along with a simultaneous shortage of available and suitable candidates, presaged a downturn in the economy. Nonetheless, the country seemed steady on a
course most found familiar.

During this era the power of the church persuaded the business community and government to set aside Sunday as a day of worship and contemplation trains did not operate, and stores, and entertainment venues shut down for the day. This symbiotic relationship served both church and state, since religion was channeled as another form of nationalism in support of the state.

Religious practice also helped to further the notion that the far-flung dominions were all part of the same British whole. The family, religion, and monarchy continued to be the supports of the state. A conservative English, tradition-bound image was internalized by the king's subjects. Furthermore, this image of steady, unflappable, British omnipotence projected well abroad.

One singular event marred the apparently serene face of Britain in the 1920s: the General Strike of May 1926. As a way to express displeasure with their low wages and unemployment, the coordinated strikes of miners, transportation workers, and other municipal workers brought the entire country to a standstill. The message was clear: workers were unhappy with their economic lot. However, the abrupt end of the strike, however, did not force the government into a reevaluation of its course. The General Strike led to divisiveness rather than unity in British society; a divisiveness that would only be reconciled on the eve of the Second World War.

Economic Woes

For most people, the Great War created an expectation that they could aspire to some of the comforts of middle-class life—new leisure-time activities and mechanical devices. Also, housing became more affordable for the middle classes. In 1919 the head of the housing authority, Neville Chamberlain, instituted legislation that helped subsidize private home building.

Another significant change during the early twenties involved land redistribution, thereby increasing the number of smallholder farmers to an unprecedented degree. The economy received one final reconfiguration when the government, encouraged by Winston Churchill returned to the gold standard in 1925.

Women, at the end of the 1920s, won the right to vote and gained the right to live their lives more in concert with their own desires and less according to the restrictive dictums of the pre-war period. As in other countries, they could engage in activities that were once considered shocking. Women's forays into sexual liberation, smoking, and wearing revealing clothing spearheaded a revolution in social mores.

Great Britain experienced the Depression of 1929 as an economic downturn that the Labor government was unable to mitigate. The Depression's effect was felt world wide, as each industrial state found that itself was caught in an economic vice of overproduction and loss of markets, while trading partners experienced the exact same phenomena.

For Britain, recovery did not begin until the mid-1930s. All the while, the government, and British political parties and intellectuals struggled to put forward an effective solution. Every possible political and economic sobriquet was offered as a salve to the national distress: utopian constructs, socialist solutions, communism or collectivism, corporatism, fascism specifically fitted to the British situation, or New Deal solutions à la the United States of America.

This environment of self-doubt and uncertainty also let loose the impulse to apportion blame. After the public chastised the Labor government for being ineffective, the other scapegoat was "the Jew"; the 1930s witnessed a rise in anti-Semitism.

Of the generation of politicians who survived the 1920s the most prominent figure of the 1930s Britain was Prime Minister Neville Chamberlain. He was credited with Britain's economic recovery after the Depression. His program for affordable working class housing, economic support for the farming community, and for an improved transportation grid gained him widespread support, made him popular and inflated his stature.

International Quandaries

As the international political climate deteriorated noticeably in the 1930s, British domestic stability remained bound by tradition to its class system. While other Europeans faced the rise of totalitarian governments, the British remained unscathed by such change on their island kingdom. The sincere rejoicing that accompanied the silver jubilee celebrations of King George V (r. 1910-1936) in 1935 is evidence of this internal tranquility. When, in the following year, the abdication of Edward VIII (r. 1936) could have undermined British society, the event was noticeably unable to shake the public's faith in its government and the system it espoused.

Life at Blair Drummond

Blair Drummond, the Muir estate in Perthshire, Scotland, was built on the shores of the river Teith, and located in the gateway to the Scottish highlands. The late Victorian grand mansion, built on the site of an early eighteenth-century mansion and constructed in the British tradition of solid, substantial family estates, included a plethora of turrets, leaded glass windows, and towers.

Perthshire was renowned for its legendary beauty, and Blair Drummond was in keeping with this environment, with sculptured grounds ensconced at the foothills of the Grampian Mountains. From Blair Drummond, Castle Doune and Stirling, the closest notable sites, can be made out in the distance.

Sir John Kay willed the property to Sir Kay Muir in 1916. Lord Kay Muir had apprenticed himself to his uncle as a tea merchant and had spent years learning the trade in India. The next master of Blair Drummond, Sir Jamie Muir (Lord Kay's nephew), was eventually compelled to sell the property to a charity in the late 1970s.

During Nadejda's life at Blair Drummond the gardens and greenhouses provided a profusion of flowers and fruits. Orchids, ferns, and rare plants peeked among peach and fig trees trained on the wall, along with climbing geraniums.

Gardening was a shared passion so tending to plants in the green house or on the property beyond the glass walls was something Kay and Nadejda enjoyed doing together.

The estate was magnificent and represented the best a Scottish residence could offer: a river full of salmon, grouse and other game in abundance, a heath garden, a pond, forested knolls, and a rose garden. For Nadejda, who adored natural beauty and was sensitive to the change seasonal transition brings to a landscape, the magnificence of her new home was intoxicating. Blair Drummond was a comforting abode as for Nadejda, it recalled not only *Les Trois Sources,* in many respects, but also some of the exceptional estates she had visited and admired throughout her life.

The main building of Blair Drummond had survived a fire in 1921, but Lord Kay had it rebuilt to its former grandeur. It included fifteen bedrooms, and seven bathrooms for the Lord's family and guests. Domestic staff apartments included seven staff bedrooms and two bathrooms, along with a staff dining room, a butler's room, the butler's pantry, a gunroom, a lumber room, plus two cellars. The garages housed two elegant Bentleys and the house had an elevator. The staff responsible for the gardens, the grounds keeper, and others had residences apart from the main house.

The library, a splendid room at the center of the house, contained book-lined walls that framed elegant furniture, writing desks, and a fireplace. Its size was enormous by any standard, and the sweeping views of the park enhanced the room's magnificence. It was the meeting place for weekend guests after church on Sundays and the place of congenial congregations at other times. At the time of Sir Kay's death, his personal collection in the library contained well over 500 volumes. The topics were as wide-ranging as butterflies of England; histories of England; the French Revolution; fiction by authors such as Thomas Hardy and the Brontes, poetry by Robert Browning and Emerson, the eleventh edition of the Encyclopedia Britannica, books on famous artists and scores of books on diplomacy and the history of Europe and the Orient.

The Stancioff Touch

Although the manor ran much as it had before the Nada's arrival, the Stancioff influence introduced a distinct change in the rapport between master and servants. Although British masters talked about their servants in their presence as thought they were not there, in Nada's household, servants were addressed and talked to as friends might have been. Nada famously fired an overbearing housekeeper during one of her first days in residence when the woman surprised Nadejda in the act of making her own bed. When the housekeeper objected that this behavior was unacceptable, Nada responded by dismissing her from service! Nadejda would have things done her way.

The Stancioffs had a history of playing dress-up and being unabashed jokesters. The tradition was so ingrained that Nadejda carried it on with her staff and guests alike in Scotland. She often chose to wear flowing kaftans, with long strings of large amber beads, which made her resemble a theatrical version of an oriental woman. Lady Muir could play the role of the exotic "other" before her guests, because she could rely on the authority of her professional experience to affirm her membership among the elites.

She adored shocking, although quite mildly, her proper English guests and often made verbal puns. For example, when serving Turkish coffee in the small demitasse appropriate to that beverage, she would quip, to those who had not had a cup before, "N'agitez pas le fond," which, although correct, in French sounds a bit risqué.[8] Moreover, in this way, she could produce a chuckle from her English guests, who were admonished not to agitate their bottom!

Hunting was a way of life at Blair Drummond. Mr. McQueen, the game-keeper, was in charge of keeping the rifles and guns prepared for use, of training and supervising the beaters, placing shooters in such a way that their abilities matched their placement. He confided to young Dimitri Stancioff, Ivan's first-born son, that he was certain that his arrangements of the field were "safe for the guns, safe for the beaters, safe for the birds."[9]

The gamekeeper could report on the nature of every shooter in his hunt, whether the shooter was sporting or not—easy shots were unsporting—wounding the birds and not killing them outright was also a misdemeanor. Apparently, Dimitri's father, Ivan, was the kind of shooter who was safe for all three: shooters, birds, and beaters.

When her nieces and nephews visited their Aunt Nada in Scotland, the children experienced Blair Drummond as a fantastical backdrop for all sorts of make believe. As teenagers and adults they anticipated a sophisticated entrée into English society. The estate, the grounds, the mansion, and the staff bore a close resemblance to all sorts of English fiction that was part of their children's vocabulary.

Before Dimitri, Nadejda's eldest nephew, gained permission to dine with the adults in the dining room, he ate with the key staff in their own domain downstairs. He took his meals with the housekeeper, Mrs. Brown, in her dining room, where the butler, the cook, and a nurse or nanny might also dine. In the servant's hall, the lower rank served the housekeeper and others on the A-list of service. In that cozy group, the child heard the gossip about the goings-on upstairs as well as the details of the life of the downstairs community.

In supervising a large staff and property, Nadejda had to rely heavily on her domestic staff to run a household more in keeping with the staffing requirements of a large estate. She needed to be aware of staff disputes, staffing shortages, and to avoid jeopardizing the smooth running of so large a property when guests were present.[10] The task was as time consuming as running a substantial business enterprise.

Bulgarian Domestic Politics in the 1920s and 1930s

Bulgaria under Aleksandûr Stamboliiski and the Agrarian Party did not react the way the other loser states did to compensate for the burden of enormous reparation payments and unjust territorial revisions imposed by the peace treaty of 1919. Born from the Paris Peace Conference of 1919, the country reeled under the burden but did not choose fascism, despite a national sense of frustration and anger with the peace settlement. Instead, from 1919 to1923 the country focused on strengthening its economy and making reparations payments.

Throughout the interwar period, the Balkan states were almost uniformly hostile toward each other and especially toward Bulgaria. As the biggest territorial loser after the peace treaty of 1919, Bulgaria was kept at the greatest distance as a potential revanchist state. At first, the international climate appeared equanimious toward Bulgaria but later grew neglectful and even hostile.

Bulgaria's government had few options for friendly cooperative associations. Over time the League of Nations seemed more inept and vulnerable to criticisms. While in England, Nadejda spoke to the need to have the League compel the Balkan states to fulfill their obligations toward minorities. At the other end of the continent inter-state relations in the Balkans deteriorated.[11] In the Balkans, the League appeared to be ineffectual.

Tsankov's Regime

Following Aleksandûr Stamboliiski's brutal murder, (he was tortured, his right hand cut off, and, finally, he was decapitated) Bulgarian political life took a turn for the worse. Those who carried out the coup formed a new government under Aleksandûr Tsankov. A motley coalition of former conspirators held power in Sofia. This new party alliance initially tempered its violent ascension with moderate domestic reforms. However, actions taken by the Bulgarian Communist Party (BCP) took against the regime led to increasingly repressive and authoritarian measures on the part of Tsankov's regime.

The BCP had chosen not to defend Agrarian policies or causes while the Agrarians were in power. Compounding the error, the BCP did not support the Agrarians' disorganized attempts at rebuffing the coup in June 1923. Chastised by Moscow, the BCP finally took action, undertaking some inept activities culminating in a plot to kill or injure a large number of military and political leaders, including the king, who had gathered for a state funeral in a Sofia cathedral in 1925. The plot failed, although scores of people died in the explosion at the cathedral.[12]

The government, in retaliation, purged the BCP. Its leaders and a majority of its followers disappeared, were imprisoned, executed, or forced into hiding. The violence and severe repressive measures of Tsankov's government, coupled with poor economic policies, made the government increasingly unpopular.

Unwilling or unable to do otherwise, the king was forced to acquiesce to the change in political power in 1923.The changeover did nothing to alleviate Boris' precarious position. A monarchy had no formal role to play in an agrarian led government and even less under the Tsankovists. Furthermore, the king felt imprisoned—if not imperiled—by the political parties that came to power. He felt equally used by all factions the Agrarians and those who replaced them saying

"Both the Agrarians and the Rights who replaced them use me like a rag, they wipe their hands with me."[13]

Boris was in an untenable situation once the Tsankovite regime was in control of the country. He could not be sure that his rule would be utilitarian enough to survive a de facto military dictatorship. He was unhappy and disillusioned with his standing and commented openly on his indefensible situation: "The Agrarians were simple...spoke out openly against me but did not have the perfidy of the bourgeoisie."[14]

The needs of country had dictated the life of Bulgaria's monarch from the year of his ascension in 1918 until 1926. He had not dared leave the country. It was not until 1926 that he took his first trip abroad. By then, Andrei Liapchev had replaced Tsankov and Bulgaria's domestic situation settled into some form of normalcy. King Boris could leave the country with no fear of there being another coup.

Boris' sister, Princess Nadejda, had married in 1924 and lived in Germany. When his sister, Princess Eudoxie, returned to Bulgaria, from an extended visit with their father, the former King Ferdinand, she became her brother's closest confidant. Their brother, Prince Cyril, too, returned, hounded by creditors and with a trail of unsuccessful initiatives behind him.[15] The three royal siblings lived together in Bulgaria once more.

On the heels of the political upset caused by the Right-backed coup, engendered, Bulgaria experienced the economic upheaval of the Great Depression. Economic dislocation, the rise of workers' parties and their communist directors from abroad, as well as the continual agitation of members of the Internal Macedonian Revolutionary Organization thoroughly confused the domestic political situation. Arguably, the agitation by Macedonian nationalists and partisans' agitation of either position regarding the future of that territory created the greatest domestic political turmoil. Repeated violence and assassinations continued to project an image of the country as backward, savage, and uncouth.

Balkan Isolation

Overall, the decade, despite some optimistic turns, became increasingly difficult. King Boris pressed to change that negative perception of Bulgaria in the Balkans and abroad and attempted a royal rapprochement with Yugoslavia's King Alexander. Until Alexander's assassination in 1934, it seemed that the two countries might reconcile their differences.

Despite the monarchy's attempts to forge ties with other states, especially other monarchies, the damage to Bulgaria's foreign policy was difficult to sidestep. With a political system that was still in its nascent stage, fixed on unending political turf-battles and the scrambles for patronage; there seemed to be no viable end in sight.

Furthermore, the Balkan entente, which was signed by all her neighbors, Greece, Romania, Turkey, and Yugoslavia, in 1934 excluded Bulgaria. The Bulgarian government could not make commitments to foreswear territorial revanchism. To do so would risk domestic political chaos on an even greater scale than the country had experienced during the decades-long grip the Macedonian party members had over domestic life. Their bloody party squabbles had destabilized the country. The tightening of the bonds among Bulgaria's neighbors in the entente, who also represented the coalition of belligerents during the Second Balkan war, sent a chill through the Bulgarian foreign affairs establishment. Their neighbors were clearly turning their backs on Bulgaria and at the same time forming a menacing circle of alliances. As Bulgaria became increasing isolated abroad, the domestic situation seemed to spiral out of control.

Zvenari—Another Military Coup

Finally, another military coup in Bulgaria in 1934 sealed the fate of political pluralism. A group of military conspirators led the coup. It was an expression of the military's impatience with the civilian government's mishandling of the country. By 1934, Macedonian inspired violence as well as fascist inspired political organizations appeared to be the most prominent political expressions in Bulgarian public life. The military found this political chaos unacceptable and guided by a group of like-minded military reformers, organized as Zveno (Circle). The coup leaders inaugurated severe repression of all opposition groups including IMRO. To their credit, Zveno managed finally to neutralize that disruptive portion of the polity. However, they also purged every other potential opponent, political parties, as well as trade unions.

The Zveno-led Velchev-Georgiev government managed to control the unruly elements in Bulgarian society. They reorganized the productive population into a guild system that resembled the Italian model of work divisions, which offered options for the government to influence the Narodno Sûbranie. Despite suspending civil rights and getting a firm grip on the legislature the coup nonetheless did nothing to assure Bulgaria's Balkan neighbors of their country's pacific intentions.

The King Rules

When in 1935 King Boris took his turn at controlling the country, Bulgaria bent in another direction entirely. Easily dismissed as a dictatorship King Boris' own coup was more an expression of his distrust of the military leadership of Zveno, which had managed to wipe the established parties from existence.

Although not uniformly champions of the monarchy, the party system had been easier to work with than the military, which was uncertain about the role a king could play in their new structure. Aiming to find a negotiable middle ground, the king ended by declaring Bulgaria a democracy, which was hardly that. Yet the declaration did satisfy some desire for political expression. The king's quiescent minister, Kioseivanov, managed to manipulate the domestic scene to the king's satisfaction until the two disagreed on foreign policy in 1939.

Building a Dynasty

King Boris managed to secure the prospect of a dynasty through his marriage in fall 1930. His union with Princess Giovanna, the daughter of King Victor Emmanuel, blossomed into a successful, affectionate union. The marriage was a personal coup and a political stroke of brilliance. Bulgaria was once again linked to the Italian royal family. Italy's star seemed to be on the rise, both domestically and abroad, and Bulgaria gained a strong ally.

The couple married in Assisi, then traveled to Bulgaria via ship, for a benediction ceremony. Feo became lady-in-waiting to the new queen from the moment the newlyweds took their first cross-country trip. The royal couple disembarked in the port of Burgas, and took a slow train to the capital city.[16] Feo Stancioff and the young queen became genuine companions who enjoyed each other's company.

The Ivan Stancioffs

Ivan Stancioff and Marion Mitchell met at a dance. Their lives had been somewhat similar, Ivan had experienced the transient and rich life of a diplomat's child and Marion, who had been born in Brazil, traveled extensively and had been raised primarily in England. Culturally, they were both Europeans, and both were devoted to intellectual and enriching pursuits, that emanated from their class and educational experiences. Marion exhibited her willingness to join the Stancioff fold most fully by converting to Catholicism.

Ivan insisted on taking an extended honeymoon in Bulgaria with his new bride. Weeks after their marriage in 1925, the newlyweds traveled for a two-week interlude to *Les Trois Sources* where they enjoyed the countryside and gardening. The trip presented an opportunity for Marion to be acquainted with the country. She was enticed, perhaps *Les Trois Sources* itself, to take on the family passions for gardening and nature as part of her entrée into the clan.

On that first visit, the king and his sister Eudoxie hosted Marion and Ivan for dinner at the palace at Vrana.[17] The meeting was a first for Ivan after many years of estrangement from the royal family. He noticed that Boris looked careworn; there had been two assassination attempts on his life that year. That night, in a flood of information, Marion was introduced to Bulgarian domestic realities.

The small group discussed first the violent coup that toppled the Agrarian government. Then the king bemoaned the repressive tactics the Tsankov government used, which had led to the imprisonment and torment of hundreds of opposition members. The attempt to wrest the country from the reactionary group, in turn, led to the most recent disorder. Bulgarian politics were in turmoil.

In the interwar period, cycles of coups, repressions, counter coups, and repeated offenses against the political opposition combined with a deterioration of the economy, created a downward spiral in public life. This was Marion's first image of Bulgaria's political realities and was a sobering reminder for Ivan of domestic politics in his homeland.

The Young Couple

Ivan and Marion raised a large family of seven children. Marion's fist child, was born in 1926, and the last, in 1937. The seven offspring were born in an alternating pattern or male and female children beginning with Dimitri (b. 1926), Anne, (b. 1927), Johnny, (b.1929), Feodora, (b.1930), Peter, (b. 1932), Nadejda, (b.1934), Andrew, (b.1937). The children lived the lives of diplomats, just as their father before them. Ivan entered the Bulgarian diplomatic service in 1927 as a cipher clerk, then worked in protocol. He was eventually promoted to third secretary to the legation in Rome in 1931. There he took on a second duty as a military intelligence officer. His primary responsibility was to observe, undetected, the work of the Bulgarian military attaché at the legation.[18] Once Italy and Bulgaria united in a personal union with the king's marriage to an Italian, Bulgaria had to keep a watchful eye on its reputation in Italy.

When Ivan was recalled from Italy in 1936, he had attained the position of chargé d'affaires. His children did not speak Bulgarian, and the family hired, as a tutor, a retired gymnasium teacher, who began their lessons in spring 1937. The children had come to know their extended family through infrequent visits to Bulgaria, mostly to enjoy the properties on the Black Sea.

When Ivan bought a home in Sofia, the children became better acquainted with the capital city as well. Their Stancioff relations spoke either Bulgarian exclusively, like their Aunt Bina, or if they spoke another language, it was German and Russian, like their Uncle Nic. The children communicated freely in German with him and in halting Bulgarian with everyone else. They, of course, spoke German with the royal family.

Royal Playmates—The Next Generation of Friendships

The Ivan Stancioffs carried on their father's family experiences in another respect. Over time, the young couple developed a close relationship with the Bulgarian royal family. The Coburgs eventually had two children, who became the playmates of the Stancioff children. Marion and Ivan had an intimate rapport with the Coburgs, they became confidants during troubled times. Their children, amused each other. Maman reported to Nadejda that, "the children were invited two times to play with their peers and their elegant outfits were admired so much that Mrs. Soden [Queen Giovanna] asked the address of our tailor for her children."[19]

Their contacts with the royal siblings were frequent enough for the Stancioff children to formulate impressions of Bulgaria's royal family. Both King Boris and Prince Cyril were easy with the children, but the prince was much more fun loving. He was the kind of adult who did not mind being silly and entertaining children in the way they found most amusing. They recalled that he made funny and rude noises, while King Boris was more serious and composed.

Dimitri, the eldest Stancioff child, remembered the king's witticism about a doll tossed out of an upper story window; the doll landed hapless in the branches of a tree, caught suspended by its hair. "Absalom, is that your doll's name?" quipped King Boris.[20]

The royal sisters were different from each other in character as well. From the children's perspective, the Princess Nadejda was infinitely approachable and likeable. Her sister, Princess Eudoxie, although a frequent visitor to their home, and a very close friend of the children's Aunt Feo, was less approachable, and was most like her father King Ferdinand; reserved, even haughty, and difficult to engage in conversation.

Ivan and Marion built their own villa by the Black Sea a short walk behind *Les Trois Sources*. They bought the property in 1933 and expanded an existing structure to house their growing family. The children remembered their summers at the *Marion Cottage* (their parents' home at *Les Trois Sources* property) as an idyllic time. The children described the place as paradise, glorious, and magical. The two homes on the cliffs overlooking the Black Sea were a gold mine for adventure-seeking children who could roam at will, satisfy childhood fantasies and realize games of make-believe. With an abundance of fruits, vegetables, and the gifts of the sea, the young family's lives were the stuff of endless summers filled with perfect memories and dreams.

The young Stancioff family hosted interesting visitors to their homes over the years. Ivan and Marion's lives had permitted them to build friendships with all sorts of personalities. Marion's education in England introduced her to some notable individuals, and these lifelong friends visited the family in Bulgaria. Steven Runciman became a close friend. The pre-eminent historian of the Byzantine Empire and the Crusades, the second son of a viscount, enjoyed the easy banter of a party as much as he enjoyed exploring the Bulgarian countryside. Among his many posts, he served as press attaché at the British Embassy in Sofia during World War II. As one of his obituaries stated, he collected anecdotes and people; both were equally splendid and colorful.

George Rendell, the British minister to Sofia was young Dimitri's confirmation godfather, and his daughter, Ann Rendell, was good friends with Ivan and Marion. The list of Bulgarian friends is extensive. Former colleagues carried on a relationship long after the professional one ended. These colleagues and friends included: Mimi Balabanoff, Ilia Belinoff, the Peevi of the Bulgarian brand Peev Candies, and Stoyan Petroff Chomakoff, who was first secretary in London with Dimitri. Furthermore, former domestic help who eventually became friends with the young Stancioff couple were also part of this cadre.

The Stancioff tradition of treating everyone with the same degree of respect and kindness was borne out on several occasions. For example, their Italian chauffer, Amato, followed the family to Bulgaria with their maid Caesera. Amato and Caesera married in Bulgaria, and Amato learned Bulgarian. The couple remained in the Stancioffs' service until the outbreak of World War II. The two couples remained in contact even after the war was over.

Nadejda Influences Public Opinion—Her 1920s and 1930s

The elder Stancioffs habitually involved themselves in charitable activities. Maman set the example by immersing herself in fundraising for needy causes, and nursing. She was one of the founders of the District Nursing Association of Bulgaria. Her two eldest daughters followed her example by nursing the wounded in times of war. Nadejda spoke of those experiences years later, saying "I started sweeping floors, making beds, and finished administering anesthetics."[21] Feo, Chou, and Nadejda participated in charitable activities with the Red Cross, the YWCA, Women's Rural Institute, Save the Children, and others. The Stancioff sisters raised money for Bulgarian causes as well as English charities.

As Lady Muir, Nadejda was called upon to do her part, as a member of the Peerage, and she enthusiastically took up the role. She organized and patronized charity events throughout her life. Only one year after her marriage, she and a neighbor, Peggy Stirling, organized a Gleneagles Ball to raise funds for the District Nurses Association.[22] She donated to charities, like the one her friend Katia Galitzine headed to benefit White Russian officers in Britain.[23]

Chou and Feo actively involved themselves charity work both in Bulgaria and when they visited Britain. When an earthquake devastated many Bulgarian towns in 1928, the family worked in both Britain and Bulgaria to help their countrymen to collect and distribute donations to the needy. Each member of the family used their talents and time to help further respectable causes. They also used their considerable notoriety as diplomats and valuable contacts among the wealthy and powerful to encourage others to contribute to their causes.

During the interwar decades, Nadejda was busy with a variety of projects. Her notoriety grew—she had an entry dedicated to her life in *The Ladies' Who's Who*—as did her active participation in national discourses. She wrote articles, solicited by the Encyclopedia Britannica. on Aleksandûr Stamboliiski's life and on contemporary Bulgarian literature.[24] Lord Kay was extremely flattered that the Encyclopedia addressed the request to his new bride.[25] Newspapers continued to solicit articles from her too. In 1925 *Courrier de Genève* solicited a piece for their readers.[26]

She produced programs for the British Broadcasting Corporation (BBC) and gave talks on the Balkans to various organizations. In addition, she and Sir Kay hosted King Boris' stays in Britain, supporting and nudging their contacts in the press and keeping up and even increasing Nadejda's valuable contacts in the foreign office establishment.

Nadejda Stancioff Muir used her position as the wife of a Scottish baronet to conduct a campaign to win over British public opinion and British government policy in favor of Bulgaria. She took upon herself the role of shaper of public opinion voluntarily and willingly indeed she saw it as a duty. She emphasized her experience as a diplomat, and combined this authority with her position as a member of titled society, to lend credibility to her message. She spoke with an authoritative professional voice with plans to inform and change public opinion.

Soon after she became a British citizen, published reports and private communications urged her to run for Parliament. Instead, she chose private life and other means of remaining in the public eye. She modernized the notion of noblesse oblige and felt that the aristocratic elites, who knew the world, who had first hand experience with international politics, had to share their expertise; it was incumbent on them to do so. This was her approach to public and private debates on foreign policy as well as domestic policy. In addition, while she promoted policies in the best interests of Britain, she kept in mind the best interests of the country of her birth, Bulgaria, working for what (she believed) was best for both.

Therefore, for example, when speaking at a flower show in Shirlingshire she chided the British government for "encouraging the dumping of foreign produce. It [the government] has made people buy foreign fruit to make jam and foreign flowers to decorate their houses . . . [but] it [the government] must encourage Scottish fruits and vegetables to be used to more profitable ends."[27] She had made similar pleas in Bulgaria.

Maman's Memoirs

Over the years, Maman had begun keeping notes on her métiers as a lady-in-waiting and a diplomat's wife. Once Papa retired, Anna felt free to begin the process of writing her book, *Recollections of a Diplomatist's Wife.*[28] Anna de Grenaud Stancioff had lived an interesting life that propelled her from her home in Savoy to the Bulgarian Principality in the 1880s, and then to various European capitals as a diplomat's wife. It was those experiences, the acquaintances, and the friendships she created that she chose to record and publicize in her memoir.

Even as Anna wrote on her experiences, she and her "editors," virtually the entire family, were careful to make even their former ruler, King Ferdinand, appear in the best possible light. There are no intimate revelations in the book about the king's character. Rather the work is a soft narrative account of the Bulgarian domestic scene, the court, and its denizens.

Anna Stancioff's memoirs did not presume to discuss any contentious bit of information. Instead, she chose to end the memoir in 1918, a year when the darker future of Bulgaria had yet to materialize. The narrative evinced no rancor and leveled no accusation at any individual or state for the ultimate fate of Bulgaria.

She accomplished the work with her family's help—clarifying recollections, editing sensitive passages, and typing the manuscript. Although all her daughters helped with the revisions, her husband was the ultimate editor. By fall 1931, the book was ready to present to a publisher. Nadejda arranged for the book to be published in England. By spring 1936, with an introduction written by Lord Newton, it appeared to some acclaim and garnered favorable reviews.[29]

Travel: Luxury, Power, and Comfort

Masters of the world, as Nadejda had once described them, British citizens were free to travel everywhere, and they did. The Muirs traveled on an annual basis. In addition to visiting family in Bulgaria, they frequented tourist destinations and also spent time touring tea plantations and commercial concerns related to Kay's business interests.

In Western Europe, their favorite mode of transportation was the Simplon Express Blue Train and Pullman, along with its eastern brother, the Orient Express. When they traveled beyond the continent, they frequently engaged the services of Cooke, Lloyd, or similar travel agencies to book first-class accommodations on ocean liners, steam ships, trains, and with private guides. With all-inclusive plans, they enjoyed amenities like orchestras, costume balls, and on-board cinema.

Like other British, the Muirs, with some notable exceptions, relished the company of their compatriots and sought them out when traveling abroad. Moreover, the foreign backdrops did not soften the requirements of etiquette and decorum.

Often Feo accompanied the Muirs on trips abroad Nadejda, Kay, and Feo traveled the world over—Egypt, Kenya, Greece, the Caribbean, and South America. Nadejda and her husband also traveled on their own as well, visiting Chou while her sister lived in the United States. Later, the couple took extended trips to Japan and China.

As children, Feo and Nadejda were already well-traveled. Initiated into a tradition of educational travel to foreign destinations by their parents, the sisters were part of a growing number of women travelers who explored the world.30 On recurring trajectories across Europe, as experienced tourists, they could look upon a familiar site and mentally note the historical features and curiosities it offered a visitor. They satisfied their natural curiosity about parts of the world they had not visited by reading authors known for their travel writing and who used certain countries as stages for their fiction. For example, they read Henry de Regnier for Venice, Maurice Barrès for Spain, Robert Hitchen's novels to get a glimpse of Egypt and Sicily, and Pierre Loti for Constantinople.

Their expectations and images of unfamiliar lands, which copious reading of fiction and nonfiction created, led the sisters to make assumptions that were sometimes shattered by reality. In Italy, traveling in the Veneto, they could not imagine that Titian had used locals as models, since the locals they observed were rather dour looking, as opposed to Titian's ethereal subjects.[31]

The Stancioff sisters enjoyed noting the ubiquitous Orient in everything they observed in Italy and even in non-European locations, such as South America. The flavor of the Orient, in unexpected locations, reminded them of home, the Orient of the European imagination that began so near the heart of the continent. The two Stancioff sisters worked on maintaining that special relationship with each other begun in childhood, and they experienced new adventure and encounters of foreign environments together, as they traveled the far-flung destinations of the world. As Europeans, they craved exploring the inscrutable other, and they sought it out in every direction of the compass.

In spring 1927, the Muirs and Feo Stancioff took a three-month trip to what they perceived as the New World. It was the first of numerous such excursions with sister Feo. After New York City, they headed south to cross the Panama Canal on their way to Chile, Argentina, Brazil, and a few other South American countries. Their voyage combined the pleasure of undiscovered terrains with some business matters of Kay's. Nadejda notes that "The Anglo-Saxon servants find our far off destination completely natural."[32]

They traveled first class on the Cunard liner, the Berengaria, a top-of-the-line luxury liner. Except for Ivan and Marion, who were away on their own travel adventures, the entire combined clan was there to see them off. Nadejda described the ocean liner as

> an immense palace, a floating hotel, with stairs, ball room, winter garden with palm trees and hyacinths, immense concert hall, designated rooms for repose and writing supplied with all possible books, newspapers; cabins with beds and furniture, immense bathrooms, dining rooms like the Ritz; Roman bath, Turkish bath, exercise rooms, about 12 floors with elevators, 2000 person staff alone; provisions include caviar, oysters, [and] select wines.[33]

During their voyage across the Atlantic Ocean, the sisters shared a copy of Paul Bourget's 1893 book *Outré Mer,* about the New World they were about to encounter. Kay presided over a charity concert for the Maritime Society. The games, teas, and social interactions continued as dictated by their kinship in class with fellow travelers.

As members of the Old World, Feo and Nadejda both felt drawn to the temperament of the New World while they worked on a translation of their father's work—the manuscript that would be published as his memoirs.[34] "Feo and I, looking like two poorly paid stenographers write all day long in the elegant "Palm Court" of the luxury ship!"[35] The book was a project that occupied the sisters from their teenage years until it was published in 1957.

New York City was a shock for Feo and Nadejda. They experienced the city first as the dirty disordered ports of call of their childhoods: the train stations of St. Petersburg, Warsaw, and Budapest, but the city center impressed them. Nadejda describes her experience:

> An entirely different city reveals itself; the skyscrapers! . . . city of iron and steel, triumph of modern science, a dream realized by modern technology, the combination of all that we can produce and accomplish by the biggest engineers and architects of the world . . . Along with this negligence, the filthiness of the streets, no feeling of cosmopolitanism.[36]

New York, and by association, the United States of America, had many deficiencies that jarred their European sensibilities. Although they stayed at the Plaza Hotel, they judged the rooms to be the quality of "a good country hotel of

France with good bathrooms and heating apparatus," and felt, at least, that the food was excellent.[37]

Their first experience of a Broadway show was also quite shocking; Nadejda described *Lulu Belle* as a "dirty, barbaric, and savage" It seemed to the English tourists, to display the "mores of Jews-Negros of New York."[38]

The Metropolitan Museum of Art hit its mark, but in their estimation, it too was poorly maintained and somewhat rundown, despite its eye-opening collections.

After lunch at the India House Club and a visit to the Cotton Exchange, the travelers felt more at ease. Touring the principal sights, such as the Brooklyn Bridge, climbing to the top of the fifty-ninth floor of the Woolworth building, shopping, and dining in an elegant English restaurant, also led the three to find the city more agreeable.

The final impressions of the city, according to Nadejda were as follows: "Exaggerated heating of apartments; glasses of water everywhere with ice; constant noise; ugly men, women in the street elegant and well put out . . . higher prices than London everywhere, except for the taxis."[39] The travelers also observed something else about New York City: Americans seemed determined to destroy the old in order to build the new, with no grand design to guide them.

Although their first impressions of New York were "frankly detestable," the city finally managed to charm them. They felt for the city "as one would feel for a child who is very talented, who needs encouragement and advice. . . . a city where," according to Feo, "dreams develop in [numbers] of floors!"[40]

The next leg of their journey was a cruise on a Chilean liner that departed from the Brooklyn docks. After traveling through the Panama Canal, they traversed the South American continent at a leisurely pace via train and car.

At each destination, they made contacts with the members of whatever British colony existed. They were reminded of old Europe as they apprised themselves of the domestic political situation, the deportations, camps for detainees, political coups d'état, and government corruption. The Old World and the New World were not so far apart after all.

Buenos Aires appeared to have French blood, even Parisian, since the main arteries were aligned wide boulevards that gave way to very narrow streets. The overabundance of beef on the menu made the travelers crave vegetables, but they enjoyed the diversity of the views, and especially the bay. Sao Paolo also made a good impression; Nadejda described the city as a "superb modern city very well built and constructed; well situated on a plateau with a distant view of hills; Superb light. . . . . City of energy. . . . Remarkable cleanliness. Formidable electricity, superb autos, tramways."[41] Marion's father had been responsible for leading the team who constructed the light and power station, so the travelers felt a special pride in the electrification of the city.

Where is Egypt?

On their first trip to Egypt in 1933, the three travelers' initial impression was one of disagreeable odors that marred their experience of Alexandria as a grand city of ancient Egypt. The present, as opposed to the imagined ancient past, was quite earthy, as the travelers toured in a fiacre and observed little that was graceful; and, according to Nadejda, they found only "pyramids of cabbage!"[42]

They traversed the Suez Canal at night, and an orchestra played Viennese waltzes while they experienced the heat of the desert. Recalling Bible stories of Moses in the Sinai, the travelers marveled that they had come so far in one week—from Victoria Station to the heart of the Sinai. Travel, which transcended time and place, served to underscore both the travelers' proximity to the foreign while reminding them of the common cultural roots of civilization.

When Nada and Kay revisited Egypt in 1937, their impressions of that dusty destitute population changed little. As much as they attempted to evoke the ghosts of Antony and Cleopatra or a shadow of the Library of Alexandria, they continued to be jarred into the present by streets teeming with people. Porters plied their trade along streets lined with modern stores and the ubiquitous piles of cabbages. The poverty they observed from the train, which took them to Cairo, was pitiful. Dusty villages with biblical processions of lines of camels, and white asses indicated an Egypt frozen in time. Against a backdrop of destitution, the white-colored egrets in the fields were bright spots, pallid against a barren landscape.[43]

Egypt was still very much a land of mixed influences, with both the ancient past and its evolving modern incarnation coexisting. While at a small airport Nadejda noted that, the facilities were guarded by camel corps "aerodrome airplanes, autos, asses, and camels . . . A very strong impression of the immensity, complexity, and diversity of Cairo."[44]

In Cairo, the Muirs resided at the British Embassy, a cross-shaped building, with an enclosed garden of palm trees, roses, and pleasantly odiferous trees. Armed soldiers guarded the grounds and buildings. Still exuding power, the British were losing some of their privileges as the Egyptians asserted their sovereignty.

At a tea for the English colony, the Muirs had an opportunity to mingle with generals, officers, and British functionaries. Their accommodations were rather cavernous, poorly-heated rooms. Nonetheless, they could call on the services of an English butler, a Greek cook, a *femme de chambre*, and a valet for the guests. As Nadejda said, "Luxury, power, and comfort!"[45]

The impression of British power and resilience was thrust before the Muirs at a cocktail party given in a baroque palace where the Louis Philippe décor recalled the elegance of the continent. Cairo society was as distinguished as any in the world. European royalty, cultural elites, and even notorious Englishmen like Robert Hichens (infamous for his conduct during the Titanic disaster in 1912) made up the social life in Cairo. Nadejda notes that the English race could crisscross the universe yet not be influenced in the slightest by it but rather maintain its British essence: "The sensation of Britannic omnipotence . . . Very amusing the world is very interesting, immense, and very tiny for cosmopolitans and the English!"[46]

Visions of India

On a trip to India in 1933, progressing along on the Indian Ocean, the Muirs experienced the sensation of isolation, serenity with a routine of meals, interspersed with activities, games, bridge, music, and golf. Their environment was so properly put together that at a shipboard ball, they were transported to the Savoy.

When they reached Bombay, the impact of the crowds of "flowers," since both male and female natives wore colorful attire, was their first impression. They saw a people who were "intense, thin, innumerable! We see Ghandis [sic] everywhere!"[47] Nadejda writes that the crowd appeared to be celebrating a holiday. The atmosphere was replete

> with wandering merchants, snake charmers, women carrying babies the color of spice bread. Vendors of doubtful looking liquids . . . All hiding their microbes and their political opinions despite the bright penetrating light of the climate![48]

The English by contrast were clean looking in white with the "topee" (pith helmet). Sliding back and forth between cultural comfort zones was at once invigorating and slightly repugnant the Europeans. Seeking the familiar, while surrounded by the unfamiliar, the travelers sought a balance of sensations.

The public garden at Malabar recalled that of Euxinograd, and the local yacht club gave some echo, as Nadejda says, of the "Ranelagh of London reconfigured for the tropics."[49] Nadejda noted that although British émigrés were well cared for in Bombay, their lives were difficult. So many British families lived separated by the long distances that divided the motherland from her dominion.

Africa, Land of Contrasts

For the Muirs, travel in Africa in 1937 presented some of the same dilemmas as travels elsewhere in the world, especially in the British dominion lands. Looking for the familiar in an alien world, the Muirs found it at Thika, in the heart of Africa.

Invited to coffee and scones as guests of a local coffee farmer, the Muirs noted his tortured English garden.[50] The farmer had lived alone for a year; his wife was back in England taking care of the children. His well-designed garden required extraordinary effort to maintain, since English flowers could not adapt to a climate of extremes—deluges or dry seasons.

The landscape of his homeland, embodied by a traditional English garden, symbolized the essence of Englishness. Importing England to Africa was untenable, yet he persisted. He did compost his coffee plants with elephant grass, as was the local custom, but in the garden surrounding his home, he tried to recreate the familiar landscape of home.

The effort to reconcile native and familiar lifestyles led the British travelers to the conclusion many Europeans made about their cultural superiority and its desirability to the less-developed world. When natives complied with European customs, those natives exhibited superior traits as a people, in the eyes of Europeans.

In Africa, Nadejda commended the Kikuyu when they made an effort to take on the trappings of European civilization. On their reservation, she noted that they were "less pretty [than other natives] . . . but they are imitative and do learn [;] presumably they picked up European culture and civilized living."[51]

On the plains of Nairobi, while touring in the area of Mount Kilimanjaro, Nadejda, unexpectedly, was reminded of her past. The Muirs' guide had hosted none other than King Ferdinand on the latter's tour of Kenya, Uganda, and Tanganyika—on safaris, and to the sources of the Nile. Nadejda remembered their, Stancioffs' and Coburgs', shared histories fondly. Time spent with King Ferdinand she recalled inevitably included: "[his] bonbons and [his] remedies; the gloves and the rings"[52]

The Muirs stumbled onto the trail of King Ferdinand there too, and made a pilgrimage to the hotel where the king stayed while on a butterfly hunting expedition. Mombassa had a cosmopolitan history, the city part Swahili, part Indian, and part Arab, was founded by the Portuguese and later occupied by Arabs, only to be taken over by the British navy. The baobab trees, with dry foliage and trunks as large as elephants, stood in stark contrast to the Shell and Pratt Oil Companies' constructed forests of steel.

For British tourists, the mark of Empire was distinctly stamped on the land: here too, the expatriate colony was discernible by their stalwart efforts to recreate their English gardens in Africa.

The white population of Kenya, which was relatively small, settled on modest private properties that some developed into farms. Nadejda remarks that, "Kenya is a land of contrasts and views that appear to change every twenty kilometers."[53]

The abundance of Indians astounded the Muirs. Many of the Indians were Sikhs working as foremen directing the natives in their work. For the most part, the towns seemed to be cut from the same design: a train station, one general store with one English employee, one post office, and one hotel. The Muirs duly noted the predominant English influence when they happened upon a "perfectly organized hunt for jackal with master of equipment and hounds and etiquette. Horses imported and crossbred. Golf course." They remarked, "The English are admirable!"[54] Although travel evoked change and reflection, it also permitted the traveler to return to the familiar.

Traveling in first class, on steamships and trains, the Muirs inevitably met some bright and distinguished passengers—both British and foreign. A Chinese businessman told them about the current conditions in China and that the Japanese held large swaths of Chinese territory. The British journalists apprised the Muirs of the machinations of Hitler and the Nazis' domestic political movements.

The political changes that percolated steadily in Europe and elsewhere formed the backdrop of international travel. In the 1930s, traveling through Italy, the couple saw large numbers of Black Shirts and armed young fascists on parade. Nadejda declared them "the ugliest people in Europe except maybe the

Scots!"[55] She made no other comment about their policies, for example, in her journal.

Political Instability in Italy, Spain, Germany, and France

Italians felt their allies had betrayed them in 1919, when Italy was not permitted to claim all the territories promised her in secret treaties signed during the Great War. As the Italian economy took a precipitous decline immediately after the war, civilians and returning soldiers alike, drove the public outcry for justice. Therefore, it was a relatively simple process for Italians to be inspired by a new type of leader and a new ideology fascism.

What Benito Mussolini (1883-1945) and his followers created was a totalitarian state that brooked no domestic opposition and sought to redress the inadequacies of the peace through foreign adventurism. Even more damaging for Europe, was the fact that Mussolini's model served to inspire imitators.

Drawing on war-weary populations' feelings of anger, resentment, and frustration, fascists everywhere garnered support for their plans to dominate society and control the military. Leaders who proposed fascism inspired their followers to hope for a better future and improved living conditions. This hopeful mood coincided with the consequences that war exhaustion and devastation had introduced into Europe. In addition, theories of racism, nationalism, and conservatism, as well as the economic cost of war all combined to make populations receptive to notions of racial superiority and historic destinies of nations as absolutes.

The Italian example of fascism, as Mussolini envisioned it, inspired others to create their own domestic varieties of totalitarianism in rabidly exclusionary yet aggressive regimes. Spain under Franco and Germany under Hitler became the most prominent states to apply the new totalitarian ideology.

Russia, where a popular revolution and a Bolshevik coup drove the country out of the Great War, became the spawning ground for another form of totalitarianism—communism. The Soviet state posed a challenge to the rest of Europe. The Bolshevik Party, and the communist state it created, threatened the stability of the continent. There were also many people in Europe who found communism inspirational.

The Paris Peace Conference of 1919 ignored Russia. Civil war and the dissolution of much of the westernmost former imperial Russian territories destabilized the nascent Soviet state. The Bolsheviks spent most of the 1920s trying to find a middle ground between the strict application of communist ideology and the permitting of limited market forces to return the devastated country to domestic equilibrium. The European states ostracized the Soviet Union for the better part of the 1920s and 1930s.

France suffered the greatest amount of physical damage of all the belligerents in the Great War. In addition to sustaining the largest number of dead and wounded, the French territorial, economic, business, agriculture, housing, and transportation infrastructure losses were so great that the French attitude during the peace was one of complete intransigence. Vengeance and revenge motivated their negotiating agenda as the French focused on recouping all the material losses of the war by extracting the largest possible reparations payments, especially from the Germans.

Moreover, the French fixated on assuring their future security by hobbling the Germans' capacity to rearm and reconstitute offensive armed forces. Those dual aims, fueled by the bitter results of war, put the French in an entirely cantankerous posture throughout the 1920s and 1930s.

France based its security first on the formation of alliances with smaller states; Czechoslovakia, Romania, and Yugoslavia made up the Little Entente. Poland, too, was allied with France. France also created a fortified line of defense works on its border with Germany—the Maginot Line.

In addition, the French had to contend with tensions the war had left unresolved among the various political blocs that had begun to emerge at the turn of the century. A significant communist and socialist party presence caused domestic unrest as French Communists clashed with groups of the right. These conflicts came to a head in 1934 when a political crisis led to serious street fighting in Paris and disrupted the entire country. (Nadejda's friend, Clare Sheridan, witnessed the clashes in Paris and wrote detailed accounts in letters). Although a popular-front government formed in 1936, the Left could not sustain its popularity and instead bowed out to a radical government that steered a country splintered by dissension toward the brink of war.

European reliance on collective security and the power of the League of Nations to keep the peace faltered over the course of the 1930s. France and Britain, the main forces behind the Versailles treaties, had the most to lose by letting other powers dominate the continent. However, these two countries were increasingly at odds with each other. The failure of their relationship, in great part, led to the emasculation of the League and helped destabilize Europe.

A Broadcasting Career

Nadejda Muir's career as a radio personality began with the help of British historian Arnold Toynbee who recommended her to the British Broadcasting Corporation (BBC) in 1930. Then, in 1931, Mr. Evelyn Wrench, editor of the *Spectator,* approached her about a specific broadcasting project. The letter of invitation assured Lady Muir that the series of broadcast talks for that summer would "discuss with an Englishman the essential differences of outlook and temperament which find expression in their [the smaller countries of Europe] respective nationalities."[56] The title of the talk on Bulgaria, *A Nation Trained to Work,* aired on May 14, 1931 as part of the *World and Ourselves Hour.* Nadejda's debut into broadcasting became an opportunity to use innovative recording equipment, a first for the BBC. Lady Muir and Mr. Wrench were the first to use a Stille recording device, which had the ability to record and re-broadcast later. The speakers could rehearse their "discussions," hear the results, and work on the rough spots in their presentation before broadcast.

A transcript of their broadcast was published in the *Listener* on May 20, 1931 with a photograph of Gabrovo.[57] Nadejda received accolades from friends for her talk. Edward Boyle wrote to praise her for adroit presentation of Bulgarian views on the outlet to the Aegean and other territorial revisions "without giving your neighbours an opportunity to take offence."[58]

The *Observer* commented on Nadejda's "discussion" with Mr. Wrench, noting that "she gave an astonishingly packed lecture, playing the complete ambassador for Bulgaria and not shirking political pleas." [59] The observation confirmed what Nadejda wrote in her journals and what she announced in her letters home—that she set herself on a course to influence British public opinion through whatever means possible and garner support for Bulgaria and her policies. Although the *Observer's* columnist was scandalized that her talk was "certainly not a discussion as advertised,"[60] the commentary underscored Nadejda's fearless pursuit of her self-appointed mission to serve as an unofficial representative of Bulgarian interests abroad.

Her talk stressed the usefulness and benefits inherent in Bulgaria's program of mandatory volunteer work during the 1920s, for young people of both genders; was required to perform ten days of unpaid service to the state. According to Nadejda "every year about 18,000 youths are called to work...handed a grey suit of clothes and a cap with a medallion bearing the words 'Work for Bulgaria.'...Since 1925 the amount of work done ...has been of greater value to the State than the cost of their food, the salaries of their chiefs, overhead expenses and cost of materials."[61] Despite the scolding tone of the *Observer,* in the end, the columnist was convinced that Bulgaria's "example of applied altruism" was worth considering, since the country had managed to shrink its national debt to below its pre-war level. The writer also expressed admiration for the products of a Bulgarian public education in a country largely comprised of an agrarian population. He learned all this from Lady Muir's broadcast!

The year 1931 was a busy one for Nadejda. She wrote newspaper articles, broadcast for the BBC, gave public addresses, traveled, and hosted the Bulgarian king, among other distinguished guests.

Soon after her broadcasting debut, Lady Muir became a frequent radio program host. Over the course of the next decade and a half, she was asked to prepare a variety of talks for the BBC and for the National Radio of London, and finally for Radio Sofia. Her talks were on subjects that were as personal as travel experiences and as topical as wartime life for women in England. As her broadcasts became popular, she acquired a following who wrote letters to her. She answered some of these letters on the air.

In 1933, she broadcast travelogues for the BBC called *Through Three Continents,* in which she shared her growing number of international travel experiences.[62] On a completely different topic, on a National Radio broadcast, she rendered a descriptive essay she called "The International Housewife." In this broadcast, she portrayed a "typical" peasant household and contrasted that family with a small urban ménage in Bulgaria.[63] She also developed and broadcast a series called *Europe and Its Peoples* (1935) for Scottish schools; this radio classroom stressed the importance of geography and natural resources in the historical developments of the Balkans.[64] Nadejda also had a series of talks called the *Balkan States Lectures.*[65]

In 1937 and 1938, Nadejda broadcast a series of vignettes titled *Personalities I Have Met*. In this series, she described her impressions of continental notables like Queen Marie of Romania (1875-1938), Queen Giovanna of Bulgaria (1907-2000), Queen Elena of Italy (1873-1952), Mussolini, Edvard Beneš (1884-1948), Ismet Inonu and others.[66] In 1938, her family in Bulgaria heard her BBC broadcast on Greece, during its early morning transmission, at the home of their English friends the Bakers. Maman complimented her daughter on a "beautifully conceived and delivered talk" and wrote, furthermore, that she, Papa and Feo were proud of the "world renown of [their] eldest."[67] Soon after hearing their daughter, for the first time, during her broadcasts, Ivan secured a radio for his parents and listening to it became a daily ritual at *Les Trois Sources*.

In addition to an *Empire Transmissions Series* (1938), in which she discussed Albania, Greece, Hungary, Turkey, and Bulgaria, Lady Muir also prepared and delivered broadcasts for Radio Sofia sponsored by Empire Products. In these broadcasts, she described the process of cultivating various exotic products such as cocoa, tea, bananas, and coconuts.[68] She related her first-hand experiences traveling to the plantations around the world that produced these commodities that Empire Products marketed to countries like Bulgaria. During the 1930s, Nadejda's talks on the Balkans were a constant over the radio waves.

She and her family fumed over the complete disregard among the European community of nations for Bulgaria's consistent efforts to remain nonbelligerent, to abjure any foreign adventurist policies. Despite the injustice meted out to the country in of 1919, distrust and paranoia increased throughout Europe, and Bulgaria found no sympathetic partner in international relations.

In 1937, when the Balkan current of mutual distrust intensified, and the tense atmosphere led to increasing resentments, Maman wrote, "What to say of our [Bulgaria's] weakness in comparison to all these Balkan states who have given us nothing in exchange for the security which we have guaranteed [on the Peninsula]! My old blood is revolted by all this."[69] Bulgaria wanted respect and consideration from other European states and especially her neighbors.

The Bulgarian Cause in Great Britain

Nadejda and Sir Kay invited King Boris to pay a personal visit to them in Scotland in fall 1927. They invited the king to a hunting party, but they made certain also to invite people with influence in government as well as "lay" people who could be swayed to take up Bulgarian causes once they were charmed by her monarch.[70]

Five years later, the king visited Blair Drummond once more—this time with his new Queen Giovanna of Parma. The couple made an even better impression on the Muirs' guests as charming and affable people than the king had done alone. Henceforth, King Boris' visits to the Muirs' became an annual event until the outbreak of war in 1939. The Muirs invited the British elites of their acquaintance to spend leisure time with the king on these royal visits to their Scottish estate. They created contacts through hosting weekend parties and shoots.

Nadejda and her husband did their best to be useful to the monarchy by popularizing the Bulgarian dynasty their entire lives. Personal contacts mattered, and the British Foreign Office was still an exclusive organization.[71] Using social associations to professional or personal advantage was acceptable among the elites who perceived no fault in advancing class-based power based on personal connections. Social status commanded authority. Thus, when Nadejda Stancioff married Lord Kay, she could use that fact to advocate for her causes.

It was natural for Lady Muir to promote the Bulgarian sovereign to his equals in England. She and the king had been devoted friends since childhood. When it came to the movements of King Boris, the Muirs were especially vigilant, lest they let an opportunity slip by unexploited to advance his positive image. "Certain ordinary newspapers have mentioned that he will hunt possibly this year," Nadejda wrote home to Bulgaria; "It is probably the servants talking to the press. I read the Bulgarian press carefully."[72]

Nadejda was so committed to helping Bulgaria's foreign image that she even directed Stancioff propaganda efforts in Bulgaria, long distance, via her letters to her family—letters that were always full of directives and suggestions for initiatives. She insisted, for example, that her family pass on favorable press clippings to the royal family:

> I hope Mrs. Soden [Queen Giovanna's pseudonym] will start hatching soon! The articles enclosed are excellent . . . [s]ince they [the royal couple] do not read anything, send him [King Boris] the Times and the Guardian articles from me; and tell him that the Allendale ménage adores him. That they are overwhelmed by his royal generosity; that she adores her bracelet and him his links; that the butler showed me his tie tack . . . that they are as rich as Croesus, tells me Kay! but they are simple and good.[73]

Clearly the Stancioff family worked around their king's weaknesses to make their efforts as effective as possible. On the premise that the birth of an heir would help the dynasty's prospects, they prayed for a royal pregnancy. The entire Stancioff family was involved in the process since they read the press on both sides of the continent and kept each other abreast of political and social developments.

Meanwhile, Nadejda, the primary power broker at this point, attended covert shoots with the Elgins and the Allendales, while keeping up a commentary on current events with her companions and touting wonderful Bulgaria.[74] She used her status and her contacts to make new acquaintances that were even more valuable to the cause, as she described: "Was at a Balkan meeting at Carlisle ... duties! Then a nuptial cocktail party in Yorkshire, dull; then diner and evening at the Allendales. In automobile from nine until midnight—then from 2:30 to 6:30; then 7 to 7:30 a little day for Papa!"[75]

All the while, she kept her family informed of her plans and initiatives to build a support base for Bulgaria. Remarkable in her tirelessness in this regard, Nadejda continued to be her king's champion, even on her annual summer visits to Bulgaria with Lord Kay in tow. There, while the king offered reciprocal hospitality to his Scottish hosts, Nadejda continued to maintain and cultivate her diplomatic contacts and her husband's connections among his countrymen abroad. Therefore, the Muirs, made a point of accepting invitations from the British legation in Sofia and other notable expatriates, chatting all the while about the wonderful king and his progressive governing style. Meanwhile, in Bulgaria, the rest of the Stancioff clan had settled into their lives with spouses, children, and new occupations.

Villa Les Trois Sources and Villa Marion

During the interwar period, Nadejda's retired parents and sister Feo often visited the Muirs in Blair Drummond and in London. Nadejda and Kay visited Bulgaria almost annually for extended stays in spring and early summer.

When at home in Bulgaria, Feo took on the duties of managing the *Trois Sources* property and also played the role of lady-in-waiting to Queen Giovanna. Feo took on the responsibilities of running the household, of ferrying her parents to and from social calls or errands in an old Studebaker, and keeping the gardens productive and beautiful. Ivan and Marion filled in when possible, and the combined households were a rather well coordinated family enterprise where children and grandparents enjoyed an ideal environment in each other's company.

As the Ivan Stancioff family grew, the seven children and their parents spent increasingly more time by the Black Sea. Their *Diado* (Grandpa) Dimitri, Granny Anna, and *Lelia* (Aunt) Feo enjoyed observing the children's progress as the lives of the two households commingled on the joint properties. Their grandparents enjoyed witnessing how the children matured physically and intellectually and how they learned Bulgarian from their tutor and governesses. Everything was reported to the absent members of the family.[76]

Feo and Ivan had been close as children. In 1928, the two experienced an adventure together when they undertook a road trip across Europe. The ultimate goal of the trip was to deliver the car they were driving, a Standard, to *Les Trois Sources* for the family's use.

While Marion and Nanny Cowles, with baby Dimitri, traveled via train from London to Varna, Feo, Ivan, and dog Punch drove across Europe on an epic journey. Their road trip wound its way via France, Germany, Austria, Hungary, and Romania delivering the car in Varna. Brother and sister were quite pleased with the adventure and shared driving duties over miles of poorly paved and unkempt roads. They endured ferry crossings, flat tires, and the temporary defection of Punch, who at one point left Romanian territory in preference for Hungary and a Hungarian bitch, while the Bulgarians were negotiating a border crossing. They traveled over 3000 kilometers in just 72 hours.

Feo wrote to Nadejda about their adventures and published an article on the trip in the *Near East and India* called *From London to the Black Sea by Car* in 1928. She noted to her sister in Britain that the first sense of coming closer to the Orient was when at the "rustic" Austro-Hungarian border, just 50 kilometers from Vienna, they were greeted by a Hungarian soldier who was "not very elegant and brandished a bayonet that was three meters long!" The travelers discovered that once in Hungary "no one wants to speak German" and that once in

Romania they noted that Temešvar was more Hungarian and Romanian.[77] Feo observed that Romania appeared to be full of soldiers who were stationed at sensitive spots, like Temešvar, partially in readiness to offset an attack from Bolsheviks.[78]

That summer, in Varna, the senior Stancioffs, Feo, and the two sets of new-lyweds, the Stancioffs and the Guepins, shared the splendor of *Les Trois Sources* as Marion awaited the birth of her second child. The king, according to Feo, was in a "very sociable mood this year. I think that in eight days he has visited us six times!"[79] She also reported to Nadejda, in a letter written two weeks later, that the king appeared unannounced at some boat races at the Sea Garden in Varna and was simply stampeded by the crowd who could not curb their enthusiasm and rushed to shake his hand, shouting "tsarcheto (the kinglet)," and singing Shumi Maritsa (a patriotic song).[80]

The cycle of visits to and from Great Britain by the Stancioffs, the Muirs, and the royal family permitted the Muirs and the Stancioffs in Bulgaria to keep well informed about each other. The king made certain to update the Stancioffs on his latest visits or written communications, as did they in return. The bonds of family, obligation, duty, friendship all blended to bring the royal family and the Stancioffs closer.

The royal couple finally started a family Princess Marie-Louise was born in 1934. When Prince Simeon was born in 1937 Nadejda wrote a letter of con-gratulations to King Boris. He replied by reporting to her that he had been taken aback by the "explosion of joy the likes of which I have never seen here" on the occasion of the birth of a royal heir. He included, in that letter, a photo of the newborn with his older sister.[81]

The Stancioffs in Bulgaria remained neighbors and friends with the royal family. Dimitri and Anna found themselves cast in the role of Diado and Granny for the royal offspring, as the little ones toddled in their garden. Maman reported to Nadejda, "we are royal all the time here...visit of the King with the charming Princess Maria Louise who fed the chickens with Diado Stancioff...dinner at the palace with the majesties."[82] Dimitri was especially thrilled to take on the role of grandfather as he stewarded mixed groups of grandchildren, his own and the royal family's, through his gardens in Varna. Papa wrote to his eldest, "the heir apparent Simeon is magnificent... he runs in his play room, when visitors ap-pear he salutes them military style, shakes hands with everyone, ...may god protect him!"[83]

Nadejda's bond with Feo remained undiminished in its intensity. Typical of their feelings for each other was a reminder from Feo, to Nadejda, in a letter, of their "precious childhood" in Sofia 1912–1913: "Our children [Stancioff chil-dren and grandchildren were raised by the entire family] go often to Vrania to play...and it seems to me as though it all begins once more."[84] This and other written communications of their precious memories attest to the sisters' close-ness.

It seemed the Stancioff cycle of life repeated itself as before, grandparents Anna and Dimitri, on hand to supervise when the parents were busy, and the Stancioff children close to their relatives and becoming the playmates of royalty.

Nadejda was kept current on every niece and nephew's triumphs and peculiarities in character, as five adults kept her informed of each and everyone of the brood of seven.

Chou and husband, Felix Guepin, who worked for Shell Oil as an executive, spent some years living in England after their marriage. Chou was involved in charitable activities as well as broadcasting. She prepared talks on her experiences as a traveler and as a guest at royal weddings. *Radio Times* linked Chou's name, now Hélène Guepin, to her sister's, Lady Muir, to highlight her qualifications as a broadcaster by associating her with her better-known sister.

Chou and Felix lived primarily in the United States after 1937 because of his work-related assignments. Thus, the distances and costs involved constrained their contacts and visits with their extended families. Their departure from Europe in 1937 was traumatic for the entire family. Papa had grown feeble with age and could not travel to London to see them off. However, he did manage to ask King Boris to award Felix with a civilian decoration of merit to the Bulgarian nation as a memento. He enjoined Felix not to forget the Old World in a letter laboriously written in an unsteady script.[85] From this point on, Chou maintained her family connections through letters and telegrams.

For Chou, after the birth of her daughter, Karin, in 1935, the child whose physical and cognitive dysfunctions put a heavy burden on her time and energies, the efforts to sustain her contacts with the family were enormous.

Although her family, at times chafed under their forced ignorance, they did what they could to fill in for her inability to keep connected. Ivan and family, Nadejda and Kay, invited mutual friends who visited the United States to dinner expressly so that the family could get first-hand information about their distant sister. Also, the family shared press releases in the society pages on both sides of the Atlantic. In this manner, all the Stancioffs managed to keep the flow of information steady.

Furthermore, Nadejda's visits to Chou in the United States helped to keep the Guepin household within the embrace of the close-knit family. Chou had given birth to a second daughter in America, Felicia, in 1938. Felix's situation was comfortable enough so that they could live at ease. Apart from the separation from her family, the Guepin ménage survived the war years in comfort.

Publishing Her Message

By the time she had become a British citizen Nadejda had become a prolific writer and her articles appeared in journals such as *Foreign Affairs, Near East, Contemporary Review, Journal of the Royal Institute of International Affairs,* as well as in the *Encyclopedia Britannica.* In addition to these venerable publications, she also submitted hundreds of articles and letters to the editor in British, Bulgarian, and French newspapers. She acted as an agent for her sister Feo's articles on more than one occasion using her contacts among journalists to get Feo's pieces published.[86]

She wrote sympathetic vignettes—about Bulgaria and her royal family— and published them in local Scottish newspapers as well as in national British papers. King Boris III was grateful. He thanked her for her "useful activities in England."[87]

Nadejda also encouraged compatriots, whom she knew to be sympathetic to Bulgaria, to publish positive accounts of the country.[88] When Rosita Forbes, traveler, accomplished author, and lecturer, was headed to Bulgaria in fall 1928, Nadejda secured letters of introduction for her to members of the royal family. Furthermore, Nadejda arranged with her own family in Bulgaria that Rosita and her husband would have an appropriately memorable reception from the Stancioffs and all the notable Bulgarians they would meet. She created the circumstances so that in the end Rosita Forbes, wrote a sympathetic article for the *Daily Telegraph*. "Bulgaria: A Nation of Natural Democrats" was published on December 28, 1928, part of a Balkan Travels series.[89] Since Forbes was published in Britain and known for her travel accounts to exotic locales such as Abyssinia, and Libya, her article on Bulgaria most likely would garner according to Nadejda, a wide audience. The Stancioffs unabashedly asked influential friends to lobby other important people to support Bulgaria's position.[90]

Nadejda understood the power of the press to disseminate her point of view and shape public opinion. She was careful to employ every means at her disposal to popularize her messages and to rebut those whose views would sway opinion in other directions. She was delighted when the king received positive press; she noted that "Soden [King Boris] . . . [was] getting marvelous press in England!"[91]

In order to keep track of King Boris' reputation in addition to keeping her finger on the pulse of foreign affairs, Lady Muir employed press-clipping services. She collected all articles that even remotely touched on her interests—especially those that mentioned the king. On one occasion, when she read a published piece about King Boris' plans to travel to England, she was annoyed that the "leak" did not emanate from her camp.

Nefertiti—Profiles in Beauty

In the world of elites, one's image, whether real or invented, was supremely important. Society pages published photographs of the upper classes enjoying their status in every conceivable type of activity. Photographs splashed across the pages of society gossip magazines. Newspapers offered glimpses of the elites at rest as well as in attendance at soirées, balls, teas, and charitable events. When a magazine such as *Sketch* published an issue with a dramatic cover page, the subject was inevitably members of the elites.

On October 29, 1930, Lady Kay Muir and her sister, Mrs. Hélène Guepin, appeared on the cover in dress and makeup created to resemble the well-traveled bust of Queen Nefertiti of Egypt. The three heads were posed in profile. Regal and idealized paragons of contemporary beauty the Stancioff sisters posed with Queen Nefertiti for a British, culturally, west European audience. The live models' contours were blended with the stately headdresses of Egypt to accentuate the sisters' resemblance to the Egyptian queen. The caption reads "Profile Parity—of Old Egypt and Modern Beauty." The image of power and beauty combined in that striking composition, presented two contemporary beauties posed beside a classic.

The Stancioff sisters embodied an archetypal beauty which their contemporaries admired. The cover photograph of *Sketch* would have projected a message of belonging to the social elites of the West but at the same time being of another world as well. Nadejda and Hélène were two aristocrats who were from Bulgaria, had been presented at court but were also of the oriental other. The message could have only enhanced Nadejda's prestige among her adopted compatriots. She was intelligent, erudite, and a classic beauty.

Bolshevik or Fascist England?

By the end of 1935, a new atmosphere pervaded public and government discourse in Great Britain. There was a pronounced tone of alarm about the state of the world and Britain's ability to face possible aggression from hostile states. A cry for preparedness in the event of an emergency gradually replaced the pacifist stance. The two largest alarmist camps were the anticommunist and the antifascist groups. Well-known public figures supported each position.

Largely pro-fascist media moguls used their newspapers to introduce a bias in favor of fascism in public discourse. They aimed to garner public support for the notion that, indeed, the British people and the German people were of the same valiant ethnic stock that together could stop communism's insidious spread.

At the same time, prominent aristocrats like the Astors who nurtured about them a group of politicians and journalists held that communism was a much preferable system to fascism. Communism, they maintained, was a system whose time had come, and a system that could benefit Britain. In any event, the Foreign Office ignored the right-wing forces of General Franco, who illustrated fascist regimes in action.

The timbre of British public discourse, which seemed alarmingly left-leaning, distressed Lady Muir and her husband. Annoyed that Bulgaria was not getting a fair appraisal in England because of the stain of participating on the German side in the Great War, Nadejda fumed in private correspondence. In her view, the British were ignorant of the Balkans and of Bulgaria in particular. That ignorance, she believed, would lead to dangerous decisions in domestic and foreign affairs. The British public was especially oblivious to the dangers of bolshevism.

The Muirs believed the "British terribly misguided" in their perceptions about Bolshevik propaganda. The British were well meaning and thoughtful but mistaken.[92] When one of their journalist acquaintances resigned from his position at the *Times* to protest that paper's official antifascist position, Nadejda's triumphant mood diminished when he confided in her that he was as suspicious of fascism as of bolshevism. She grumbled instead, "Very English! But alas, the world does not belong yet in its entirety to the Anglo-Saxons! Instead, it eludes them."[93] She expounded on what she called "popular errors [of judgment] about

Russia."[94] She maintained that her Bulgarian family's physical proximity to the Soviet state permitted them to have a clearer image of that regime.

Her positions on the social and political movements that disturbed the continent in the interwar period hinged on her belief that the peacemakers had botched the Peace of Paris, creating a dysfunctional world. Hence, the mistakes were coming home to roost, and Europeans had to prepare. Instead, however, the English seemed stunningly oblivious to the dangers swirling about them.

Nadejda kept abreast of the Bulgarian political climate as the Stancioffs' impressions of the goings-on in Europe flew back and forth in letters and shared thoughts. Living in the Balkans, the Stancioffs knew the realities of life in the Soviet Union. Britons, living "conveniently" far away from the Soviet Union could not get sufficient first-hand information. Instead, they had to rely on the few misguided travelers to that country, according to Nadejda. Moreover, Nadejda Lady Muir advised her audiences, on the radio and at her lectures, that travelers to Soviet Russia visited a few restricted venues that were heavily controlled, and even staged, for foreigners' consumption.

The Muirs saw the British as hoodwinked when they believed, as late as fall 1940, that the Soviet Union would be reliable in a showdown against the Nazis. Nadejda and Kay had just hosted a grouse shoot with British generals at Blair Drummond, and Nadejda wrote to her family about her frustrations: "The good people here persist in believing that the Neva is *against* the Spree and *with* the Thames . . . blindly, which is in its own way pathetic!"[95]

From the Stancioffs' and Muirs' perspective, the most dangerous threat to the continent was the rise of Soviet communism and its attempts to spread the ideology beyond its borders. Their experiences in diplomacy, and their understanding of the reality of the Soviet domestic regime, led them to conclude that rebuffing, at all costs, the insidious allure of a proletariat-run world was necessary. Both a class perspective and an experiential lens affected their position on the dangers in the changing European political landscape. This view chiefly supported fascism and opposed bolshevism.

Living Close to the Bolshevik Peril

The Stancioffs' contacts with Russians, primarily émigrés, but also foreign business people who traveled in the Soviet state, gave them a realistic understanding of the goings-on behind the country's borders. Papa kept up his interests in all matters concerning international relations and made a point of seeking out informants on these matters. He then discussed his insights with his clan.

For example, he purposefully interrogated an industrial chemicals representative who landed in Varna. The man, a German, had just returned from the Soviet Union after years of working there in the early 1930s.[96] He predicted imminent famine because of agricultural mismanagement. He pointed out that the soviets planted cotton and tea in the Batum region and expected the plants to adapt to the climate in order to reap a good harvest! The businessman also observed to Dimitri that an uneducated officer corps led the military who controlled their troops with "the knout [brute force]."

Finally, the businessman responded to the question of whether there was a possibility of rebellion by stating that "the people do not have the courage nor the energy . . . a change of regime would not be possible to provoke except from a foreign power . . . the Bolshi[e]s are very afraid of a war!"[97] Dimitri related his conversations to his daughter in Britain and she continued to drive home the message of the grave danger of communism.

Much of the message in Nadejda's broadcasts, public addresses, and articles included warnings about the dangers of the spread of bolshevism. As a counterbalance to that cautionary tale, she would offer the example of a democratic state, Bulgaria, as bulwark against that insidious Red danger in the Balkans.

Naturally, she defended fascist governments because they appeared to support monarchy and the church. As a Catholic and a monarchist, Nadejda Lady Muir perceived that fascism was "although not ideal for all nations," a much preferable, reasonable, and constructive state system than the Bolshevik option.[98] Moreover, she pressed these points home repeatedly, saying that "It seems to be an absolute anachronism for a country like Great Britain to side with those Governments which are doing their utmost . . . to wreck civilization and to shatter all our sacred beliefs."[99]

She also maintained an engaged correspondence with two Members of Parliament, Jock McEwen, and the Duchess of Atholl (1874-1960). She admitted, in a letter to her family in Bulgaria, that she wrote "informative . . . and anti-Bolshi [letters]."[100] A constant in her life was her campaign to convince everyone within earshot that "...anything in the world is preferable to sovietism."[101]

The Muirs were staunch supporters of the Conservatives in British politics in the interwar period. Traditionalists, whose incomes were dependent on plantations in the dominions and prudent domestic investments, believed, along with the majority of their compatriots, that controlled government spending, deflation, and little foreign involvement would eventually return Britain to her pre-1914 economic and political splendor. Social unrest, in their view, was primarily due to Red agents fomenting discontent among the working classes.

Engaging Speaker

Lady Muir was a popular and an experienced speaker who appeared before a continual stream of charitable organizations and scholarly groups, throughout her life in Britain. Her talks focused on Bulgaria and foreign affairs in general. Subjects included "Bulgaria and the Balkan Pact," "Bulgaria Today," the "Difficulties of Bulgaria," "The Problems of Bulgaria," "Balkan Crosscurrents," and "Foreign Affairs Made Homely." She spoke to audiences as small as fifty and as large as 1,600.

For example, in 1924, two months before her marriage, Nadejda Stancioff gave a talk to the Near and Middle East Association; a digest version of her lecture was printed in the *Near East* six days later.[102] In another talk, Nadejda continued to champion her former chief, Aleksandŭr Stamboliiski, by exposing the motives of those who had overthrown his regime. She then focused on the diplomatic issue that had absorbed her time since Neuilly: securing a Bulgarian outlet to the Aegean and the port of Dedeagach. A few months later, in October 1924, Nadejda, now as Lady Muir, addressed the Danube Literary Society with a general survey of Bulgarian history.

In 1926, at the Royal Institute of International Affairs she addressed the pressing issues of the refugee crisis in Bulgaria and used the forum to stress the peaceful intentions of the king, who represented "stability, sincerity and honour" for the country, which only aimed for peace "The Present Position of Bulgaria" which was later published by the society's journal.[103]

Dr. Seton-Watson, a historian of Central and Eastern Europe, invited Lady Muir to give a series of lectures on "Modern Bulgaria" at the School of Slavonic Studies starting in January 1928.[104] She made an exhaustive excursion of the problematic themes in Bulgarian politics: territorial and minority issues, as well as the Macedonian Question. Her first talk covered Bulgarian history from the liberation in 1878 to 1887. One month later, a second lecture, discussed Bulgaria from the beginning of the reign of Prince Ferdinand to the Balkan Wars. Her audience was "impressed by the masterly treatment of her subject, her rapid review never failing to hold the interest of those who followed it."[105]

Women and Diplomacy

Nadejda also spoke in public forums on the subject she knew well: women and diplomacy. She took on the challenge to use her unusual experiences, her public reputation as one of the first women diplomats, to encourage other women to pursue their career goals. When she first discussed the topic in 1921, she was quite enthusiastic about the positive change female diplomats could make. She stressed the point that women needed to enter the diplomatic service, since they had so much to offer and could benefit their nation.

The British Foreign Office did not permit the admission of women to its ranks and Nadejda spoke out against the practice, admonishing the government that the only thing that kept women from serving their country was male prejudice.[106] She enumerated the progressive countries that had welcomed women into their diplomatic and consular ranks, including Bulgaria and the United States, and wondered why Britain kept the doors of the Foreign Office firmly shut to women.

She pointed to the example of Gertrude Bell who had become her country's unofficial ambassador to Mesopotamia. Bell's international reputation had not diminished even eight years after her death. Nadejda chose wisely to use her name as a symbol of what women could accomplish. If women could be just as useful as men abroad, Nadejda opined, why were they not permitted to use their considerable talents?

When given an opportunity, she did not resist aiming a barb at the British foreign office establishment by intoning the following pronouncement in 1931:

> But were women and their intuition to introduce into our diplomacy an element of constructive imagination, we British, should find ourselves before long, ex-

posed to the danger of having a foreign policy, and be robbed of the blessed privilege of having no policy at all![107]

As Great Britain continued to bar women from the diplomatic corps Nadejda's criticism grew more pointed when she said "I see very little hope for the British women, owing to the well-known fact, that the members of the Foreign Office actually dread women and are even known to encourage bachelorhood!"[108] She cited Sir Hubert Montgomery, assistant under secretary of the foreign office who, when questioned on the admission of women in the diplomatic service, replied: "Such ladies might be exposed to bad climates and even danger . . . certain items of the work involved might be repugnant to women."[109] Nadejda brushed these comments aside as excuses by pointing out that the wives and daughters of ambassadors managed to survive at postings all over the world.

Described as "one of the most a public-spirited and intelligent women in Scotland," Lady Kay Muir spoke at the third national conference of the National Union of Soroptimists Clubs of Great Britain along with others who came together for the cause of opening up careers for women.[110] Nadejda told her audience that a "[diplomatic] career is not more difficult than others, and . . . women could easily acquire the technique, while their intuition would be valuable . . . qualifications necessary are two or three languages, a good classical education, knowledge of law and history, manners, good temper and the gift of concealing first impressions."[111]

In May 1931, Nadejda, a member of the governing council of the Foxcombe Hall Appeal volunteered to give a talk to an audience of 200 on the subject "Women in Diplomacy.[112] She reviewed the merits of some famous women who had a direct or indirect impact on European diplomatic events. The thrust of her talk was that these women exerted their influence through their contacts with men in power.

She specifically focused on Princess Clementine, the mother of the former King Ferdinand of Bulgaria. She ascribed to the princess what she calls "the error free reign" of her son. Nadejda states that the princess "scored success after success without having to resort to warfare and managing to avoid internal complications."[113] The mother, it seems, was the one in power. As proof of this assertion, Nadejda went on to state that after Princess Clementine's death, her son made many errors in judgment. Another example of women controlling the policies of state was Queen Marie-Christina, mother of King Alfonso who was regent of Spain while her son was a minor.

Through a variety of similar examples, Nadejda conceded that "there have been few instance of it's [the influence of women in diplomacy before the War] having been very direct; but it would be impossible to deny the great importance of the unofficial influence of women over diplomatic relations in Europe."[114] Nadejda wished to deepen the pool of eligible candidates for diplomatic positions by helping to make the career accessible to women.

Bulgaria in the Public Eye

In the winter of 1932, Nadejda Muir addressed the Overseas League Club on "Some Views on the Problem of Disarmament."[115] The talk was timed to coincide with the Disarmament Conference, which was proceeding simultaneously in Geneva. She pointed out that it was incumbent on every nation to disarm so that Germany could not justifiably rearm.

She said: "One cannot expect her people and government to wait forever for the conditions of a ratified treaty to be carried out."[116] She believed that in conjunction with the League of Nations, disarmament and keeping peace could be achieved if all nations worked together. She stressed the need for "moral disarmament."[117]

In an era when France and her dependent states focused solely on building up their collective security in case of attack instead of building lasting relationships with their European neighbors, Nadejda undertook extra efforts to popularize the Bulgarian position on international developments. That summer she gave a talk on "Bulgaria Today" still on the theme of the disarmament of Europe.

The British Institute of International Affairs invited her to talk to their society in 1934 on "Bulgaria and the Balkan Pact." She was forceful in pointing out that on the heels of recent Balkan conciliatory meetings among all the nations there, that the next step in cementing the warming of relations would be solid economic support for Bulgaria. If the French and British governments would extend the necessary financial assistance in the form of trade and industrial development, then the situation would stabilize and all Europe would benefit.[118]

A few months later, Nadejda published an article in the *Contemporary Review* called "Bulgaria Under a New Government." In this article, she assured her readers that the coup of May 1934 had not disrupted the good work of the previous six months. On the contrary, the article was positive about the changes in Bulgaria and the leadership at the helm. She stressed the constants of Bulgarian unity, devotion to king and country, and the industriousness and guilessness of her people, the peasant classes.

In an interview for the *Bulletin and Scots Pictorial* in 1937, Nadejda focused on the solid Bulgarian monarchy and intoned that "royalty are simple and human people; statesmen I consider the vainest of men, and influenced by flattery more than any others."[119] In this vein, she spoke the name of King Boris in the same breath as King George and Queen Mary. Monarchism notwithstanding, the rise of fascism, especially in Germany, put a new perspective on what qualified as capable leadership in state governments.

Nazi Party in Germany 1933–1938

Hitler and his party came to power in 1933. Over the course of the next few years, the Nazi Party managed to dominate the country and stifle political opposition professing to be leading the country to recovery, the fascist way.

Racism, especially anti-Semitism was a Nazi credo. By oppressing and eventually exterminating undesirables of all types: racial inferiors, physically and mentally imperfect people, homosexuals, and others, the Nazi Party aimed to produce the ultimate, pure Aryan state that would dominate its "lesser" neighbors.

Meanwhile, German industrial workers, small and large farmers, and professionals all came increasingly under state control as job choice, mobility, wages, and prices were state controlled. Central control permitted the party to advance its ultimate goal of acquiring *Lebensraum* or living space for the Aryan race, the perfect embodiment of humanity, according to Nazi doctrine.

As Nazi Germany began to break its Versailles treaty commitments, the atmosphere of distrust and timidity on the part of the League of Nations and its signatories emboldened aggressive states to disregard treaty obligations on the continent.

German rearmament began officially in 1935 and secretly much earlier. In the same year, Mussolini attacked Ethiopia. The League of Nations did little to combat these breaches of international treaties. In addition, the success of the fascists in the Spanish civil war encouraged more domineering acts. Europe was becoming increasingly tense.

A Change of Course?

As supportive as Lady Muir was of women pursuing a career of choice in 1931, she carried out a startling about-face a few years later. In 1936, she wrote an article for the *Evening Standard* with the headline "No Women Diplomats!"[120] In response to yet another public pronouncement in which the British Government barred the admission of women into the diplomatic and consular service, Nadejda Muir wrote a commentary on this prohibition.

Although she began affirming her belief that women could discharge their duties as well as men, she continued by stressing specific reasons why it would *not* be a good idea for them to do so. First she emphasized that female diplomatic representatives would be a liability in countries where there was no gender parity as in Britain. Second, on the question of marriage, she plainly stated that it would be unthinkable to ask a man to support his wife's diplomatic career; therefore, any woman would have to be prepared to give up her career once she decided to marry. Her third point was that there existed an overabundance of candidates for British diplomatic posts. Presumably, women should not take jobs away from men. Finally, she focused on the importance of maintaining Britain's prestige abroad. She maintained, also that women diplomats would be held to higher standards as representatives of the great nation; therefore, the position would be more difficult than for men. This was perhaps her most gender-biased remark.

While she offered the wisdom of her own experience, she also "reminded" women that diplomacy was not a very happy career. Although women were capable of the work, she stressed that the liabilities of dull routine, uncongenial colleagues and postings, small salaries, lack of opportunity for rapid advancement, and short and irregular holidays might dissuade them. Although she stated in the article that single women should not be barred from the service, she had mixed feelings. This was her last public pronouncement on the issue of women in diplomacy. At the end of her piece, she opined that diplomacy was "not a career specially suited to women."[121]

Therefore, it is no surprise that on the eve of a general European war, Lady Muir revised her position even more. She advocated excluding women from the diplomatic process completely. She came out publicly to assert that the "direction of foreign affairs should always be left to men." A report of her talk in the *Bulletin and Scots Pictorial* claimed that Nadejda believed that men were "more objective," able to "see more sides of a question," and were "less sentimental and impulsive" than women.[122] Her views changed as she grew alarmed over the increasingly grave situation on the continent from being a promoter of women in traditionally male professional realms to denying them a voice at the highest levels of decision making in government. Did she doubt her own role in the diplomatic process when she was active in helping to shape policies? Possibly her mature age (44) and her innate conservatism held sway over Nadejda's approach to the rights of women.

Causing a Stir—Are Fascists Undesirable?

On January 10, 1938, when Lady Muir addressed the National Council of Women, Stirling Branch, as its president, she proposed to give a talk that would elucidate the confusing and increasingly alarming European political situation. Her address was entitled: "Foreign Affairs Made Homely." Her talk, on the one hand, proposed to simplify and make accessible an international climate that was in turmoil and already upset by local wars.[123] On the other hand, she also intended to explain the root of all that unrest by visiting the peace treaties post the Great War, then extrapolating the errors of those negotiations into the contemporary morass of localized wars and the rise of interracial tensions.

She insisted that "the sacrifices that must be offered to the altar of peace" were still worth making, an oblique reference to concessions to Hitler's demands for treaty revisions regarding Germany. Her talk emphasized the pacific intentions of the Nazis and that despite the Anschluss and the occupation of the Sudetenland, which were both relatively bloodless, these acts attested to Germany's desire to only gain that of which Germany had been deprived unjustly in 1919.[124] Lady Muir assured her audience that essentially the events of 1938 could be categorized as marvels of German achievements that should not raise alarm. She maintained that Mr. Chamberlain had the right idea, regardless of criticisms abroad and at home.

Despite her lengthy excursus on the "Continental Jig-saw Puzzle" Lady Muir still made time to bring up the humble and hardworking Bulgaria, which asked for nothing after Munich. She pointed out that Bulgarian tact and discretion, vis-à-vis her territorial desiderata, had made the country invisible to the less prudent European states.[125] She reminded her audience that there were still tens of thousands of Bulgarians living beyond her borders, especially in Dobrudja.

Nadejda's address made its way into the local newspapers and caused comment. She received ninety letters in response, and, according to the *Scotsman*, 75 percent of the mail was supportive of her position. At least seven other newspapers published excerpts of her address; her lengthy talk ran fourteen typed, double-spaced pages.[126]

She had touched on the virtues of fascism over bolshevism.[127] She had also pronounced Italian fascism to be of no threat to Great Britain. In fact, she had congratulated the Italians on their ability to balance fascism with the two institutions that she felt were a bulwark for European civilization: the Crown and religion. She had voiced approval for the fact that the "power and dignity of the Crown" were still in tact and not endangered by fascism in Italy.[128]

She had maintained that German fascism had no interest in foreign adventures as long as the Germans were left alone to do what was best for their country; her position was live and let live. She supposed that Hitler's plans in *Mein Kampf* were the unrealistic gymnastics of an immature mind. She believed that a work written so many years before the apparent political maturity of the writer could not be a realistic manifestation of Hitler's current goals.

Instead, she, and others like her, focused on other fascist regimes. Spain and Franco's people were a good example of how hard a government had to fight to ward off outside influences, according to Nadejda. The Spanish imbroglio showed what dangers lay in allowing the proliferation of Bolshevik propaganda to penetrate a state.[129] According to Lady Muir, Bolshevik propaganda had been at work in that country since 1928, and the fact that Franco's nationalists had managed to keep the conflict local was another testament to the preferability of fascist over Red ideology.

Thus the *Scotsman* published a piece entitled "Bolshevist Perils Should Be Obvious to Britain."[130] Nadejda believed that fascism was distasteful to the British simply because the British loved democracy. But democracy was not suited to all peoples' temperaments, in her opinion; therefore, she inferred that fascism obviously suited the Germans better than the British. She felt that the British did not need to judge the Germans harshly for their preferred method of government.

The *Edinburgh Evening News* chose specifically to print "Lady Kay Muir's Views on Bolshevism and Fascism" as its headline. The newspaper's synopsis, brought up her point that "if European civilization was to be preserved . . . Franco [who] represented law and order . . . [had to prevail] . . . he stood for religion and a democratic government."[131] Other newspapers ran their own headlines on the same talk: "Scots Lady Praises Franco and Fascism," "Dictator Hailed as Democrat," and "League 'Powerless' in Politics: Lady Muir on World Unrest."[132]

The *Stirling Journal* took up her remarks on fascism being more acceptable to Britons than bolshevism. While tempering its commentary by noting that it did not to wish to "cross swords with so doughty an opponent, on her own ground so to speak," the editorial came out in opposition to her assertion by claiming Britons to be equally distrustful of fascist regimes.[133] They judged fas-

cist powers based on their international policies. As an example, the writer noted
that

Italian fascism . . . regards it as a worthwhile achievement to attack an ignorant
and almost defenseless nation of blacks and take their country from them. . . .
Germany has a . . . policy of arrogant buccaneering that has impressed only
timid neighbors and fellow freebooters. . . . Britain and all other nations upholding democratic government, watch with mistrustful eyes the doings of fascism and Nazism. . . . . the one hope of Europe . . . is the intelligence of Britain's common crowd that made them so distrustful of the dictatorships.[134]

Dundee Courier & Advertiser published a letter of rebuttal by someone who
identified himself as one of those "good, steady, honest, British citizens" Lady
Muir used as her focus group in her remarks about the favorable reception of
bolshevism in Britain.[135] The writer was surprised "an intelligent, cultured
woman like Lady Kay Muir should hold those opinions."[136] The writer claimed
that his class was attracted to neither ideology and instead was aghast at the obvious denial of freedoms that the British held dear. He went on to disparage her
remarks about the aristocracy and about Roman Catholicism being in any way
bulwarks of civilization.

Other readers wrote letters in complete agreement with her point of view. In
the *Scotsman,* a writer agreed wholeheartedly that British public opinion was
primarily blind to the dangers of communism. According to the letter, not only
was communism a threat that should be banned as illegal but also the British had
to fear "Bolshevist scheming against [Great Britain] in India and Palestine."[137]
The latter remark went to the heart of the argument of those in Britain who still
lived with their map of Great Britain stretched across the globe. Russia's
enlargement to the east in the bygone era of the epic conflict between the Russian bear and the British whale had menaced Britain's interests in Asia. Britons
still perceived that danger in the present.

Lady Muir and her neighbor, the Duchess of Atholl, an MP had already discussed this issue, on the merits of one ideology over the other, in private correspondence and in public.[138] This address, and the stir it caused, was just a continuation of their epistolary dialogue—or battle of wills—the two women had
already carried on. The battle stemmed from an earlier article the duchess had
published. The two opinionated and outspoken women's views were diametri-
cally opposed on the issue of which ideology was more dangerous. The Ladies
had carried their correspondence throughout 1937, each trying to convince the
other, politely but insistently, of her point.[139]

In April 1937 the duchess had pointed out to Nadejda's attention the fact
that although intelligent people in Germany might not "read *Mein Kampf* willingly, as it is long and diffuse and violent, but surely what matters to us is ...the
policy of the government which controls Germany under an administration infinitely more unified and far stronger than was the case in 1914."[140]

In a previous letter to the duchess, Nada had dismissed the importance of
the book by claiming that it was due to the hysteric reaction on the part of Hitler's detractors. The Duchess of Atholl went on to ask if Nadejda was willing to

let Britain sacrifice Czechoslovakia by not upholding its integrity as pledged to the League of Nations: "You yourself have . . . attended meetings of the assembly. Are you prepared to throw all obligations under the League to the winds?"[141]

Remaining unconvinced of the dutchess' arguments, Lady Muir followed the Spanish civil war with avid interest and "rejoiced when the Whites retook Toledo."[142] She could be sanguine about the win because she perceived it as another victory against bolshevism and against what she viewed as the insidious ideological threat it posed to the rest of the world. She noted that "few things were destroyed; few deaths and the treasures remain more or less intact in that city of somber beauty."[143] At the same time as her fascists were winning, her contacts and words of influence dropped on important ears: "We ate excellent cotes for lunch—much approved by Sir William Erskine come from Alloa House and talking about nothing but Soden [King Boris]."[144]

Appeasement for Germany

Late in the 1930s, tensions among the larger powers began to unsettle the European climate at a rapid pace. This situation aided the Bulgarians temporarily as the British government sought to solidify the Balkan entente, pressing for Bulgaria's admission to it. A few short months in 1938 witnessed the unraveling of the entente.

In 1938 Germany called for and accomplished the Anschluss, unification with Austria, something that was denied them in 1919. Soon after, Hitler began agitating for the self-determination of Czechoslovak Germans, the "liberation" of the Sudetenland, the swath of territory historically part of Bohemia, but with a German-speaking majority.

German agitation caused unrest in Czechoslovakia, which eventually led to the imposition of martial law to maintain order. Neville Chamberlain, British Prime Minister, conducted hopeful missions to Germany to help maintain peace and appease the Fuhrer's desiderata.

Hitler's firm refusal to budge from his demand for autonomy for the largely German-populated region of Sudetenland led to a curious international conference at Munich in September 1938. With no Czechoslovak representative present—Chamberlain represented Britain, and Daladier represented France—Hitler and Mussolini dismembered Czechoslovakia. Not only did Germans take the Sudetenland but also neighboring states helped themselves to small bits of the defenseless state. Slovakia broke free and gained autonomy.

The dismemberment of Czechoslovakia had repercussions southward; the action weakened Yugoslavia's defensive position, and Bulgaria's own search for security also foundered because of the Czechoslovak partition.

The Stancioffs believed that safeguarding peace should be the primary objective for politicians. Papa intoned what was the prevailing family sentiment with respect to chamberlain's policy of appeasement. Dimitri believed that Chamberlain could possibly "convince the Fuhrer to be reasonable in his desiderata!"[145]

The Stancioffs, along with thousands of his admirers, called Chamberlain "the savior of the Peace, before those few haranguing mites, [who are] jealous and above all ambitious [a reference to Anthony Eden and Winston Churchill among others]".[146] However, British policy seemed divided, and this division troubled the Stancioffs deeply, since they wished to perceive their idealized empire as a perfect example of united patriotism.

King Boris had been to Britain on another visit and had informed the Bulgarian Stancioffs of his satisfaction with the trip. Maman reported to Nadejda by writing "Your schedule was quite full during this short visit, but the King must have been extremely satisfied. He wrote of his pleasure to us with a post card sent from Balmorals. Now he is in Berlin."[147]

On the European scene, the situation had turned alarming for the continent. In the fall of 1938, it appeared that peace had been preserved with the territorial concession of the Sudetenland to Germany. By mid-March, however, the future of peace looked less assured than ever.

In 1939, Hitler's military invasion obliterated the remains of the Czech state. Papa was at a loss about the "lack of clairvoyance of English diplomacy . . . [and] how . . . the ambassadors . . . in Berlin [did] not foresee the 'migration' of Hitler into Prague." Dimitri was stunned by the developments in Europe.[148] Appeasement was a failure. By the spring of 1939 general war was inevitable.

Appeasement Fails

Although the British government had begun to rearm its military, focusing most on the air force, Chamberlain's "peace in our time" philosophy was finally seen as a failure. The cry for rearmament and preparedness was taken up by an alarmed British population.

When Hitler invaded Prague in 1939, the British public outrage led to a promise to defend Poland's borders. Britain finally issued a challenge to Hitler. The invasion and dismemberment of Czechoslovakia so horrified the British that the government considered the heretofore untenable option of an alliance with the Soviet Union.

The crisis precipitated by this profound change of circumstances precipitated on the European continent coalesced public opinion and unified the nation behind the war effort. Citizens of all classes and realms of the British Isles, as well as her subjects in the dominions, would fight to defend the rights of subjugated Europeans.

Although King Boris was inclined to favor supporting the British in the war political and economic realities intervened and he declared neutrality. Possibly, to appease the Germans and buy himself some time, the king accepted the resignation of his prime minister, Kioseivanov, and took on board the German-educated Filov.

As long as the Russians were allied with the Germans, King Boris' neutral position in the war brought an added benefit: the support of his subjects. In this manner, he was able to sail through turbulent 1939.

By March 1939, the Stancioffs were alert to the possibility of imminent war when Maman refered to the rise of the Nazi state as "the new barbarian invasion."[149] Keeping the peace had been an ineffectual tactic; facing an invasion, Europe had to defend itself.

Bulgarian Stancioffs

As Papa deteriorated physically, in 1939 he was 75 years old, the elder Stancioffs prepared to spend their winter months in Sofia, near the Ivan Stancioffs. There, all three adult children took care that their parents would be comfortable and well provided for. Ivan and Feo negotiated for a temporary lease on an apartment adjacent to the Stancioff house in Sofia, while Marion took charge of decorating the five-room apartment. Maman was so pleased with the arrangement that she reported "Marion decorated our apartment so well that the wife of the French Minister who finds all Sofia interiors horrid was astonished."[150] She assured her eldest in Scotland that they wanted for nothing, and well into 1940, rail links with Europe, the Simplon, and the Adriatic line, were fully functional. They had all the necessities of life. All was well in Bulgaria.

Notes

1. *Bulletin* 15 July 1932.
2. Nadejda used this moniker to describe herself on numerous occasions from public speeches to ceremonial events such as dog shows, flower shows. Cambusbarron Flower Show Stirling Journal 3 September 1931. See reference to her as a "cosmopolitan," Lady Muir stated, "generally the word [is] translated as mongrel."
3. Nadejda Stancioff, unpublished letter from Blair Drummond, 2 July 1925, TsDIA F 143 ae 25.
4. Ibid.
5. Nadejda Stancioff, unpublished letter from Blair Drummond, 16 July 1925, TsDIA F 143 ae 25.
6. Ibid. She enumerated her engagements with or without Lord Kay beginning in July through her "first big party here, with all the Peerage! ... *Sir* Kay and *Lady* Muir [she began to list the invitees] Lord and Lady Douro (oldest son of the Duke of Wellington Gotha!) [the list continues on with explanations, as necessary, and room assignments]." Her letter mentions her social engagements through the hunting season into December. An earlier letter, 2 July 1925, had run on in a similar vein, with all the breathless excitement of young bride as she listed visits with Kay's family and public functions they would attend together.
7. Ibid.
8. Interview with Mr. Dimitri Stancioff, Camden, ME, August 18, 2002.
9. Ibid. Ivan Stancioff quoted Mr. MacQueen "Mr. Ivan is orright. He's safe forr the beaters, he's safe forr the guns and he's safe forr the birds." Stancioff, *Diplomat and Gardener Memoirs*.
10. Nadejda Stancioff, unpublished letter from Blair Drummond, 16 July 1925, TsDIA F 143 ae 25.

11. *Dundee Courier,* 27 April 1931, *Apathy to League of Nations* and on the same date the *Scotsman.* Nada not only pled for justice for Bulgaria's minorities but reminded her audiences that Bulgaria had come very far indeed in a mere 50 years while hinting broadly that other states had not accomplished nearly as much in a century.

12. Stancioff, *Diplomat and Gardener Memoirs.* 48. The two assassination attempts commingled in this rather bizarre incident when the king was delayed to go to the Requiem Mass for the assassinated general because he stopped to pay his respects to the widow of the man who had been killed riding next to him in his car during the first attempt. The bombing of the cathedral had been planned based on the assumption that the general targeted for the assassination would be important enough to lure the entire government and the king to his funeral. Neither plot was successful in their original intent nor did they instead serve to restore tranquility. Instead they created an ever more tense, violent, and chaotic domestic environment.

13. Gruev, *Korona Ot Trûni Tsaruvaneto Na Boris Iii 1918-1943.*182.

14. Ibid. 183.

15. Ibid.

16. Dimitri Stancioff, unpublished letter, 25 October 1930, Nada X, PASF.

17. Stancioff, *Diplomat and Gardener Memoirs.* 47-48. See too Gruev, 190-191.

18. Ibid.

19. Anna Stancioff, unpublished letter to Nadejda, 2 October 1939, Nada XI, PASF.

20. Interview with Dimitri Stancioff, 5-7 August 2000, Camden, ME.

21. *Stirling Journal,* 21 July 1932, *Infirmary Awards.*

22. Nadejda Stancioff, unpublished letter to family, 22 September 1925, TsDIA F143K a.e. 19, l. 28b.

23. Ibid.

24. Ibid.

25. Ibid. Furthermore, Nadejda was proud of the fact and permitted herself to feel somewhat superior about the project when she turned the Encyclopedia editors down for a proposed article that would have been a dry political overview of Bulgaria and instead recommended Edward Boyle. She then had "the pleasure to tell Beatrice [Edward Boyle's wife] that I recommended *her husband.*"

26. Ibid. "I will work on it between hosting my guests! Mimi Tachet [the editor who solicited the article] wants is soon. I hope to get it to her in six days! We are in eternal correspondence!"

27. *The Scotsman* 1931.

28. Stancioff and Muir, *Recollections of a Bulgarian Diplomatist's Wife.*

29. *Observer,* 15 February 1931, *"Bulgaria Under King Ferdinand"* by Dr. G. P. Gooch Nada clipped the review, scribbled *Bravo* and sent the piece along to her Maman.

30. There exists a growing body of literature of female travelers. In the Balkans the most well known pair is MacKenzie and Irby who traveled, recorded, and published on their intrepid journeys. Clare Sheridan, Nadejda's friend, had traveled alone to exotic destinations that eventually seduced her into settling down; she lived for years near the desert in northern Africa. Gertrude Bell's travels were well known beyond Great Britain. See Melman, *Women's Orients, English Women and the Middle East, 1718-1918 : Sexuality, Religion, and Work.*

31. Nadejda Stancioff, unpublished journal, 10 February 1933, PASF.

32. Nadejda Stancioff, unpublished journal, 1 March 1927, PASF.

33. Ibid.

34. Muir, *Dimitri Stancioff Patriot and Cosmopolitan.*

35. Nadejda Stancioff, unpublished journal, 1 March 1927, PASF.

36. Nadejda Stancioff, unpublished journal, 9 March 1927, PASF.
37. Ibid.
38. Ibid.
39. Nadejda Stancioff, unpublished journal, 10 March 1927, PASF.
40. Ibid.
41. Nadejda Stancioff, unpublished journal, 25 April 1927, PASF.
42. Nadejda Stancioff, unpublished journal, 13 February 1933, PASF.
43. Nadejda Stancioff, 1937, PASF. Nadejda observed "an abundance of camels, bulls, sheep, lambs, children, and cabbages!"
44. Ibid..
45. Ibid..
46. Ibid. 23 January 1937.
47. Nadejda Stancioff, unpublished journal, 22 February 1933, PASF.
48. Ibid.
49. Ibid.
50. Nadejda Stancioff, unpublished journal, 11 February 1937, PASF.
51. Ibid. 7 February 1937.
52. Ibid. 10 February 1937.
53. Ibid. 7 February 1937.
54. Ibid.
55. Ibid. 17 February 1937.
56. Unpublished letter from British Broadcasting Corporation to Lady Muir, 7 January 1930. Nada XVII, PASF.
57. Listener, 20 May 1931 in The World and Ourselves series – VI, 858-859.
58. Edward Boyle, unpublished letter, 19 May 1931, BBC Talks File, PASF.
59. *Observer* 17 May 1931. See the *Programme* and the *Listener* on the same date.
60. Ibid.
61. Listener, 20 May 1931 in The World and Ourselves series – VI, 858.
62. Nadejda received glowing letters from ordinary listeners of her talks such as a housewife in Surrey who wrote to praise and bemoan the end of her series. "I arranged my work so that I could always have ¼ of an hour with *you*. I used to get out a good Atlas, enjoy a cup of coffee and sitting by the fireside I would travel round with you." Margaret A. Smith, unpublished letter, 18.12.33, BBC Talks File, *Through Three Continents* 1933, PASF.
63. National Radio, *The International Housewife*, 1933.
64. BBC, *Europe and Its Peoples*, 1935.
65. BBC, *Balkan States Lectures*
66. BBC, *Personalities I Have Met* 1937 and 1938.
67. Anna Stancioff, unpublished letter to Nadejda, 26 September 1938, Nada XI, PASF. She also wrote, of the continental political climate, "one can despair of the wisdom of humanity...where are we going? Is carnage decreed for the safety of the few millions of Czechs?"
68. BBC, *Empire Transmissions Series,* 1938.
69. Anna Stancioff, unpublished letter to Nadejda, 19378, Nada XI, PASF.
70. King Boris was grateful for the Stancioffs' efforts on his behalf. He corresponded with the entire family; his communications were typed or sometimes, hand written by him personally. He sent thank you cards and letters, photos he had taken during his visits with the Muirs, and tokens of his affection. See RH, PASF.

71. "A Bulgarian Hostess" 31 August 1931 in *Portsmouth Evening News*. In the article Nadejda is identified as an "ideal hostess with the gifts of tact and charm." The *Evening Standard*, on the same date, headlined the article as "Hostess to a King."

72. Nadejda Stancioff Muir, unpublished letter, date unclear – 1930s, TsDIA, F 143K, 9, 30 October 1936.

73. Nadejda Stancioff, unpublished letter, 22 October 1934, TsDIA F143, ae l 100.

74. Ibid. l 54.

75. Nadejda Stancioff, unpublished letter, 1936 (no date), DSF, PASF.

76. Nadejda Stancioff, unpublished letter, 1937 (no date), Nada XI, PASF.

77. Feo Stancioff, unpublished letter, 2 June 1928, Feo IV, PASF.

78. She does not specify but I believe she meant the soldiers would forestall any internal coup by Bolshevik sympathizers.

79. Feo Stancioff, unpublished letter, 23 July 1928, Feo IV, PASF.

80. Feo Stancioff, unpublished letter, 12 August 1928, Feo IV, PASF.

81. King Boris III, unpublished letter, 26 December 1937, RH II, PASF. "The arrival of Simeon...caused an immense and unanimous enthusiasm in the entire country...your parents are well."

82. Anna Stancioff, unpublished letter to Nadejda, 4 November 1938, Nada XI, PASF.

83. Dimitri Stancioff, unpublished letter to Nadejda, 4 November 1938, Nada XI, PASF.

84. Feodora Stancioff, unpublished letter to Nadejda, 18 October 1939, Nada XI, PASF.

85. Dimitri Stancioff, unpublished letter to Felix Guepin, 27 October 1937, DS? PASF.

86. Nadejda Stancioff, unpublished letter to family, 5 May 1925, TsDIA F 143K a.e. 19 l. 23. "I have sent it to M. Bell, asking him to publish it this Thursday, I hope this pleases you...

87. Nadejda Stancioff, unpublished letter to family, (no day) June 1926, TsDIA F 143K ae 19 l 55.

88. Nadejda Stancioff, unpublished letter to family, 21 September 1922, Nada II, PASF. From Lausanne, Nada refered them to recent positive articles in the *Sunday Times* and *Daily Mail* and encouraged her family to "work the press" and to "make friends work too."

89. Nadejda Stancioff, unpublished letter to family, 21 June 1928, TsDIA F 143K ae 19 l 982? (unclear). "Rosita Forbes is coming to Bulgaria September 15 with husband. She is traveling for the *Observer* and several other newspapers, and he is on a mission from the *War Office*. She has been quite celebrated here [in Great Britain] for some time, and he is important ...I will give her letters [of introduction] for the Princess...Helene; Ivan, Marion, Mme. Liaptcheff; ...in my opinion it is essential that she spend two days with you before her husband [is there]. *Much* more important and above all much *more interesting than Sam Green* [a reporter]!"

90. Nadejda Stancioff, unpublished letter to family, 28 August 1939, Nada XVII, PASF. Nadejda wrote to a friend, on the eve of the invasion of Poland, that she remained hopeful but [finally] understood that Hitler was not a "normal man." She asked her friend to explain to other influential people what Bulgaria's foreign policy position really was. "...what I am telling you is absolutely the truth....I don't want you to think that Bulgaria is pro-German."

91. Nadejda Stancioff, unpublished letter, (date unclear, she mentions King Edward's divorce), TsDIA F 143, l 60.

92. Ibid.

93. Nadejda Stancioff, unpublished letter, 31 Aug 1936, TsDIA F143 ae l73.

94. Ibid.

95. Nadejda Stancioff, unpublished letter, October 1940, Nada XII, PASF.

96. Dimitri Stancioff, unpublished letter to Nadejda 17 June year unknown, possibly mid-1930s, Nada X, PASF.

97. Ibid.

98. Nadejda Stancioff, address "Foreign Affairs Made Homely" National Council of Women, 1938, PASF.

99. *Bulletin and Scots Pictorial* 11 January 1938.

100. Nadejda Stancioff, unpublished letter, January no date 1936, TsDIA F143 l 61-62.

101. Nadejda Stancioff, unpublished letter, 31 August 1936, TsDIA F143 l 44.

102. *Near East* 31 January 1924. Over the course of the next decades Nadejda Stancioff Muir addressed the following organizations: the British Institute of International Affairs, the Near East Association at the Royal Empire Society, the League of Nations Union, the National Council of Women, the Balkan Committee, the Overseas League Club, the Danube Literary Society, she also spoke at the University of St. Andrews. This is not an exhaustive list.

103. *Journal of the Royal Institute of International Affairs* March 1927 Vol VI no.2, pp.88-104.

104. Her first talk covered Bulgarian history from the liberation in 1878 to 1887. One month later Lady Muir presented a talk from the beginning of the reign of Prince Ferdinand to the Balkan Wars.

105. *Near East and India*, 9 February 1928, 169-70.

106. The *Vote* 15 July 1932 *Women and Diplomacy.*

107. The *Vote*, 22 May 1931 Women and Diplomacy, 11.

108. Ibid.

109. Ibid.

110. *Bulletin* 15 July 1932.

111. *Dundee Record and Mail* 27 June 1932 *Conference of British Soroptimists.*

112. The society was organized in order to build a Hostel for International Students near Oxford.

113. Nadejda Stancioff, address, "Women in Diplomacy" for Foxcombe Hall Appeal fundraiser, May 1931, PASF.

114. Ibid.

115. Talk to Overseas League Club in 1932 "Some Views on the Problem of Disarmament," 11 pages.

116. Ibid., 2.

117. Ibid.

118. Talk to British Institute of International Affairs 1934 "Bulgaria and the Balkan Pact."

119. *Bulletin and Scots Pictorial* 25 November 1937, attached to BBC Talks file, PASF.

120. *Evening Standard* 2 May 1936.

121. Ibid.

122. *Bulletin and Scots Pictorial* 11 January 1938.

123. Talk to National Council of Women, Stirling Branch,1938 "Foreign Affairs Made Homely"

124. Ibid.

125. Ibid.

126. The following newspapers published all or parts of her talk: *Stirling Journal, The Glasgow Herald, the Glasgow Weekly Herald, The Scotsman, Dundee Courier & Advertiser, Liverpool Daily Post, Edinburgh Evening News, Daily Record and Mail.*

127. *Scotsman* 1938.

128. Ibid.

129. Ibid.

130. *Scotsman*, 14 January 1938.

131. *Edinburgh Evening News*

132. *Daily Record, Dundee Courier,* and *Advertiser Glasgow Herald.*

133. *Stirling Journal*

134. Ibid.

135. *Dundee Courier & Advertiser*

136. Ibid.

137. *Scotsman*

138. *Liverpool Daily Post*

139. Nadejda Stancioff, unpublished letters, Nada X, PASF.

140. Duchess Atholl, unpublished letter, Nada X, PASF.

141. Ibid.

142. Nadejda Stancioff, unpublished letter, 30 September 1936, TsDIA, F143 l45.

143. Ibid.

144. Ibid.

145. Dimitri Stancioff, unpublished letter to Nadejda, 24 September 1938, Nada XI, PASF.

146. Anna Stancioff, unpublished letter to Nadejda, 14 October 1939, Nada XI, PASF.

147. Anna Stancioff, unpublished letter to Nadejda, 24 September 1938, Nada XI, PASF.

148. Dimitri Stancioff, unpublished letter to Nadejda, 18 March 1939, Nada XI, PASF.

149. Anna Stancioff, unpublished letter to Nadejda, 24 September 1939, Nada XI, PASF.

150. Anna Stancioff, unpublished letter to Nadejda, 14 December 1939, Nada XI, PASF.

9

The End of an Era

"The Stancioffs have always loved each other too much but that has been forced on them by their lives."
Ivan Stancioff, unpublished letter [1]

The peace of 1919, in part, along with the economic and social changes which emerged after the peace, laid the groundwork for World War II.[2] While Europeans fixed their sights on the past as an ideal, the environment of the continent was in transition. A vague sense of grievances and mistrust, of wrongs unjustified, and of lost opportunities among great and lesser states replaced the Great Power relationships which had previously defined so much of inter-state communications.

Conditions for War, 1939–1940

As Europe attempted to find its balance, powerful ideologies grew and prospered. These ideologies ultimately pulled Europe into a state of imbalance and heightened malaise. Totalitarianism, (bolshevism and fascism) arose virtually unchallenged within a Europe overwrought by guilt, loss, and a desire for revenge. Smaller states attempted to find Great Power patronage, hence protection, as they had come to expect it, but found instead powers eager to first secure their own interests before considering another's. In sum, systems of alliances were hardly dependable, and a general sense of defenselessness, in the face of rising aggressive states, pervaded the continent.

After Hitler's rise Chancellor of Germany in 1933, the pace of change quickened through out the continent. Change rippled in Germany as the Nazi party consolidated control and executed its increasingly demanding policies. Change coursed through the rest of Europe as well, either in the form of demands for territorial revisions or in the development of defensive postures. Power relationships and alliances were formed based on one-dimensional goals. Public discourse led governments to consider increasingly extreme options for domestic change.

The rapid evolution of major international developments of the late 1930s— the Anschluss, the Munich accords, and the rise in persecutions based on race in Nazi Germany—all led to the one final act of aggression that triggered general war: the invasion of Poland on September 1, 1939.

Since the war gravitated first to the east toward Poland and later to the west, France, Britain, and the southern tier of Europe remained relatively unscathed at the outset of the war. However, the Nazis' blazing successes left no doubt about their ability to pose a threat to the entire continent. War, invasion, death, and destruction were simply a matter of time.

Bulgaria's Triumphs

Bulgarian foreign policy had a few modest triumphs in the 1930s. It appeared that King Boris' frequent visits abroad would bear fruit. Late in the decade, the territorial revisions Bulgarians had anticipated seemed near completion. In October 1939 Maman reported to Nadejda that "the king enjoys his prestige and his successes; we place our hope in the revision of unjust treaties."[3]

The hope was that Dobrudja, with its Bulgarian population, would finally be returned to Bulgaria. However, no territorial changes came free and clear in an increasingly intricate international climate, and King Boris felt the weight of the complex situation.

As Maman observed and reported to Nadejda and Kay in Scotland, the king, "appear[ed] . . . preoccupied," [and she] . . . suppose[d] that his political horizons . . . [were] not restful." In the same letter Maman also commented on the prevailing political environment in the Balkans, where the Romanians enjoyed growing prestige. She wrote, "King Carol [r.1930-1940] is hailed as a big deal politician by the papers [because] he focuses on [his use of the seduction of his trading partners] oil and wheat."[4] As King Boris continued to visit the both Stancioff families on a regular basis, they could keep a watchful eye on his moods. Despite the king's discretion regarding issues of state, the Stancioffs accurately gauged the political climate based on his general demeanor and willingness to engage in pleasantries. Years with the royal family had given the Stancioffs opportunity to study their characters, royal family members' personal habits and peculiarities.

Stancioffs Fear Disaster

As diplomats, the Stancioffs understood the dangers inherent in the situation between the fascists and the rest of Europe as it evolved from broken promises to a shooting war. Among the lessons they had gleaned from years of diplomatic experience was that larger powers, with more military power to enforce their own foreign policies, would inevitably jostle the small powers. Geographic realities such as proximity to important bodies of water or other geo-politically important sites, or national borders could be the blueprints for good fortune or an appalling fate.

For Bulgaria, neutrality was the only option. Keeping the country out of the melee was the most prudent course. However, neutrality could be maintained only as long as the powers at war fought at a safe distance. The geopolitical realities soon changed the choices for Bulgarian, which had no genuine local friends and no substantive support from the Allied Great Powers.

France had worked to bolster her national security to the detriment of the defensive alliance system of her own creation, the Little Entente (Czechoslovakia, Romania, and Yugoslavia) plus Poland. In 1936, the Franco-Russian rapprochement caused consternation among the French. Uncle Robert de Grenaud commented to his sister in Bulgaria when he wrote her a letter full of distress. He called the move monstrous, "[it] alienates us from all the nations who still have their wits about them. . . . France will only have the province of Monaco as an ally since I am convinced that Poland, Romania, and Yugoslavia will also turn to Germany for which Czechoslovakia will become a large province!"[5] The outraged Frenchman showed uncanny vision; Uncle Robert was prescient about the fate of Central Europe.

In Bulgaria, the rapid Nazi advances limited the country's options. As the German armies advanced and appeared unstoppable the prospects for remaining out of a continental war diminished. For Bulgaria, the year, 1939, was one of constant badgering by the Italians, the Russians, the Nazis, and the Allies, all attempting to entice the king with attractive territorial and alliance offers each of which he rejected, keeping neutral.

Last Interview with King Boris

Nadejda traveled back to Bulgaria in the period labeled "Britain's phony war" (September 1939–April 1940). This arrested period of declared war with no substantive military action created an inflated sense of fortitude among Britain's citizens. Although war preparations proceeded—the building of air-raid shelters, the sandbagging of buildings, and the evacuation of children—the immediacy of war had not yet visited British shores.

In January 1940, Nadejda traveled to Bulgaria via train across the continent. Shortly after arriving in Sofia, Nadejda assumed her broadcasting activities. On January 31, 1940, she gave an evening address, via Radio Sofia, entitled "From London to Sofia." She spoke of her observations and experiences in London shortly before she left, She then discussed what it was like to traverse Europe in wartime. Nadejda reported to Bulgaria that she saw "more uniforms in the streets but no apparent reduction of traffic," and that "[p]eople . . . [were] gradually returning to the town after the first days of hurried evacuation."[6]

She drew her Bulgarian listeners into the greater radio listener community of the BBC. Lady Muir praised Bulgarian radio, in her friendly transmission, with a message from their Bulgaria's British counterparts in London. Her broadcast assured Bulgarians that the British listening public and the British Broadcasting Corporation (BBC) held "very favorable impressions of the Bulgarian Radio Service and a particular appreciation of the musical programs." Also, she "was asked [in London] to give a cordial salutation to the Bulgarian Radio from the British!" Nadejda confided to her Bulgarian audience.[7]

The Bulgarian press published her radio address and those who missed the radio transmission could read it.[8] She described life in London and Paris. The City of Light was still lively, piles of sandbags were heaped around monuments, and the population had become accustomed to rationing and meatless days.

Nadejda presented a complete and engaging overview of her travels, her impressions, and her experiences of all the countries she traversed. She included a report on train travel and meals as well as the general mood in the streets. She even reported her first impression of the population of Sofia. Since her protracted absence, the denizens of the city appeared "satisfied, happy, and full of joie de vivre."[9] She concluded with an uplifting message about the economic and industrial progress she noticed in her native land. Nadejda referred to Bulgaria as "our beautiful motherland" and pronounced her hope that, with God's help, hardworking Bulgarians would remain in peace and tranquility, a state she knew Bulgarians valued above all.[10]

During her visit to Bulgaria in January 1940, Nadejda encountered at firsthand the kind of German pressure that pro-Nazi elements already exerted in the country. The pro-Nazi forces used her broadcast on Sofia radio to justify their bid for a similar program—an address by a German woman who had recently traveled from Berlin to Sofia. Sofia Radio turned down that request on the grounds that Lady Muir was a former Bulgarian citizen and thus had some affinity for her listeners and they to her.

In Sofia, Nadejda also had what would be a last meeting with King Boris III. They met alone and spoke late into the night. She reconstructed the conversation, from a hastily jotted shorthand version of the original interview when she left him. The following is a partial transcription of her notes:

He[King Boris]: ...you could have stayed here for a few more weeks. After April, it will not be so easy.
Me [Nadejda]: ?[response not recorded]
He: No, I know nothing specific; but a declared war must begin one day!
Me: ?
He: I have been the messenger for Bulgaria since my first trip in 1927. Beyond my frontiers, they were all amiable but non-committal! I feel I have done my duty to the best of my ability . . . the intra-Balkan rapprochement has been successful to a certain degree [the Salonika accord and the Pact of Friend-

ship with the Serbs] but France and England preferred to "Carolize" because of oil! I do not owe anything to the Allies. Perhaps they have positioned themselves not to owe me anything! However, theirs is the cause of good; it is a ray of light, the other is darkness. The power of Shadows and the Twilight of the Gods! I prefer the light. . . .

If you told the Allies that Carol [King of Romania] has deceived them since mid-October, they would not believe you.

I will remain neutral . . . but I am powerless like a caterpillar under the foot of an elephant—an English or a German elephant.

Me: May God preserve you.

He: Yes, no one else can help me. I am alone.[11]

King Boris felt isolated and helpless; he had few options, and his country was facing unbearable pressure to relent to the demands of one or another warring block.

Death in the Family

That visit to Bulgaria in January 1940 was also to be her last contact with her beloved father. In February he fell and suffered a fracture, that caused him to be bedridden. A few short weeks later he expired. The terrible news of her father's death was a hard blow to his eldest daughter. She could not forgive herself for having returning home to Scotland when she did and she sent agitated messages of regret and remorse to her family in a number of subsequent letters. She was devastated and could not reconcile herself to the idea that she would never see him again. Recalling her father, Nadejda writes:

Oh, how he spoiled me, always. I told myself several times that once married to this love, to another unique man, I would no longer have enough . . . for Papa. I hope he never thought that; that he knew that he was always the First . . . In life, it seems to me that I belonged only to him.[12]

Her faith guided her to find a place of peace soon after his death. Nadejda began to write to her family and to believe that she could see God's plan for their father: that God would not have wished to keep him longer in a world that would quickly disintegrate and destroy all that he held dear: institutions, traditions, cities, and the millions of people who would die in the war.

Dimitri Stancioff's funeral was a state affair. As a former prime minister and minister of foreign affairs, he country honored him one last time. King Ferdinand remembered him from exile when he wrote a touching letter of condolence to Anna on May 6, 1940. Ferdinand was eloquent in his praise as he had been eloquent in his vitriol. He described Dimitri as "one whose patriotism was so warm, so wisely precocious."[13]

Nadejda had spent an all-too-brief visit to Bulgaria in January. Early in February of 1940 she returned home to Scotland after only a few weeks' stay with her family. In her own inimitable way, she kept in touch with her loved ones left in Bulgaria by writing detailed accounts about everything she saw and experienced as she traveled back to Britain and her husband.

The Trip Back to London

On her journey home through warring Europe, Nadejda wrote descriptions of her stop in Paris and her trip to London.[14] Paris was not quite marching to a martial beat but felt tense and full of people: there were few comforts. The city occasionally still managed to appear its usual gay, beautiful, albeit dirty self, however. The old city center, the Louvre, the Champs Elysée, the Opera, and Place de la Concorde appeared quaint. Signs of Anglo-French solidarity were everywhere with tricolor ribbons, oriflammes (flags), the Union Jack, wreaths, and standards. The façade of Paris appeared so reassuring.

Her train trip to Calais was rough; the train was not lighted, and she used a flashlight to read Harold Nicolson's book *Peacemaking* comprised of his recollections of the Paris peace conference of 1919, which she, too had witnessed, although from an entirely different perspective. Nadejda noted that the book was "infuriating at times but often quite good!" and that the book was "quite a fear programme for the future after *his own* absurd past!"[15] Her other reading option was the report of the last British ambassador to Warsaw; she judged the report pathetic.

In Calais, she was further inconvenienced by having to spend hours in a waiting room, since there were no hotel rooms to be had. She slept fully dressed, on a bench in the room, which, although heated and lighted, was crammed with luggage, packages, skis, golf clubs, and a few guns. In a letter to her family in Bulgaria, Nadejda described her discomfort as "an experience that presages perhaps the communal future that is in store for Europe."[16]

She wrote to her family of her next plan of attack regarding pro-Bulgarian propaganda to cultivate Lloyd George and the BBC, presumably to aid Bulgaria.[17] Nadejda was tireless and single-minded in her pursuit of supporting Bulgaria before the British general public and presented her homeland in the best possible light to her radio and print media audiences.

The War Intensifies

By 1940, the war on the continent prompted Nadejda to redouble her efforts in Great Britain. She gave interviews and wrote articles to draw attention to the idea that Bulgaria was completely on the side of sane neutrality and that her king was a dependable democrat. Her campaign to make King Boris appear a man Britons could trust prompted her to give talks and interviews that presented her as a friend and a "counselor" to the Bulgarian king and, therefore, a reliable source. She did what she could to keep up the perception of Bulgaria among the Foreign Office establishment as a cool-headed and unflinching member of the community of nations that would not be swayed by "blandishments of the Hun."[18]

Her stature as a broadcast personality became so considerable that the Joint Broadcasting Committee approached her about preparing programs in English for broadcast to Sofia in 1940. Therefore, in addition to her broadcast in Sofia to

Bulgarian audiences she took on a new task. Nadejda Muir prepared broadcasts in Bulgarian for distribution in Bulgaria. The first two broadcasts had the following titles: *British Courage in the Hour of Danger* and *The Ordinary People of Britain*.[19] What was the intent of those broadcasts at a time when Europe was well into a general war? Were they a gentle reminder to Bulgarians that Britain was the side to join should Bulgaria choose to shed her neutrality? For example, Nadejda's broadcasts discussed conditions in Britain, such as the introduction of rationing. She commented that

> soon we shall all be getting our ration tickets, but we can register with any shop we like. . . . the English are—as a nation—so methodical and thorough. They do not—like the Slavs—enjoy improvisation or anything they are not quite used to . . . This explains perhaps the unity and spirit of cooperation of the empire. They [the English] certainly do not like innovations of any sort.[20]

Was this a way to preserve some sense of community among like-thinking, like-feeling ordinary citizens, Britons and Bulgarians, all coping with the radical changes in daily life in wartime just on different sides of the same continent? She also spoke on the issue of evacuees and the logistics of housing them:

> In Bulgaria, you are familiar with refugee questions and you will all remember how once when the housing problem was acute—Bulgarian families were compelled by a law, of the Agrarian Government then in power, to take in strangers, for a certain time, under their roof. The British public had never been faced with such happenings before . . . the people in Britain have assisted the governmental authorities to make the evacuation of over 3 million children, thousands of mothers, invalids and infants, a success. After the first excitement dies down – you know the Bulgarian proverb, "no sensation ever lasts more than two days" [vsiako chudo za dva dena; Nadejda misspoke; the expression is three days] there were many adjustments to be made between the hosts and the guests.[21]

From London, under the guise of answering her Bulgarian correspondents, Lady Muir addressed the issues that would affect most civilian citizens' lives: ration cards, air-raid shelters, and conditions of the blackout regiment. She answered questions about Britain's royal family and their activities in wartime. At least some of these letters from her so-called correspondents were actually a creative way to introduce subjects she and the producers believed important. Two of her "correspondents'" names were those of her siblings, however, and at least one other name was that of a family friend. Above all, the tone of her broadcasts was of cool, competent Britain managing, once more, to deal with adversity and not be cowed. Once the Luftwaffe began to bomb London and other targets, that attitude changed.

Pressure Comes to Bear on Bulgaria

King Boris was keenly aware of the pressures accumulating with each passing week. His revelations to Nadejda in January 1940 were searingly accurate. Pressure, for Bulgaria to join one or another warring block, was applied in many forms on the king. In February, the Balkan entente (Greece, Romania, Turkey, and Yugoslavia had signed the agreement in 1934) finally extended an offer for Bulgaria to join, but by that point, joining would have meant committing the country to the Allied side and immediate participation in the war.

Germany's alliance with the Soviets did force King Boris to accept a commercial treaty with the Russians in 1940. By May 1940, the dramatic German victories in Europe and the rest of the world made it difficult for Bulgaria to maintain neutrality. As Italy's forces mired in their bid to capture Greece, Germany's response of sending troops to the Italians' aid, via a direct line through Romania and Bulgaria, quickened the pressure on the Balkan states to cooperate with the Axis.

German pressure ultimately redesigned Romania's borders with the Treaty of Kriaova, which in September 1940 finally returned to Bulgaria the Southern Dobrudja, a territory with a majority Bulgarian population. Remarkably, despite Germany's role in helping to restore the region, Bulgaria still maintained her neutrality.

The Bulgarian outlook on its own prospects was increasingly grim by the end of 1940, since the situation across the continent was progressively more alarming. With thousands already dead or wounded, European destruction occurred on an unimaginable scale. Maman was shocked when she wrote to her daughter what millions across the world must have thought, "Science has become just a machine perfected for the most total destruction."[22] Demagogues in political power could use mass movements first to control and then to crush people. The Stancioffs voiced, with Maman's letter to Nadejda, a universal thought, "We have but to pray! To hope!"[23]

The Stancioffs had to acknowledge that the world that they had once understood, a world in which the ideas of honor and human dignity seemed to prevail, was vanishing. Maman commented in a letter to Nadejda, "While Francis I once said: all is lost but honor one could say today that all is gained without honor."[24] Nonetheless, Nadejda did not lose heart and continued to write editorials for public consumption and letters to private individuals about Bulgaria's position and perspectives on the war.[25] Her brother too voiced cautious optimism.

Ivan's career changed with the course of Bulgarian diplomacy, as the war affected the southern tier of Europe and spread to the Balkans. Between 1937 and 1941, Ivan worked at the Ministry of Foreign Affairs in Sofia. His older sons went to school, initially to the French College in Plovdiv, just as Ivan had done years earlier. Later, when the French College transformed into a field hospital for the German Greek campaign, the eldest boys, Dimitri and Ivan, went to the Kniazhevo French College instead.

As late as fall 1939, Ivan had believed that Bulgaria could maintain her neutrality. In a letter he wrote to his sister in Scotland, he insisted that neutrality was possible as long as no enemy invaded from without.[26] By 1940, he too had to acknowledge that it was only a matter of time before Bulgaria was drawn into the continental war.

Bulgaria Joins the Axis Powers

At the outbreak of World War II, Bulgaria was in an untenable situation—neither a friend to the Nazis' nor a sympathizer with the Soviets. Although the country had improved its economic situation, and ordinary people fared better, in foreign policy, her government still faltered.

What the Stancioffs had feared, and what King Boris had perceived as the reticence of his peers to accept his overtures in the interwar period, came to be. Bulgaria was friendless and held at a distance by potential allies. Once more, an unfortunate geographic location—in close proximity to Constantinople and the Straits—coupled with historic prejudice, placed the Bulgarians in an untenable position. As the Nazis advanced across Europe, there was no recourse but to give in to the pressure which a victorious, powerful juggernaut exerted. Promising his people to maintain neutrality at all costs, King Boris was aware that this position was contingent on factors beyond his control.

Throughout 1940, Bulgaria's monarchy rebuffed several attractive offers from both the western Allies and Nazi-allied states. Each offer was appealing, in and of itself. However, accepting any offer laid the fate of Bulgaria in the hands of a belligerent bloc of states and, therefore, put the country in harm's way. The king's prime minister pressured the king to accede to the Nazis. Internal pro-Nazi groups ratcheted up their demands for Bulgaria's inclusion in the Axis, but the king remained steadfast and refused to commit the country to war.

In October 1940, the Muirs received word from King Boris while they entertained British generals at Blair Drummond. Nadejda reported to her family, "Soden telegraphed me with some touching words and gave me the latest news of you all . . . since then however the clouds are gathering once again over the . . . orient."[27]

As German military gains became increasingly dramatic, the Bulgarians' ability to negotiate neutral status diminished proportionately. Nadejda worked feverishly in February 1941 to keep Bulgaria's point of view in the public eye in Britain. She sent a multitude of letters to the influential members of the Balkan Committee, Lord Newton, and Teddy Boyle, feeding them information she extracted from the Bulgarian legation in London.[28] The West made one last attempt to lure Bulgaria to their side, until Bulgaria joined the Axis powers in spring 1941. By then, the luxury of choice was a chimera.

When Bulgaria joined the Axis powers early in March 1941, the one obvious benefit was that the alliance allowed the incorporation of Macedonian and Thracian territories held dear in the Bulgarian nationalists' breast. Once their lot was thrown in with the Nazi-led Axis powers, the country's future became entwined with the Germans' successes and failures.

By May 1941, German invasions of Yugoslavia and Greece were largely successful. The invasion of the Soviet Union by Nazi Germany in June 1941 spread the war in Europe farther a field. The fascist armies were victorious, and the map of Europe was figuratively and literally littered with the triumphant

German standard. The Allies, meanwhile, found themselves increasingly on the defensive and losing even modest toeholds on the continent.

Bulgaria did manage to salvage some of its dignity as an independent state by refusing to commit Bulgarian troops to fight on the Russian front. In fact, Bulgarian troops were primarily kept busy occupying Thrace and Macedonia. The king even refused to send Bulgarian pilots to bomb Russians.[29]

The monarchy also deserves credit for maintaining some national dignity by withstanding Nazi pressure to exterminate Bulgaria's Jewish population. That victory was an affirmative moment in the country's history as well as a noble accomplishment for her monarch.

War years brought privation to Bulgaria's civilian population and eventually bombardments by Allied air forces. The end of the war was an even more bitter dénouement. The Red Army invaded Bulgaria in September 1944, even though Bulgaria had steadfastly resisted sending troops to the Russian front. As a country that had sought to join defensive alliances throughout the interwar period, Bulgaria suffered a catastrophic defeat in 1944. A state that had resisted involvement in the war, at the outset and for a remarkably long time afterward, Bulgaria was sucked into the vortex of the conflagration.

Furthermore, Bulgaria's geographic position sealed the country's fate long before the end of the war. Bulgaria's people faced a future they could not have imagined during the war, since no postwar world in living memory had ever been as radically reshaped as Europe in the 1940s. As Nadejda wrote to a friend on September 14 1944,

> it does not really matter now what any of us say, think, or write; for the future of the Balkan Peninsula is in the hands of Russia . . . some day we shall know the truth [about what motivated Bulgarian foreign policy in the critical period leading up to and during the war until she gave up neutrality.][30]

War Years at Blair Drummond

During the war years, Nadejda and Kay remained at Blair Drummond. They were comfortable and lived off the estate's produce with a reduced domestic staff. The manor house was converted into Blair Drummond Auxiliary Hospital, and well into 1946, the temporary facility housed patients. The hospital had seventy beds, forty of which were occupied by wounded soldiers in 1940. A small staff of efficient nurses ran the hospital. Despite the rearrangement of their living space, the Muirs were not terribly put out, as they did not have to be on fuel rations, since the hospital had priority.[31]

The entire hospital ran smoothly, except for the necessary red tape, which required that Nadejda be responsible for some accounting of expenses. At roughly the same time, Nadejda was president of the Scottish Red Cross and contributed, through her work with that organization, toward the war effort as well.

While war raged on the continent, Nadejda, an unstoppable Bulgarian patriot, persisted in using every opportunity to campaign for her homeland and her former playmate, the king. In a letter to Ivan and Marion, she reminded them of her efforts by writing "We [Nadejda and Kay] do our best to add a few drops of water to the most useful glasses!! . . . I work as best I can and where I can."[32]

Nadejda reported to her brother, in a letter written in 1940, what she understood of the British domestic mood. She observed that

> the British people—individuals—show wonderful courage, strength, and determination. As usual, they will get what they want with time . . . One wonders how all this happened. You and I, dear Ivan, know the answer only too well. And so far so good, but times change from hour to hour! I love you all and please des letters, des letters, and des letters![33]

By March, in her next letter to Ivan, Nadejda bemoaned the drop in the value of the pound. But something much more alarming for Nadejda was the precipitous drop of traditions and privileges "that took centuries to build up."[34] The rapid changes Nadejda noticed in social convention sped along even faster than those that alarmed the Stancioffs on heels of the previous war.

A visit to London in May 1940 left the Muirs with an impression of a country proceeding with business as usual; the stores were full of goods, pre-war normality seemed to reign, at least in shop windows, and prices were not unusually high.

Nadejda continued to work with the BBC on radio broadcasts, but the climate was decidedly a suspicious one regarding King Boris III and his foreign policy goals. The good news from that trip was that a private visit with the Bulgarian minister to London encouraged her to believe that Ivan might be assigned to work in London. She wrote:

> Ivan may be named to London according to Momtchilov. Poor London attacked day and night; but all continues [as usual] and the nightclubs have special programs during the raids . . . The servants send you their greetings . . . spirit excellent, even jovial, I would say![35]

The family was hopeful for the potential appointment but perhaps somewhat perplexed by the British cheerful attitude of survival at all costs. They shared impressions of the European situation, and the prospects were decidedly foreboding.

The year 1940 was a turbulent one, not only because of the capitulation of France but also because the war against the French underscored that the Nazis were bent on dominating the continent. From Scotland, the Muirs were concerned for the future, victory was uncertain for the western allies. Even if victory came what kind of a future. Victory was uncertain for the western Allies. Even if victory came, what kind of a future would, it be? Kay seemed to believe that the Communists would be triumphant and that his world would irretrievably vanish. With centuries of traditions wiped away, he foresaw only ugliness to come, even though he believed, as Nadejda related to her family in Bulgaria, "that Wagner is a colossus with feet of clay," and that the Allies would ultimately triumph.[36]

Life continued relatively serenely for most Britons. The German Blitz campaign failed to destroy its military targets and instead fueled a feeling of invincibility and even superiority among the British who viewed themselves and their island as once again separate from continental Europe.

When rationing became ordinary, when acquiring of everyday goods like food, fuel, and clothing became a daily challenge, the British public seemed steeled to face the worst the enemy could employ against them. They were determined not to buckle under the strain.

The Stancioff family continued to support each other as best they could. The most difficult factor militating against day-to-day security was the rapid devaluation of national currencies. For the Bulgarian family branch of the Stancioffs, the situation rapidly became dire. Cut off from their French investments, and desperate to supplement their Bulgarian incomes with hard currency, the Bulgarian Stancioffs had to rely on their British, and ultimately their American branches of the family.

First, the Muirs helped from Great Britain. Nadejda wrote Feo and Maman, saying:

> Don't worry about finances, if you need to borrow in Bulgaria . . . we will pay
> it later with shares or I will pay it . . . I hope later to help Ivan pay for the education of his children as long as the Hare[Kay] will not be forced to reduce my
> salad; and the quid lowers in value! [37]

Later when the pound began to quiver and deflate, when the British government forbade sending money abroad the Stancioffs created another plan. Chou would infuse the Bulgarian Stancioffs with cash from the United States, and Nadejda would send money abroad via her youngest sister. Nadejda would continue her primary role as caretaker of the family, but now she would transfer some of the duty over to Chou, so "the stiff stuff," the American dollar, would be sent to Bulgaria. "Her [Chou's] brand [of currency] . . . will suit you better anyhow," Nadejda assured her family.[38] The Stancioffs managed to survive.

At Home in Bulgaria

When Maman and Feo were alone in Bulgaria during the war, their lives were, along with their compatriots, focused on day-to-day survival and amassing life's necessities. Food, shelter, and fuel came first. Their roots in Varna helped them circumvent some discomforts. Their friends and acquaintances, former employees, or the tradesmen who had been regular suppliers of services and goods before the war considered them another sort of "quality." The Stancioff custom of making everyone with whom they came in contact comfortable and feel as though they were in the presence of an equal paid dividends during those stressful, uncertain times. The family's innate populism put them in a separate category from their elite peers.

Feodora Stancioff had become something of celebrity among the lower brow and could carry on lengthy theoretical discussions with avowed communists about the state of inequality in the world. She maintained contacts with a wide variety of people and did not remain attached exclusively to her social equals.

Whether because of a sense of populism, or because she had chosen to remain single, she cultivated all sorts of people. She had no spouse to impose any restrictions on her interactions with others. With her wide array of acquaintances, she could tap into the changes in wartime Bulgarian society. In conversations with her mechanic and tradesmen friends, between drags of shared cigarettes and strong coffee, Feo and Bulgarian communists dissected the state of the world and the possible scenarios that the future might hold. These tête-à-têtes left an impression.

She recorded that at least on one occasion that a Bulgarian communist in Varna assured her that "come the revolution," she and her family would be spared because they were a different sort than the rest of the elites. He said, "Do not worry, if we come to power one day: we will take care of you; some of the "others" will pay."[39] The Stancioffs were acceptable and would not be molested by the change over of power from the dictatorship of the capitalists to the dictatorship of the proletariat.

In fact, her car mechanic revealed that he had already planned how the family would be useful to the new regime. He said that her brother would be made mayor of the town and that they the Stancioffs could keep their home; it would not be converted to a communal property. The king, he said, could also keep his palace, since the mechanic, although a communist, considered the king to be "a good friend of the people."[40]

During that downward economic spiral of wartime marked by skyrocketing unemployment, economic collapse, and the rationing or unavailability of basic needs, communists had gained a great deal of support for their beliefs. These wartime stressors would eventually lead to a complete break down in the political and economic order of the country.

After Bulgaria joined the Axis powers, Ivan's position in the diplomatic corps was somewhat precarious. His family ties did not inspire trust in Bulgaria's new Nazi partners. His wife was American, his mother French, one sister was in England married to a British citizen, and his father had famously resigned his position rather than be associated with a government that allied itself with Germany during the Great War. In many respects, Ivan's motivations and allegiance were suspect in a Nazi-allied Bulgarian state.

One of Ivan's last assignments in Bulgaria proper occurred after he and his superior and friend, Ilia Belinoff, witnessed the Russian and German exchange of diplomats once the two countries were at war. Ivan was assistant to the chief of protocol, and Ilia was chief of protocol at Svilengrad, Bulgaria, that summer of 1941.

After work at the ministry of foreign affairs in Sofia, Ivan's new assignment in June 1942 was to Galatz, Romania, a few hours east from Bucharest. He was dismayed with the appointment, but King Boris was personally responsible for his post and assured him that he was doing what was in Ivan's long-term best interest.[41]

Ivan's posting to Galatz proved to be a boon for him personally, despite the disappointment of not being able to reprise his father's former post in London or some other prestigious capital. His deployment to a virtual war zone also negated the possibility of having his family join him.

He spent the remaining years of his service helping Bulgarian expatriates in Bessarabia with visas and material assistance as necessary. There were approximately 300,000 Bulgarians in Galatz at that time, and Ivan Stancioff headed the office seeing to their needs in wartime.[42] His accommodations, rudimentary and even primitive, made working and living conditions a trial. Ivan amused himself by reading Ovid's *Dacian Exile* and commiserated with the Roman who once looked out upon the same terrain, centuries earlier.

While being in Galatz from 1942 to 1944 removed him from a position in which he might have influenced state policy in Bulgaria, Ivan's post, later in the war, offered an opportunity to escape west when the change in atmosphere in Sofia would not be congenial for former Bulgarian patriots and monarchists.

In spring 1943, the Ivan Stancioff family made a decision to leave Bulgaria and find a safe, neutral retreat in Fribourg, Switzerland. After the children and Marion visited Ivan in Galatz, the eight Stancioffs, mother and seven children, took a circuitous route to the Swiss border. Marion insisted that they remain in Budapest for three days so the family could enjoy the beauty of the city and take in some of the principal sights. Then they spent one day in Vienna doing as much sightseeing as possible.

In a queer bit of *déjà vu*, the Stancioffs found themselves in Fribourg, the city where Ivan had studied in the 1920s. This time it was the female members of the family who found refuge and who took advantage of the cultural and economic bounty. Marion found accommodations in an old Fribourg hotel. The three older boys went away to boarding schools while the girls of school age attended day school.

As the war continued to drive the lives of civilians, the family relied on letters and packages to feel connected, some delivered by friends in the diplomatic service. Hope and faith sustained them.

1943 Brings a Power Shift

By early 1943, Nazi forces were in retreat on all fronts, imperceptibly at first, and then at a quickened pace as the year progressed. The battle for Stalingrad was the turning point in the east. The Nazis suffered defeats in Europe and in Africa. Italy backed out of the Axis. Would Bulgaria do the same? After all, King Boris was King Victor Emmanuel of Italy's son-in-law.

Once the Soviet armies regained some of their composure, the rollback of the German occupation of European territories began. For the Balkan states, the changes in the front came at an excruciatingly slow pace. German and Italian occupations of the peninsula were deeply entrenched, and despite heavy losses on the eastern front, the Germans were not loosening their hold on their southern European holdings, even after the collapse of the Italian fascist regime.

Death of the King

Hitler had repeatedly pressured King Boris to permit the use of Bulgarian troops beyond Bulgaria's borders, and Boris had consistently refused. He also remained adamant about the fate of Bulgaria's Jewish population, whom he dispersed in villages throughout the country but refused to deport to death camps.

In mid-August 1943, Boris returned from a visit with Hitler in Germany. Their meetings had been heated and stressful. Although no record remains of the substance of their talks, the men parted under strained circumstances. Shortly after his return home, King Boris complained of physical malaise and chest pains. He eventually collapsed and died within days of his return. The king's death was premature; he was only 49 years old. In Bulgaria, rumors were rife that Boris was murdered.

Bulgaria's fate, however, was determined well before the untimely death of her king in August 1943. Nonetheless, fear coursed through the population; now Bulgaria would be fully incorporated into the Nazi behemoth, since the only man who had kept the Germans at bay was dead.

King Boris' death, of natural causes, an autopsy proved he had a congenital heart condition, prompted the creation of a regency of three co-rulers; one of whom was Prince Cyril , Bogdan Filov, and General Mihov. The king's little son, now King Simeon II of Bulgaria, became the figurehead of the Bulgarian nation while his father's grave at Rila Monastery became a site of pilgrimage and veneration.

In Britain, King Boris' death prompted news commentary that was, on the whole, negative. Nadejda countered the criticism with an interview broadcast on Scottish radio. Her praise of the king and his government was perceived as unpatriotic with respect to the Allied cause. Nonetheless, Nadejda continued her unqualified support of her king, even after his death.[43]

Leaving Varna

Feo and her mother had to be coaxed, cajoled, and begged to leave Bulgaria. Marion wrote letters from Switzerland begging them to come to Fribourg to help her with the children. In fact, Ivan spent part of his precious leave time in 1943 not only visiting his family in Switzerland but also paying one last visit to his mother and sister in Varna. He tried to entice them to leave Bulgaria for good.

Ivan, keeping Nadejda and—via Nadejda—Chou abreast of developments in the family living in Bulgaria, wrote a letter to the Muirs from Switzerland describing his last visit to *Les Trois Sources*. He reassured the Muirs that Maman and Feo were in good health and spirits and were well provided for. They had fruits, vegetables, and poultry they raised with a hired man, who helped with the heavy work.[44] The women were not in any material need, although the death of King Boris was a blow to them, and they mourned his passing. Ivan hoped that the onset of winter would convince them to finally leave Bulgaria. Despite finally agreeing to go to Switzerland, the women never fully believed that their departure from Bulgaria would be permanent.

International Intrigue

To label Ivan's leave, in the fall of 1943, eventful would be a gross understatement. In September 1943, Ivan had two remarkable experiences that could qualify as material for spy thrillers and war stories of the most chilling kind. When he went to visit Marion in Fribourg Switzerland, he arrived with the expectation that she had something important to relate. The reason for this suspicion was that a month earlier he had received a letter from her. The letter was a cryptic and obviously coded narrative full of oblique references that only he might understand. The code had been so carefully constructed that he had not been able to guess its intent.

Upon arrival in Fribourg, he found out that none other than Allen Dulles, the station chief for the Office of Strategic Services, the precursor to the Central Intelligence Agency, had contacted her indirectly via Chou, who now lived in New York. In his capacity as chief of covert operations, the American spent World War II gathering intelligence from anti-Nazi groups, German émigrés, and other political refugees. Ivan Stancioff husband and his wife met with Dulles in Berne for a rather sobering conversation on the future of the postwar Balkans.

At the time of the initial contact, three months before the meeting with Ivan, the American had hoped to lure King Boris to the side of the Allies. When Marion originally met with Dulles in June 1943, he had warned her that the Russians would occupy Poland, Romania, Bulgaria, and Hungary; the Allies perceived this occupation as inevitable. It was imperative, according to the American, that Bulgaria join the Allies while the Allies continued to insist on supplying and supporting the Soviets. Although the Allied states understood the costs, they were willing to sacrifice their East European allies to the cause of crushing the Nazis. Marion was appalled but agreed to communicate with Ivan in a coded letter, to urge him to find a way to speak with the king in private.

However, the changes in the front by the fall of 1943, when Ivan finally met with Dulles, and the continuing negotiations among the Allies, had reached a point of increasing rigidity. By then, King Boris had passed away, and Allen Dulles was in "a completely negative mood as far as the Balkans were concerned."[45] Ivan left Switzerland hoping to find a chance to speak with Prince Cyril, who was now one of three regents, but no chance materialized, and events forced his hand.

While in Sofia, after his strange encounter in Berne, Ivan experienced yet another odd interview. The following is excerpted from his published memoirs:

> I was awakened at dawn to find a most unexpected visitor. At the foot of my bed stood an immense German Air Force, NCO [noncommissioned officer]. He saluted and said that the "'Herr Major'" had sent him with this message: "Leave Sofia at once. The Browns are out to get you." I asked him why this

Major—who was . . . the head of Military Intelligence in Bulgaria—took an interest in my welfare, [the officer replied] "Weil Sie doch ein Offizier und ein Herr sind," [You are an officer and a gentleman] . . . saluted smartly and left.[46]

Ivan heeded the advice, left immediately, and heard subsequently that indeed a group of Gestapo had arrived at his residence looking for him later that morning. Ivan made a narrow escape.

Although Ivan's mission to convince mother and daughter to leave Bulgaria was successful, they insisted that they could not abandon their home, their familiar and comfortable lives, for the unknown. By late 1943, however, the situation called for realism. In the fall of that year, they left *Les Trois Sources* for good. They planned to join Marion and the children in Switzerland.

While they waited for their Swiss visas, they stayed with Queen Giovanna at the royal palace in Vrana. Queen and former ladies-in-waiting comforted each other and spent a few days in each other's company. The queen, in her mourning clothes and veil, was thin and pale.[47] She seemed to have a far-off look in her eyes as though expecting her husband to enter the room at any time. Her mourning was extremely tortuous, and she often had tears in her eyes. Prince Cyril seemed more composed and recovered from the shock.

Together, the women recalled the last time they had all been at Vrana together, when King Boris had been alive, the previous April. Then, the Stancioff women remembered that he had been calm, very affectionate, tired, and had even retrieved an old photo of *Trois Sources* from his wallet to show them how closely he treasured their times together among his happy memories.

In November 1943, the palace and its memories seemed morbid for the Stancioffs. The small company, queen and the Stancioff women, visited King Boris' grave together at Rila Monastery. On their return drive, at various stops in villages along the way, the peasants greeted the queen with warmth, love, gifts, and tokens of esteem. The Stancioffs were impressed and comforted that the royal family still had the support of its populace. In fact, the king's grave had become an instant site of pilgrimage.

The war was visited upon them in a new and horrifying way when during their stay, Stancioffs and Coburgs experienced an air raid together.[48] Although not the one that would later damage the palace and destroy part of the building, the raid and the damage caused by the bombardment in November was a shocking reminder of how imminent the charnel of war could be.

Feo described her experience of an air raid in Sofia; which caught her off guard and exposed in the streets as she crossed Aleksandûr Nevski Place.[49] The noise of the aerial bombardment and the explosions of the bombs were deafening. She felt as if the cobblestones in the streets were jumping into the air and that the entire city was rising and falling like a volcanic cone about to burst its confines.

Eventually mother and daughter left Bulgaria and undertook a journey, first to visit Ivan in Galatz, and then to continue west to Switzerland. Nadejda wrote telling them how she followed their final week in Bulgaria in her imagination. She empathized with them about each agonizing decision about what to take and what to leave and about the uncertainty of the future. Most of all, she reminded them to cling to "seven treasures" that no one could take from them: Faith, Hope, Family, Prayer, the Past, Tenderness, and the beauty of Nature.[50]

Mother and daughter began their migration out of the country in Sofia, progressed to the Danube, then via rowboat, across the great river to the Romanian shore, since ferry service had stopped due to the danger of mines.[51] They pressed on by train to Bucharest, where Ivan welcomed them and whisked them to his apartments in Galatz.

In the bosom of the Bulgarian colony, Maman, Feo and Ivan celebrated Christmas Eve. New Years Eve was ushered in at the home of the Portuguese consul, who offered a rich banquet to his guests. Considering wartime privations and the shortages civilians encountered, his tables were well-stocked with caviar, turkey, ice cream, and champagne.[52] Feo recorded that when they left the celebrations, barefoot beggars, shifting from one foot to the other in the snow, pleaded for handouts. It was a brutally cold winter that year.

When mother and daughter left for their final destination in Switzerland, their journey by train, in January 1944, was an ordeal, as it was for any traveler who would venture to cross a Europe exhausted by years of war. In Bucharest, they had to be hoisted into their car via the window to claim their seats on the train. Those benches became a test of endurance, since they could not and would not have dared leave their seats for fear of losing the precious berths. Their luggage was wedged in about them, and cramped conditions kept the two imprisoned for the duration of their trip. Fortunately, by the time they reached the Swiss border, most of their fellow passengers had left the train cars, and the two women spent the end of their trip in relative comfort.

Mother and daughter had left Ivan on the frozen Bessarabian territories. His job required that he look after the Bulgarian populations, who although born and raised in the area, were now in a rush to apply for and to receive Bulgarian passports and visas.[53] The material situation for many declined at a critical pace as the war progressed and the Russian front began to moved west. There were hordes of desperate refugees who attempted to escape the inexorable advance of the Russian armies. For Ivan, the post and his duties as a representative of the Bulgarian government kept him busy as he saw to the needs of these refugees.

Life in a Safe Haven

In Switzerland, Mother and daughter reunited with daughter-in-law Marion and her seven children. The two settled into life in exile. The mixed family visited monasteries and attended concerts. In the winter, the children skied and sledded. In the summer, they swam in the lakes, hiked, biked, and played while enjoying their temporary Swiss "citizenship."

The Ivan Stancioff family corresponded, as the children tried to keep their father current on all the details of their lives. Some letters included sketched illustrations of various daily occupations of the motley congeries of Stancioffs. The illustrations, accompanied by mixed language prose, described what ironing and laundry day looked like, or Granny reading in her rocking chair, or mother putting on her hat to go to church, or the boys soaking their frozen feet after walking home. One illustration that rendered the exterior and floor plans of the house they occupied contained endearing explanations of their accommodations. One of the seven children wrote, "There is no bath, but a *cheshma* [spigot] in the garden. There is a little river beside the house quite deep enough for Andrew [the youngest] to drown himself."[54] The letter offered discomfiting images for their father from one of his well-meaning progeny.

In Switzerland, the truncated family followed news of the war, of loved ones, and of acquaintances who managed to find refuge there over time. Nada and Chou were together in England in 1944 and managed to celebrate their twentieth anniversaries of their respective marriages. Felix was doing work-related traveling, first to Cairo and later to Persia.

In May, the Stancioffs heard the news of their uncle Ernest's death in Paris; at that point, Maman was the last of her family left alive. They worried about and anticipated Ivan's return from Galatz any day. Nadejda kept vigil from Scotland and prayed for her brother's safe return to his family and, ultimately, for the safe reunification of the entire family. She wrote:

> If God permits it soon we . . . will share, as in other times, the beauties of nature, that no one can manage to rest from us, and that of religion and that of family; and we will all have dear mementos like a stash of precious pearls hoarded by a pearl diver.[55]

Ivan Leaves Bulgaria

When Romania left the Axis alliance, Bucharest and other cities experienced retaliatory Nazi strikes. Ivan and a few expatriates experienced bombings and air raids from both the Germans and Allied aircraft. By summer 1944, the situation in Romania was deteriorating rapidly, and the Romanians encouraged the consular corps in Galatz to leave for their own safety.

Between June and August of that year, Ivan made his way out of Romania and passed through Bulgaria one last time on his odyssey to the West. With a convoy of four private automobiles, he managed to shepherd a few remaining compatriots across the Danube and to the relative calm of Bulgarian territories.[56]

He spent a short time in Sofia. While waiting for a decision about his subsequent posting, he worked on repairs on his home on Oborishte Street; which had been seriously damaged during a bombardment. He also spent time visiting with friends in the city. He paid a visit to the King's sister, Princess Eudoxie, who now lived and gardened on a property on the road to the Vrana.[57] She had been a good friend to both Ivan and Marion.

Toward the fall of 1944, it was clear that it would not be advisable for Ivan to remain in the Bulgarian diplomatic service. The Soviet invasion of Bulgaria was imminent, the so-called "liberation" of the country from its capitalist "oppressors" was underway, and he represented the persona non grata category of civil servant. Under the guise of taking up a new post in Istanbul, he left Bulgarian territory for the last time.[58]

He left Bulgaria days before the Soviet declaration of war on Bulgaria and the invasion by the Red Army. His official position, tenuous at best, lasted a few months in Turkey. By December, Ivan relinquished his position in the Bulgarian diplomatic service.[59]

Ivan spent his time harbored by friends in Turkey, especially the British ambassador, Lord Maurice Patterson. Ivan worked on acquiring an ordinary Bulgarian passport and waiting for permission to travel and to enter Great Britain. He made it to England through a series of convoluted airplane journeys. He ran out of money just as he made it to London and called his sister Nada on a borrowed coin so she could wire him money for a train ticket. He then spent the rest of the war in England trying to obtain a visa to rejoin his family in Switzerland.

All of the Stancioffs were reunited for the last time in Fribourg, for Noel, in 1945. The Muirs, Chou and her daughters, and the Ivan Stancioffs celebrated the holidays together at Villa Garcia, as they might have in the past. They sang Christmas songs, exchanged presents, attended midnight mass, ate supper after, and went to bed at 3:00 a. m. The end of the war would effect profound changes in their lives.

End of World War

The war in Europe finally came to an end in May 1945. A moment to celebrate freedom from the tyranny of warfare on civilian populations also signaled the migration of millions of people across the continent. Among them were refugees who trekked toward their homes, concentration camp survivors, prisoners of war, decommissioned armies and civilians who took the first steps toward a resumption of normalcy.

The end of the war signaled the rapid degeneration of allied relationships from amicable cooperation to suspicion, mistrust, and ultimately outright hostility. In Bulgaria, the Communists abolished the monarchy in September 1945 and declared Bulgaria a republic.

The new atmosphere among the allies affected the lives of millions of Europeans. For those who lived in the Soviet occupied zones, life took on a new harsh reality. While Europeans contended with post-war shortages and hardships of all sorts, those living in the eastern part of the continent experienced even greater losses: of freedom of thought, expression, and movement.

Europe reverted from a battlefield where firepower and guns determined destinies to a new type of proving ground. As the former allies exhibited inimical postures, ideological battles quickly replaced firefights with a Cold War. Suspicions of ideologies, both communist and capitalist, gave the post war world an aura of paranoia. The new atmosphere, to a large extent, supported an environment of cloak-and-dagger attitudes among ordinary citizens as well as their national secret service establishments. The lives of ordinary citizens were co-opted into the war of ideologies on both sides of what Winston Churchill dubbed the Iron Curtain. Civilians found themselves embattled once more.

The Stancioffs' Postwar Lives

The end of the war initiated further fragmentation of the close-knit Stancioff clan. For Ivan and Marion's large brood, the security and relative economic prosperity of the United States was a much more attractive option than war-devastated Europe. Therefore, they and their seven children began a new chapter in their lives by choosing to head to Marion's native land and to make a life there. They left Europe in August 1946.

In the United States, the American cultural norms, behaviors, and attitudes that were vastly different from their own European ones posed a severe test for the family's deeply held beliefs. In the end, they survived and thrived in a house they bought and renovated in Urbana, Maryland. Everyone in the family helped with those renovations, and the inevitable gardens that seemed to sprout whe-rever there were Stancioffs in residence came to life once again.

On the property in rural Urbana, the Stancioff family recreated, as much as the soil and climate of Maryland would permit, the verdant, pastoral, and agri-cultural splendors of *Les Trois Sources* and the *Marion* villas in Varna. As the children matured, the Stancioffs supplemented their income by producing their own vegetables, fruits, and eggs.

Feo and Maman obtained permission to live in Britain in November 1945. They settled in the country, dividing their time between their apartment in Lon-don, at 29 Courfield Gardens, and Blair Drummond. Chou and Felix divorced after the war, and Chou established herself in her own apartment in London. Nadejda remained, as ever, the glue of her family—the one who kept the rest of the family abreast of news in each of their lives, the one who fretted over their far-flung abodes, and the one who constantly conspired to reunite the clan.

The Stancioffs also used their many international contacts to glean what bits of information they could about increasingly distant communist Bulgaria. [60] In November 1946, they found, through a contact with the Red Cross, that although the queen and her children were adored by ordinary Bulgarians, the former king and his brother were publicly criticized. And that the Stancioffs were refered to, in the press, as *Dvortsovi Hora*, (palace people) who were not fit for contempo-rary Bulgaria.[61]

After Lord Kay passed on in 1951, Nada relinquished Blair Drummond to his heir and moved to a flat in London, at 19 Albert Court, close to her mother and sisters. She missed her life in the country, "the blessed stillness, the space, the dignity of large, well ordered, well kept rooms, the writing tables all ready, the silver gleaming, the efficient butler; that rare British feeling, known and ap-preciated by me for 27 years, of the combination of leisure, culture, beauty, na-ture! All so courteous and calming!"[62] However, life in London had other plea-sures and Nadejda most enjoyed being in the company of her family.

Notes

1. Ivan Stancioff, unpublished letter, 12 August 1933, IS I, PASF.

2. See a new evaluation of the peace in Patrick O. Cohrs, *The Unfinished Peace after World War I America, Britain and the Stabilization of Europe, 1919-1932* (Cambridge: Cambridge University Press, 2006).

3. Anna Stancioff, unpublished letter, October 1939, Nada XI, PASF.

4. Anna Stancioff, unpublished letter, 4 November 1938, Nada X, PASF.

5. Robert de Grenaud, unpublished letter, 20 July 1936, Nada X, PASF.

6. Talk on Radio Sofia, 31 January 1940 "From London to Sofia."

7. Ibid.

8. Article from unknown Bulgarian newspaper in PASF.

9. Ibid.

10. Ibid.

11. Nadejda Stancioff, notes on last interview with King Boris and unpublished letter to family regarding that conversation, Nada XVI, PASF.

12. Nadejda Stancioff, unpublished letter, 16 May 1940 TsDIA, F143 .

13. King Ferdinand, unpublished letter-typescript, 6 May 1940, DS Obituary File, PASF.

14. Nadejda Stancioff, unpublished letter, 2 July 1940, TsDIA, F143.

15. Ibid.

16. Ibid.

17. Nadejda Stancioff, unpublished letter, 7 February 1940, TsDIA, F143.

18. *Star* 29 November 1940.

19. Nadejda Stancioff, transcripts of broadcasts, 8/40 and 10/40, BBC file, PASF.

20. Ibid.

21. Ibid.

22. Anna Stancioff, unpublished letter, 14 December 1939, Nada XI, PASF.

23. Dimitri Stancioff, unpublished letter, 25-27 December 1939, Nada XI, PASF.

24. Anna Stancioff, unpublished letter, 14 December 1939, Nada XI, PASF.

25. Nadejda Stancioff, unpublished letter, 4 March 1941, Nada XVII, PASF. Draft of a letter to the editor responding to a letter on her editorial of February 11, (newspaper unknown) "My remarks were based on information supplied to me...by the Bulgarian minister in London, who has since resigned [when Bulgaria joined the Axis]...I would do exactly the same if I had been in his place."

26. Ivan Stancioff, unpublshed letter to Nadejda, 13 November 1939, Nada XI, PASF.

27. Nadejda Stancioff, unpublished letter, October 1940, TsDIA, F143.

28. See Nada XVII, PASF. Nadejda wrote letters to both men on February 17, 1941 in reaction to a particularly anti-Bulgarian radio address by Winston Churchill on February 9, 1941, when he used the "colloquial style of a soap-box orator of Hyde Park." She believed it was a deliberate departure from his well-known "literary, magnificent" style of speech in order to influence his listeners more negatively regarding Bulgaria. In that month, Nadejda published articles in the *Contemporary Review* and the *Queen*.

28. Crampton, *A Concise History of Bulgaria*.

29. Nadejda Stancioff, unpublished letter, 14 September 1944, Nada XVII, PASF. Nadejda wrote to Graves, "I am sad that as regards Bulgaria you should still see things in such a bitter way. You write that the Rumanians were robbed; a Bulgarian could say that the Dobrudja and Western Thrace were stolen from Bulgaria. Why underline the viola-

tion of some pledges; and not of others?.I entirely agree with you on one point, Bulgaria should have been a second Denmark."

30. Nadejda Stancioff, unpublished letter, 5 April 1947, Nada XIII, PASF. The hos-- pital closed at the end of the month. Over the course of its existence 2840 wounded were accommodated there. Once closed, the Muirs had to face steep heating costs that led them to reconsider their household expenditures in general. In anticipation of the reduced comforts such as hot baths, and central heating Nadejda wrote "I knew what I was doing when I kept it [the hospital] on!" and although Kay's annual income was quite high, 5000/year (the Duke of Westminster apparently could expect approximately the same amount according to Nadejda in the same letter.) The costs of maintenance, repairs, finding and keeping personnel, as well as other expenses, had been manageable until the war. Now, Kay was concerned about living expenses, leaving something for his heir, John Muir, for his other relatives, and leaving something for his wife.

31. Nadejda Stancioff, unpublished letter, 12 February 1940, Nada XIII, PASF.

32. Ibid.

33. Nadejda Stancioff, unpublished letter, 3 March 1940, Nada XIII, PASF.

34. Nadejda Stancioff, unpublished letter, 3 May 1940, Nada XIII, PASF.

35. Nadejda Stancioff, unpublished letter, 6 July 1940, Nada XIII, PASF.

36. Nadejda Stancioff, unpublished letter, 23 May 1940, Nada XIII, PASF.

37. Nadejda Stancioff, unpublished letter, 20 June 1940, Nada XIII, PASF.

38. Stancioff, Nadejda Memories of Love, 108.

39. Ibid.

40. Stancioff, *Diplomat and Gardener Memoirs*.

41. Ibid. I use Ivan's figures as stated in his memoir on page 130.

42. Ibid., 114.

43. Ivan Stancioff, unpublished letter, Nada XVI, PASF.

44. Stancioff, *Diplomat and Gardener Memoirs*. 141.

45. Ibid., 141-142.

46. Stancioff, Nadejda Memories of Love, 115.

47. Ibid.

48. Stancioff, Nadejda Memories of Love,

49. Nadejda Stancioff, unpublished letter, 17 November 1943, Nada XIII, PASF. Nadejda wrote the letter trying to maintain some feeling of connection to her loved ones as they undertook their odyssey.

50. Stancioff, Nadejda Memories of Love, 117.

51. Ibid., 116-117.

52. Stancioff, *Diplomat and Gardener Memoirs*.

53. Ivan Stancioff, unpublished letter, 13 April 1944, IS I, PASF.

54. Nadejda Stancioff, unpublished letter 20 June 1942, TsDIA, F143, ae 65 1 37.

55. Stancioff, *Diplomat and Gardener Memoirs*.

56. Ibid.

57. Ibid.

58. Stancioff, *Diplomat and Gardener Memoirs*.

59. Nadejda Stancioff, unpublished journal, Easter Sunday 1954 "Christ is risen. I think of dear Bulgaria (very often!)." PASF.

60. Nadejda Stancioff, unpublished letter, 19 November 1946, Nada XIII, PASF.

61. Nadejda Stancioff, unpublished journal, 1 April 1954, PASF.

Epilogue

In the centuries, leading up to the Great War European elites created a standard of culture, a kind of universal European blend of an elite ideal of civilization. European transnational elite culture mandated a hierarchical system of social ranking, staunch support of monarchy, and the church.

Civilization and the Other

As European states emerged from the middle ages, French language and culture became, overtime, the European standard of good breeding. In the west, other European, non-French, elites came to imitate the culture of the French and acquire the language as a universal marker of good breeding. By the nineteenth century Russian elites succeeded in acquiring that exemplary culture to a remarkable degree. In the East, the Russian aristocracy managed to abjure the use of their native language, dress, and manners in favor of western cultural norms, and specifically French models. The conclusion of this process, throughout Europe, began with the defeat of Napoleon Bonaparte.

Elites began to be affected by the rise of nationalism during the period of Romanticism in the nineteenth century, just as other citizens. Nationalism was a force that compelled all citizens to respond to official power with fresh demonstrations of devotion, loyalty, and sacrifice. With this novel ideal, European elites acquired new duties and responsibilities. They now served the nation and her monarch.

The advent of nationalism in Europe precipitated the reexamination of the state. What did the citizens value about their nation? Greatness would no longer be measured just by martial victories and concomitant regal displays of might. National grandeur would now be defined by the unique and special characteristics of the "people;" the indigenous language, dress, cultural habits of the nation.

European states began to differentiate among themselves based on new criteria that made a nation unique. Peasants and their culture were now held up to be the only true representatives of the ethnos and therefore deserving of preservation and even emulation.

Savage Orientals

In the differentiation process of discovering and defining the nation, the taint of being of the East and the Orient, attached a specific type of stigma to the Slavs. Furthermore, those Slavic groups who were also Orthodox (Bulgarians, Russians, Serbs, for example) were more likely to be perceived as part of the inscrutable "Other" by the rest of Europe. Catholicism was more familiar to West Europeans therefore Slavs like the Poles and Czechs found their place more readily among the western European national order. Orthodoxy was alien to Europe; autocephalous, national churches represented a foreign, eastern, and mysterious society to a largely Protestant and Catholic Europe.

Slavic elite societies examined their eastern roots during the Romantic era of the nineteenth century, and accepted or rejected their status as "Other" in Europe. As the forefathers of nationalism, Fichte and Herder (those German thinkers identified with the spread of nationalism in Eastern Europe) insisted, the *Volksgeist* and the *Volk*, were the essence of the nation and therefore sacred. However, Orthodox Europeans, a substantial part of the Slav peoples, had to contend with their dualistic cultural influences. Being European and culturally Orthodox created barriers to the Balkan Slavs' incorporation into culturally western Europe. How did they cope with being Europeans but orientals too?

The Russians, Orthodox Slavs, managed to avoid overt stigmatization because until the dawn of the twentieth century Imperial Russia's presumed military superiority, the very extent of the state's geographic dominance, and Russian cultural preeminence in the fields of music and literature, assured them preferential consideration by other Europeans. Imperial Russia was one of the Great Powers.

Among other Orthodox Slavic countries, the situation was more complex. National Orthodox churches were also nationalist actors. In the nineteenth century, priests and freedom fighters were often in league against foreign oppressors and sometimes priests picked up weapons and joined the revolutionaries.

In order to rise above the negative identification of coming from oriental roots, the Balkan Slavs, sought to change over the eastern elements of their identity into a new, native identification with their peasant cultures while also embracing western cultural norms—a daunting task.

The Bulgarians wrestled with their oriental, "savage" origins. In 1878, national liberation of Bulgaria from the Ottomans set the process of separation from the Orient in motion. Latecomers to the national definition process by comparison to most of their Balkan neighbors, the Bulgarians, sought to "join" Europe: they sought inclusion into the European cultural family.

Transnational Elites

A rigid system of semiotic indicators of belonging identified aristocrats and nobles across the continent as the transnational European elites. Implicit in this system was the exclusion of anything or anyone who represented elements alien to Western European culture—in this case, oriental cultures. It was assumed, with few exceptions, by both West and East Europeans, that western culture was superior and desirable.

With no contemporary paradigm of tolerance, for a plurality of alternative cultural templates, Europeans of the East and West gazed at the world through the same West-centric prism. West Europeans felt free to impose their will on others by imagining "Others" as inferior because they lacked the "universally" accepted markers of western culture.

According to West Europeans, Europeans from the eastern parts of the continent people of the East were oriental, inferior, and subject to the will of the westerners. Failure to accede to this logic proved the point that westerners maintained: members of the Orient were irrational, inferior, savage, and unpredictable. In this atmosphere, racism was accepted by Europeans and legitimated the practice of imperialism "at home" on the European continent.[1]

The superiority of the West in the eyes of Europeans included cultural and governmental institutions built up over centuries, the fact that the marginalized nations of Europe, such as the Balkan states, could not immediately erect or graft similar institutions on to their societies, proved their inherent inferiority as a people. Using this judgment as infallible, the Balkan states, Bulgaria among them, struggled to acquire the polish of the west and shed the taint of the Orient.

The Stancioffs—Hybrid Elites

In Bulgaria, Stancioff patriotism combined with de Grenaud European cosmopolitanism, to create a hybrid sense of national loyalty. However, this process was not linear. The Stancioffs traveled back and forth, literally and metaphorically, from civilization in the West to disorder in the East. Each train trip back to a diplomatic posting in "Europe," from Bulgaria-orient, Russia-east, gave rise to laments, as Nadejda recorded in her journals, about leaving the dear, disordered, free, ardent, warm, Orient for the restrictive, constraining, rule-bound, oppressive European world.

In St. Petersburg, the Stancioffs mingled with a social network of aristocratic elites and observed the Russians wrestle with their own sense of "otherness," on a daily basis. For the Stancioff children the self-identification with the "Other" began in St. Petersburg, they internalized the symbolism of separate selves for the private and public realms.[2] They witnessed how the private and public self could reconcile the clash of cultures from East and West.

The Stancioff family lived on that problematic boundary, identifying themselves in a unique way that kept them consciously both together and apart from both Bulgarian and European elites. In their effort to contain the Orient within, they were able to project expertly the European civilized persona without. As rational "western" nationalists, they had to represent a state that was the very epitome of the oriental "Other" for most Europeans.

From the late nineteenth century to World War II, being the diplomatic representative of an oriental state required certain fortitude. Just as *haiduts*, marauding bands of freedom fighters that harassed Ottoman troops before the liberation of Bulgaria, diplomats fought the good fight at a front made up of skeptical, even hostile, European elites. Diplomats of marginalized countries on the cultural periphery of Europe embodied that same fearless panache with which a young man would run to the hills to devote his life to fighting for a just cause and for the greater good. If the Stancioff family had a tradition of helping *haiduts* like the famous Vasil Levski, then certainly their descendants were comfortable in taking on the cause of nationalism before the withering gaze of Europe's cultural elites.

The Making of Patriots

While surrounding themselves with the décor of European culture in their legation homes—Louis XVI furniture, damask wall coverings, grand pianos and elegant tea service sets and similar, widely accepted cues of elite culture—the Stancioffs also created, with their one authentic home, *Les Trois Sources*, the embodiment of their true selves. Both the interior of the house and the grounds were a counterpoint to their residences abroad.

To be sure, Maman's elegant touch in decorating the public spaces was evident in the fine imported furnishings. However, the focus of the main reception hall was a large wooden reproduction of the Madara horseman; a dramatic, eighth century bas-relief carved in a vertical cliff about twenty yards above the ground, not far from Varna.[3] On the other end of the room, and in all the other public spaces, the Stancioff crest was fashioned in bas-relief into the walls. The décor of *Les Trois Sources* underscored the sentiment: We are of this place, we belong, and we are proud to belong yet we appreciate western European culture and décor.

The grounds had a cultivated flower garden, a pergola, a fountain, fruit, and nut trees. The cultivated area was sophisticated yet also included elements of a French-style garden in which domesticated plants seemed to burst forth from the surrounding native landscape. A staircase made of knotted and twisted trees wound gracefully to the shore along the cliff side, beneath the property, ending in an artfully constructed pier of twisted vine limbs.

Les Trois Sources became the site of the Stancioffs' other, freer nature—the picture of an oriental style of life, where the family dined sitting outside, at a white table and arched bench constructed to fit under a pear tree, eating fresh home made bread they cut with "a good sturdy knife of Samokov," where peasants picked the grape harvest in colorful native garb, where the Stancioffs cultivated their fruits and vegetables and enjoyed the fruits of their labors in the domestic environment they created. As Nadejda noted numerous times in her journals, all pretence, all formality could vanish at *Les Trois Sources* and the

Stancioffs could luxuriate, as they did in the balmy weather and the welcoming sea, in being free of European civilizing constraints.

Being of the Orient made the Stancioffs' self-image an antipode to being fully European. Furthermore, their oriental self-identification brought them closer to Bulgarian self-identification and could separate them from the European cosmopolitan image of the aristocratic elites. Becoming more Bulgarian, they were showing their true allegiances, to the nation and all it represents.

Stancioff Patriotism—Models of Iconographic Prototypes

The cultural traditions of the Stancioffs bound them to the nineteenth century. Their development, as individuals and as a family, parallels the birth of the twentieth century world.

The lives of a family of diplomats exemplify how a mixed family of national transients, a type of "displaced people" (albeit self-selecting), invent, and preserve patriotism. The entire family, except the father, had to learn the language of their homeland as foreigners. Nonetheless, during sporadic years or just months of habitation in their homeland they developed a fierce love that was nurtured by several factors.

First, despite, or perhaps because of their hybrid religious life, for the Stancioffs, religion served as the foundation of their strength. A Catholic and Orthodox hybrid family should have presented difficulties in shaping nationalism. However, the Stancioffs were Catholics who maintained their identification with Bulgaria and its largely Orthodox population. They were Bulgarian patriots who supported their "country" while they lived comfortably in the western, non-Orthodox Europe of the twentieth century.

Next, the family was universally seduced by the splendors of nature; the Bulgarian native landscape became a metaphor and a real tangible manifestation of the country's greatness: the landscape of the nation offered objects to venerate like rivers, mountains, valleys of roses, fields of tobacco, which became metaphors for national distinction among other states.

Finally, the Stancioffs practiced a delicate balance between traditional socially accepted cultural norms and alien cultural markers. They understood that their family strength emanated from the pillars of traditional social stability: the church, the monarchy, and a class system. However, they blended western and eastern cultural traditions to find a middle ground.

The Stancioffs believed themselves Bulgarian citizens because they developed a strong bond with their homeland through their professional positions and through their personal connection with the royal family. For them the embodiment of the state was a powerful and benevolent figurehead (the king). As the state's subjects (citizens), they were ready to fulfill their obligations by working for the good of the state. The head of state—monarch or prime minister—also had to exemplify greatness.

The Stancioffs perceived King Ferdinand and later, King Boris, as well as Aleksandûr Stamboliiski, as noble, wise, powerful, and benevolent leaders.

They were ready to show their loyalty through diligent work for them and their country.

The Stancioffs understood hierarchy in the lives of individuals and in the historical developments of states. The traditional, class-based society segregated classes into spheres of power and influence, just as nations were a part of a system of greater and lesser players. National greatness could be judged based on cultural or physical characteristics, as in the natural landscapes of a state, or literary and artistic achievements, or based on martial exploits and influence over colonies.

As long as the state managed to evoke feelings of patriotism and nationalism from its citizens, then patriotic citizens like the Stancioffs would sustain the state. When Bulgarian patriots were swept up in the enthusiasm of the heady days of victories in domestic and foreign affairs, Bulgarian unification in 1885, the declaration of independence in 1908, and the First Balkan War of 1912, the Stancioffs perceived their country and its sovereign as superior, as successful in scaling the heights of power and status among "great" European states. They combined the learned patriotism of diplomats with pride in the growing power and prestige of their nation-state.

At the turn of the twentieth century Bulgaria and the Stancioffs were uniquely positioned to straddle a cultural divide between the "civilized" West and "oriental" East. Both the country and the family had a unique cultural background that could become their strength.

Nadejda Stancioff Muir was an enormously intelligent, gifted, and family-oriented woman whose single-minded dedication to worthy causes was staggering. Although she had opportunities to break free from her traditional upbringing, she embraced tradition and remained primarily a conservative her entire life.

She was a member of the transnational European elites, a pious Catholic, at times a Bulgarian nationalist and patriot, always a Bulgarian monarchist, and occasionally a modest feminist. Her public persona did not stray far from her private mien. As a member of elite society, she found it difficult to fully enter the worlds of other social groups. Travel, international experiences, and exposure to a variety of cultures did not shake her free of her roots. Although she could fantasize about being a woman of the Orient, she was clearly a member of the European elites and a complex woman of her times.

Using this family's life as an example of how individuals coped with modernization at the beginning of the twentieth century, this family biography parallels how Bulgaria undertook the process of modernization. Since Bulgaria is still a bridge to the "Orient" and a conduit for Europeanization to the East, serving as a middle ground for both cultures could enhance the country's value to international forums. Just as the Stancioffs used their status as marginal "others" before West Europeans cultural elites, Bulgaria could employ the same dual nature to present a hybrid European state that is comfortable being of the East and the West and uses that dichotomy to national advantage.

Notes

1. Said, *Orientalism*. Edward Said's work is best known for this discussion however, there are many other sources on this discourse. See too Goldsworthy's *Inventing Ruritania: The Imperialism of the Imagination*.

2. Bolenko, ""Ruskii Vel'mozha, Evropeiiskii Grand Seigneur I Tatarskii Kniaz'" N.B. Iusupov: K Voprosu O Samoorientalizatsii Rossiiskovo Dvorianstva V Poslednei Treti XVIII-Pervoi Treti XIX Vv.."

3. The sculpture has been associated with an early medieval Bulgar ruler or Thracians. It portrays a mounted rider with a dog running at his side and an eagle flying overhead. The work and the very site are impressive since they are dramatic. Caves at the foot of the site were inhabited by stone age human societies.

Bibliography

Unpublished Primary Sources

Private Archive Stancioff Family (Varna, Bulgaria)—PASF
   Family letters
   Family mementos
   Family journals
   Comte de Bourboulon "Ephémérides De Bulgarie," manuscript.
   Feodora Stancioff "Nadejda Memories of Love," manuscript.

Bulgarian Historical Archives (Sofia, Bulgaria)—BIA

Central Government Archives (Sofia, Bulgaria)—TsDIA

Hoover Institution Archives (Stanford, California)—HIA

Secondary Sources

Adie, Kate. *Corsets to Camouflage Women and War*. London: Hodder & Stoughton, 2003.
Allen, Ann Taylor. "Feminism, Social Science, and the Meanings of Modernity: The Debate on the Origin of the Family in Europe : And the United States, 1860–1914." *American Historical Review* 104, no. 4 (1999).
Alpern Engel, Barbara. "Mothers and Daughters: Family Patterns and the Female Intelligentsia." In *The Family in Imperial Russia New Lines of Historical Research*, edited by David Ransel. Urbana: University of Illinois Press, 1978.
———. *Mothers and Daughters Women of the Intelligentsia in Nineteenth-Century Russia*. Cambridge: University of Colorado, 1983.
———. "Engendering Russia's History." *Slavic Review* 51 (1992): 309-21.
Anderson, Mosa. *Noel Buxton a Life*. London: Allen & Unwin, 1952.
Aries, Philippe. *L'enfant Et La Vie Familiale Sous L'ancien Regime*. Paris: Libraire Plon, 1960.
Atkinson, Dorothy, Alexander Dallin, and Gail Warshofsky Lapidus. *Women in Russia*. Stanford, Calif.: Stanford University Press, 1977.
Avramova, Rumiana, Nikolai Genchev, Krasimira Daskalova. *Bûlgarskata Vûzrozhdenska Inteligentsiia: Uchiteli, Sveshtenitsi, Manasi, Visshi Dukhovnitsi, Khudzhitsi, Lekari, Aptekari, Pisateli, Izdateli, Knizhari, Tûrgovtsi, Voinni: Entsikolopediia*. Sofia: Durzhvano izdatelstvo "Dr P. Beron", 1988.
Badinter, Elisabeth. *Mother Love Myth and Reality Motherhood in Modern History*. New York: Macmillan Publishing Co., Inc., 1981.
Bell, John D. *Peasants in Power Alexander Stamboliski and the Bulgarian Agrarian National Union, 1899-1923*. Princeton: Princeton University Press, 1977.
Bell, Susan Groag, and Karen M. Offen, eds. *Women, the Family, and Freedom 1880-1950*. Vol. II. Stanford: Stanford University Press, 1983.
Bell, Susan G., and Karen M. Offen. *Women, the Family, and Freedom : The Debate in Documents*. 2 vols. Stanford, Calif.: Stanford University Press, 1983.
Bolenko, Konstantin. ""Ruskii Vel'mozha, Evropeiiskii Grand Seigneur I Tatarskii Kniaz"" N.B. Iusupov: K Voprosu O Samoorientalizatsii Rossiiskovo Dvorianstva V Poslednei Treti Xviii-Pervoi Treti Xix Vv." *Ab Imperio* 3 (2006): 161-

216.
Braybon, Gail. *Women Workers in the First World War.* London ; New York: Routledge, 1989.
Bridenthal, Renat, and Claudia Koonz, eds. *Becoming Visible Women in European History.* Boston: Houghton Mifflin Co., 1977.
Buchanan, George William. *My Mission to Russia, and Other Diplomatic Memories.* 2 vols., London ; New York: Cassell and Co., 1923.
Buchanan, Meriel. *Recollections of Imperial Russia.* London: Hutchinson & Co, 1923.
———. *Queen Victoria's Relations.* London: Cassell, 1954.
———. *The Dissolution of an Empire.* 2nd edition London: John Murray, 1932.
———. *Diplomacy and Foreign Courts.* London: Hutchingson, 1928.
———. *Ambassador's Daughter.* London: Cassell, 1958.
Burgess, Ernest W., Locke, Harvey J., Thomes, Mary Margaret. *The Family from Traditional to Companionship.* New York: Van Nostrand Reinhold, 1971.
Buxton, Noel. *Travels and Reflections.* Boston: Houghton Mifflin, 1929.
Childers, Kristen Stromberg. "Paternity and the Politics of Citizenship in Interwar France." *Journal of Family History* 26, no. 1 (2001): 90-111.
Clyman, Toby W., and Judith Vowles. *Russia through Women's Eyes : Autobiographies from Tsarist Russia, Russian Literature and Thought.* New Haven: Yale University Press, 1996.
Cockburn, Cynthia. *The Space Between Us: Negotiating Gender and National Identities in Conflict.* London, New York: Zed Books, Distributed in the USA by St Martin's Press, 1998.
Cohrs, Patrick O. *The Unfinished Peace after World War I America, Britain and the Stabilization of Europe, 1919-1932.* Cambridge: Cambridge University Press, 2006.
Constant, Stephen. *Foxy Ferdinand Tsar of Bulgaria.* London: Sidgwick & Jackson, 1979.
Conwell-Evans, T. P. *Foreign Policy from a Back Bench 1904-1918.* London: Oxford University Press, 1932.
Corley, Christopher. "Preindustrial "Single-Parent" Families: The Tutelle in Early Modern Dijon." *Journal of Family History* 29, no. 4 (2004): 351-65.
Cova, Anne. *Maternite Et Droits Des Femmes En France (Xix-Xx Siecles).* Edited by Jacques-Guy Petit, *Historiques.* Paris: Anthropos, 1997.
——— *Au Service De L'eglise, De La Patrie Et De La Famille Femmes Catholiques Et Maternite Sous La III Republique.* Paris: L'Harmattan, 2000.
Crampton, Richard. *Bulgaria 1878-1918: A History.* Vol. CXXXVIII, *East European Monographs.* Boulder: Columbia University Press, 1983.
———. *A Short History of Modern Bulgaria.* Cambridge, New York: Cambridge University Press, 1987.
———. *A Concise History of Bulgaria.* Second ed. Cambridge: Cambridge University Press, 2005.
———. *Bulgaria.* Oxford History of Modern Europe. Oxford: Oxford University Press, 2007.
Crapol, Edward P., ed. *Women and American Foreign Policy Lobbyists, Critics, and Insiders.* 2nd ed. Wilmington: Scholarly Resources Inc, 1992.
Daskalov, Doncho. *Politicheski Ubiistva V Novata Istoriia Na Bûlgaria: Ubiistva, Atentati, Sûdebni Protsesi.* Sofia: Petûr Beron, 1999.
———. *Bialata Emigratsiia V Bûlgariia.* 1. izd. Sofia: UI Sv. Kl. Okhridski, 1997.
———. *Anarkhizmût V Bûlgaria.* 1. izd. Sofia: Universitetsko izdatelstvo "Sv. Kliment Okhridski", 1995.
Daskalov, Rumen. *Mezhdu Iztoka I Zapada : Bûlgarski Kulturni Dilemi.* 1. izd. Sofia:

Lik, 1998.

———. *Bûlgarskoto Obshtestvo 1878-1939*. 1. izd. 2 vols. Sofia: IK "Gutenberg", 2005.

Daskalova, Krassimira. "The Women's Movement in Bulgaria in a Life Story." *Women's History Review* 13, no. 1 (2004): 91-103.

———. "Women, Nationalism and Nation-State in Bulgaria (1800-1940s)." In *Gender Relations in South Eastern Europe: Historical Perspectives on Womanhood and Manhood in Nineteenth and Twentieth Century*, edited by M. Jovanovic and S. Naumovic, 15-37. Belgrade-Graz, 2002.

———. "The Politics of a Discipline: Women Historians in Twentieth Century Bulgaria." *Storia della Storiografia* 46 (2004): 171-87.

———. *Literacy and Reading in Nineteenth Century Bulgaria*. Seattle, WA: Henry M. Jackson School of International Studies, Univ. of Washington, 1997.

———."A Life in History: Fani Popova-Mutafova." *Gender and History* 14, no. 2 (2002): 321-39.

———. *From the Shadows of History: Women in Bulgarian Society and Culture (1840-1940)*. Sofia: Bulgarska Akademia na Naukite, 1998.

———."Bulgarian Women's Movement (1850s-1940s)." *Networks and Debates in post-communist countries in the 19th and 20th centuries* (2006): 413-37.

———."Bulgarian Women in Movements, Laws, Discourses (1840s-1940s)." *Bulgarian Historical Review* 1-2 (1999): 180-96.

Davidoff, Leonore. *Worlds Between: Historical Perspectives on Gender & Class*. London: Routledge, 1995.

———. *The Best Circles Women and Society in Victorian England*. Totowa, New Jersey: Rowan and Littlefield, 1973.

Dimitrov, Ilcho Ivanov. *Kniazût, Konstitutsiata I Narodût*. 2. izd. Sofia: Akademichno izd-vo "Prof. Marin Drinov", 2001.

Dimitrov, Ilcho Ivanov, and Elena Boianova Statelova. *Vûnshnata Politika Na Bûlgariia : Dokumenti*. 1. izd., *Bûlgaria. Ministerstvo Na Vûnshnite Raboti*. Sofia: Univ. izd-vo "Sv. Kliment Okhridski", 1995.

Edmondson, Linda Harriet. *Women and Society in Russia and the Soviet Union*. Cambridge, New York: Cambridge University Press, 1992.

Elenkov, Ivan, and Rumen Daskalov. *Zashto Sme Takiva : V Tûrsene Na Bûlgarskata Kulturna Identichnost*. Sofia: Izd-vo Prosveta, 1994.

Elias, Norbert. *The Civilizing Process*. 1st American ed. New York: Urizen Books, 1978.

Engel, Barbara Alpern. *Between the Fields and the City: Women, Work, and Family in Russia, 1861-1914*. Cambridge [England], New York: Cambridge University Press, 1994.

Engelstein, Laura, and Stephanie Sandler. *Self and Story in Russian History*. Ithaca: Cornell University Press, 2000.

Enloe, Cynthia. *Bananas, Beaches and Bases Making Feminist Sense of International Politics*. Berkeley: University of California Press, 1990.

Fernandez-Azabal, Lilie Bouton de. *Romance and Revolutions*. London,: Hutchinson & Co., 1937.

Figes, Orlando. *Natasha's Dance a Cultural History of Russia*. New York: Holt and Company, 2002.

Finch, Janet. *Married to the Job: Wives Incorporation in Men's Work*. London: G. Allen & Unwin, 1983.

Firkatian, Mari A. "Armenian Émigré Communities in Bulgaria." *Balkanistica* 9 (1996): 63-66.

Folbre, Nancy. *The Invisible Heart Economics and Family Values*. New York: The New Press, 2001.

Frader, Laura and Sonya Rose, ed. *Gender and Class in Modern Europe*. Ithaca: Cornell

University Press, 1996.

Fuchs, Rachel G. "Introduction to the Forum on the Changing Faces of Parenthood." *Journal of Family History* 29, no. 4 (2004): 331-38.

Gapova, Elena, ed. *Zhenshtinii Na Kraiu Evropi*, Minsk: EHU, 2003.

Gapova, Elena, Usmanova A., Peto A., ed. *Gendernie Istorii Vostochnoi Evropi*, Minsk: EHU, 2002.

Genchev, Nikolai. *Bûlgarska Vûzrozhdenska Inteligentsiia*. 1. izd. Sofia: Universitetsko izd-vo "Sv. Kliment Okhridski", 1991.

Genchev, Nikolai. *Ochertsi : Sotsialno-Psikhologicheski Tipove V Bûlgarskata Istoriia*. 1. izd. Sofia: Dûrzh. izd-vo "Septemvri", 1987.

Genov, Georgi. *Bulgaria and the Treaty of Neuilly*. Sofia, Bulgaria: H. G. Danov & co., 1935.

Georgiev, Georgi. *Sofia I Sofiantsi 1878-1944*. Sofia: Nauka i Izkustvo, 1983.

Gheith, Jehanne M., and Barbara T. Norton. *An Improper Profession : Women, Gender, and Journalism in Late Imperial Russia*. Durham, [N.C.]: Duke University Press, 2001.

Gilman, Charlotte Perkins. *Women and Economics a Study of the Economic Relationship between Men and Women as a Facet of Social Evolution*. New York: Dover Publications Inc., 1998.

Gilmour, David. *Curzon: Imperial Statesman*. New York: Ferrar, Straus and Giroux, 1994.

Goldstein, Joshua. *War and Gender: How Gender Shapes the War System and Vice Versa*. Cambridge: Cambridge University Press, 2001.

Goldsworthy, Vesna. *Inventing Ruritania : The Imperialism of the Imagination*. New Haven: Yale University Press, 1998.

Grant, Rebecca and Kathleen Newland, ed. *Gender and International Relations*. Buckingham: Open University Press, 1991.

Gruev, Stefan. *Korona Ot Trûni Tsaruvaneto Na Boris III 1918-1943*. Sofia: Bulgarski Pisatel, 1991.

Haan, Francisca de, Krasimira Daskalova, and Anna Loutfi. *Biographical Dictionary of Women's Movements and Feminisms in Central, Eastern, and South Eastern Europe : 19th and 20th Centuries*. 1st ed. New York: Central European University Press, 2005.

Hankey, Lord. *The Supreme Control at the Paris Peace Conference 1919*. London: Allen and Unwin, 1963.

Harris, Barbara J. *English Aristocratic Women, 1450-1650 Marriage and Family, Property and Careers*. Oxford: Oxford University Press, 2002.

Healy, Maureen. *Vienna and the Fall of the Habsburg Empire Total War and Everyday Life in World War I*. Cambridge: Cambridge University Press, 2004.

Hegermann-Lindencrone, Fru Lillie Moulton. *The Sunny Side of Diplomatic Life, 1875-1912*. New York and London: Harper & brothers, 1914.

Hellerstein, Erna Olafson, Leslie Parker Hume, and Karen M. Offen. *Victorian Women : A Documentary Account of Women's Lives in Nineteenth-Century England, France, and the United States*. Stanford, Calif.: Stanford University Press, 1981.

Hickman, Katie. *Daughters of Britannia the Lives and Times of Diplomatic Wives*. New York: William Morrow, 1999.

Higonnet, Margaret Randolph et al., ed. *Behind the Lines Gender and the Two World Wars*. New Haven: Yale University Press, 1987.

Higonnet, Patrice. *Paris Capital of the World*. Cambridge: Harvard University Press, 2002.

Hinton, James. *Women, Social Leadership, and the Second World War Continuities of*

Class. Oxford: Oxford University Press, 2002.

Hoff-Wilson. In *Women and American Foreign Policy Lobbyists, Critics, and Insiders,* edited by Edward P. Crapol. Willmington: Scholarly Resources Inc, 1992.

Hooson, David, ed. *Geography and National Identity.* Oxford: Blackwell, 1994.

Hughes, Katherine L. *The Accidental Diplomat Dilemmas of the Trailing Spouse.* Putnam Valley, New York: Aletheia Publications, 1999.

Ilchev, Ivan, ed. *Noel I Charls Bukston Misiia Na Balkanite.* Sofia: Kliment Ohridski, 1987.

Ivanov, Martin, *Politicheskite igri s vûnshniia dulg. Bûlgarski siuzheti na stonpanski krizi i vuzhod, 1929-1934,* Sofiia: Zlatiu Boiadzhiev, 2001.

Jalland, Pat. *Women, Marriage and Politics 1860-1914.* Oxford: Clarendon Press., 1986.

Jeffereys-Jones, Rhodi. *Changing Differences Women and the Shaping of American Foreign Policy, 1917-1994.* New Brunswick: Rutgers University Press, 1995.

Jelavich, Barbara. *Russia's Balkan Entanglements, 1806-1914.* Cambridge [England] ; New York: Cambridge University Press, 1991.

———. *History of the Balkans.* 2 vols. Cambridge ; New York: Cambridge University Press, 1983.

Jelavich, Charles, and Barbara Jelavich. *The Establishment of the Balkan National States, 1804-1920, A History of East Central Europe ; V. 8.* Seattle: University of Washington Press, 1977.

Jiricek, Konstantin, and Stoian Argirov. *Bûlgarski Dnevnik, 30 Oktomvri 1879-26 Oktomvri 1884 G.* Plovdiv, Sofia, Knigoizd. Kh. G. Danov, 1930.

Kaiser, Robert J. *The Geography of Nationalism in Russia and the USSR.* Princeton: Princeton University Press, 1994.

Kaser, Karl. *Vom Nutzen Der Verwandten: Soziale Nezwerke in Bulgarien (19. Und 20. Jahrhundert).* Wien: Bohlau Verlag, 2000.

———. *Mact Und Erbe. Mannerherrschaft, Besitz Und Familier Im Ostlichen Europa (1500-1900), Zur Kunde Osteuropas Ii/30.* Wien: Bohlau Verlag, 2000.

Kertzer, David I. and Barbagli, Marzio, ed. *Family Life in the Long Nineteenth Century 1789-1913.* III vols. Vol. II, *The History of the European Family.* New Haven: Yale University Press, 2002.

Khristov, Khristo, ed. *Aleksandûr Stamboliiski: Zhivot, Delo, Zaveti.* Sofia: Bûlgarska Akademia na Naukite, 1980.

Kinnear, Mary. *Woman of the World : Mary Mcgeachy and International Cooperation.* Toronto ; Buffalo: University of Toronto Press, 2004.

———. *Margaret Mcwilliams: An Interwar Feminist.* Montreal ; Buffalo: McGill-Queen's University Press, 1991.

———. *In Subordination : Professional Women, 1870-1970.* Montreal ; Buffalo: McGill-Queen's University Press, 1995.

Klein, Yvonne M. *Beyond the Home Front Women's Autobiographical Writing of the Two World Wars.* New York: New York University Press, 1997.

Kostadinova, Tatiana. *Bulgaria 1879-1946.* Boulder: East European Monographs, 1995.

Landes, Joan, ed. *Feminism, the Public and the Private, Oxford Readings in Feminism.* Oxford: Oxford University Press, 1998.

Leverson, Albert. *Tsar Boris III Shtrihi Kûm Portreta.* Sofia: Sv. Georgi Pobedonostsev, 1995.

Lyons, Martyn. "Love Letters and Writing Practices: On Ecritures Intimes in the Nineteenth Century." *Journal of Family History* 24, no. 2 (1999): 232-39.

MacMillan, Margaret. *Paris 1919.* New York: Random House, 2001.

Margadant, Jo Burr, ed. *The New Biography: Performing Femininity in Nineteenth-Century France.* Berkeley: University of California Press, 2000.

Markov, Georgi. *Vûrhovete Privlichat Mûlni Pokushenia i Politika v Bûlgariia 1878-*

1919. Sofia: Partizdat, 1989.

McCaffree, Mary Jane, and Pauline B. Innis. *Protocol: The Complete Handbook of Diplomatic, Official, and Social Usage.* Rev. ed. Washington, D.C.: Devon Pub. Co., 1985.

McDermid, Jane, and Anna Hillyar. *Women and Work in Russia, 1880-1930: A Study in Continuity through Change, Women and Men in History.* London ; New York: Longman, 1998.

Meininger, Thomas A. *The Formation of a Nationalist Bulgarian Intelligentsia, 1835-1878, Modern European History.* New York: Garland, 1987.

Melman, Billie. *Women's Orients, English Women and the Middle East, 1718-1918: Sexuality, Religion, and Work.* London: Macmillan, 1992.

————, ed. *Borderlines: Genders and Identities in War and Peace, 1870-1930.* New York ; London: Routledge, 1997.

Muir, Nadejda. *Dimitri Stancioff Patriot and Cosmopolitan.* London: John Murray, 1957.

Nazûrska, Zhorzheta. *Universitetskoto Obrazovanie i Bûlgarskite Zheni, 1879-1944.* Sofia: BAN, 2003.

————. *Bûlgarskata Dûrzhava I Neinite Maltsinstva 1879-1885.* Sofia: LIK, 1999.

Neikov, Petur. *Zavchera I Vchera : Skitsi Ot Minaloto.* 2. izd. ed. Sofia: Izd-vo na BZNS, 1981.

————. *Spomeni.* 1. izd. ed, *Poreditsa "Dnevnitsi I Spomeni Za Bulgarskata Istorìa".* Sofia: Izd-vo na Otechestvenìa front, 1990.

Newton, Judith. "Engendering History for the Middle Class: Sex and Political Economy in the Edinburgh Review." In *Rewriting the Victorians Theory, History, and the Politics of Gender,* edited by Linda M. Shires. London: Routledge, 1992.

Nicolson, Harold George. *Portrait of a Diplomatist.* New York: Harcourt, 1939.

————. *Peacemaking, 1919.* London: Constable and Co. Ltd., 1933.

Nicolson, Harold George, and Nigel Nicolson. *Harold Nicolson Diaries and Letters 1907-1964.* London: Weidenfeld & Nicolson, 2004.

Nicolson, Juliet. *The Perfect Summer : Dancing into Shadow : England in 1911.* London: John Murray, 2006.

I. Ilchev. *Misìa Na Balkanite.* 1. izd. ed. Sofiëìa: Univ. izd-vo "Kliment Okhridski", 1987.

Norton, Barbara T., Jehanne M. Gheith, ed. *An Improper Profession Women, Gender, and Journalism.* Durham & London: Duke University Press, 2001.

Offen, Karen. *European Feminisms 1700-1950.* Stanford: Stanford University Press, 2000.

Offen, Karen and Ruth Roach Peirson, and Jane Rendall, ed. *Writing Women's History International Perspectives,* Houndmills, Basingstoke, Hampshire: MacMillan, 1991.

Panaiotov, Panaiot. *Vûnshnata Politika Na Bûlgaria.* Rio di Janiero, 1986.

Pantev, Andrei. *Za Stefan Stambolov V Chasa Na Bûlgariia: Statii, Eseta, Ochertsi.* Sofia: Edem 21, 1995.

Pateman, Carol. *The Sexual Contract.* Stanford, CA: Stanford University Press, 1988.

Petersen, Jeanne. *Family, Love, and Work in the Lives of Victorian Gentlewomen.,* Bloomington: Indiana University Press, 1989.

Petrov-Chomakov, Stoian. *Duhût Na Diplomatsiata.* Translated by Gocho Chakalov. Sofia: LIK, 2002.

Popiel, Jennifer J. "Making Mothers: The Advice Genre and the Domestic Ideal, 1760-1830." *Journal of Family History* 29, no. 4 (2004): 339-50.

Popov, Radoslav and Vasilka Tankova, ed. *Ivan Evstatiev Geshov Lichna Korespondentsiia.* Sofia: Marin Drinov, 1994.

Psarra, Efi Avdela and Angelika. "Engendering 'Greekness': Women's Emancipation and Irredentist Politics in Nineteenth-Century Greece." *Mediterranean Histori-*

cal Review 20, no. 1 (2005): 67-79.

Pushkareva, Natalia Eve Levin translator and editor, ed. *Women in Russian History.* New York: M. E. Sharpe., 1997.

Radev, Simeon. *Stroitelite Na Sûvremenna Bûlgariia. [Dokum.-Khudozh. Khronika]. V 2 T.* [2. izd.] ed. Sofia: Bûlg. pisatel, 1973.

Ransel, David, ed. *The Family in Imperial Russia. New Lines of Historical Research.* Urbana: University of Illinois Press, 1978.

Roshwald, Aviel and Richard Stites, ed. *European Culture in the Great War: The Arts, Entertainment, and Propaganda, 1914-1918.* Cambridge: Cambridge University Press, 1999.

Runciman, Steven. *A Traveler's Alphabet.* New York: Thames and Hudson Inc., 1991.

Said, Edward W. *Orientalism.* 1st Vintage Books ed. New York: Vintage Books, 1979.

Schlogel, Karl. *Der Grosse Exodus. Die Russische Emigration Und Ihre Zentren 1917 Bis 1941.* Munich: C.A.Beck, 1994.

Schorman, Rob. *Selling Style : Clothing and Social Change at the Turn of the Century.* Philadelphia: PENN/University of Pennsylvania Press, 2003.

Schwartz, Katrina. "The Occupations of Beauty: Imagining Nature and Nation in Latvia." *East European Politics and Societies* 21, no. 2 (2006): 259-93.

Scott, Joan. *Only Paradoxes to Offer.* Cambridge, Ma: Harvard University Press, 1996.

Sells, Michael. *The Bridge Betrayed: Religion and Genocide in Bosnia.* Berkley: University of California Press, 1996.

Shires, Linda M., ed. *Rewriting the Victorians Theory, History, and the Politics of Gender.* New York: Routledge, 1992.

Shorter, Edward. *The Making of the Modern Family.* New York: Basic Books, 1977.

Smith, Bonnie. *Ladies of the Leisure Class: The Bourgeoisies of Northern France in the Nineteenth Century.* Princeton: Princeton University Press, 1981.

Stamboliiski, Asen. *Aleksandr Stamboliiski Snimiki Ot Edin Zhivot.* Sofia: Dûrzhavna Pechatnitsa, 1934.

Stancioff, Anna, and Nadejda Muir. *Recollections of a Bulgarian Diplomatist's Wife.* London: Hutchinson, 1931.

Stancioff, Ivan D. *Diplomat and Gardener Memoirs.* Sofia: Petrikov, 1998.

Statelova, Elena Boianova. *Politika, Partii, Pechat Na Bûlgarskata Burzhoaziia 1909-1912.* Sofia: Nauka i Izkustvo, 1973.

Statelova, Elena Boianova, Radoslav Popv, Vasilka Tankova. *Istoriia Na Bûlgarskata Diplomtsiia, 1879-1913.* Sofia: Fondatsiia Otvoreno obshtestvo, 1994.

Statelova, Elena Boianova. *Biografiia Na Bulgaskiia Dukh: Rodut Panitsa.* Sofia: Marin Drinov, 1997.

Statelova, Elena Boianova, and Radoslav Popov. *Stefan Stambolov I Negovoto Vreme : Nepublikuvani Spomeni.* 1. izd. Sofia: IK "Detelina 6", 1993.

Steans, Jill. *Gender and International Relations.* Cambridge: Polity Press, 1998.

Stites, Richard. *The Women's Liberation Movement in Russia: Feminism, Nihilism, and Bolshevism, 1860-1930.* Princeton: Princeton University Press, 1978.

Thurer, Shari L. *The Myths of Motherhood How Culture Reinvents the Good Mother.* Boston: Houghton Mifflin Company, 1994.

Tilly, Louise. "Linen Was Their Life: Family Survival Stategies and Parent-Child Relations in Nineteenth-Century France." In *Interest and Emotion Essays on the Study of Family and Kinship*, edited by Hans and Sabean Medick, David Warren, 300-16. Cambridge: Cambridge University Pres, 1984.

Tilly, Louise with Joan Scott. *Women, Work and Family.* New York: Holt, Rhinehart and Winston, 1978.

Todorova, Maria Nikolaeva. *Imagining the Balkans.* New York: Oxford University Press, 1997.

———. *Balkani, Balkanizûm*. 2. prerab. i dop. izd. Sofia: Univ. izd-vo "Sv. Kliment Okhridski", 2004.

———. *.Balkan Identities : Nation and Memory*. Washington Square, N.Y.: New York University Press, 2004.

Todorova, T. Tsvetana. *Probleme Der Modernisierung Bulgariens Im 19. Und 20. Jahrhundert, Collegium Germania ; 1*. Sofia: Universitätsverlag "Hl. Kliment Ochridski", 1994.

Tovrov, Jessica. "Mother-Child Relations among Russian Nobility." In *The Family in Imperial Russia*, edited by David Ransel, 1978.

Trumbach, Randolph. *The Rise of the Egalitarian Family Aristocratic Kinship and Domestic Relations in Eighteenth-Century England*. New York: Academic Press, 1978.

Tuttle, Leslie. "Celebrating the Pere De Famille: Pronatalism and Fatherhood in Eighteenth-Century France." *Journal of Family History* 29, no. 4 (2004): 366-81.

Urdanez, Gracia Gomez. "The Bourgeois Family in Nineteenth-Century Spain: Private Lives, Gender Roles, and a New Socioeconomic Model." *Journal of Family History* 30, no. 1 (2005): 66-85.

Viroubova, Anna. *Memories of the Russian Court*. New York: The Macmillan Company, 1923.

Wallach Scott, Joan. *Gender and the Politics of History*. New York: Columbia University Press, 1999.

Whitney, Susan B. "Gender, Class, and Generation in Interwar French Catholicism: The Case of the Jeunesse Ouvriere Chreienne Feminine." *Journal of Family History* 26, no. 4 (2001): 480-507.

Wingfield, Nancy M., and Maria Bucur. *Gender and War in Twentieth-Century Eastern Europe, Indiana-Michigan Series in Russian and East European Studies*. Bloomington: Indiana University Press, 2006.

Winter, J. M. *Sites of Memory, Sites of Mourning : The Great War in European Cultural History, Studies in the Social and Cultural History of Modern Warfare*. Cambridge ; New York: Cambridge University Press, 1995.

Winter, J. M., and Jean-Louis Robert. *Capital Cities at War : Paris, London, Berlin, 1914-1919, Studies in the Social and Cultural History of Modern Warfare*. Cambridge [England] ; New York: Cambridge University Press, 1997.

Yeo, Eileen Janes. "The Creation of 'Motherhood' and Women's Responses in Britain and France, 1750-1914." *Women's History Review* 8, no. 2 (1999).

Yuval-Davis, Nira. *Gender and Nation*. London: Sage, 1997.

Zheliazkova, Antonina, Bozhidar Aleksiev, Zhorzheta Nazûrska, ed. *Miusiulmanskite Obshtnosti na Balkanite I v Bûlgaria*. Sofia: IMIR, 1997.

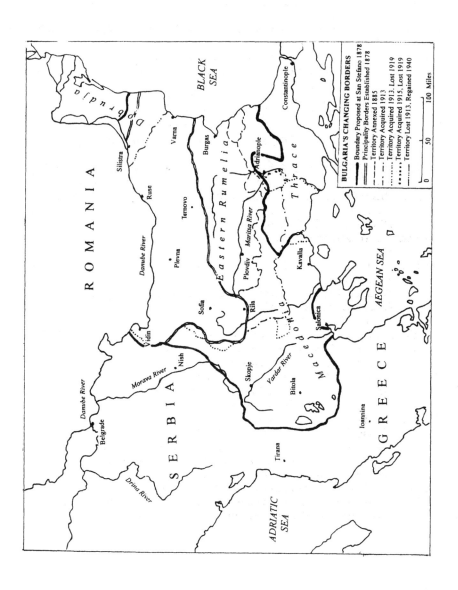

BULGARIA'S CHANGING BORDERS

Boundary Proposed at San Stefano 1878
Principality Borders Established 1878
Territory Annexed 1885
Territory Acquired 1913
Territory Acquired 1913, Lost 1919
Territory Acquired 1915, Lost 1919
Territory Lost 1913, Regained 1940

0   50   100 Miles

ROMANIA

BLACK SEA

Dobrudja

Silistra

Ruse

Varna

Danube River

Tarnovo

Burgas

Plevna

Eastern Rumelia

Sofia

Maritsa River

Adrianople

Thrace

Plovdiv

Rila

Constantinople

Vidin

Kavalla

Danube River

Morava River

Nish

Skopje

Vardar River

Macedonia

Salonica

SERBIA

Bitola

AEGEAN SEA

Belgrade

Ioannina

GREECE

Drina River

Tirana

ADRIATIC SEA

Index

About the Author

Mari A. Firkatian is Associate Professor of History at the University of Hartford. Currently president of the Bulgarian Studies Association, she was born in Bulgaria. As a researcher and a traveler she has lived in most of the European countries and has spent extended periods of time in the former Soviet Union and Eastern Bloc countries.

Among other works, Mari Firkatian is the author of the *Forest Traveler: Georgi Stoikov Rakovski and Bulgarian Nationalism*, a chapter "Retaining Ethnic Identity: The Armenians in Bulgaria" in *Cultural Education–Cultural Sustainability: Minority, Diaspora, Indigenous, and Ethno-religious Groups in Multicultural Societies*, articles in Journal of Family History and Teaching History.